50+1

作者:保罗·J.克里斯托弗
主译:方华文
译者:陆小明

英汉对照
Greatest Cities in
the World You Should Visit

50+1个最该游览的伟大城市

安徽科学技术出版社
Encouragement Press, LLC

图书在版编目(CIP)数据

50+1个最该游览的伟大城市 / (美) 克里斯托弗著；
方华文，陆小明译. -- 合肥：安徽科学技术出版社，
2009.06
（50+1系列）
ISBN 978-7-5337-4434-2

Ⅰ. ①5… Ⅱ. ①克… ②方… ③陆… Ⅲ. ①城市-
简介-世界 Ⅳ. ①K915

中国版本图书馆CIP数据核字(2009)第079289号

50+1个最该游览的伟大城市

(美) 克里斯托弗(Christopher,P.J.)著　方华文　陆小明　译

出 版 人：黄和平
责任编辑：姚敏淑　孙立凯
封面设计：朱　婧
出版发行：安徽科学技术出版社(合肥市政务文化新区圣泉路 1118 号
　　　　　出版传媒广场，邮编：230071)
网　　址：www. ahstp. net
E - mail：yougoubu@sina. com
经　　销：新华书店
排　　版：安徽事达科技贸易有限公司
印　　刷：合肥瑞丰印务有限公司
开　　本：787×1092　1/16
印　　张：19.75
字　　数：546 千
版　　次：2009 年 6 月第 1 版　2022 年 1 月第 2 次印刷
定　　价：46.00 元

译 者 序

巴黎，"光之城"，恐怕是世界上最美丽的城市了。这儿弥漫着浪漫的气息和文化情调。香榭丽舍大道、罗浮宫、巴黎圣母院……小仲马笔下的"茶花女"经常徜徉于香榭丽舍大道，那儿绿树成行、莺往燕来、鸟语花香。大道的尽头是闻名遐迩的凯旋门，那是拿破仑为纪念奥斯特利茨战争的胜利而建立的。由于香榭丽舍所处的显赫位置，法国许多重要事件常常选在这里举行。比如每年七月十四日国庆游行，环法自行车赛终点冲刺等。当您漫步在香榭丽舍街头时，很有可能会碰上一个国际巨星或世界名人。罗浮宫是法国历史上最悠久的王宫，也是世界上最古老、最大、最著名的博物馆之一。它的藏品多达2.5万件，其中有被誉为世界三宝的《维纳斯》雕像、《蒙娜丽莎》油画和《胜利女神》石雕。至于巴黎圣母院，它的第一块基石于1163年奠下，全部工程完成于在1220年。著名作家雨果以《巴黎圣母院》为名写了一部催人泪下的长篇小说，给这座教堂增添了无限的文化色彩。这就是巴黎……历史和文化赋予它魅力和基础！

本书所介绍的51座城市均为世界名城，如埃及的亚历山大、荷兰的阿姆斯特丹、希腊的雅典、泰国的曼谷、西班牙的巴塞罗那、中国的北京、德国的柏林、英国的伦敦和印度的孟买等。它们各具特色，但有两个共同之处——风光旖旎、文化底蕴深厚。你愿意旅游吗？会旅游吗？我建议你不要流连于摩天大厦和百货商场，那样有些"肤浅"，而应该去参观法罗岛灯塔、荷兰风车、希腊神庙、曼谷的佛教寺、巴塞罗那的毕加索博物馆、北京的故宫、柏林的威廉皇帝纪念教堂……这样多有味、多"深沉"！旅游是"玩"，但这是获取信息(特别是文化知识)的"玩"，是有价值的"玩"！到世界名城去享受文化艺术的熏陶，会产生美丽的梦幻，会产生缥缈的遐想。你在迷雾蒙蒙的伦敦街头散过步吗？狄更斯经常踟蹰于那儿的大街小巷，在那儿体验生活，把观察到的情况用艺术手法写入作品。到了那儿，你的文化素养将大大提高，文学欣赏力也会上一个台阶。

人类文明为什么越来越繁荣和强盛？那是因为每一代都有杰出的人物产生，是他们创造了一个个的"奇迹"，推动了社会的进步。大多"杰出人物"都以这些名城为舞台演出"大戏"。是这儿的历史沉淀塑造了他们的细胞，是这儿的文化环境为他们补充了养分。他

1

们一朝奋起便气冲霄汉！有人开玩笑地说：就连巴黎空中的老鹰也文质彬彬！虽为笑谈，可也说明了一个问题：文化氛围可以改变一个人的气息，令一个人脱胎换骨。世界名城还有许多闪光点，从街道布局、房屋形状、居民谈吐到古董店、画廊……一切的一切，散发出"古香古色"的摄人心魄的感染力，这是"俗地"所不具备的！

方华文

2009年5月于苏州大学

方华文简介

方华文，男，1955年6月生于西安，现任苏州大学外国语学院英语教授，著名学者、文学翻译家及翻译理论家，被联合国教科文组织国际译联誉为"the most productive literary translator in contemporary China"（中国当代最多产的文学翻译家，Babel.54:2，2008，145–158）。发表的著、译作品达1 000余万字，其中包括专著《20世纪中国翻译史》等，计200余万字；译著《雾都孤儿》《无名的裘德》《傲慢与偏见》《蝴蝶梦》《魂断英伦》《儿子与情人》《少年维特之烦恼》《红字》《从巅峰到低谷》《马丁·伊登》《套向月亮的绳索》《君主论》《社会契约论》以及改写本的《飘》《汤姆叔叔的小屋》《查特莱夫人的情人》《大卫·科波菲尔》《苔丝》《高老头》《三个火枪手》《悲惨世界》等；主编的译作包括《基督山伯爵》《红与黑》《简·爱》《汤姆·索亚历险记》《茶花女》《金银岛》《鲁滨孙漂流记》《巴黎圣母院》《莎士比亚戏剧故事集》《精神分析引论》《论法的精神》和《国富论》等；并主编了多部英汉对照读物。以上均为单行本著作，所发表文章不计在内。

Imagine holding the whole world in your hands—or at least the greatest cities of the world! That is exactly what this book is about: The excitement and allure of the exotic, beautiful, legendary and famous cities of the world. Each is a center of art, culture, architecture, business and cuisine. Each has its own unique appeal, its own charm, and its own fascinating and fact–filled history.

Part travel book, part travelogue and part wish book, *50 plus one Greatest Cities of the World You Should Visit* is an intimate, easy and satisfying visit to the world's most wonderful cities. Imagine how helpful a book like this will be when planning that trip of a lifetime. With just a quick read, you can narrow down your travel choices to those most attractive to you.

Fascinated by history, geography, travel and culture? This is the perfect book for those interested in knowledge for its own sake. *50 plus one Greatest Cities of the World You Should Visit* provides information on everything from geography and climate to the history and sites you must see when you travel.

Love trivia? Sure, everyone does! Each chapter contains little–known facts and figures, unique to the city, its people and its culture.

While all the cities are presented in alphabetical order—there were too many disagreements to rank them otherwise—one city is our *50 plus one* favorite: Paris! As many world travelers know well, Paris is the most popular and important travel destination in the world. Paris is alive with culture, art, history and cuisine. What is more, the city's compactness makes for easy and pleasant exploration. Paris is a walker's dream come true.

Enjoy your visits to Paris and the other greatest cities of the world. Happy reading and happy traveling!

Paul J. Christopher

想象一下把全世界 —— 或者至少将世界上最伟大的城市握在手中会是一种什么样的感觉！而这正是本书的宗旨：将世界上那些或异域、或美丽、或传奇、或著名的城市中令人激动和沉醉的地方展示给你。每个城市都是一个中心，艺术的、文化的、建筑的、商业的、美食的中心；每个城市都拥有其独特的魅力、迷人的特征以及自身引人注目的丰富历史。

作为一本融合了导游手册、旅行见闻以及美好祈愿的书，《50＋1个最该游览的伟大城市》将带你进行一次轻松而愉快的旅行，去亲身体验一下世界上那些最美妙的城市。设想一下，当你计划平生难得的旅行时，这样的一本书该是多么有用！只需一次快速的浏览，你就能将目的地锁定到那些最吸引你的地方。

旅行中什么最令你兴奋，历史、地理、旅行本身，抑或各地的文化？假如你是一个对知识本身感兴趣的人，那么这本书是你完美的选择。《50＋1个最该游览的伟大城市》为你提供了从地理、气候、历史，到游览中的最佳景点等所有必备的信息。

喜欢猎奇吗？当然，人人都喜欢！针对不同的城市、人群和文化，每一章都包含了一些鲜为人知的事实和数据。

尽管所有的城市都是按照字母顺序编排介绍的 —— 不然的话，要给这些城市排序还真不容易 —— 有一个城市是50＋1的例外：那就是巴黎！许多在世界各地游历的人都知道，巴黎是世界上最受欢迎的、最重要的旅行目的地，巴黎因其文化、艺术、历史和美食而深入人心，此外，这个城市的景点密集也使得游客可以很容易地安排一次愉快的探寻之旅，巴黎令步行者美梦成真。

尽情享受你在巴黎以及世界其他伟大城市的旅行吧！祝大家开心阅读、愉快旅行！

保罗·J.克里斯托弗

Table of Contents

目 录

Introduction   1
前言

Paris, France   2
法国巴黎

Alexandria, Egypt   10
埃及亚历山大

Amsterdam, The Netherlands   16
荷兰阿姆斯特丹

Athens, Greece   22
希腊雅典

Auckland, New Zealand   28
新西兰奥克兰

Bangkok, Thailand   34
泰国曼谷

Barcelona, Spain   40
西班牙巴塞罗那

Beijing, China   46
中国北京

Berlin, Germany   50
德国柏林

Bombay, India(Mumbai, India)   56
印度孟买(孟巴)

Boston, United States   62
美国波士顿

Brussels, Belgium   68
比利时布鲁塞尔

Budapest, Hungary   72
匈牙利布达佩斯

Buenos Aires, Argentina   76
阿根廷布宜诺斯艾利斯

1

Table of Contents
目　录

82　Cape Town, South Africa
南非开普敦

88　Caracas, Venezuela
委内瑞拉加拉加斯

92　Chicago, United States
美国芝加哥

98　Cologne, Germany
德国科隆

104　Copenhagen, Denmark
丹麦哥本哈根

110　Hong Kong, China
中国香港

116　Istanbul, Turkey
土耳其伊斯坦布尔

122　Jakarta, Indonesia
印度尼西亚雅加达

128　Jerusalem, Israel
以色列耶路撒冷

134　Johannesburg, South Africa
南非约翰内斯堡

140　Las Vegas, United States
美国拉斯维加斯

146　Lima, Peru
秘鲁利马

152　Lisbon, Portugal
葡萄牙里斯本

158　London, England
英国伦敦

166　Madrid, Spain
西班牙马德里

Table of Contents

目 录

Mecca, Saudi Arabia 172
沙特阿拉伯麦加

Mexico City, Mexico 178
墨西哥墨西哥城

Montreal, Canada 184
加拿大蒙特利尔

Moscow, Russia 190
俄罗斯莫斯科

Nairobi, Kenya 196
肯尼亚内罗毕

New York City, United States 202
美国纽约

Prague, Czech Republic 210
捷克共和国布拉格

Rio de Janeiro, Brazil 216
巴西里约热内卢

Rome, Italy 222
意大利罗马

San Francisco, United States 230
美国旧金山

Seattle, United States 236
美国西雅图

Shanghai, China 242
中国上海

Singapore 248
新加坡

St. Petersburg, Russia 254
俄罗斯圣彼得堡

Stockholm, Sweden 260
瑞典斯德哥尔摩

3

Table of Contents
目　录

266　Sydney, Australia
　　　澳大利亚悉尼

272　Tokyo, Japan
　　　日本东京

278　Toronto, Canada
　　　加拿大多伦多

284　Vancouver, Canada
　　　加拿大温哥华

288　Venice, Italy
　　　意大利威尼斯

294　Vienna, Austria
　　　奥地利维也纳

300　Washington D.C., United States
　　　美国华盛顿

50+1个最该游览的伟大城市

Plus one

Paris, France

The Basic Facts

Paris is the capital of France and is its largest city. Many consider Paris one of the most beautiful cities in the world, and it has been nicknamed the City of Light. During the late 20th century, Paris underwent a major facelift: modern structures replaced unusable buildings, but historically and aesthetically valuable buildings were restored and preserved. Some Parisians believe that the construction of skyscrapers has ruined the overall beauty of the city. Paris, however, continues to be a treasure trove of art, music, architecture and great food, and is one of the most visited cities in the world.

Geography

Paris lies at 48 degrees 51 minutes north latitude and 2 degrees 20 minutes east longitude. The city is located in the heart of a lowland called the Paris basin, some 100 miles southeast of the English Channel. The Seine River, an enduring symbol of the city, winds its way roughly eight miles through Paris from east to west. The Right Bank (La Rive Droite) and the Left Bank (La Rive Gauche) are located north and south of the river, respectively.

The layout of the city has evolved over hundreds of years. The Ile de la Cité, an island in the Seine, is the site on which Paris was founded and is considered the heart of the city. Paris contains many broad avenues, of which the most famous is the Champs-élysées.

Climate

The Paris climate is moderate throughout the year and rarely reaches extremes of either cold or warmth. Winter temperatures average in the mid-40s Fahrenheit and summer temperatures average in the mid-70s Fahrenheit. Spring is considered the most beautiful time of year in Paris.

Government

Paris is divided into 20 arondissements, administrative divisions that are governed by independent commissions and mayors. Paris also has a central government that handles overall municipal services and laws; a mayor and 109 city council members are elected for 6-year terms.

Demographics

Paris is one of the most densely populated cities in the world. Gentrification and congestion have contributed to a rise in the cost of housing. As a result, the population of the city proper has decreased over the years, and many city residents have relocated to the nearby suburbs. Paris is a multicultural city; nearly 20 percent of its current population originated elsewhere in France or in other countries. Most city residents are of European background, but recent immigrants have come mainly from China, Africa and the Middle

法国巴黎

概况

　　巴黎是法国的首都和最大的城市，巴黎是全世界公认的最美的城市之一，并美其名曰"光之城"。20世纪后期，巴黎经历了一次大规模的城市改造，现代化的建筑取代了那些废弃的楼房，然而一些具有历史及美学价值的建筑却得以保存和修复。尽管有些巴黎人认定摩天大楼式的结构破坏了城市整体的美感，但是至今巴黎仍然是一座艺术、建筑和美食的宝库，是世界各地游客最常光顾的城市之一。

一、地理

　　巴黎位于北纬48°51′，东经2°20′，地处英吉利海峡东南方100英里左右的名为巴黎盆地的低地中心。作为该城恒久象征的塞纳河全长大约8英里，自东向西蜿蜒穿过城市，右岸地区和左岸地区分别位于塞纳河的北面和南面。

　　巴黎市的布局历经数百年的衍变。西岱岛，作为塞纳河中的一个小岛，是巴黎最初的发祥地，并被冠以城市的"心脏"。巴黎市区有许多宽阔的街道，其中最著名的是香榭丽舍大街。

二、气候

　　巴黎全年气候温和，很少有极端寒冷或炎热的天气。冬季平均气温在华氏40度上下，夏季则在华氏70度左右。春天是巴黎一年中最美的季节。

三、政府

　　巴黎市分为20个行政区，各区由自己独立的委员会和区长管理，全市还有一个中央政府负责提供全面的市政服务及制定法律法规，市长和109位市政官员每6年选举一次。

四、人口

　　巴黎是世界上人口密度最大的城市之一。城市区域的"贵族化"和交通拥堵成为居住成本上涨的主要因素，结果造成市区人口逐年下降，许多城市居民重新选择到郊区定居。巴黎是个多元文化的城市，现有人口的近20%来自于法国其他地区或世界其他国家。大多数居民属欧洲血统，但是近些年的移民主要来自于中国、非洲及中东国家。目前，巴黎

East. Paris currently has about 2.1 million residents.

Economy

Paris and the surrounding area comprise France's major industrial center.Products manufactured here include automobiles, chemicals, dyes and electronic equipment. Paris is also a center for printing and publishing. Smaller manufacturers in the city create Paris' world-renowned jewelry, perfume and haute couture women's clothing.

Paris is France's center of financial, marketing and distribution services. Tourism accounts for much of the city's economy and attracts thousands of visitors every year who seek the city's rich mixture of art, culture, architecture, music and food.

The History

The first residents of the area (on the Ile de la Cité around 250 B.C.) were a Celtic tribe named the Parisii. Roman invaders established a colony in the area in 52 B.C.. The colony expanded quickly on both banks of the Seine and the settlement became known as Paris around 300 A.D.. Paris was first made the capital of France in 512 by Clovis, the first ruler of the Frankish kingdom. As France and its rulers grew in power, so did Paris, and by the early 13th century the city was already recognized as a center of culture, education and government.

During the Renaissance, new boulevards, palaces and squares were styled to reflect ancient Greek and Roman architecture. The French monarchy held total control of France until the bloody French Revolution of 1789—1799, during which Paris served as the focal point. After a period of instability following the revolution, Napoléon Bonaparte (later Napoléon III, emperor from 1852—1870) took control of the government and made further improvements to the city, including banks, hospitals, theaters and infrastructure.

Long-range German cannons damaged Paris during World War I, but the city survived. In World War II, however, the German army occupied Paris during the years 1939—1945. Nevertheless, Paris became a center of the French underground (known as La Résistance).

The Sights and Sounds

Paris is undoubtedly the *plus one* city of the world. Visitors are overwhelmed by the city's richness, sophistication and artistry, and each neighborhood has its own characteristic sights and sounds. Paris' city center is compact and its transit system is first-rate, making it a wonderful city for visitors to explore.

One of the standouts in Paris is certainly Notre Dame de Paris, the famous cathedral that stands on the eastern half of the Ile de la Cité. For nearly 2,000 years, Parisians have worshipped on this site. The present cathedral is actually the fourth church built on the site. Construction began in 1163, and the cathedral was not completed until the mid-14th century—nearly 300 years later! Take the 422-step hike to the top of the Bell Tower for a wonderful view of Paris and the cathedral itself. Notre Dame was heavily damaged during the French Revolution by mobs who viewed it as a symbol of the hated monarchy. Restorations in the mid-1800s added modern touches to the cathedral. It is known for its flying buttresses,which strengthen the walls while enabling natural light to shine through rose windows of beautiful stained glass.

4

的居民大约有210万。

五、经济

　　巴黎及其周边地区构成法国主要的工业中心，这里加工的产品包括汽车、化学制品、燃料和电子设备等。巴黎还是印刷及出版业的中心，令巴黎闻名世界的珠宝、香水和高级女装就是由这里的小型制造商生产的。

光影流金

　　巴黎地区(公元前250年左右的西岱岛)最初的居民是一个名为"巴黎人"的凯尔特人部落。公元前52年罗马入侵者在这里建立了一个殖民地，这一殖民地在塞纳河两岸迅速扩张，到了大约公元300年发展成为著名的巴黎城。公元512年，法兰克王国的第一任统治者克洛维首次将巴黎定为法国的首都。随着法国及其统治者们权利的扩张，巴黎也在发展壮大。到了13世纪初期，巴黎已然成为公认的文化、教育和行政中心。

　　文艺复兴时期修建的新式林荫大道、宫殿和广场反映了古希腊、古罗马的建筑特色。法国原本一直处于君主统治之下，直到1789~1799年血腥的法国革命之后，这一制度才被废除。而巴黎作为此次革命的核心地区，后来也经历了一段时间动荡。随后拿破仑·波拿巴(即后来的拿破仑三世，1852~1870年在位)控制了政府，并对城市进一步改造，修建了银行、医院、剧院等城市基础设施。

　　第一次世界大战期间，德国军队的远程大炮对巴黎造成了一定破坏，但是巴黎城还是得以幸存。在第二次世界大战中，德国军队曾于1939至1945年期间占领巴黎，尽管如此，巴黎仍成为法国地下组织(被称为"抵抗组织")的中心。

声光景点

　　巴黎无疑是世界上顶尖的城市，游客们无不为这个城市丰富的内涵、成熟的发展和其艺术特质所倾倒。这里的每一个街区都有着独特的声光色彩。巴黎的中心城区非常紧凑，交通设施一流，从而使巴黎成为各地游客探幽寻秘的绝佳场所。

　　巴黎最突出的景点之一当属巴黎圣母院，这是一座位于西岱岛东半部的著名大教堂，在近2000年的历史当中，这里是巴黎人朝拜之所。事实上，现存的教堂是在此地址上建起的第四座教堂，教堂始建于1163年，但是直到14世纪中期，也就是300年之后才得以完工！沿着422级台阶踏上钟楼的顶部，教堂自身的建筑以及巴黎全城的景色都尽收眼底。法国革命期间，巴黎圣母院遭到严重破坏，因为在这些人眼中，教堂是他们所仇视的君主制度的象征。开始于19世纪中期的教堂重建工作为教堂的建筑风格注入了一些现代化的元素。最有名的是悬吊式扶壁，一方面它们加强了墙壁的稳定性，另一方面又能让自然光透过嵌有漂亮彩色玻璃的圆窗照射进来。

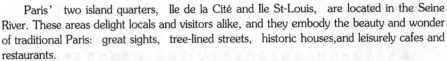
Paris' two island quarters, Ile de la Cité and Ile St-Louis, are located in the Seine River. These areas delight locals and visitors alike, and they embody the beauty and wonder of traditional Paris: great sights, tree-lined streets, historic houses,and leisurely cafes and restaurants.

While Notre Dame de Paris is known throughout the world, many visitors rave about the Holy Chapel, La Sainte-Chapelle. This chapel was built in the years 1246—1248 for Louis IX, who became its patron. Its stained glass—perhaps the oldest in Paris—constitutes most of the upper chapel's walls. To construct the chapel in this way must have been a remarkable feat for its time!

New York has Fifth Avenue, Chicago has Michigan Avenue, but Paris has the Champs-élysées: the world's greatest and most chic (read: expensive) shopping and restaurant center. This avenue, a little over a mile long, is not what it used to be; fast-food restaurants and car dealerships now encroach on this historic area.

Still, visitors flock to this avenue, often beginning their tour of Paris at the Arc de Triomphe. The Tuileries Gardens offers a beautiful end to a tour of this district.This 63-acre formal garden, which has often been painted by Paris' greatest artists, is so majestic that visitors enjoy lingering in its environs.

Perhaps Napoléon's finest contribution to Paris is the Arc de Triomphe, which towers more than 165 feet over the Champs-élysées. It was commissioned to celebrate Napoléon's great military successes; ironically, construction was completed many years after his death. The Tomb of the Unknown Soldier is located under the Arc, and memorializes the French who perished in the First and Second World Wars. French victories and other special events are typically celebrated here.

Napoléon is buried in Mansart's Dome at Les Invalides, founded in 1674 as a home for older, ailing soldiers. Fittingly, the army museum is near by and famous of its collection of arms and armaments.

What can be said about a royal palace that is today the world's greatest art museum? The Louvre has everything to satisfy the artistic eye. There is simply no end to the degree and depth of this museum's collection. Exhibits include the 140-carat Regent Diamond, the Venus de Milo, and Leonardo da Vinci's renowned Mona Lisa. The Louvre's Egyptian collection is world famous, but its Greek,European, French and Arab collections are just as impressive.

The Place de la Concorde is a large—and congested—quarter of Paris worthy of attention. In this square, neoclassical buildings surround a 75-foot-tall,3,000-year old Egyptian obelisk and its two nearby fountains. The annual Tour de France bicycle race ends here, as do most parades.

Care for a bird's eye view from 1,000 feet? Take the elevator to the Eiffel Tower, which was built for the World Exhibition of 1889. Although most French considered the tower to be an eyesore, it now stands as the most recognizable symbol of this great city.

The Pompidou Center is a museum with a decidedly futuristic appearance: the building's steel beams and its heating, water, and electric systems are located on the exterior. The museum's main attraction, naturally, is the National Museum of Modern Art, encompassing most every conceivable style and school of 20th century art.

The Orsay Museum, while not exclusively French in character, contains an expansive collection of Impressionist art. In many ways, this museum's collection complements that of

巴黎的两大岛屿地区,即西岱岛和圣路易岛都位于塞纳河中,这些区域受到当地人和观光客的共同喜爱,因为它们拥有传统巴黎的美丽与神奇:迷人的景致、树木密布的街道、古典的建筑、闲适的咖啡屋和餐馆。

在巴黎圣母院名闻天下的同时,许多游客对于神圣教堂,也就是圣夏佩尔教堂也赞不绝口。这座教堂建于1246~1248年,是为国王路易九世而修建的,因此,路易九世也就成为该教堂的庇护人。这所教堂的彩色玻璃或许是巴黎最为古老的,它们构成了教堂四壁最上层的部分,以此种样式修建教堂必定是那个时期非凡的技艺!

纽约有第五大道,芝加哥有密歇根大街,巴黎则有香榭丽舍大街:世界上最美妙、最时髦(意即:最昂贵)的购物及餐饮中心。如今,这条长约1英里多的街道已非昔日模样,快餐馆、汽车经销店业已占据了原有的历史街区。

如果说纷至沓来的游客常将凯旋门作为他们巴黎之旅的开端的话,那么杜伊勒里花园则为该旅程画上了完美的句号。这座占地63英亩、以规则的几何图形布局的花园,常常成为巴黎绘画大师们笔下的创作对象,它是如此庄严华贵,令游人陶醉其中、流连忘返。

也许拿破仑对巴黎最杰出的贡献就属凯旋门了,这座高高耸立的超过165英尺的建筑横跨于香榭丽舍大街之上。这一建筑的初衷是为庆祝拿破仑伟大的军事胜利,然而具有讽刺意味的是,直到他死后多年这座建筑才得以完工。位于凯旋门下方的无名烈士墓,是为纪念在第一和第二次世界大战中阵亡的法国人而修建的,如今,法国人为胜利和其他一些特殊事件而举行的庆祝活动都在此举行。

拿破仑葬于位于荣军院的芒萨尔圆顶教堂。荣军院建于1674年,是为老人及伤残军人修建的福利院。与之相应的,是近旁的军事博物馆,以收藏有大量武器装备而著称。

对于一座现今已成为世界最著名的艺术博物馆的皇家宫殿,我们能说些什么呢?卢浮宫拥有所有吸引艺术家眼球的东西,这家博物馆的藏品其范围之广、价值之高无与伦比。其中包括重达140克拉的摄政王的钻石,米洛的维纳斯,列奥纳多·达·芬奇最著名的《蒙娜丽莎》。不仅卢浮宫的埃及馆藏举世闻名,而且其希腊馆、欧洲馆、法国馆和阿拉伯馆也同样令人难以忘怀。

协和广场是巴黎一个大型的人口稠密地区,值得关注的是在这个广场上,围绕一座高75英尺,拥有3 000年历史的埃及方型尖塔及近旁的两座喷泉,有许多新古典主义风格的建筑,每年一度的环法自行车赛以及大多数的狂欢游行活动都是以这里为终点的。

想从1 000英尺的高空来个鸟瞰吗?那就乘上埃菲尔铁塔的电梯吧!这座铁塔是为1889年举办的世界博览会而修建的,尽管大多数法国人觉得铁塔实在难看,但这并不妨碍它成为巴黎这座伟大城市的象征和标志性建筑。

蓬皮杜艺术中心是一座外观明显带有未来主义特征的博物馆,建筑的钢梁及其供暖、供水和供电系统都架设在外部,博物馆的主要吸引力无疑来自于其中的国家现代艺术博物馆,它囊括了几乎所有20世纪艺术流派以及任何一种想象得到的艺术风格。

奥塞博物馆不仅具有典型的法国特色,而且拥有印象派艺术的全面展示,从许多方

the Louvre.

Paris, like many of the world's greatest cities, is on the go 24 hours a day. The cafes, clubs, sights and sounds are exhilarating and at times exhausting for visitors. The French and particularly the Parisians consider their city home to the greatest cuisine and chefs in the world. Why argue? Splurge a little and enjoy the other side of Paris: its food, wine, beer and coffee. Stay out after dark and take a boat ride along the Seine.

The Trivia

Fact: The Louvre, constructed in the 12th century and arguably the most famous art museum in the world, began as a fortress. The building was razed and rebuilt as a royal palace in the 1500s; additions over the years made it the largest palace in the world. In 1793 parts of the palace became a public museum, which displayed artwork formerly held by the deposed French royalty.

Fact: In 1914, during World War I, the Germans came within 15 miles of Paris.The French army used taxicabs to transport fresh soldiers to the front. This taxicab army helped the French defeat the Germans in the First Battle of the Marne,thereby averting a quick German victory.

Fact: Paris is laid out according to plans that evolved over the centuries. The Ile de la Cité is in the heart of the city. The Seine River runs from east to west through the city and divides it into the Right Bank and the Left Bank. The Right Bank contains the city's offices, small factories and some shops. The Left Bank has traditionally been a center for artists and students.

Fact: Victor Hugo's famous character, Quasimodo, found sanctuary in the cathedral of Notre Dame de Paris; this fictional character is almost as famous as the church itself.

Fact: To save Paris from destruction by the Nazis in World War II, the French government declared it an open city, which meant that the French did not defend it. German troops entered the city without opposition and marched down the Champs Elysees in triumph.

Fact: During the height of the French Revolution, executions were carried out on the Place de la Concorde. It is estimated that more than 1,000 people, including King Louis XVI and Queen Marie Antoinette were guillotined on this site.

Why Paris Is First Among World Cities

Paris was chosen as the first among the world's greatest cities because it has everything a city should have: nightlife, culture, art, architecture, history,fine cuisine and sophistication. Throughout history, the city was caught in the middle of political and social change and intrigue, yet the city and its treasures have survived and thrived to this day. Governments come and go, but Paris lives on. It is the symbol of style, haute culture, luxury and fine living. Who can visit Paris and not want to return?

面来看,该博物馆的收藏很好地弥补了卢浮宫馆藏的不足。

正如世界上许多最伟大的城市一样,巴黎一天24小时忙碌运转。咖啡馆、夜总会,都市的声光景致令人兴奋,有时也使人疲惫。法国人,尤其是巴黎人,认为这里是全世界大厨及美食的家园。不信?你不妨小小地挥霍一下,体验一下巴黎的另外一面:它的美食、葡萄酒、啤酒和咖啡。待在户外直到天黑,然后沿着塞纳河享受一次泛舟的乐趣。

奇闻轶事

之一:卢浮宫修建于12世纪,号称世界上最著名的艺术博物馆,然而起初这里却是一座避难所,后被拆除并于16世纪作为皇家宫殿重新修建,历经多年扩建逐步成为世界上最大的宫殿。1793年,这座宫殿的一部分成为公共博物馆,用以展出前法国皇室所拥有的艺术作品。

之二:1914年,第一次世界大战期间,德国军队入侵到距离巴黎15英里的地方,法军用出租车将入伍的新兵送往前线,这一出租车队帮助法国人在马恩河首役中击败了德军,阻止了德国军快速取胜的步伐。

之三:巴黎城市的布局经过了几个世纪的规划,西岱岛作为城市的心脏,塞纳河由东至西穿城而过将其划分为右岸和左岸。右岸包括城市的办公大楼、小型工厂和一些商店,左岸则成为传统艺术和学生活动的中心。

之四:维克多·雨果笔下著名的人物:卡西莫多在巴黎圣母院找到了他的避难所,这一虚构的人物几乎同教堂本身同样出名。

之五:为了在第二次世界大战中,从法西斯手中拯救巴黎,使其免遭毁灭,法国政府宣布巴黎为开放城市,意思是法国不作任何抵抗,因此,德军没费吹灰之力,就长驱直入,由香榭丽舍大街开进巴黎。

之六:法国革命的巅峰时期,死刑都在协和广场执行。据估计,有超过一千人在这里被处死,其中前国王路易十六和王后玛丽·安托瓦内特就是在这里上的断头台。

为什么巴黎入选世界50 + 1个城市之首?

巴黎之所以成为世界上最伟大城市的首选,是因为它拥有一个城市必须拥有的一切:夜生活、文化、艺术、建筑、历史、美食和成熟。在历史的长河中,这座城市经历了种种政治动荡、社会变迁和错综发展,然而直到今天城市的建筑及其宝藏依旧保存完好,生机勃勃。尽管政府换了一届又一届,巴黎始终没有变,它是风格的象征,洋溢着文化,彰显着奢华,展示着生活的美好,有哪一个到过巴黎的人不想再次踏上这片热土呢?

Alexandria, Egypt

The Basic Facts

Alexandria is the second largest city in Egypt and the country's largest port. The city is often called the Pearl of the Mediterranean, as its culture and atmosphere tend more toward pan-Mediterranean than Middle Eastern.

Geography

Alexandria lies 31 degrees 12 minutes north latitude and 29 degrees 58 minutes east longitude. The city is located on the Mediterranean Sea in northwest Egypt, about 140 miles from Cairo. It is a mile from Lake Mariout and near the outlets of the Salam Canal and Rosetta River, which emanate from the Nile. Alexandria is built on the former island of Pharos, which was eventually connected to the mainland.

Climate

Alexandria has a relatively moderate climate for Northern Africa. Annual precipitation amounts to a mere eight inches, most of which falls during the months of December and January. Annual temperatures range from the mid-50s Fahrenheit in winter to the low 80s Fahrenheit in summer. This mild weather enables tourists to wander comfortably throughout the city.

Demographics

The vast majority of Alexandria's population was born in Egypt, although there are small concentrations of Bedouins, as well as Palestinian and Sudanese refugees.Islam is the majority religion, constituting nearly 90 percent of the inhabitants;the remaining residents are primarily adherents of Coptic Orthodox Christianity.Alexandria is estimated to have between 3.5 million and 5 million residents.

Economy

Alexandria's strategic location along the southern Mediterranean Coast has made it an important industrial center and port in Egypt. Major natural gas and oil pipelines originate in the nearby Suez Canal. Nearly 80 percent of Egypt's imports and exports flow through the city's harbors. Tourism is a vital facet of the economy as well. International tourists visit to explore Alexandria's rich historical past, as well as to escape nearby Cairo when the summer heat becomes unbearable.

The History

The city is named for Alexander the Great, who founded the city in 323 B.C. after conquering ancient Egypt. Under Ptolemy, Alexandria later became the capital of Egypt. The city had already become a major trade center, and its population grew rapidly. After Rome conquered Egypt in 30 B.C., the Roman Empire took full advantage of Alexandria's

埃及亚历山大

概况

　　亚历山大是埃及第二大城市，也是埃及最大的港口。虽地处中东，但因其文化及环境氛围更倾向于地中海，时常被人们称为"地中海的珍珠"。

一、地理

　　亚历山大市位于北纬31°12′，东经29°58′，地处埃及西北部的地中海地区，距离开罗大约140英里，距离迈尔尤特湖一英里，在萨拉姆运河和发源于尼罗河的罗塞塔河河口附近。亚历山大最初创建于法罗斯岛上，后来该岛和大陆连接了起来。

二、气候

　　作为北非的一个城市，亚历山大气候相对温和，年降水量只有8英寸，且大多集中在12月至1月间，年平均气温冬季在华氏55度左右，夏季在华氏80度以下。温和的天气使得游客能够在舒适的环境里畅游城市。

三、人口

　　尽管有一小部分贝都因人、巴勒斯坦人和苏丹难民，亚历山大市的人口大多还是当地出生的埃及人。伊斯兰教是大多数人信仰的宗教，占总人口的近90%，其余居民主要属于科普特东正教派。据估计，亚历山大市有350万~500万居民。

四、经济

　　亚历山大市位于地中海南部沿岸，其战略性的位置使之成为埃及的一个重要的工业中心和港口，主要的天然气和石油管道发源于附近的苏伊士运河，埃及近80%的进出口货物都必须经过亚历山大港进行吞吐。旅游业也是其经济很重要的方面，世界各地的游客有的来亚历山大探寻其过往丰富的历史，有的则在夏季酷热难耐时，从附近的开罗来这里避暑。

光影流金

　　亚历山大市是以亚历山大大帝的名字命名的。公元前323年，在征服了古埃及之后，他建立了这座城市。托勒密王朝时期，亚历山大市成为埃及的首都，并且已经发展成为一个主要的贸易中心，城市人口迅速增长。公元前30年，罗马人征服了埃及，罗马皇帝充分

port to expand its reach in the Mediterranean.Over the next 2 millennia, various entities controlled the city: the Arabs, who moved the national capital to Cairo; the Ottomans; the Napoleonic French; and finally the British, who employed Alexandria as a naval base in both World Wars.The British withdrew from Egypt in the early 1950s and the country became a sovereign nation.

The Sights and Sounds

Unfortunately, little of the ancient city of Alexandria survives today. Prominent buildings were destroyed either by natural forces or were razed for reconstruction.Among the few monuments that remain to this day is Pompey's Pillar, located in the acropolis next to the Arab cemetery. The pillar is a 99-foot edifice of red granite that was once part of a temple colonnade.

Kom al Sukkfa, the catacombs of Alexandria, are a short distance from Pompey's Pillar. This labyrinth of graves and chambers is on several levels and contains ancient pillars, statues and sarcophagi accentuated with Egyptian and Roman inscriptions. Kom al Dikka is a contemporary excavation in the city proper; to date archaeologists have discovered the ruins of an ancient theatre and Roman baths.

The oldest section of Alexandria lies along the causeway that links the former island of Pharos to the mainland. The city districts that comprise the Turkish Quarter are Gumrok, Anfushi, and Ras el-Tin. The Quarter forms a T-shape that divides Alexandria's eastern and western harbors. The Bibliotheca Alexandrina attempts to recreate the Library of Alexandria, famous throughout the world as the storehouse of countless ancient papyrus scrolls. The contemporary granite-andglass structure is a fascinating complex of museums, galleries, and research laboratories, and also has a planetarium and large reading room.

Alexandria's Greek Quarter is one of the finest residential districts in the city.Wealthy Greeks lived here at the turn of the century and the street names still reflect its Greek heritage. Notable landmarks here include the church of St. Saba and the Shallalat Gardens, on the site of the former Bab Rosetta fortification. The Zoological Gardens, the Museum of Natural History, and the Fine Arts Museum are located in close proximity, and public gardens extend into the surrounding area of the Antoniadis Palace.

Among the famous Islamic sites in the city are the Attarine Mosque, once a Christian church; Fort Qaitbey, built in the 1480s on the site of the ancient lighthouse at Pharos; the Mosque of Abu al-Abbas al-Mursi, Alexandria's largest and most important shrine; the Mostafa Kamel Graveyard, with four tombs that date to the 2nd century B.C.; the Muntazah Complex, a 115 acres palace with magnificent gardens; Shatby Tomb, the oldest of its kind in the city; and Terbana Mosque, one of the few remaining ancient mosques in Alexandria.

The Trivia

Fact: Another famous Muhammad Ali—no apparent relation to the world-famous boxing champion—was an Ottoman army officer who ruled Egypt after the French were ousted from the country. Ali helped to revive Alexandria's regional importance, which had waned for centuries as the city languished as a fishing village.

Fact: The Lighthouse of Alexandria is considered one of the Seven Wonders of the Ancient World, and the only one with a practical usage. This lighthouse ensured sailors a

利用亚历山大港有利的位置,将势力扩大到地中海地区。在接下来的2 000年时间里,各种政权交替统治该市:首先是阿拉伯人,是他们将埃及首都迁往了开罗,其次是奥斯曼人,以及拿破仑统治时期的法国人,最后是英国人。在两次世界大战当中,英国人把亚历山大市变成了军事基地。20世纪50年代初,英国人从埃及撤军后,埃及成为独立的主权国家。

声光景点

令人遗憾的是,古老的亚历山大市如今几乎已消失殆尽,其辉煌的建筑要么由于自然界力量的破坏,要么因为城市改造而被夷为平地,在硕果仅存的几处历史遗迹当中,有一根庞贝神柱,位于阿拉伯公墓旁边的卫城,这根高99英尺的巨大而雄伟的柱子,是由红色花岗岩制成的,过去曾经是一座庙宇廊柱的一部分。

在距离庞贝神柱不远的地方,是孔姆索嘎法,亚历山大大帝的地宫,这座由墓穴和地宫构成的迷宫有上下几层,包括古代的石柱、雕塑及刻有埃及和罗马文字的石棺等。孔姆拉索嘎法地宫是一座于当代发掘的位于城区的遗址,至今,考古学家已经在此发现了古代的剧院和罗马时期的浴场等遗迹。

亚历山大市最古老的部分位于过去连接法罗斯岛和大陆的砌道两侧。城里土耳其居民区部分由冈姆洛克、安福诗和拉斯埃丁组成,这一区域形似T型,将亚历山大港分成东西两部分。亚历山德拉藏书馆的修建是试图恢复亚历山大图书馆,那座以收藏了无数古代纸草卷轴而闻名天下的宝库的原貌,这座修建于当代的由花岗岩和玻璃构成的建筑,是一个集博物馆、画廊、研究实验室为一体的综合性大楼,并且还配有一个天文馆及一个大型阅览室。

亚历山大市的希腊区是该市最好的居住区之一,就在世纪之交的时候,富足的希腊人就住在这里,这里的街道名称仍然反映出希腊的传统。街道两边有历史意义的著名建筑物包括圣·萨匹教堂和建在过去巴布·塞塔塔城堡旧址之上的萨拉拉特花园。此外,动物园、自然历史博物馆、美术博物馆也坐落于邻近地区,公共花园延伸到周边的安东尼帝斯宫殿地区。

在城市著名的伊斯兰教地区有埃塔塔瑞清真寺,过去曾经是基督教教堂。修建于15世纪80年代的奎特贝要塞,其旧址是古代法罗斯岛上的灯塔。阿布阿巴斯·阿莫斯清真寺是亚历山大市最大也是最重要的圣地。穆斯塔法·卡梅尔墓地拥有四座公元前2世纪的陵墓。占地115公顷的蒙塔扎宫是一座有着华丽花园的宫殿群。沙特比陵墓是城中最古老的墓园。特巴纳清真寺是亚历山大市少有的几座保存至今的古代清真寺之一。

奇闻轶事

之一:另一位著名的穆罕默德·阿里 —— 和世界拳王没什么明显关系 —— 是奥斯曼帝国军队的一位军官,他在法国人被驱逐之后统治埃及,并帮助亚历山大恢复了其区域的重要性,而这一重要性在几个世纪里曾因城市沦落为渔村而逐渐减弱。

之二:亚历山大的灯塔被公认为世界古代七大奇迹之一,而且是唯一一个具有实际用途的奇迹。这座灯塔保证了海上船员平安返航,曾经一度成为那个时代世界上最高的

safe return to the harbor. It was the tallest building in the world at the time; with its foundation, the lighthouse stood nearly 400 feet. Its mirror reflected the sun's rays during the day, and could be seen more than 35 miles offshore. A large fire was the source of nighttime light for the structure; fuel for the fire was lifted through the tower's internal core. The building's summit was adored with a statue of Poseidon, the Greek god of the sea.

Fact: The Library at Alexandria once boasted a collection of half a million delicate papyrus scrolls, its contents detailing the vast body of knowledge discovered by the scientists and historians of the ancient world. Papyrus was invented by the Egyptians and was a primary export during that era.

Why Alexandria Is a 50 plus one City

So many civilizations have left their mark on this fascinating city. Although much of its history is lost to the ages, what remains offers tourists a glimpse into the importance of this Mediterranean city. Today the city thrives as a vibrant center for regional and international trade. Alexandria is a great city because it is cosmopolitan, known for its rich culture as well as for its historical prominence.

建筑,加上地基,灯塔高度近400英尺。白天灯塔上面的镜子所反射的太阳光线,在35英里之外都能够看见。而夜间一束巨大的火焰成为灯塔的光源,供火焰燃烧的燃料是由灯塔内部核心部位提升上来的。灯塔的顶端装饰有一个希腊神话中海神波塞冬的雕像。

之三:亚历山大图书馆曾经收藏有50万册精致的纸草卷轴文献,其内容详细介绍了古代世界科学家和历史学家广博的知识。纸草是古代埃及人的发明,也是那个时代主要的出口商品。

为什么亚历山大市入选50＋1个城市?

如此众多的文明在这一充满魅力的城市留下印迹,虽然随着岁月的推移,众多历史事实已然消失风化,但是残存下来的部分依然为游客提供了一个粗略了解这一地中海城市重要性的可能。今天,这个城市作为地中海地区及世界贸易活跃的中心地区,正在迅速发展,亚历山大是一个伟大的城市,因为它是世界性的,其丰富的文化和曾经显著的历史地位人所共知。

Two

Amsterdam, The Netherlands

The Basic Facts

Amsterdam is the capital of the Netherlands and the country's largest city. Second only to Rotterdam as the Netherlands' busiest port, Amsterdam is undoubtedly the cultural and financial center of the nation. Its name is derived from the Amstel River which flows through its confines.

Geography

Amsterdam lies at 52 degrees 21 minutes north latitude and 4 degrees 52 minutes east longitude. The city is located in North Holland Province on the banks of the IJsselmeer near The Hague. Amsterdam is a flat city, most of which is below sea level. The metropolis rests on a foundation of piles driven through peat and sand to the underlying clay substratum. The city's many canals are famous the world over and are a popular attraction for visitors. Amsterdam is linked to the North Sea and to other European countries by a network of railways, highways and canals. Amsterdam Schiphol Airport is one of Europe's busiest and continues to expand with increasing traffic to and from the Netherlands.

Climate

Amsterdam has a temperate climate similar to that of England; winters are mild and summers are rarely uncomfortably hot. Annual temperatures range from the mid-30s Fahrenheit in winter to the mid-50s Fahrenheit in summer. The city receives a considerable amount of rain throughout the year—a boon to the area's well-known symbol, the tulip, its blooms becoming a colorful carpet each spring.

Government

Amsterdam's government consists of a mayor, aldermen, and a municipal council. During the 1980s, as a means to improve municipal services, Amsterdam was divided into 15 boroughs. Local decisions are made at the borough level, but matters that concern the entire city, such as infrastructure improvements, are Amsterdam, The Netherlands decided by the municipal council. Although Amsterdam is the official capital of the country, the seat of government is located in The Hague.

Demographics

The population of Amsterdam numbers approximately 735,000 and the metropolitan area's population is roughly 1.3 million. More than 170 nationalities are represented among the citizens, making Amsterdam one of the world's most culturally-diverse cities. Roman Catholicism is the dominant religion; minority groups include Protestant Christians and Muslims. Nearly 86 percent of the population is under the age of 65.

荷兰阿姆斯特丹

概况

　　阿姆斯特丹是荷兰首都和最大的城市。作为荷兰最繁忙的港口,其地位仅次于鹿特丹居第二位。阿姆斯特丹无疑是荷兰文化和金融中心,它的名字来源于流经这一地区的阿姆斯特河。

一、地理

　　阿姆斯特丹位于北纬52°21′,东经4°52′,地处靠近海牙的艾瑟尔湖两岸的北荷兰省。阿姆斯特丹是一个平坦的城市,大部分处于海平面以下。这个大都会建在由泥炭和沙子经堆积成为地下的黏土层,并进而形成的地基之上。城里的许多运河在世界上都非常有名,同时也深受旅游者的欢迎。阿姆斯特丹和北海相连,并且通过铁路、公路和运河网同其他欧洲国家联系。阿姆斯特丹史基浦国际机场是欧洲最繁忙的机场之一,由于进出荷兰的运输量逐年增大,机场仍在不停地扩建。

二、气候

　　阿姆斯特丹和英国一样气候温和,冬季温暖,夏季很少出现闷热天气。年平均气温冬季在华氏35度,夏季在华氏55度左右,全年降水丰富——这对于该地区著名的象征,郁金香的生长非常有益。每年春天,郁金香花盛开,为大地铺上五彩斑斓的花毯。

三、政府

　　阿姆斯特丹市政府由市长、市政官员和市政委员会组成。20世纪80年代,作为改善市政服务的措施,阿姆斯特丹市被划分为15个区。地方决策由区一级来制定,但是诸如基础设施改善之类涉及全市的事务,则由市政委员会决定。虽然阿姆斯特丹是荷兰的官方首都,但是政府的真正所在地却设在海牙。

四、人口

　　阿姆斯特丹市区人口接近73.5万,大市范围的人口大约有130万。荷兰公民由具有代表性的170多个民族构成,这使得阿姆斯特丹成为世界上文化最为多元的城市之一。罗马天主教是占主导地位的宗教,人数较少的宗教包括新教和伊斯兰教。近86%的城市人口年龄在65周岁以下。

Economy

Amsterdam's strategic location in the European Union (EU) makes the city an important commercial center. The European headquarters of many international corporations are located here. Amsterdam's leading industries are shipbuilding, sugar refining, publishing, beer brewing, and manufacturing. Goods produced here include heavy machinery, paper products, textiles and clothing, porcelain, glass, aircraft parts, automobiles, and chemicals. Amsterdam is also recognized worldwide as a center for diamond cutting and polishing. The service industry is a major employer as well, and includes banking, insurance, and tourism.

The History

Amsterdam was founded in the 13th century and joined the Hanseatic League in 1369. By the middle of the 16th century, the city was swept up in the Protestant Reformation. Religious tolerance attracted Flemish merchants, Jewish diamond cutters, and French Huguenots, thus enhancing the size and diversity of the city's population. Amsterdam quickly became a burgeoning trade center, as merchants moved their goods through its ports to the rest of the Netherlands and to Western Europe.

Amsterdam became the capital of the Kingdom of the Netherlands. Even today, royals are typically crowned in Amsterdam, although they reside in a palace outside the city. The Nazi occupation during World War II devastated the city, and the government—which by then had been taken over by the Nazis—nearly wiped out the city's considerable Jewish population. Amsterdam slowly but steadily recovered from the destruction of the war to once again become a great European city.

The Sights and Sounds

Amsterdam, being a compact and flat city, is a walker's dream. The streets of the old city radiate outward from the many canals. Veteran tourists often suggest beginning at Central Station, which was built in 1903 and remains an important hub for intercity rail transportation.

The Beurs van Berlage is the home of the former Amsterdam Stock Exchange and is considered an architectural masterpiece. The building was designed by the architect Hendrick Petrus Berlage and constructed of red brick. The Weighthouse, which dates from 1616, was originally used to weigh the large quantities of hennep (cannabis) that passed through the city's ports. This building is located in an area called New Market, the oldest part of the city.

Amsterdam is famous as the hiding place of the diarist Anne Frank, her family and friends. The young author hid for 2 years in an attic in her father's office building, desperate to avoid discovery by the Nazis. The group was later betrayed and captured, and in 1945 Anne Frank died of typhus in 1945 while interned in a concentration camp. Her father Otto published her writings in 1947. *The Diary of a Young Girl,* as it is known in English, is a much-beloved autobiography that details her struggle to survive amid the Nazi occupation of Amsterdam. The book became an international sensation and was adapted for stage and screen. The building where she lived for those 2 years is now the Anne Frank Museum, and is dedicated to her memory and to the eradication of persecution and discrimination.

五、经济

阿姆斯特丹所处的位置使之成为欧盟(EU)重要的商业中心,许多国际公司的欧洲总部都设在这里。阿姆斯特丹最主要的工业是造船业、蔗糖提炼、出版业、啤酒酿造和加工制造业。这里生产的商品包括重型机械、造纸产品、纺织品和服装、瓷器、玻璃、航空零部件、汽车及化学制品等。此外,阿姆斯特丹还被认为是世界上钻石切割和加工的中心。服务行业也是主要的就业领域,例如,银行业、保险业和旅游业。

光影流金

阿姆斯特丹建于13世纪,1369年加入汉萨同盟。16世纪中期,新教改革之风吹遍阿姆斯特丹,宗教上的宽容吸引了许多佛兰芒商人、犹太钻石切割匠、法国的胡格诺派教徒来到这里。因此,城市人口的数量和多样性进一步加大。阿姆斯特丹发展迅速,很快就成为一个贸易中心,各地商人纷至沓来,将他们的商品从阿姆斯特丹港运往荷兰或欧洲其他地方。

阿姆斯特丹是荷兰王国的首都,即使在今天,尽管王室成员都住在城外的王宫里,他们仍会在阿姆斯特丹举行象征性的加冕仪式。第二次世界大战期间,纳粹占领了阿姆斯特丹,城市惨遭践踏,当时的政府 —— 由于已被纳粹接管 —— 几乎将城里的犹太人全部杀死。然而,阿姆斯特丹还是缓慢地、稳步地从战争的创伤中恢复了过来,并再次成为欧洲最伟大的城市之一。

声光景点

作为一个平坦而紧凑的城市,阿姆斯特丹是步行者的天堂。这座古老的城市中有许多条运河,城里的街道以众多运河为出发点向四周伸展。经验丰富的游客常建议以中央车站为游览的出发点,这座建于1903年的车站至今仍是城际间轨道交通的重要枢纽。

伯尔拉赫交易所是以前阿姆斯特丹证券交易所的旧址,被认为是建筑上的杰作。由建筑师亨德里克·P.伯尔拉赫所设计的这座大楼全部用红砖砌成。过磅房的历史可以追溯到1616年,起初是为大量经过阿姆斯特丹港的汉尼普(即大麻)计重用的。过磅房位于一处名曰"新市场"的区域,是城中最古老的部分。

阿姆斯特丹作为日记作家安妮·弗兰克及其家人、朋友的藏身地而闻名遐迩。这位年轻的作家在她父亲办公大楼的阁楼里躲了两年,竭力想避免被纳粹发现。然而后来,他们这群人因为有人出卖而被捕,1945年,在被关押的集中营里,安妮·弗兰克死于当年爆发的斑疹伤寒。1947年,他的父亲奥托将她的手稿发表出来,众所周知,这本取名为《一个年轻女孩的日记》的英文版是一本深受读者喜爱的自传,书中详细地描述了在被纳粹占领的阿姆斯特丹她是如何艰难求生的。这本书在全世界轰动一时,被改编成戏剧,并被搬上了银幕。那座她曾住过两年的大楼如今成了安妮·弗兰克博物馆,作为对她、同时也是对消灭种族歧视和迫害的纪念。

The Netherlands Maritime Museum has an extensive collection of restored sailing ships and vessel. The Weepers' Tower is a 15th century lookout, where women scanned the seas for their seafaring husbands, in hopes of a safe return from their long voyages abroad. The Golden Bend on the Gentleman's Canal is known for its beautiful 17th century homes where the wealthy merchant class moved in their search for upward mobility.

The Dutch artist Rembrandt was perhaps the greatest portrait painter in European history. His legacy lives on in several museums in Amsterdam. His house in the city, where he worked for 20 years, displays a collection of his etchings among other exhibits. The State Museum is the pearl of Dutch museums, holding the crème-de-la-crème of the 16th- and 17th century Dutch Masters. Rembrandt's works are prominently displayed along with those of Franz Hals, Jan Steen and others. The Museum of Modern Art has an excellent permanent collection of modern artworks and frequently displays traveling exhibits from around the world. The Van Gogh Museum contains a vast collection of artworks by the renowned Dutch artist. Nearly 700 of his works are represented, including his paintings and drawings. Works of his contemporaries are also displayed here, as well as traveling exhibits of temporary shows of 19th and 20th century artists.

The Leidseplein is the center of Amsterdam's nightlife, which is internationally known for its permissiveness. Brown cafés dot the city, and are a wonderful way to meet the typically friendly Dutch. They are so named for the color of their interiors, darkened over the years from copious amounts of tobacco smoke.

Amsterdam has many beautiful churches. Dutch sovereigns are crowned at the New Church, which is ironically one of the oldest buildings in the city. The Old Church is, however, aptly named; the building dates from the 13th century and was dedicated to St. Nicholas, the patron saint of Amsterdam.

The Trivia

Fact: Amsterdam is built upon pilings driven into the marshy land. These pilings do not rot, however, because there is so little oxygen in the ground. Houses are built to lean against others for support. Homeowners are taxed according to the number of pilings needed to support their houses; as a result, the thrifty Dutch tend to build rather narrow houses.

Fact: One of the city's cultural attractions is its infamous Red Light District, where prostitution is legal. Unfamiliar tourists are often surprised to see women displayed in windows, offering their services to passersby.

Fact: Beer was first brewed at the Heineken Brewery in the 16th century and continued uninterrupted until 1988. Brewery tours and beer sampling are available.

Why Amsterdam Is a 50 plus one City

Amsterdam is beautiful and welcoming, tolerant and diverse. The city's history is reflected throughout the metropolitan area. Amsterdam is an engineering marvel that has kept the North Sea at bay for centuries. Thoroughly modern, the city's intimate feel attracts visitors from all over the world.

　　荷兰海洋博物馆收藏有大量复原的帆船和货轮。哭泣者之塔是一座15世纪时修建的瞭望台，从那里妇女们眺望大海，搜寻着她们以航海为生的丈夫的踪影，期盼他们在经过长时间海外航行之后能够平安归来。绅士运河上的黄金弯地区非常有名，那里有许多漂亮的17世纪风格的住宅，是当时有钱的商人们为了能够进入上流社会而修建的。

　　在欧洲历史上，荷兰画家伦勃朗或许称得上是最伟大的肖像画家了。他的绘画遗产在阿姆斯特丹的几家博物馆得以留存。在他曾经工作过20年的房子里展出的有他全部的蚀刻画，当然还包括其他一些作品。国家博物馆是荷兰博物馆中的明珠，拥有16~17世纪荷兰大师们的精华之作，伦勃朗的作品同弗朗茨·哈尔斯、简·斯藤以及其他一些画家的作品一道被摆放在显眼的位置。现代艺术博物馆是现代艺术作品完美的永久性收藏馆，这里还时常展出一些来自世界各地的流动性展品。凡·高博物馆拥有这位著名荷兰画家大量的艺术作品，近700件展品包括他的油画和素描，以及一些风格前卫的作品。此外，这里也能看到一些临时展出的19世纪和20世纪画家的流动性展品。

　　莱顿广场是阿姆斯特丹夜生活的中心，以其放纵的生活而世界闻名。遍布城中的褐色酒吧是你结识典型而友好的荷兰人的好去处，之所以称之为褐色酒吧，是因为这些酒吧的内部都因经年累月被大量烟草熏烤而变成了黑色。

　　阿姆斯特丹有许多漂亮的教堂，荷兰国王的加冕仪式就是在"新教堂"举行的，有意思的是，这座教堂却是城中最古老的建筑之一。不过，另一座"老教堂"却是名副其实的，它修建于13世纪，是专门为了献给圣·尼古拉斯 —— 阿姆斯特丹的神圣庇护人而建造的。

奇闻轶事

　　之一：阿姆斯特丹市是建造在无数被打入湿地中的木桩之上的，然而，这些木桩却并不会腐烂，因为在地下几乎没有氧气。此外，房屋在建起之后，还需倚靠其他的支撑。房主必须根据自家房屋所依靠的木桩数缴纳税款，结果就是，那些精明的荷兰人都把房子盖成了窄窄的。

　　之二：城中臭名远扬的娱乐景点之一是红灯区，那里的妓女拥有合法的身份，初来乍到的游客常惊讶于那些窗子后面的女人，她们搔首弄姿地向过路人招揽生意。

　　之三：啤酒最早从16世纪起就在喜力酿造厂开始酿造，此后，这种不间断的酿造生产持续到了1988年。如今，参观啤酒厂和啤酒样品也成了旅游项目。

为什么阿姆斯特丹市入选50＋1个城市？

　　阿姆斯特丹是个美丽、亲切、宽容而又多变的城市，它的历史在大都会的每个角落得以反映。几个世纪以来，阿姆斯特丹控制了北海，从而造就了一项工程上的奇迹。完完全全的现代以及怡人舒适的感觉，让它吸引了来自世界各地的游客。

Three

Athens, Greece

The Basic Facts

The capital of Greece, Athens is renowned the world over for its history and importance to Western culture. It is the cultural, economic, governmental and educational center of Greek life. Unfortunately, much of its former glory has been replaced with modern architecture, leading many people to refer to contemporary Athens as a concrete jungle.

Geography

Athens lies at 38 degrees north latitude and 23 degrees 38 minutes longitude. It is located in the plane of Attica and surrounded by mountains, the highest of which is Mount Parnitha, at nearly 5,000 feet. The highest point in Athens, which covers roughly 15 square miles, is the pine-covered Lykavitos Hill.

Climate

The weather in Athens is generally mild, pleasant, and frequently sunny—the ideal tourist environment. Annual temperatures range from the mid-50s Fahrenheit in winter to the mid-90s in summer. Regrettably, the surrounding mountains prevent winds from reaching Athens, and so urban pollution can be problematic in the summer. In fact, the city's pollution is generally considered the worst in Europe.

Government

Athens is one of 54 towns and villages that have been subsumed into the Municipality of Athens. A mayor and several district councils govern the municipality. The city itself is divided into seven districts that administer their respective city services.

Demographics

Nearly a third of the entire population of Greece calls Athens home. The population of the city Athens is estimated at 750,000, although the metropolitan area has some 3.2 million inhabitants. More than half of the population is between the ages of 15 and 64, and nearly all residents are ethnic Greeks. Greek Orthodox Christianity is the dominant religion.

Economy

Athens has a mixed capitalist economy and is one of the poorest countries in the European Union. Reconstructing the economy and reducing unemployment are currently the city's major challenges. Tourism and shipping are the main industries of Athens. The city welcomes millions of tourists every year, and its shipping sector is one of the most important in the world. Agriculture accounts for a mere 15 percent of the economy.

第三章　希腊雅典

概况

希腊首都雅典因其悠久的历史和对西方文化的重要性而享誉全球，它是希腊文化、经济、政府和教育的中心。令人惋惜的是，往昔古城那辉煌的容颜大多已被现代化的建筑所取代，在许多人眼里，如今的雅典已经成了钢筋混凝土的丛林。

一、地理

雅典位于北纬38°，东经23°38′的位置，地处群山环绕的阿提卡平原地区，这里最高的山脉是海拔近5 000英尺的帕尼撒山，而雅典境内的制高点则是面积约15平方英里的被松林覆盖的利卡维多斯山丘。

二、气候

一般来说，雅典气候温和、舒适怡人、阳光明媚 —— 理想的旅游环境。年均气温在冬季的华氏55度到夏季的华氏95度。遗憾的是，由于周围山脉的阻挡，风很难吹进雅典，到了夏天，城市的污染就成了一个头疼的问题。事实上，雅典的污染通常被认为是欧洲最严重的。

三、政府

雅典是已经纳入雅典自治区所辖的54个市镇和乡村之一，该自治区由一个市长和若干个区议会来管理，雅典市划分为7个区，各区负责相应的行政事业服务。

四、人口

整个希腊人口的近三分之一都将雅典称为他们的"家"。据估计，雅典市区人口有75万，不过，大市范围的居民却有约320万。超过半数的人口年龄在15至64岁之间，几乎所有的居民都属于希腊族。希腊东正教是他们主要信仰的宗教。

五、经济

希腊属于混合型的资本主义经济，是欧盟最穷的国家之一。重组经济体系和减少失业人口是当前城市所面临的主要挑战。旅游和造船业是雅典主要的工业，每年，雅典要迎接数百万计的游客，而雅典的造船业使之成为世界造船业最重要的区域之一。农业在雅典经济当中仅仅占了15%的比例。

The History

Athens is named for Athena, the Greek goddess of wisdom. It is unclear when the city was actually founded. It is known, however, that the Greeks occupied Attica as early as 1900 B.C.; Attica became one of the first Peloponnesian city-states. Royalty was replaced by democracy in 510 B.C. with the creation of an unwritten constitution. The 2 century Golden Age of Greece followed; at this time Athens became a center of culture and intellectualism, which led to the advent of Western civilization.

Athens lost its political leadership in the Peleponnesus after its defeat in the war against its rival city-state Sparta. By the Byzantine era, Athens was little more than an insigni.cant provincial town. In 1458 A.D the city fell to the Ottoman Empire led by Sultan Mehmet the Conqueror. Ironically, the conquest proved beneficial to the preservation of the city's ruins; the sultan declared that they were to be left unspoiled. The Parthenon, for example, was spared after being converted to a mosque.

By the 17th century, the Ottoman Empire began to fail, and the ancient buildings of Athens were once again neglected. The Venetians laid siege to the city in the late 17th century, and the famed Parthenon was largely destroyed by enemy attack.

The Ottomans relinquished control of Greece in the mid-19th century, and Athens became the capital of the new kingdom, despite the fact that the population now languished at a mere 5,000 inhabitants. The city flourished after being rebuilt in a neoclassical style, and its population grew. As evidence of the city's return to prominence, Athens hosted the first modern Olympics in 1896.

Italy and Germany occupied the city during World War II. Athens was an open city, meaning that it would neither fortify nor attempt to defend itself without risking massive destruction. Soon after the war, archaeologists and preservationists began considerable efforts to restore and protect the city's ancient buildings. Their work has contributed to the city's current blend of modern and ancient architecture.

In anticipation of hosting the Summer Olympics in 2004, Greece overhauled many parts of the city, constructed new housing, improved its public transportation system, expanded its airport, and built state-of-the-art facilities for athletes.

The Sights and Sounds

Although Athens is a sprawling city, most of the key sights and sounds can be found in its compact city center. The Acropolis is the focal point of Athens, a rather flat hill crowned by the Parthenon. The imposing structure has a magnificent presence regardless of the time of day. Even before its completion in 438 B.C., the building was considered a marvel of sophisticated art and architecture. Its original red and blue decorations are long gone, however, and the marble pillars have lost their shine. The largest surviving relic of the original frieze is now in London's British Museum, and Greece has been petitioning for its return for some time.

The National Archaeological Museum displays an extensive collection of antiquities, including the world's largest collection of Greek art and artifacts. The collection at the Goulandris Museum of Cycladic and Greek Ancient Art spans nearly 5,000 years of art history; 100 exhibits date to 3000 B.C.. The Acropolis Museum has a significant number of koria, female figures that were sculpted in dedication to Athena. The Byzantine Museum, housed in a 19th century mansion, is dedicated solely to preserving the Byzantine history of

光影流金

雅典是以智慧女神雅典娜的名字命名的，这个城市究竟何时建立已经无从考究，然而，我们已知的是早在公元前1900年，希腊人就占领了阿提卡。而阿提卡是最早建立起来的伯罗奔尼撒城邦之一。公元前510年，随着一部非书面宪法的诞生，民主制度取代了封建皇权，随后，希腊进入了长达两个世纪的黄金时期，那时候，雅典成为文化和理智主义的中心，进而引起西方文明的萌芽。

在同敌对城邦斯巴达的战争中，雅典战败，并失去了对伯罗奔尼撒半岛的政治掌控。到了拜占庭时期，雅典仅仅算一个不起眼的地方小镇。到了公元1458年，它又沦为征服者苏丹·穆罕默德统治的奥斯曼帝国的一部分。耐人寻味的是，事实证明此次征服，对于古城遗址的保护却是非常有益的，因为苏丹宣布所有古迹都将原封不动的保留下来，例如，帕台农神庙在被改为清真寺之后就得以幸免于难。

到了17世纪，奥斯曼帝国开始衰落，雅典的那些古建筑再次被人忽视。17世纪后期，威尼斯人围攻雅典，著名的帕台农神庙在敌人的炮火声中大部分被毁坏了。

19世纪中期，奥斯曼人将雅典的政权交还给了希腊人，雅典成为新王国的首都，尽管当时的事实是雅典的人口仅剩下5 000人。在以新古典主义风格进行重建之后，雅典日益繁荣起来，人口数量不断增加。作为城市地位回升的见证，1896年，雅典主办了第一届现代奥林匹克运动会。

第二次世界大战期间，意大利和德国占领了雅典，当时的雅典属于一个开放的城市，换句话说，它既没有防御工事，也不打算进行防御，以此来避免大规模的伤亡。战争一结束，考古学家和文物保护专家便开始投入精力恢复及保护城市的古建筑，正是由于他们的工作，造就了今天的雅典市内现代与古典建筑的完美融合。

在力争主办2004年夏季奥运会期间，希腊将城市许多地区进行了拆除改建，盖起了新的大厦，改善了公共交通，扩大了机场，修建了最新的体育设施。

声光景点

虽然雅典是一个布局散乱的城市，但是大多数重要的景点都可以在密集的市中心找到。雅典卫城是雅典市的焦点景区，在一处相当平坦的山丘上矗立着帕台农神庙。尽管岁月沧桑，这座雄伟的建筑依然有一种恢宏的气势。即便是在公元前438年，神庙尚未完工的时候，它就被当成复杂工艺和建筑学上的奇迹。然而，如今原有的红色和蓝色装饰早已消失殆尽，大理石柱也失去了应有的光泽，幸存下来的原有顶柱雕带的最大残片，现今陈列于伦敦的大英博物馆，希腊政府则一直请求英国能够归还。

在国家考古博物馆，能够看到大量展出的文物，其中汇集了世界上最大的希腊艺术和手工艺品。古兰德立的基克拉迪文化和古希腊艺术博物馆，其藏品跨越了近5 000年的历史，有100件展品来源于公元前3000年。卫城博物馆拥有相当数量的克丽亚，这是一种用来供奉给雅典娜的女性雕像。拜占庭博物馆是一座建于19世纪的大厦，专门用来保存雅典及周边地区在拜占庭帝国时期的历史文物。宗教人物的圣像是希腊拜占庭教堂模式

Athens and the surrounding area.   Religious icons accent models of Greek Byzantine churches,constructed as they might have appeared in their prime.

The Odeon of Herod Atticus is a restored 2nd century Greek theatre built into a hillside; the theatre continues to stage performances. Panathenaic Stadium is a recreation of the ancient Roman stadium building in Athens. This 80,000 seat venue of marble gleams in the bright sun and was built for the 1896 Olympics.Hadrian's Arch was built in 131 to commemorate Roman control of Athens.Constitution Square was built in 1838 as the new royal palace when the Greeks finally separated themselves from the Ottomans; today it is the home of Parliament. The transit station in the square displays fragments and artifacts recovered during construction.

The modern section of Athens also offers several reasons to visit including the shopping center between Omonia Square and Constitution Square.   Stores and fine restaurants abound, and trolleys are available from Omonia Square for tourists with tired feet. The Plaka is one of the most popular tourist districts; its neoclassical buildings and traditional tavernas make it one of the most beautiful neighborhoods in the city center. The nightlife of Athens is also a draw; most bars and nightclubs are open until 3 a.m.. Betika is a uniquely Greek form of the blues,enjoyed by many.   The Psiri neighborhood is the hot new club area with the latest music and dance.

The Trivia

Fact: The Greeks built Athens on and around a large rocky hill with a flat top.   This became known as the Acropolis, from the Greek akro (high) and polis (city).The Acropolis gradually became a center of temples and public buildings; ruins of these structures remain to this day.

Fact: The Parthenon has an interesting history. At various times it was a Roman brothel, a Christian Church, a Turkish mosque, and a storage depot for gunpowder.

Why Athens Is a 50 plus one City

Thousands of years of Greek, Roman and Byzantine culture, art and architecture are represented in Athens. No European city has had a greater influence on Western culture, civilization, and democracy.

的重点,从中可以领略到其全盛时期的风貌。

希律·阿提卡斯剧场是一座依山重建的公元2世纪的古希腊剧场,剧场的演出延续至今。泛雅典娜体育场则是一座再造的位于雅典的古罗马竞技场,这座能够容纳八万人的大理石会场是专为1896年的奥运会而修建的,今天它仍然在阳光下闪闪发光。

哈德良拱门修建于131年,为的是纪念罗马人统治雅典。宪法广场建于1838年,当希腊人最终和奥斯曼人分离之后,它被当做新的皇宫,如今这里则是议会大厦,在广场的地铁转乘站能够欣赏到广场建设时期发现的一些艺术作品或残片。

这里有理由向你推荐一下雅典的现代部分,其中包括位于协和广场和宪法广场之间的购物中心,这里有很多的商店和很好的餐馆,走累了的话可以在协和广场乘无轨电车。普拉卡是最受人们欢迎的旅游区之一,新古典风格的建筑加上传统的咖啡馆使之成为市中心最靓丽的街区。雅典丰富的夜生活也是吸引游客的一个原因,大多数酒吧和夜总会都营业到凌晨3点,贝提卡是一种深受游客喜爱的希腊特有的蓝调音乐。普西里街区属于热门的新兴夜总会区,在那里能够欣赏到最新潮的音乐和舞蹈。

奇闻轶事

之一:希腊人围绕一座有着平顶的巨大的石头山建起了雅典,这就是著名的雅典卫城,这个名称取自希腊语的"阿克罗"(高)和"波利斯"(城市)。渐渐地,雅典卫城成为庙宇和公共建筑的中心,这些建筑的遗迹残存至今。

之二:帕台农神庙有一段有趣的历史。在不同的时期,它曾先后充当过罗马人的妓院、基督徒的教堂、土耳其人的清真寺以及存放枪炮的军火库。

为什么雅典入选50 + 1个城市?

雅典代表了几千年历史的希腊、罗马以及拜占庭的文化、艺术和建筑。它对西方文化、西方文明,乃至西方民主思想的深远影响是任何一个欧洲城市都无法企及的。

Auckland, New Zealand

The Basic Facts

Auckland is the largest city in New Zealand and is nicknamed the City of Sails. The city is a combination of well-preserved historical buildings and modern architecture.

Geography

Auckland lies at 36 degrees 53 minutes south latitude and 174 degrees 45 minutes east longitude. Auckland covers 419 square miles along the Hauraki Gulf of the Pacific Ocean and is one of the few world cities to have harbors on two bodies of water. Auckland is located in the North Island of New Zealand.

Climate

Winters in Auckland are cool and damp, while its summers are warm and humid. Annual temperatures range from the mid-50s Fahrenheit in winter to the low 80s Fahrenheit in summer. Because Auckland is located south of the equator, the winter and summer months are opposite from those in the northern hemisphere; winter occurs between June and August, and summer occurs between December and February.

Government

Auckland is governed by a mayor and city council. In 1989 the center city was merged with other areas to form a new Auckland City.

Demographics

The population of metropolitan Auckland is roughly 1.3 million, most of whom speak English. Auckland's transportation systems have not met the needs of its residents, a typical consequence of urban sprawl. Nearly one in seven people are of Maori descent, giving Auckland a significant Polynesian population.

Economy

Tourism and the service industry are important factors in the city's economy. Auckland's trade industry deals in sheep, timber and dairy, and most of New Zealand's shipping and manufacturing is centered in Auckland.

The History

The Auckland region was settled by Maoris around A.D.450. The area was hotly contested for hundreds of years by groups vying for its rich surrounding lands. In fact, the region's initial name was Tamaki, which in Maori means battle.

European explorers began to visit New Zealand in the late 1700s, and by the end of the century seal and whale hunters and traders took advantage of the area's natural riches. Many were former British convicts from the penal colony in nearby Sydney; as a result,

新西兰奥克兰

概况

奥克兰是新西兰最大的城市,有"帆船之都"的美称。这座城市既有保存完好的古建筑,也有现代化的摩天大楼。

一、地理

奥克兰位于东经174°45′,南纬36°53′,地处太平洋的豪拉基湾沿岸,面积达419平方英里,是世界上仅有的几个在两大洋水域都拥有港口的城市。奥克兰地处新西兰的北岛。

二、气候

奥克兰的冬天凉爽潮湿,夏季则温暖湿润,年平均气温在冬季的华氏55度左右至夏季的华氏81~83度。由于奥克兰位于赤道以南,所以冬夏两季的月份与北半球正好相反,冬天出现在6月到8月,夏天则为12月至2月。

三、政府

奥克兰市由一位市长和一个市政委员会管理,1989年,其中心城市与周边其他几个地区合并组成了新的奥克兰市。

四、人口

奥克兰大市范围的人口约有130万,绝大多数人讲英语。奥克兰目前的交通系统尚无法满足城市居民的需求,这是城市无计划扩张造成的典型后果。该市人口的近1/7是毛利人的后代,它们构成了奥克兰人口中一个重要的毛利人分支。

五、经济

旅游业和服务行业是奥克兰经济的重要组成部分,城市的贸易往来主要包括绵羊、木材和奶制品,此外,新西兰大部分的造船和加工业也都集中在奥克兰。

光影流金

大约在公元450年,毛利人在奥克兰地区定居下来,在之后的几百年间,为了争夺周边肥沃的土地,人们不断进行激烈的战斗。事实上,该地区最初的名字"塔玛梯",在毛利语中就是"战斗"的意思。

18世纪后期,欧洲的探险家们开始登陆新西兰,到了18世纪末,海豹和鲸鱼的捕猎者及贸易商们从当地富饶的自然资源中获利颇丰,他们中的许多人都是从附近的悉尼流放地入境的先前英国的囚犯。可见,早期的新西兰和奥克兰地区只是充斥着不法分子的

early New Zealand and the Auckland area were lawless frontiers.

Decades of fierce intertribal confiict made for an easy conquest by the European settlers, and by 1840 the British had a firm grasp on the area. Captain William Hobson, New Zealand's first governor, named Auckland the country's capital in honor of Lord Auckland, Hobson's patron and past commander.

Although the South Island flourished immediately after colonization, settlers on the North Island, including the Auckland area, experienced mounting tensions with the Maori. From 1845 to 1872 the New Zealand Wars pitted the British colonists against the Maori; the British prevailed and the Maori leaders withdrew to a remote area of North Island.

The Great Depression of the 1930s devastated the country's economy and led to the rise of the Labour Party, which promised work and social programs to free the city from the economic disaster. Auckland's economy revived somewhat during World War II, when New Zealand troops fought alongside the Allies; the country also aligned with the United Nations in the Korean War and with the United States and its allies in the Vietnam War.

The Sights and Sounds

Acacia Cottage dates from the 1840s and is one of the oldest wooden houses in the city. The cottage is in Cornwall Park in the heart of the city center. Highwic House, built mid-19th century, is a timber Gothic-style period home filled with antique furniture, paintings and all the trappings of the good life. The Auckland Town Hall was built in the early 20th century, an Italianate building quite different from the rest of Auckland's architecture. The building's two large halls are regularly used for concerts and other public events.

A popular modern attraction is the 1,066-foot-tall Sky Tower, built in 1997. The tower has a hotel and casino, a revolving restaurant, and observation decks for a fine view of the city. Adventurous tourists with strong stomachs can try sky jumping—with a harness, of course.

The New Zealand National Maritime Museum contains a large collection of historical maritime artifacts. The museum gives visitors a sense of the importance of ocean trade and sport in the life of the city. The War Memorial Museum is dedicated to the memory of the New Zealand Wars between the settlers and the Maori; the museum's collection includes a variety of Maori arts and crafts. The Auckland Art Gallery is the city's largest permanent collection of paintings by international artists; it is housed in a classic Victorian building.

Auckland Harbour Bridge, built in the 1950s, spans Waitemata Harbour and connects the city to the Hauraki Gulf. The Grafton Bridge that spans Grafton Gully is an engineering wonder of the early 20th century. It was constructed of reinforced concrete, and when completed it was the world's largest single-span bridge.

The metropolitan area has more than 100 marvelous beaches, where visitors can sunbathe, swim, scuba, snorkel and surf. The beaches closest to the city center are the East Coast beaches located on Tamaki Drive. Nearby are a host of restaurants, cafés and pubs, along with family-friendly playgrounds and open spaces.

The Auckland Botanic Gardens are south of the city center and offer a sampling of New Zealand's natural beauty. The vast collection of plants includes exotics generally unknown to visitors from the northern hemisphere. Also here are delightfully landscaped green spaces, fountains and walking paths, some of the finest in New Zealand.

蛮荒之地。

　　部落间几十年的激烈冲突使得来自欧洲的殖民者们轻而易举就统治了这一地区,到了1840年,英国人牢牢地掌控了这里,威廉·霍布森船长作为新西兰的第一任总督,将奥克兰命名为国家首都,以纪念奥克兰勋爵——霍布森的赞助人和已故的指挥官。

　　虽然在殖民化之后,新西兰南岛迅速地繁荣起来,但是在北岛,包括奥克兰在内的地区,早期的开拓者们同毛利人之间的关系却越来越紧张。从1845年到1872年,新西兰的几场战争使得英国人同毛利人不断相互争斗,最终,英国人取得了胜利,毛利人的首领们退回到了北岛的一个偏僻的地方。

　　20世纪30年代的经济大萧条,将新西兰的经济彻底摧毁,并导致了工党的崛起,该党承诺了就业及社会保障项目以使城市能够从经济灾难中摆脱出来。第二次世界大战期间,当新西兰的军队和盟军一起作战之时,奥克兰的经济略有复苏。之后的朝鲜战争,新西兰也站到了联合国的一边,而在越南战争中,它则成为美国的盟友。

声光景点

　　金合欢屋始建于19世纪40年代,是奥克兰市最古老的木制房屋之一,该房屋位于市中心的康沃尔公园内。海威克屋建造于19世纪中期,是一所木制的哥特式住宅,里面摆满了古色古香的家具、绘画以及彰显优裕生活的各类服饰。奥克兰市政厅修建于20世纪早期,迥异于奥克兰市内其他建筑,这座建筑完全是仿意大利式风格的,大楼内部的两个大厅定期被用来举办音乐会或其他公共活动。

　　建于1997年的高1066英尺的天空塔是一座深受游人喜爱的现代化魅力景点, 大厦内设一座酒店、一家赌场、一处旋转餐厅以及可以将城市美景尽收眼底的多层观景台。敢于冒险且性格坚强的游客不妨尝试一下摩天弹跳——当然,是戴着保护带的。

　　新西兰国家海洋博物馆拥有大批年代久远的海洋手工艺制品,从中游客能够感受到海上贸易和娱乐在城市生活中的重要性。战争纪念馆是为纪念殖民者和毛利人之间所进行的新西兰战争而修建的,博物馆内的藏品包括各种各样的毛利人的手工艺品。奥克兰美术馆是市内最大的永久性收藏国际艺术家作品的地方,其建筑属于古典的维多利亚风格。

　　奥克兰港湾大桥修建于20世纪50年代,横跨怀特玛塔港,将豪拉基湾与该市连接起来。格拉夫顿大桥横跨格拉夫顿溪谷,是20世纪早期的一项工程奇迹,它以钢筋混凝土建造,完成后成为世界上最大的单拱桥。

　　奥克兰市周边有100多处迷人的海滩,在那里游客们可以进行日光浴、游泳、戴水肺或呼吸管潜水,还可以进行冲浪。距离市中心最近的海滩是位于塔玛梯大道的东海岸沙滩,它的附近有很多餐馆、咖啡屋和酒吧,还有适合家庭聚会的游乐场及空地。

　　位于市区以南的奥克兰植物园为游客提供了一个新西兰自然美景的样本。通常情况下,对于那些来自北半球的游客来说,这里展出的大量奇特的植物他们根本就叫不出名。此外,这里有令人赏心悦目的景观式绿地、喷泉和小径,其中有不少在新西兰也是首屈一指。

One of the most exciting and invigorating ways to see Auckland and the North Island of New Zealand is a balloon trip over the city. Trips leave daily from the Albany district of Auckland, and a champagne toast is included. If terra firma is more your style, take a tour of the city's northeastern coastline aboard one of the many cruise ships. Tour guides provide commentary on the city and its history, and some voyages include meals. Cruises are scheduled throughout the day and into the evening.

The Trivia

Fact: In 1984 New Zealand banned from its ports all ships carrying nuclear weapons or powered by nuclear fuel. This policy led to a contentious situation with the United States, after a naval destroyer was denied access to a port; U.S. officials refused to say whether the vessel's cargo included nuclear weapons. As a result of the dispute, the United States suspended its obligations under the ANZUS treaty, a military alliance between Australia, New Zealand, and the United States.

Why Auckland Is a 50 plus one City

Auckland has an idyllic location, and the physical beauty of the land and surrounding sea are compelling to any first-time visitor. Simply to visit Auckland is an event, as it is so far from the big cities of Europe and North America.

欣赏奥克兰以及新西兰北岛自然风光的一个最令人兴奋刺激的方式是来一次城市上空的热气球旅行,该项行程每天从奥克兰市的奥尔巴尼区出发,包括一次香槟酒庆祝。假如你更喜欢站在坚实的土地上,那就乘上一艘游船,沿着城市的东北海岸线来一次海上之旅吧,沿途导游会向你介绍城市以及它的历史,有些航程还包括用餐,此类水上游项目根据时间从早晨一直持续到傍晚。

奇闻轶事

1984年起,新西兰禁止一切运输核武器或由核燃料驱动的船只靠岸,这一政策与美国引起了广泛的争议,原因是一艘美国海军驱逐舰被禁止靠近港口,而美国官员拒绝透露该船运输的货物是否包含核武器。争论最终的结果是:美国暂停了其在ANZUS协议中的义务(ANZUS协议是一份由澳大利亚、新西兰和美国签署的军事盟约)。

为什么奥克兰入选50+1个城市?

奥克兰拥有田园诗般的牧场,无论是陆地还是其周围的海洋都是那么的美丽、自然,令任何初来乍到的游客心醉神迷。于是,看一眼奥克兰,就成为许多人生活中的一件大事,因为它距离那些欧洲及北美的大城市是如此遥远。

Bangkok, Thailand

The Basic Facts
Bangkok is the capital of Thailand and is the country's largest city. It is still known as the Venice of the East, although most of the city's canals have now been replaced with paved roads.

Geography
Bangkok lies at 13 degrees 50 minutes north latitude and 100 degrees 29 minutes east longitude. The city is located in the delta of the Great Chao Phraya River near the Gulf of Thailand, in the heart of Thailand's agricultural region.

Climate
Bangkok has a tropical monsoon climate and is considered one of the hottest urban centers in the world. The city swelters in a humid environment where the temperature rarely departs from the high 80s and lower 90s Fahrenheit. Bangkok receives a considerable amount of rain during the monsoon season, especially in September, when the area receives up to a foot of rain.

Government
Bangkok is one of two special administrative areas in Thailand in which citizens vote for their governor. Urban sprawl in recent years led to the merger of the provinces of Bangkok and Thonburi province. The city is divided into 50 administrative districts.

Demographics
The population of the metropolitan area is estimated at a staggering nine million people, with about six million people living in Bangkok itself. The city is known for its infamous traffic jams, despite the creation of new light rail and subway lines. More than half of Bangkok residents claim Chinese ancestry, and the city has sizable numbers of European and American expatriates.

Economy
Bangkok is a leading commercial center of Thailand and the entire Southeast Asian region. Food processing, lumber and wood products, and textiles are important manufacturers, followed closely by rice milling, oil and shipbuilding.Bangkok's manmade harbor handles most of Thailand's commercial goods. The city is the hub of the continental Southeast Asian railway, and a network of modern highways advances its economic position. The city's canal system permits the inexpensive and efficient transportation of goods.

泰国曼谷

概况

曼谷是泰国的首都和最大的城市,迄今仍以"东方威尼斯"而著称,尽管现在城里的运河大多已被路面所取代。

一、地理

曼谷位于北纬13°50′,东经100°29′,地处泰国湾附近的湄南河三角洲,是泰国农业区的核心地区。

二、气候

曼谷具有热带季风气候,被认为是世界上最为炎热的城市之一,在潮湿闷热的环境里,这个城市的气温始终徘徊在华氏87~89度至华氏91~93度。在季风季节,曼谷降雨非常充沛,尤其是在9月份,该地区的降雨量可以达到一英尺。

三、政府

曼谷是泰国两个特殊行政区之一,那里的公民投票选举总督。近些年来,由于城市扩建,曼谷省和吞武里省进行了合并,整个城市被划分为50个行政区。

四、人口

据估计,曼谷大市范围的人口在900万左右,其中约600万人居住在曼谷一带,虽然修建了新的轻轨和地铁线路,曼谷的交通拥堵依然非常严重,远近闻名。曼谷有超过一半的居民具有中国血统,此外,城里还有相当数量的欧洲及美洲移民。

五、经济

曼谷是泰国和整个东南亚地区最重要的商业中心,食品加工、木材及木制品、纺织等都是重要的制造行业,紧随其后的还有稻谷加工、油料生产及造船业。泰国的大部分商业货物都经由曼谷的人工码头进出。这个城市是东南亚陆上铁路网的枢纽,此外,拥有一个现代化的公路网更促进了其经济地位的提升。市区的运河系统使得商品运输既经济又高效。

The History

Bangkok began as a small trading center and port community originally called Bang Makok, or City of Olives in a primitive Thai dialect. Thailand fought a lengthy war with neighboring Burma in the late 18th century, after which Bangkok fell to Burma.

King Rama I, the first monarch of the Chakri Dynasty, founded modern Bangkok in 1782. The King gave Bangkok a 21-word name that is commonly abbreviated (thank goodness!) as Krung Thep, meaning City of Angels. Although Bangkok is only one district in Krung Thep, most foreigners refer to the city by its more familiar name.

The city was designed in accordance with the Thai belief that the king's palace is the center of the universe. The Grand Palace was the first building to be constructed, and major temples and government structures were built nearby. Housing and other less-important buildings were relegated to areas far from the palace.

Bangkok experienced explosive growth in the 1990s; today it is a national and regional center for trade, tourism and government. The city's rapid growth came with a price, however; nearly one-sixth of the city's housing is located in slums that suffer greatly from inadequate garbage collection. Bangkok's high population density has led to constant traffic jams and air pollution due to vehicle exhaust. The land under the city has been sinking up to four inches a year for decades, and the city suffers from frequent floods, especially during the rainy season. Even so, modern Bangkok is an intriguing blend of old buildings and cutting-edge new construction.

The Sights and Sounds

Millions of world travelers visit Bangkok each year, for business and for pleasure. The city abounds with exotic sights and sounds. The Grand Palace, built in 1782, is a truly amazing building that covers some 53 acres of land. The palace is a complex of buildings, each dedicated to a specific role: a religious temple; a ceremonial complex; the royal residence and guest area; and staff and government offices.

The National Museum is the largest in Southeast Asia and was originally part of the Grand Palace. Its collection focuses on the whole of Thai history and exhibits many prehistoric artifacts. The Red House is an 18th century traditional Thai building decorated in all the splendor of the period: elephant chairs, royal emblems, wood carvings, magnificent statues of Buddha, jewelry, ceramics and religious artifacts.

Wat Phra Kaew, part of the Grand Palace, is the Temple of the Emerald Buddha and the shrine that is most revered by the people of Bangkok. The focal point is the statue itself, two feet tall atop an enormous gold base. It is said to have been carved in the 14th century.

The National Museum of the Royal Barges provides a fascinating glimpse into Thai history and culture. Thailand began as an agricultural society with settled communities near the waterways, and the river was an important means of transport and communication. Many of the country's finest historical barges are here, including:

· The Suphannahong Royal Barge, its prow resembling a mythological swan.

The vessel was completed in the reign of King Rama VI, is the highest class of Royal Barge, and was awarded the Sea Heritage Medal from the World Ships Organization of Great Britain in 1981.

· The Anantanagaraj Royal Barge, its prow carved in the form of a Naga, a seven-

光影流金

曼谷起初只是作为一个小型的贸易中心和口岸社区出现的,当时名为"邦马科克",在早期的泰国方言里意思是"橄榄之城"。18世纪后期,泰国同邻国缅甸进行了一场漫长的战争,后来,曼谷被缅甸攻陷。

1782年,查克里王朝的首位国王拉玛一世建立了现代曼谷,国王为曼谷取了一个包含了21个词的名字,通常(谢天谢地!)简称为"功贴",意思是"天使之城"。虽然曼谷只是功贴的一个区,大多数外国人还是喜欢用这个较为熟悉的名字。

曼谷城市的设计遵循的是泰国人这样一种信仰:国王的宫殿是宇宙的中心,大皇宫是第一个修建的工程,其他主要的庙宇及政府大楼也都选择建在其附近,住宅和其他次要的建筑依次建在离皇宫较远的地方。

20世纪90年代,曼谷经历了爆炸式的发展过程。今天,它已成为泰国全国及地区贸易、旅游和行政的中心,然而,城市为其快速发展也付出了代价,有近六分之一的住房处在贫民窟地区,那里的居民由于垃圾得不到及时清运而苦不堪言。曼谷过高的人口密度还造成了持续的交通堵塞以及由于汽车尾气而带来的空气污染。在过去的几十年里,曼谷的城市地面每年以四英寸的速度在下沉,城区经常遭受水灾,特别是在雨季的时候。即便如此,现代的曼谷仍然是一个融汇了古老与崭新建筑的诱人的混合体。

声光景点

每年来自世界各地数百万计的游客光临曼谷,或经商或旅游,在这座城市里,随处可见充满异域风情的景点。建于1782年的大皇宫的确是一座令人叹为观止的建筑,它占地大约53英亩,是一座由不同建筑组合而成的复杂群体,其中每一部分都有着特殊的作用:如宗教的庙宇,大典中心,皇室寝宫和会客区,以及大臣和政府办公室等。

国家博物馆是东南亚最大的博物馆,最初属于大皇宫的一部分,其藏品集中反映整个泰国的历史,另有许多史前的手工艺品。这座"红楼"是一座18世纪修建的泰国传统建筑,其装修动用了当时所有的华丽饰物:包括象椅、皇家徽章、木刻、庄严的佛像、珠宝、陶瓷和宗教手工艺品等。

菩开奥寺,作为大皇宫的一部分,又叫翡翠玉佛寺,是深受泰国人民尊崇的圣地。景区的焦点就是玉佛本身,这座伫立于巨大的黄金底座之上高达两英尺的佛像,据说是18世纪时雕刻的。

皇家龙舟博物馆为游客提供了一个奇妙的窥见泰国历史和文化的机会。泰国最初是从农业社会发展而来,人们在靠近水道的地方定居下来建立社区,因此,河流就成了交通和通信的重要手段。有很多这个国家历史上建造得最好的船舶都在这里,其中包括:

●素帕纳洪龙舟,其船头类似传说中神鸟的样子,于国王拉玛六世在位时期建造完成,是龙舟中的极品,1981年被英国的世界船舶组织授予海洋遗产奖章。

●安塔纳伽拉龙舟,其船头雕刻成那加蛇神的样子,是一个九头怪物,每到节日期

headed figure. This barged carried the statue of Buddha during festivals.

· The Anekchartputchong Royal Barge, an elaborately-painted vessel built during the reign of King Rama V.

Bangkok has more than 300 Buddhist temples; two deserve special mention and should not be missed. Wat Po, or the Temple of the Reclining Buddha, was built in the 16th century and is the largest temple in Bangkok. The main attraction is the statue itself, a staggering 150 feet long and covered in gold leaf. Wat Arun,the Temple of the Dawn, was originally a royal chapel. This temple has a stunning 282-foot-tall tower and its exterior is clad in multi-color ceramics from throughout Thailand.

Curious and adventurous tourists visit Patpong. This area is not only well known for its night market, but also for its assortment of shops that specialize in black-market goods. A more respectable and trendy nighttime spot is along Sukhumvit Road, where one can find top bars and clubs.

The Trivia

Fact: A modern business and commercial district has developed over the last few years about three miles from the Grand Palace. This area is a major tourist attraction and contains office buildings, shops, nightclubs and movie theaters.

Fact: Bangkok avoided the catastrophic damage and incomprehensible loss of life following the tsunami that overwhelmed Southeast Asia in late December 2004. Its location beyond the Malay Peninsula spared the city from the ocean's wrath.

Fact: Bangkok's official full name is Krungthep Maha Nakorn Amorn Ratanakosindra Mahindrayudhya Mahadilokpop Noporatana Rajthani Burirom Udom Rajnivet Mahastan Amorn Rimarn Avatarn Satit Sakkatuttiya Vishnukarm Prasit (whew!). The rough English translation is the city of angels, the great city, the eternal jewel city, the impregnable city of God Indra, the grand capital of the world endowed with nine precious gems, the happy city, abounding in an enormous Royal Palace that resembles the heavenly abode where reigns the reincarnated god, a city given by Indra and built by Vishnukarn. The actual translation is unknown even to most Thais, as the name is in an ancient Thai language.

Why Bangkok Is a 50 plus one City

Bangkok is exotic, dynamic and filled with history and tradition of the Thai people.The city exemplifies the increasing global influence of the Asian economy, which has come into its own in the last 40 years.

间,这艘龙舟就被用来装载佛像。

● 阿尼查菩冲龙舟是一艘绘制有精美图案的船只,建造于国王拉玛五世统治时期。

曼谷有300多座佛教寺庙,其中值得一提且不应错过的有两座。一座是涅槃寺,或称卧佛寺,建于16世纪,是曼谷最大的寺庙。其中最吸引人的就是那座卧佛,它有大约150英尺长,全身数满金箔。另一座是郑王庙,或称黎明寺,最初属于皇家寺庙,内有一座令人惊叹的高282英尺的佛塔,周身镶嵌着来自泰国各地的五彩陶瓷片。

好奇心强、喜爱冒险的游客不妨去一下帕蓬区,这里不仅有著名的夜市,而且汇集了各类专营黑市产品的商店。相对更为体面时髦些的夜间娱乐场所位于素坤逸路一带,那里你可以找到顶级的酒吧和夜总会。

奇闻轶事

之一:在过去的几年间,在距离大皇宫大约3英里的地方,一个现代贸易和商业区已经发展起来,并已成为一个主要的旅游景区,内有办公大楼、商店、夜总会、电影院等设施。

之二:在2004年12月末席卷东南亚的海啸中,曼谷有幸躲过了灾难性的破坏和难以想象的人员伤亡。因为,曼谷位于马来半岛的另一端,这一地理位置使得它避过了大海的怒火。

之三:曼谷市官方的全称是"功贴玛哈那空,阿蒙叻达纳哥信陀罗,玛哈底陆魄,诺婆叻塔纳,拉查他尼布里隆,乌童拉吉卫玛哈萨坦,阿蒙里曼阿哇丹萨蒂,萨格塔底耶,毗瑟奴卡姆普拉席"(咻!),翻译成英文大概就是"天使之城,伟大的城,永恒的宝石之城,坚不可摧的主神因陀罗之城,被赐予九颗珍贵宝石的世界之都,幸福之城,幸福遍布由神仙转世为王的美如天宫的皇家宫殿,主神因陀罗赐予、神匠毗瑟奴坎建造之城。"由于这一名称是以古代泰语写成,所以,其真正的译文即使对于大多数泰国人来说也是个谜。

为什么曼谷入选50 + 1个城市?

曼谷充满了异域风情、勃勃生机以及无所不在的泰国人民的历史和传统,在过去的40年里,亚洲经济已经显示出其真正的价值,而曼谷恰恰成为亚洲经济在全球经济中不断上升的影响力的典型范例。

Barcelona, Spain

The Basic Facts

Barcelona is the capital of the autonomous region of Catalonia in northeast Spain. The city has a rich and romantic history that attracts millions of international tourists every year.

Geography

Barcelona lies at 41 degrees 25 minutes north latitude and 2 degrees 84 minutes east longitude. Barcelona is located on the Mediterranean between the Llobregat and Besòs Rivers, a 2-hour drive from the French border.

Climate

Barcelona has well-defined seasons with high humidity throughout the year. Summers can be quite warm, winter is rather pleasant, but fall and spring are the best times to visit the city. Annual temperatures range from the mid-60s Fahrenheit in winter to the mid-90s Fahrenheit in summer.

Government

Barcelona has a mayor-city council form of government. The Municipal Council is the highest level of political representation for citizens in government; chaired by the mayor and consisting of 41 councillors, the council manages most municipal functions.

Economy

Barcelona is the second largest city in Spain, its largest port, and its chief commercial and industrial center. Manufacturing industries include textiles, machinery, automobiles, locomotives, airplanes, and electrical equipment. International banking and finance are also important to the city's economy.

Demographics

The population of the city of Barcelona is estimated at 1.6 million people. Some 230,000 residents are immigrants from the former Spanish colonies in Latin America; others come from Morocco, Pakistan, Romania, and Ukraine. Barcelona residents use both Catalan and Castillian Spanish.

The History

Barcelona was founded in 230 B.C. by the Carthaginians. Over the next 1,000 years the city was repeatedly invaded, notably by the Visigoths in the early 5th century and by the Moors in the 8th century. Barcelona's modern age began in 801 A.D., when armies from what would become France conquered the city and defeated the Moors. A succession of counts governed Barcelona from the 9th to the 12th centuries, when the city developed into an important commercial and industrial center. Barcelona later united with Aragon and

---

西班牙巴塞罗那

巴塞罗那是位于西班牙东北部的加泰罗尼亚自治区首府,这座城市拥有丰富而浪漫的历史,每年吸引着成千上万来自世界各地的游客。

一、地理

巴塞罗那位于北纬41°25′,东经2°84′,地处略夫雷加特河与巴索斯河之间的地中海地区,距离法国边境大约两小时车程。

二、气候

巴塞罗那全年湿度较大,四季分明,夏季非常温暖,冬季相当舒适,但是游览这个城市的最佳时间仍然是春秋季节。该市的年均气温在冬季的华氏65度到夏季的华氏95度。

三、政府

巴塞罗那是市长加市政委员会形式的政府,市政委员会是政府中代表公民政治权利的最高层,设有市长和41个顾问席位,该委员会负责管理大部分的市政功能。

四、经济

巴塞罗那是西班牙第二大城市和最大的港口,并且是其主要的商业及工业中心,制造业包括纺织、机械、汽车、机车、飞机和电气设备。跨国银行业和金融业在城市经济中也同样非常重要。

五、人口

据估计,巴塞罗那的城市人口有160万,其中大约有23万居民属于来自拉丁美洲原西班牙殖民地的移民。其他移民则来自摩洛哥、巴基斯坦、罗马尼亚、乌克兰等国。巴塞罗那的居民讲加泰罗尼亚语和卡斯蒂利亚(即标准的)西班牙语两种语言。

巴塞罗那市是公元前230年由迦太基人创建的。在之后的1000年里,这个城市不断地被外敌入侵,其中值得一提的包括5世纪初被西哥特人,以及8世纪时被非洲的摩尔人侵略。巴塞罗那的近代史开始于公元801年,当时攻占了这座城市的是来自即将建立法兰西共和国的军队,他们打败了摩尔人。从9世纪到12世纪,一个接一个的伯爵相继统治着巴塞罗那,这期间,城市逐步发展成为一个重要的商业和工业中心。之后,巴塞罗那与阿

became the capital of the region known as Catalonia.

During the 14th century, Barcelona ruled a small empire that included Sicily,Malta, Sardinia, Valencia, the Balearics, and parts of France and Greece. However, this empire collapsed by the 15th century, however, and the Catalans united with the nearby region of Castille. The rulers of Castille and Aragon looted Barcelona's city coffers to fund their imperial ambitions, reducing the city's importance in the region. To add insult to injury, Barcelona was prevented from trading with the newly-discovered Americas.

After Catalonia fell in 1714, Philip V, the French contender for the Spanish throne, demolished a huge section of the La Ribera (the merchants'quarter) and erected the Ciutadella. Philip was hated by his subjects, and so he watched over them from this large fort. He forbade use of the Catalan language and closed the city's university.

Catalonia finally gained permission to trade with the Americas in 1778. Spain's first industrial revolution began in Barcelona and focused on cotton manufacturing.The city was later occupied by French forces during the Napoleonic Wars. Since then it has remained under Spanish control.

During the mid-19th century Barcelona once again became a hotbed of discontent and was the center of many revolts against the Spanish monarchy. The city was the seat of the Republican government during the Spanish Civil War against the Fascist forces of General Francisco Franco. Barcelona fell to Franco in 1939 and many Catalonians fled to France or Andorra. The Spanish monarchy was re-established after Franco's death, and Barcelona regained its status as a center of culture and trade. Barcelona hosted the 1992 Summer Olympics.

The Sights and Sounds

Barcelona, at 2,000 years old, rivals Madrid as the cultural, architectural and entertainment capital of Spain. Barcelona grew and thrived at a time when Madrid was barely on the map. Barcelona is an overwhelming Catholic city and has a number of spectacular churches. The Catedral de la Seu is a symbol of local pride.It was constructed over the course of 2 centuries and completed in 1450, although parts of the church were added as late as 1892. The Lepanto Chapel within the church is highly prized by local residents. Many visitors relish Santa Maria del Mar for its wonderful 14th century Gothic architecture; most locals consider it the finest church in all of Barcelona. The Temple Expiatori de la Sagrada Familia,designed by the famous architect Antonio Gaudi, displays the history of Christianity on its façade. It remains under construction, but when finished the complex will include 18 towers.

The National Museum of Catalan Art offers a wealth of Romanesque and Gothic art from around the area. The Miro Foundation was a gift to the city from its famous son, Joan Miró; not surprisingly, many of his works are prominently displayed in the museum's exhibit halls. The Museu Picasso is housed in two 15th century buildings and houses an extensive collection of the artist's early works, including those from the Rose Period and the Blue Period.

Casa Mila is a popular home that was designed by Gaudi; its curving façade seems to slither around the block like a snake. The site also contains a museum dedicated to Gaudi's architectural creations. Famous examples of late 19th century architecture and style can be found in the area of the city called Eixample, which is also where the city's most elegant

拉贡合并成为加泰罗尼亚地区的首府。

14世纪时,巴塞罗那统治着一个包括西西里岛、马耳他岛、撒丁岛、巴伦西亚岛、巴利阿里群岛、部分法国和希腊在内的不大的王国,然而,这个王国到了15世纪却解体了。之后,加泰罗尼亚和邻近的卡斯蒂亚合而为一。卡斯蒂亚和阿拉贡的统治者们掠夺了城市的金库,以充实其自身帝国,并以此削弱了巴塞罗那在该地区的重要性。更为糟糕的是,他们还禁止巴塞罗那和新发现的美洲有任何贸易往来。

1714年,加泰罗尼亚陷落之后,西班牙王位的法国竞争者腓力五世将海岸区(商人居住区)的大片地区进行拆除,修建了修塔德里城堡。他的行为引起臣民的仇恨,于是,他时常从这座大型城堡内窥视着人们的一举一动,他下令禁止使用加泰罗尼亚语,并关闭了城里的大学。

1778年,加泰罗尼亚最终被允许和美洲通商。西班牙的第一次工业革命开始于巴塞罗那,主要为棉花加工。后来,在拿破仑战争期间,法国军队曾占领了巴塞罗那,但自此以后,这个城市的所有权一直属于西班牙。

19世纪中期,巴塞罗那再次成为敌对情绪的温床,许多反对西班牙君主制度的叛乱分子聚集于此。在针对弗兰西斯科·弗朗哥为首的法西斯势力而进行的西班牙内战期间,这个城市是在共和党政府领导之下的。1939年,弗朗哥上台,许多加泰罗尼亚人纷纷逃往法国或安道尔。弗朗哥死后,西班牙重新建立了君主政体,巴塞罗那也重新确立了其文化及贸易中心的地位。1992年,巴塞罗那主办了夏季奥林匹克运动会。

声光景点

巴塞罗那,以其2000年悠久的历史,可以同西班牙首都马德里相媲美,成为其文化、建筑和娱乐的首府。当地图上几乎压根还没有马德里的时候,巴塞罗那就已经发展繁荣起来了。巴塞罗那是一个天主教占压倒多数的城市,因此,拥有许多令人瞩目的教堂建筑,大教堂就是当地引以为荣的标志性建筑。这座教堂的修建历经两个世纪,直到1450年才得以完工,后来,教堂还进行了部分扩建,工程一直持续到了1892年。这座教堂内的莱潘托教堂是一座当地居民评价极高的小教堂。圣玛利亚教堂则是深受许多游客喜爱的一座14世纪哥特式建筑,大多数当地居民认为它是巴塞罗那所有教堂中最完美的一个。由著名建筑师安东尼奥·高迪设计的神圣家族大教堂正面显示有基督教的历史,这座教堂至今仍在建设,但是完工之后,它将是一座拥有18座塔楼的建筑群。

加泰罗尼亚国家美术馆有来自这一地区的丰富的罗马及哥特风格的艺术品。米罗基金大厦是胡安·米罗,这位巴塞罗那杰出的儿子送给自己城市的一份礼物,因此,在这座博物馆展示厅的显著位置,陈列着许多这位艺术家的大作也就不足为奇了。毕加索博物馆是两座15世纪时的建筑,内有大量这位艺术家早期的作品,其中有些出自他创作的玫瑰时期和蓝色时期。

米拉公寓是一座很多人都喜欢的由高迪设计的住宅,其弯曲的立面看上去像一条蛇从大楼上滑过,这里还有一座用来纪念高迪建筑创新的博物馆。19世纪后期建筑风格的典型代表可以在这个城市的"扩建区"里找到,那里也是巴塞罗那大部分漂亮商场以及咖

shops and cafes are to be found. The district is particularly prized for its Spanish version of Art Nouveau buildings and design.

Bullfighting is a traditional spectator sport in Barcelona that remains popular with locals despite its controversial nature. Events are held on Sundays between March and October at the Monumental; the arena also has a museum dedicated to the sport.

Evenings in Barcelona often stretch into the wee hours of the morning. The city is chock-full of cafes, cabarets, champagne bars, discos, jazz clubs and more. The many restaurants called tapas bars offer a variety of delightful dishes. Do not miss the flamenco dancers for a true sense of local culture.

The Trivia

Fact: During the 19th century Barcelona was the nexus of the Catalan Renaissance, a crusade by poets, writers and other artists to popularize Catalan as the people's language.

Fact: According to tradition, Christopher Columbus announced his discovery of the New World in Barcelona's Plaza del Rey.

Fact: Barcelona was a pioneer of early European education. The University of Barcelona, founded in 1450, continues to be a well-respected academic institution.

Why Barcelona Is a 50 plus one City

Barcelona may not be the capital of Spain, but is the country's focal point of culture, literature, and architecture. Few cities in the world can match the richness and the complexity that make up modern Barcelona.

啡屋的所在地,尤其值得称道的是,在那里你还可以发现西班牙人对于"新艺术"风潮的建筑及设计的诠释。

斗牛是巴塞罗那一项传统的颇具观赏性的体育赛事,虽然这项比赛的性质饱受争议,但是至今仍然深受当地居民的喜爱。比赛一般于3~10月的周日在纪念碑体育场举行,这个斗牛场内还有一座专为此项运动而修建的博物馆。

巴塞罗那的夜生活往往要延续到凌晨的两三点钟,这座城市里到处都是咖啡馆、卡巴莱、香槟酒吧、迪厅、爵士俱乐部及其他的娱乐场所,许多名为"塔帕斯"(餐前小吃)酒吧的餐馆都提供各式各样的美味佳肴。如果想要真正感受一下当地的文化,就千万不要错过佛拉门戈舞。

奇闻轶事

之一:19世纪时期,巴塞罗那曾是加泰罗尼亚复兴运动的中心,这是一项由诗人、作家和其他艺术家为普及加泰罗尼亚语而发起的神圣运动。

之二:据传说,克里斯托夫·哥伦布就是在巴塞罗那的国王广场宣布他发现了新大陆的。

之三:巴塞罗那是早期欧洲教育的开拓者,巴塞罗那大学始建于1450年,至今仍是一所知名学府。

为什么巴塞罗那入选50 + 1个城市?

巴塞罗那并不是西班牙的首都,但它却是这个国家文化、文学和建筑的核心,就城市的丰富性和复杂性来说,世界上几乎没有哪一座城市可以与当今的巴塞罗那相媲美。

Seven

Beijing, China

The Basic Facts

Beijing is the capital of the People's Republic of China and is the country's second largest city. The city is a regional center for politics, education, and culture, and was the site of the 2008 Summer Olympics.

Geography

Beijing lies at 33 degrees 55 minutes north latitude and 116 degrees 23 minutes east longitude. The city is located the North China plain, 100 miles inland from the Bo Gulf, and shielded by mountains to north, northwest and west. Beijing's two main rivers are the Yongding and the Chaobai.

Climate

Beijing's weather can be harsh at any time of year. Annual temperatures range from the low 20s Fahrenheit in winter to the low 80s Fahrenheit in summer.Humidity is high in summer and low in winter, and causes the temperatures to feel more extreme than they actually are.

Government

Beijing is one of four direct-controlled municipalities in the country, and has the same political status as a Chinese province. The city is divided into 18 county-level divisions and further subdivided into 273 township-level divisions.

Demographics

Nearly all Beijing residents are native Chinese of Han ethnicity; other ethnic groups represented include Manchu, Mongol and Hui. There has been an influx of R. O. Korean immigrants to the city in recent years, primarily students and international expatriates involved in global commerce. Mandarin Chinese, the country's official language, is the primary language used in the city. The metropolitan area population is estimated to be 15 million.

Economy

Beijing's economic boom of the late 20th century continues today, especially in the high-tech, real estate, and automobile sectors. As China's capital city, government entities in Beijing are major employers. Other important industries in the metropolitan area include finance, banking, construction, and trades.

The History

The history of modern-day Beijing dates back to the 13th century, when Kublai Khan attacked the city. The Khan declared Beijing as his capital city. Various dynasties over the next 3 centuries altered the face of Beijing by adding their own temples, palaces and other buildings.

China remained relatively isolated from the West until the late 19th century, when France and Britain forced the country to allow foreign diplomats into Beijing. This decision caused discontent among Chinese nationalists, and at the turn of the 20th century the bloody Boxer Rebellion attempted to expel Westerners from China.Western nations

中国北京

概况

北京是中华人民共和国的首都，也是中国第二大城市，还是地区政治、教育和文化的中心，并且是2008年夏季奥林匹克运动会的举办地。

一、地理

北京位于北纬33°55′，东经116°23′，地处华北平原，在距离渤海湾100英里的内陆地区，城市的正北、西北、正西三面都有山脉保护。流经北京的主要河流有永定河及潮白河。

二、气候

北京在一年中的任何时期都可能出现恶劣天气。年均气温在冬季的华氏21~23度至夏季的华氏81~83度。夏天湿度比较高，冬天湿度则很低，于是人们常会感到气温比实际情况更高或更低。

三、政府

北京是中国四个直辖市之一，其政治地位相当于中国的省份。整个城市被划分为18个县级区，然后再进一步划分为273个镇级区。

四、人口

北京几乎所有的居民都属于中国的汉族，其他有代表性的民族还有满族、蒙古族和回族。最近一些年，有大批的韩国人涌入这个城市，主要为学生及从事全球贸易的国际移民。中国的官方语言汉语普通话就是这个城市最早使用的语言。北京大市人口有大约1 500万。

五、经济

20世纪末北京经济迅速增长并延续至今，尤其是在高科技、房地产和汽车领域。作为中国的首都，北京的政府部门成为人们就业的主要渠道。在城市范围还有其他一些重要行业，例如，金融、银行、建筑和商贸等。

光影流金

如今现代化的北京，其历史可以追溯到13世纪，当时忽必烈的军队攻占这个城市，他宣布定都北京。在以后的3个世纪里，不同的朝代在这里所修建的庙宇、宫殿和其他各类建筑，将城市的面貌一改再改。

在19世纪后期之前，中国和西方始终处于相对隔绝的状态。直到法国和英国强迫中国允许外国大使进驻北京，这一决定引起中国民族主义者的不满，于是，在20世纪初爆发了旨在将西方列强驱逐出中国的义和团运动。作为报复，西方国家进攻了北京，并对城市

attacked Beijing in response and destroyed much of the city.

In 1949 the country became known as the People's Republic of China. Its leader was Mao Zedong, the head of CPC. Beijing is the capital of the People's Republic of China.

The Sights and Sounds

Beijing is an enigma, a modern city that belies its roots as an imperial stronghold. Westerners refer to it as the Forbidden City even today, although it is officially known as the Palace Museum. The Forbidden City itself is the former home of China's succession of emperors; its ornate buildings, gardens and courtyards cover an area of nearly 178 acres.

Tiananmen Square is at the south edge of the Forbidden City and is framed by the Gate of Heavenly Peace. On Chinese national holidays parades and fireworks are held in the square. Every year, the emperor offered prayers at the Temple of Heaven for a good harvest. Surrounded by a park, the Temple is worth a short visit. In fact, it may seem familiar from seeing it depicted on the wallpaper of Chinese restaurants. Two interesting points are the echo effect inside the temple and the stone at the entrance that amplifies the voice of the person who stands in front of it.

No visitor to China can leave without visiting the Great Wall. Although it is one of the Seven Wonders of the Medieval Mind, today considerable portions of the wall are in serious disrepair. Even so, it is one of the largest and most impressive manmade structures in the world. The Great Wall facilitated information exchange and trade in goods between regions, and also prevented invasion from outsiders.

Tourists can discover a wealth of culinary curiosities as they wander the streets of Beijing. Exotic concoctions at the night markets scattered about the city include skewered insects, seahorses and squid. More familiar Western fare is available, including street food such as dumplings, noodles and skewers of chicken, lamb or beef.

Hot pot, the local specialty, is usually only available in winter. This is essentially a fondue in which meat, vegetables or tofu are seasoned to taste and dipped in hot water. Hot pot is best enjoyed in a large group so that everyone can mix and match ingredients and sauces.

Peking duck is a local delicacy served by most local restaurants; authentic preparation of this dish takes several days. Seek out the Qianmen Quanjude Roast Duck Restaurant near Tiananmen Square. This restaurant, established in 1864, is the locals' choice for this renowned Chinese creation.

The Trivia

Fact: Beijing's houses are generally old and border narrow, tree-lined alleys known as hutongs. Newer housing developments have recently sprung up in suburbs north and northwest of the city.

Fact: The Forbidden City is so named that for many years, only emperors and authorized persons were granted access. The 1987 motion picture The Last Emperor was the first to be filmed with the Forbidden City, after having been granted special permission by the Chinese government.

Why Beijing Is a 50 plus one City

Beijing has survived 2,000 years of foreign invasion, war, and governmental and cultural change to emerge as the symbol of Chinese history and culture. Visitors to this ancient city are often captivated and frequently overwhelmed by its history and its treasures.

造成了极大的破坏。

　　1949年,中华人民共和国成立,其领袖是共产党的领导人毛泽东。北京为国家的首都。

声光景点

　　北京是一个谜,是一座扎根于皇权堡垒的现代化城市。虽然紫禁城的官方名称是故宫博物院,但是即便在今天,西方人仍称之为紫禁城。紫禁城原本是过去中国历代皇帝的住所,奢华的建筑、花园和庭院覆盖了近178英亩的土地。

　　紫禁城的南部边缘建有天安门,门外就是天安门广场,在中国的公众节假日里,一些游行及焰火表演都在广场上举行。天坛是一个值得稍作停留的地方,历史上每年皇帝都在这里祭祀,以祈求五谷丰登。环绕天坛周围的是一个公园,事实上,这里就和画在中国餐馆墙上的画差不多。寺庙里的回音效果和庙门口的那块石头是非常有意思的,因为那块石头可以把站在它前面的人的声音放大。

　　凡是来到中国的人都不会不到长城,尽管在中世纪人的眼里,它曾是世界上七大奇迹之一,但是,今天长城的许多地方都已破败不堪。即使如此,它仍然是世界上最大的、最令人震撼的人工建筑之一。长城促进了地区间的信息交流和商贸往来,并且阻止了外敌的入侵。

　　流连于北京的大街小巷,游客可以发现大量新奇的风味小吃。在散落于城市各处的夜市上,有诸如昆虫、海马和鱿鱼串成的奇特的烤肉串,也有更为西方客人熟知的食物,如随处可见的饺子、面条、炸鸡、羊肉或牛肉。

　　火锅,一种当地人喜爱的美食,通常只在冬天才能吃到。这是一种特殊的涮制菜肴,人们把肉、蔬菜或豆腐在热水中浸熟,再加上调料品尝。火锅最好是大群人在一起享用,这样每个人就可以将各种材料和调料进行混合或搭配。

　　北京烤鸭是当地的一道美食,在大多数餐馆里都可以找到,地道的烤鸭制作其准备工作就需要几天时间。建议大家去找一下天安门广场附近的前门全聚德烤鸭店,这家餐馆成立于1864年,是许多当地人享受这道著名的中国特色美食的地方。

奇闻轶事

　　之一:北京的房屋一般都很古老,四周是狭窄的、绿树环绕的小巷,称为胡同。近些年,一些较新的住宅在城市的北部和西北城郊地区迅速发展起来。

　　之二:紫禁城之所以如此命名,是因为在很长时间里,只有皇帝和获得授权的人才允许进入。1987年,电影《末代皇帝》在经过中国政府特批之后,成为第一部在紫禁城拍摄的影片。

为什么北京入选50 + 1个城市?

　　在历经2 000多年的外敌入侵、战乱纷争以及政府和文化的更替之后,北京依然傲立于世,并且成为中国历史和文化的象征。来到这座古老的城市,人们常常被它的历史所倾倒,为它的财富而沉醉。

Berlin, Germany

The Basic Facts

Berlin is the capital and largest city of Germany, and was a focal point during the Cold War of the 20th century. Today the city is a European center for culture,politics and economics.

Geography

Berlin lies at 52 degrees 31 minutes north latitude and 13 degrees 28 minutes east longitude. The metropolitan area covers more than 2,100 square miles in east central Germany, at the confluence of the Spree and Havel Rivers. Berlin is linked to the Baltic Sea by a series of canals and rivers. Government and financial offices are located in the downtown area, while housing developments and industrial firms are located mainly in the outlying areas.

Climate

Annual temperatures in Berlin range from the mid-30s Fahrenheit in winter to the mid-60s Fahrenheit in summer. Although rain is possible year-round, the wettest months are June and August. Winters can sometimes be severe, and are typically cold and dry.

Government

Berlin is comprised 23 administrative districts,   governed by a 240-member Abgeordnetenhaus (House of Representatives), which makes the city laws and elects the governing mayor. With House approval, the mayor appoints a deputy mayor and Senat (cabinet) to administer city government. The mayor and representatives serve 4-year terms. Berlin is also one of Germany's 16 states,and city residents elect representatives to the Bundestag (Federal Diet) and the Bundesrat(Federal Council).

Demographics

Native-born Germans constitute nearly 90 percent of Berlin's population.Non-German residents include Turks—the largest concentration outside of Turkey—Greeks, Italians, Poles, Russians, Americans, Asians, and Africans. The metropolitan area population is estimated at 4.2 million.

Economy

Prior to World War II , Berlin was an important German industrial center. The economy's industrial and construction sectors have lagged in recent years,   but this deficiency has been overcome by a sharp rise in both government and service jobs. Manufacturing remains an important part of the economy;   goods produced include electrical products, chemicals, clothing, processed foods, and machinery.

Berlin is a major German railway hub,   and the city has an efficient public

50

德国柏林

柏林是德国的首都和最大的城市,也是20世纪冷战时期的焦点。今天,这座城市则是欧洲文化、政治和经济的中心。

一、地理

柏林位于北纬52°31′,东经13°28′,地处德国中东部地区,施普雷河与哈弗尔河交汇处,面积超过2 100平方英里。柏林市由一系列人工及天然河流与波罗的海相连通,政府和财政办公区域位于市中心,而住宅开发和工业公司则主要在城市外围的郊区地带。

二、气候

柏林的年均气温在冬季的华氏35度左右至夏季的华氏65度变化,虽然全年都可能降雨,但最潮湿的月份是6月和8月。冬天有时天气比较恶劣,其典型表现就是非常寒冷和干燥。

三、政府

柏林市划分为23个行政区,由一个有240名成员的议会(众议院)管理,议会制定法律,选举市长。经过议会同意之后,市长再任命副市长和参议员(内阁)来行使政府的行政职能,市长和议员们任期4年。柏林还是德国的16个州之一,城市居民选举产生参加国会(联邦议院)及参议院(联邦委员会)的代表。

四、人口

在柏林的人口中,土生土长的德国人占了近90%,非德裔居民包括土耳其人——他们是土耳其境外最大的一群——以及希腊人、意大利人、波兰人、俄罗斯人、美国人、亚洲人和非洲人,柏林大市范围的人口大约有420万。

五、经济

第二次世界大战之前,柏林是德国一个最重要的工业中心。近些年来,虽然柏林经济中工业及建筑行业发展滞后,但是,这一不足却因政府和服务领域的迅速发展而得到弥补。制造行业始终是柏林经济中一个重要的组成部分,其产品包括电器、化工、服装、加工食品和机械制造。

柏林是德国铁路的一个主要枢纽,城市的公共交通系统包括地上轻轨、地铁、电车、

transportation system that operates surface rail (S-Bahn, or Schnellbahn),subways (U-Bahn, or Untergrundbahn), trams (Straßnbahn), buses, and ferries. The city's international airport is Tegel International, just outside the city. Berlin-Schöefeld International and Tempelhof serve charter flights and regional flights, respectively.

The History

Berlin was founded in the 12th century, and by the 15th century it had become the capital of the German state of Brandenburg. The city fell into decline in the 17th century due to war and medical epidemics, but under the rule of Frederick William (the Great Elector) the city revived and blossomed into a major trading and cultural center.

In the early 19th century, the city became the capital of Prussia, and later was the center of the German Empire. The Weimer Republic formed following World War I , and Berlin experienced political strife, riots, and strikes. Runaway inflation plagued the republic and the city during this period, leading to the rise of the Nazis in the 1930s and the onset of World War II.

Berlin was devastated by the Allies during World War II. Following Germany's surrender in 1945, the city was divided into sectors, of which Britain, France,the Soviet Union and the United States controlled one each. In 1948, the Soviet Union blocked surface routes to West Berlin, effectively preventing food and other necessary supplies from reaching residents of those sectors. In response, the United States military airlifted countless tons of supplies to West Berlin over 462 days in 1948 and 1949; were it not for this intervention, later known as the Berlin Airlift, untold numbers of West Berliners would have perished from malnutrition and medical neglect.

In 1961, the Soviets constructed the Berlin Wall to stem the tide of East Germans who were fleeing the city. Over the next 28 years, more than 170 people died trying to scale the Wall's barricades and barbed wire. As the Communist government waned in the Soviet Union, East Germany ended travel restrictions between East and West Berlin in 1989. In the weeks that followed, throngs of people exuberantly dismantled the Wall, a historic event that was televised around the world. Communists soon lost control of the East German government, and in 1990 the country was reunited as the Federal Republic of Germany. The German Parliament, which had moved to Bonn during the Cold War,returned to the Reichstag in Berlin in 1999.

The Sights and Sounds

The former divisions of east and west are familiar to visitors and provide a point of reference in locating the city's various tourist attractions.

In the west, begin at the Egyptian Museum of Berlin to see the magnificent 3,300-year old bust of Queen Nefertiti. The Cultural Forum is a complex of cultural jewels including the Museum of Decorative Arts, the Painting Gallery, and the New National Gallery designed by Mies van der Rohe. The Forum is also home to the world-famous Berlin Philharmonic Orchestra. The Dahlem Museum is a four-building campus displaying artifacts from around the world, including art from the early European, Indian and Asian eras.

Contemporary visitors are fascinated by the Brandenburg Gate, the 18th century landmark that is a symbol of peace. The Holocaust Memorial is located just south of this area. The Reichstag (Parliament) opened in 1894 and was originally the parliament building

公交大巴和渡轮,快速而高效。柏林的国际机场是泰格尔国际机场,就位于市郊地区,此外,柏林舍奈费尔德国际机场和坦佩霍夫机场分别提供包机和区域航线服务。

光影流金

柏林市创建于12世纪,到15世纪,它便已经发展成为德国勃兰登堡州的首府了。由于战争和疫病流行,到了17世纪,城市开始衰落,然而,在腓特烈·威廉的领导下,柏林又重新复苏并迅速繁荣,成为一个主要的贸易及文化的中心。

19世纪初期,柏林成为普鲁士的首都,进而成为德意志王国的中心。随着第一次世界大战的结束以及魏玛共和国的建立,柏林经历了一系列政治纷争、骚乱和罢工,在那段时间里,物价飞涨,通货膨胀肆虐,直接导致了20世纪30年代纳粹分子的出现和第二次世界大战的爆发。

第二次世界大战期间,柏林市几乎被盟军的炮火摧毁。1945年,随着德国投降,柏林也被瓜分,英国、法国、苏联和美国各控制其中一部分。1948年,苏联封锁了通往西柏林的地面道路,有效地阻止了运往这些地区的食品及其他必需品。针对苏联的这一行动,从1948到1949年,美国部队向西柏林提供了长达462天的无数吨的空运物资。假如没有这一后来被称为"柏林空运"的军事干预,数不清的西柏林人都可能因营养不良和缺医少药而死亡。

1961年,苏联人修建了柏林墙来堵住如潮的东德人逃离城市,在接下来的28年间,有170多人因试图翻越柏林墙,而被墙上带倒钩的铁丝障碍刺死。1989年东德取消了东西柏林间的旅游限制,禁令解除后的数周内,大批兴高采烈的市民拆除了柏林墙,这一具有纪念意义的事件在全球电视台被直播。1990年,德国重新统一成为德意志联邦共和国,在冷战时期搬迁至波恩的德国议会,也于1999年重新回到了位于柏林的帝国国会大厦。

声光景点

由于游客对于先前东西柏林的划分比较熟悉,因此,在确定旅游景点的时候也会以此作为参照。

在西柏林,从柏林的埃及博物馆出发,不妨先参观一下已有3 300年历史的奈费尔提蒂王后精美的半身雕像。文化论坛广场是一个集中了文化宝藏的建筑群,包括装饰艺术博物馆、绘画艺术馆和由密斯·凡德罗设计的新国家美术馆,同时,论坛广场还是世界著名的柏林交响乐团所在地。达勒姆博物馆是一个由4座建筑构成的广场,展出来自世界各地的手工艺品,其中包括欧洲、印度及亚洲地区早期的艺术品。

如今许多游客在看到勃兰登堡门时都会异常激动,这座18世纪的地标式建筑是和平的象征。在它的南面就坐落着犹太人大屠杀纪念广场。开放于1894年的国会大厦最初是

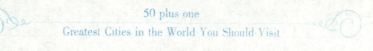

of the German Empire. The Reichstag's destruction by fire in 1933 spurred the rise of the Nazi regime. The building has been restored and is a popular tourist attraction.

For an excellent view of Berlin, climb the steps of the Siegessäule. This memorial known as the Victory Column was erected in 1873 to commemorate Prussia's victory in the Danish-Prussian war. Four tunnels lead to the top of the 220-foot-tall and provide a lovely view of the Tiergarten.

Many of Berlin's older historic sites are in the Eastern sections of the city. The Berliner Dom(Cathedral) is a 19th century church known for its large green dome. Many Prussian nobles are laid to rest here. The Hamburger Bahnhof is a beautiful restored 19th century train station; the grand interaction of color, glass and light in the new wing is a must-see. The station also contains a wonderful collection of contemporary public art.

The Old National Gallery and the Old Museum are located on Museum Island in the middle of the Spree River. The National Gallery houses 19th and 20th century paintings and sculptures, and the Old Museum has a vast collection of Greek,Roman and Old German art. The Pergamon Museum is named for its centerpiece,the Pergamon Altar. This outstanding example of ancient Greek architecture dates from the 2nd century B.C. and is 370 feet in length.

Berlin lives up to its reputation as a sophisticated yet naughty environment.There are more than 6,000 pubs, bars and clubs in the city, as well as jazz clubs,theatres, and cabarets for which Berlin is renowned.

The Trivia

Fact: An important cultural center of Berlin is the Mitte, built around Unter den Linden (the boulevard Under the Linden Trees). World-famous museums and art galleries are located in this area.

Fact: Victorious German armies traditionally paraded through the Brandenburg Gate to the delight of well-wishers.

Fact: One of Berlin's major recreation areas is the Grunewald, a forest along the Havel River. The Teufelsberg (Devil's Mountain) is a man-made hill built for climbing and winter sports; it was constructed from the rubble remaining after World War II.

Fact: Portions of the Berlin Wall have been preserved at Potsdamer Platz, in Bernauer Straße, and in the East Side Gallery along the Spree River.

Why Berlin Is a 50 plus one City

Berlin has outlasted centuries of turmoil and devastation largely because it is a resilient city. Berlin's art and architecture are unmatched in the world, drawing millions of visitors each year to stand in awe of this city's great history.

德意志王国的议会大厦,1933年, 这座大楼被火烧毁,从而刺激了纳粹组织的出现,如今,大厦重新修复并且成为受人欢迎的旅游景点。

要想更好地欣赏柏林市的全貌,可以登上凯旋塔的阶梯,这座被称为"胜利柱"的纪念塔修建于1873年,用以纪念普鲁士在丹麦与普鲁士战争中取得的胜利。塔内有4条通道直达这座高220英尺建筑的顶端,在那里,蒂尔加藤区的美景一览无余。

柏林的许多历史更为久远的景点都位于城市的东部区域,柏林圆顶屋(教堂)是一座19世纪修建的教堂,因其巨大的绿色圆顶而出名,很多普鲁士贵族死后都葬在这里。汉堡现代艺术馆是一座非常漂亮的根据19世纪原貌重建的火车站,在车站的新建部分,色彩、玻璃和灯光交相辉映的绚丽景象绝对不容错过,此外,车站内还有大量漂亮精彩的现代公共艺术展品。

老国家美术馆和老博物馆坐落于施普雷河中的博物馆岛上,国家博物馆收藏有大量19世纪和20世纪的绘画及雕塑作品,而老博物馆则汇集了大量希腊、罗马及古代德意志艺术品。帕加马博物馆因其核心展品帕加马祭坛而得名,这一古希腊建筑的杰出代表高达370英尺,其历史可以追溯到公元前2世纪。

柏林素以成熟的城市内涵和不羁的生活环境而著称,在这座城市里,有6 000多家酒馆、酒吧和夜总会,此外,还有爵士乐俱乐部、剧院以及柏林所特有的娱乐场所"卡巴莱"。

奇闻轶事

之一:柏林的一个重要文化中心是米特区,它建于林登大道(菩提树下的大街),许多世界著名的博物馆、美术馆都位于这一区域。

之二:按照传统,得胜的德国军队要列队通过勃兰登堡门走向欢迎的人群。

之三:柏林的一个主要的娱乐区叫古耐沃德,是哈弗尔河沿岸的一片森林,提奥菲兹伯格(恶魔之山)是一座供游客攀登和进行冬季体育项目的人造的山丘,它是建在二战后遗留下来的废墟之上的。

之四:原柏林墙残留的部分现分别保存在位于波恩瑙街的波茨坦广场,以及施普雷河旁的东岸美术馆。

为什么柏林入选50 + 1个城市?

经过了几个世纪的动荡和大规模的破坏,柏林依然能够屹立不倒,这都源自于这座城市的弹性与活力,柏林的艺术和建筑在当今世界上首屈一指,因而吸引着成千上万的游客来到这里,为这座城市的伟大历史而由衷地敬畏和赞叹。

Nine

Bombay, India (Mumbai, India)

The Basic Facts

Bombay (now called Mumbai) is the capital of the state of Maharashtra in India. Following Indian independence, the Bombay State was divided into the Maharashtra and Gujarat states, based upon the majority language of each area;Bombay remained the capital of Maharashtra. In 1996 the city's name was officially changed from Bombay to Mumbai, which is its name in the Marathi language; many non-Indians still refer to it as Bombay.

Geography

Bombay lies at 18 degrees 58 minutes north latitude and 72 degrees 50 minutes east longitude. The city is built on the Salsette Island (made up of seven islands connected by reclaimed land) off the western coast of India. The city is linked to the Indian mainland by several bridges, has a deep natural harbor, and is the fourth most populous metropolitan area in the world. Most of the city is at sea level, with the exception of the hilly northern part of the island. Three lakes are located within Bombay: Tulsi Lake, Vihar Lake and Powai Lake.

Climate

Bombay lies in the tropical zone and its climate reflects that fact. Spring and summer are typically humid, while fall and winter are typically dry. Temperatures depend largely on humidity; average temperatures range from the lower 50s Fahrenheit in winter to over 100 degrees Fahrenheit in summer. The monsoons that drench Bombay from June to September provide most of the city's annual rainfall.

Government

Bombay is separated into two districts, each under the jurisdiction of a District Collector. The Collectors are responsible for property records, tax collection and election administration.

The Brihanmumbai Municipal Corporation (BMC) administers the city's government departments and infrastructure. Executive power is held by the Municipal Commissioner, who is appointed by the state government. The BMC consists of 227 directly-elected Councilors, who represent each of the city's 24 municipal wards, and 5 nominated Councilors. Each ward also has an Assistant Municipal Commissioner to direct administrative services. The role of the city mayor is largely ceremonial.

Demographics

Most Bombay residents are native Maharashtrians and speak the state's official language of Marathi. However, the city reflects much of the overall flavor of India, with minority groups from every part of the country. Hindus constitute the largest religious

9

印度孟买
(孟巴)

概况

孟买(现在称为孟巴)是印度马哈拉施特拉邦的首府,印度独立之后,孟买邦被划分为马哈拉施特拉邦和古吉拉特邦两部分,划分的主要依据是各邦所使用的主要语言。划分后,孟买仍为马哈拉施特拉邦首府。1996年,这个城市的官方名称从孟买改为了孟巴,也就是它在马拉他语中的名字,许多非印度人仍然用孟买来指这座城市。

一、地理

孟买位于北纬8°58′,东经72°50′,城市建于印度西海岸之外的撒尔塞特岛(该岛是由七座经过人工填海连接起来的小岛组成)之上。孟买与印度大陆由几座大桥相通,它拥有一座天然的深水码头,是世界上排名第四的人口最为稠密的城市。除了该岛北部的丘陵地带以外,城市的大部分区域和海平面持平。孟买城内有三大湖泊:塔尔西湖、维哈湖和波瓦湖。

二、气候

孟买位于热带,其气候正印证了这一事实。春夏季节最典型的是潮湿,而秋冬季节的典型特征是干燥。气温很大程度上取决于湿度。平均气温在冬季的华氏51~53度至夏季的华氏100多度之间变化。贯穿孟买6月~9月的季风为这个城市带来了每年的降雨。

三、政府

孟买市分为两个区,各区在其区域的税务官兼地方行政长官统辖之下,这些行政长官负责财产登记、税费收缴和选举管理工作。

布里罕孟巴市政公司(BMC)管理城市的政府部门及基础设施,行政权掌握在由各邦政府任命的市政长官手中。BMC由227位直选的顾问组成。他们分别代表了城市的24个自治区和5个指定区。每个区还有一位助理市政官来监督行政服务。市长的角色很大程度上是礼仪上的,并没有实权。

四、人口

大部分孟买居民是本地马哈拉施特拉人,他们讲该邦的官方语马拉他语。不过,这也在很大程度上反映了印度整个国家的风貌,即由来自全国各个地方的少数民族共同组成。在孟买,印度教构成了最大的宗教团体,此外还有一些诸如伊斯兰教、基督教、佛教等

group in Bombay, although smaller numbers of Muslims,Christians, Buddhists, and others live in the city. Hindi is the language spoken by most residents. The total population is estimated to be more than 12 million.

Economy

Many banks and insurance companies are located in Bombay, making it a major Indian financial center. The port and trade industries are prevalent and employ many residents. The city's industries produce goods such as cotton textiles, leather articles and transportation equipment. Bombay is also the center of Bollywood,India's thriving film and television industry.

The History

Bombay was originally an archipelago of seven islands. Undocumented evidence suggests that the area may have been inhabited since the Stone Age. More credible information points to human habitation as far back as 250 B.C.. Until 1534 the islands were controlled by local rulers, when the Portuguese took the islands by force and founded what would become modern Bombay. In 1662 Portugal gave the islands to English King Charles II as a dowry for his marriage to the Portuguese royal Catherine of Braganza. The British East India Company later leased the islands to construct a major port. The port was so successful that in 1687 Bombay became the company's headquarters. The British warded off several attempts by Indian nationalists to retake the islands over the next 100 years.British governors of the city reinforced its defenses and constructed numerous bridges to the mainland.

In 1817 a major civil engineering project began that would unite the island archipelago into a single land mass. This project, completed in 1845, was known as the Hornby Vellard after William Hornby, Governor of Bombay.

Bombay became the center of the Indian independence movement in the 1940s, including the All India Congress Committee sessions of 1942. The movement eventually ended British control of the country, and in August, 1947 India formally declared its independence.

The Sights and Sounds

Visitors may initially view Bombay as a chaotic, overwhelming city. Indeed, traffic congestion is the rule, and the city teems with people rushing here are there. After a while, however, one grows accustomed to the hum of the city. In recent years,many monuments and tourist attractions have been renamed in an attempt to downplay their colonial British origins. Nevertheless, most locals still know them by their English names. In most cases, visitors should not have much difficulty finding their way around.

After the Taj Mahal, the Gateway of India is the country's most recognizable structures. Construction of this 85-foot-tall monument began in 1911 and it commemorates the first visit of King George and Queen Mary to Bombay. This monument is beautiful from a distance, but to see its architectural details requires a closer look. The Gateway is located in South Bombay and is a good place to enjoy people watching against the backdrop of the nearby waterfront.A variety of boat trips are available just across the street. Just a few miles across the water from the Gateway of India are the Elephanta Caves, which contain many

人数较少的社团。大多数居民讲印地语。据估计,孟买的人口超过了1 200万。

五、经济

　　许多的银行和保险公司都选址于孟买,使得孟买成为印度主要的金融中心。孟买的港口与贸易工业占主导地位,解决了许多居民的就业问题。孟买的工业产品有棉花纺织、皮革产品和交通设备。此外,孟买还是"宝莱坞",也就是印度繁荣的电影及电视工业的中心。

光影流金

　　孟买最初是由七个岛屿组成的群岛,尽管没有文献记载,但是大约从石器时期开始,这一地区可能就有了人类的足迹。更为可信的材料表明最晚在公元前250年,这里已经有人类居住了。1534年之前,这些岛屿一直被当地首领统治,葡萄牙人以武力占领了这些岛屿,并创建了现代孟买市的雏形。1662年,葡萄牙将这些岛屿作为嫁妆送给了当时同葡萄牙公主凯瑟琳结婚的英国国王查理二世。后来,英国的东印度公司租借了这些岛屿来建造一个大港口,而这个港口的建设非常成功,以至于1687年孟买成了这家公司的总部。在接下来的100年间,英国阻止了数次印度民族主义者试图将这些岛屿收回的努力,同时,城市里的英国总督加强了防御,建造了无数通往印度大陆的桥梁。

　　1817年,一项大型土木工程开始动工,旨在将这些岛屿群连接成一整块陆地。这项工程到1845年全部完成,并以孟买总督威廉·霍恩比的名字命名为霍恩比·维拉德。

　　20世纪40年代,孟买成为印度独立运动的中心,包括1942年举行的全印度议会委员会会议。这一运动最终结束了英国在这个国家的统治。1947年8月,印度正式宣布独立。

声光景点

　　初到孟买的游客可能会认为这是一个庞大而杂乱的城市,的确,这个城市中到处都是窜来窜去的人,交通堵塞是很常见的。然而,只要过上一段时间,你就会对它的嘈杂见怪不怪了。近些年来,许多纪念碑和旅游景点已经被重新命名,为的是弱化以往殖民地英国的烙印。不过,大多数当地人还是会沿用原来的英文名,所以,游客在孟买如果要问路的话不会有太大的困难。

　　"印度之门"是这个国家仅次于泰姬·马哈尔陵的最为著名的建筑,这座高85英尺的纪念拱门始建于1911年,用以纪念乔治国王和玛丽王后首次访问孟买。虽然这座纪念拱门远看就非常漂亮,但是,要欣赏其建筑的细节还需要近距离的观察。这座大门坐落于孟买南部,是一个可以让游客远眺附近海滨景色的好去处。仅需跨过一条街,就可以看到各种各样的船只停靠在那里。从印度之门乘船穿过数英里的海面就到了象岛石窟,这里有

centuries-old rock carvings and sculptures.

The Prince of Wales Museum houses a large assortment of Indian and Asian artifacts; visitors need more than one day to see the entire collection. Of special interest are the statues of the gods located in a gallery off the main entrance.

Mani Bhavan Ghandi Sangrahalaya is a modest home on Laburnum Road where Mohandas K. (Mahatma) Gandhi stayed while visiting Bombay. It is the former home of his friend Shri Revashankar Jhaveri and is now an important museum chronicling the life of the renowned spiritual leader. Gandhi's room on the second floor appears as it was when he last visited, and visitors can view the room from behind a glass partition. Scholars will marvel at the large collection of Gandhi's papers as well as numerous books and materials about him.

The Jehangir Art Gallery, adjacent to the Prince of Wales Museum, is a popular tourist attraction. The gallery's exhibits include photographs and oils by nationally-recognized Indian artists.

Chhatrapati Shivaji Terminus (formerly Victoria Terminus) is a historic railway station that looks more like a Gothic museum. This building was completed in 1888 and its architecture blends Gothic and Indian influences. The station is still in operation and is one of the busiest rail stations in the country.

The Trivia

Fact: The name Bombay is derived from the Portuguese Bom Bahia. The inhabitants referred to the area as Mumba, after a Hindu deity.

Fact: One of the more famous Bombay landmarks is the Parsi Tower of Silence on Malabar Hill. They were constructed in the 17th century by the Zoroastrians (Parsis). Adherents of this religion consider dead bodies to be unclean. They therefore place corpses atop the towers, and later throw the bones into an ossuary pit.

Fact: In April 1944 a mysterious fire caused the explosion of the cargo ship Fort Stikine in the harbor. Following the explosion, two million British pounds' worth of gold bars literally rained from the skies. Most were recovered and returned to the British government.

Why Bombay Is a 50 plus one City

Bombay represents the pride and spirit of India. It showcases the rise in both political and economic influence of the new India. No other city in India has quite the same combination of colonial and Indian influences as Bombay. It is a thoroughly modern Indian city, rich with Indian culture, traditions and history.

许多几个世纪前的雕刻和塑像。

威尔士亲王博物馆拥有大量形态各异的印度及亚洲的手工艺品,要欣赏完全部的藏品,需要超过一天的时间。在博物馆主入口处不远的一个美术馆里,有一些同样非常特别的神像雕塑。

位于拉伯南路上的马尼巴凡·甘地·桑格拉哈拉亚是默罕达斯·K.甘地访问孟买时住过的朴实无华的家,这里以前是甘地的朋友施里·瑞瓦山卡·贾维里的家,如今这里是一家重要的记载这位著名精神领袖一生的博物馆。甘地的房间位于二楼,至今还保留着他最后一次来访时的样子,游客可以透过玻璃挡板看到屋内的一切。来到这里的学者们会惊叹于大量甘地撰写的文章以及无数有关他的书籍和材料。

捷罕阁艺术画廊毗邻威尔士亲王博物馆,是一处深受游客喜爱的旅游景点,其展品包括照片和印度国内知名的艺术家创作的油画作品。

贾特拉帕蒂·希瓦吉终点站 (即原来的维多利亚车站) 是一处具有纪念意义的火车站,它看上去更像是一座哥特式的博物馆。这座建筑完成于1888年,其建筑融合了哥特式与印度本土的特色。火车站至今仍在使用,并且是印度最繁忙的火车站之一。

奇闻轶事

之一:孟买的名字起源于葡萄牙语"博姆–巴伊阿"。当地居民依据印度教一个神的名字而把这一地区称作孟巴。

之二:孟买更为有名的地标之一,是位于马拉巴尔山上的帕西人的安息塔。它们是17世纪由琐罗亚斯德教徒(即拜火教的帕西人)修建的。这一教派的信徒认为死尸是不洁之物,所以他们将尸体存放于这些塔顶,之后再把骸骨扔进一个存放尸骨的洞穴里。

之三:1944年4月,一场神秘的大火引起停泊在港口的斯丁凯货轮的爆炸,爆炸过后,天上下起了金雨,有价值200万英镑的金条真真切切地从天而降,但大部分都被回收并交还给了英国政府。

为什么孟买入选50＋1个城市?

孟买代表了印度的骄傲和精神,它将新印度在政治和经济上不断上升的影响力展现在世人面前,它将殖民地影响与印度本土特色有机地结合,形成独一无二的孟买特色,它既是一座完全现代化的印度城市,同时又拥有浓郁的印度文化、传统和历史。

Boston, United States

The Basic Facts

Boston is the capital and largest city in the Commonwealth of Massachusetts. It is the unofficial capital of the region known as New England and one of the oldest, wealthiest, and most culturally significant U.S. cities.

Geography

Boston lies at 42 degrees 15 minutes north latitude and 71 degrees 7 minutes west. longitude. The city covers approximately 90 square miles—46 percent of which is water—in east-central Massachusetts. Boston is 19 feet above sea level at its highest point, and much of the Back Bay and South End sections are built on reclaimed land. The Charles River separates Boston proper from Cambridge, Watertown, and Charlestown.

Climate

The weather in Boston changes rapidly; it is not uncommon for the city to experience 50-degree temperature swings over the course of several days. Summers are typically warm and humid, and winters are often cold and windy, although Boston has experienced snow in October and unseasonable warmth in February. Annual temperatures range from the mid-30s Fahrenheit in winter to the low 80s Fahrenheit in summer.

Government

Boston has a strong mayor form of government, in which the mayor is vested with extensive executive powers. The mayor is elected to a 4-year term by plurality voting. The Boston city council is elected every 2 years.

Demographics

The population of the city of Boston is approximately 590,000. The metropolitan area, encompassing parts of New Hampshire, Maine, Rhode Island, and Connecticut, has a population of 5.8 million. The largest ethnic group in the city is undoubtedly those of Irish descent, and thus makes Boston the unofficial capital of Irish America.

Economy

Boston's has a diversified economic base; important sectors include finance, health care, education, insurance, biotechnology, and business services. Area universities are among the finest in the United States and have a significant impact in the city's economy. Boston is home to a major port. The major airport in Boston is Logan International, located in the East Boston neighborhood. First-time visitors to Boston often carp about finding their way around the city, for many reasons: the streets are largely devoid of a structured numbering system; street names change often; and roundabouts confound

---

10

美国波士顿

概况

波士顿是马萨诸塞州的州府和最大的城市，是被通常称为"新英格兰"地区的非官方首府，也是美国最古老、最富有、最具文化特色的城市之一。

一、地理

波士顿位于北纬42°15′，西经71°7′，面积近90平方英里——其中46%为水域——地处马萨诸塞州的中东部。波士顿城市的最高处位于海平面以上19英尺，后湾区和南端区的大部分是在填海造地的基础上建立起来的。查尔斯河将波士顿城区与坎布里奇、水城及查尔斯镇分割开来。

二、气候

波士顿的天气瞬息万变，几天之内，气温在华氏50度之间大幅变化的情形并不少见。夏天温暖潮湿，冬天时常寒冷多风，不过，波士顿也出现过10月下雪及2月异常温暖的反常天气。年均气温在冬季的华氏35度左右至夏季的华氏81~83度变化。

三、政府

波士顿政府集中表现为强有力的市长负责制，市长被赋予广泛的行政权力，市长选举由多数选票来决定，市长任期4年。波士顿市政委员会每两年选举一次。

四、人口

波士顿市人口有近59万，其大市范围包括新罕布什尔州、缅因州、罗得岛以及康涅狄格州的部分地区，共有人口580万。毫无疑问，该市最大的民族是爱尔兰人后裔，这就使得波士顿成为爱尔兰裔美国人的非正式中心。

五、经济

波士顿拥有一个多样化的经济基础，其重要的经济领域包括金融、医疗、教育、保险、生物科技和商业服务业。这一地区的大学在全美国名列前茅，并且对城市的经济产生了积极的影响。波士顿还是一个主要的港口城市。波士顿主要的机场是洛甘国际机场，位于波士顿东部居民区附近。初来乍到的游客时常抱怨在城里找不到路，其中的原因有很多：比如城里的街道大部分都没有系统的编号标识，街道名称三天两头改变，绕来绕去的道路令原本就稀里糊涂的司机更加辨不清方向。对于那些不想自己驾车游玩的人来说，波

disoriented drivers. Boston's public transportation system is popular with those who prefer not to navigate the city on their own. The system includes buses, water shuttles, commuter rail, and a subway—the first of its kind in the United States.

The History

The area of present-day Boston was originally settled by the Massachusett Indians and inhabited by a variety of indigenous groups who called the area Shawmut. The first European settlers arrived in Boston in 1630; these were the Puritans, who initially named the area Trimountaine. The city was renamed Boston after the city of the same name in Lincolnshire, England.

In 1629 the Puritans, led by John Winthrop, signed the Cambridge Agreement to ensure self-governance for Boston and the Massachusetts Bay Colony. This Christian sect was known for its religious devotion, and had a de.nite impact on the history of early Boston. At the time, the city was said to have a special relationship with God; it was known as the City on the Hill to reference to its closeness to Heaven. Boston became the capital of the Massachusetts Bay Colony in the 1630s, and only Puritans could vote or hold public office.

Puritan Boston was a strict but stable environment in which education was emphasized. The first school in America, Boston's Latin School, was founded in 1635, and Harvard College was founded in the next year. Boston schools became the model for modern education, and the city eventually became one of the great centers of learning in the United States.

In the 1700s Boston grew rapidly and gradually abolished most strict Puritan laws.In the 1770s, however, Boston came into conflict with the British government,which attempted to exert direct control and taxation on the American colonies.

Many events leading up to and part of the American Revolution occurred in Boston: the Boston Massacre; the Boston Tea Party; Paul Revere's midnight ride;and the early Revolutionary battles of Bunker Hill, Lexington and Concord, and the Siege of Boston.

After the Revolutionary War, Boston's economy thrived with the growth of foreign trade, and by the mid-1800s manufacturing became the dominant economic sector. Boston became known as a center for literature, the arts, and the Abolitionist movement.

Boston's once-thriving industry began to show its age at the turn of the 20th century, and the city lost many jobs as a result. In the 1970s urban renewal laid the foundation for the new city of Boston. During the 1980s the city earned a national reputation for its resistance to busing and school integration. New service businesses replaced the old manufacturing base, and once again Boston is an economically vibrant city. Boston recently completed a massive public works project, the construction of a tunnel designed to ease traffic congestion;Bostonians nicknamed the project the Big Dig.

The Sights and Sounds

The Boston National Historical Park is located in the downtown area, and contains buildings and areas that figured prominently during the American Revolution. The three-mile Freedom Trail passes many of these sites, as well as Boston Common and the Boston Public Garden. Locals enjoy ice-skating on the Frog Pond at Boston Common during the winter. The Esplanade is a popular park along the banks of the Charles River.

士顿的公共交通系统自然是首选,这个系统包括公共汽车、水上穿梭巴士、通勤轻轨和地铁 —— 全美一流的地铁。

光影流金

最早定居于今天波士顿地区的居民是马萨诸塞的印第安人以及各类土著居民,他们把这一地区称为"肖马特"。1630年,首批欧洲移民抵达波士顿,他们都是清教徒,起初他们将这一地区称作特里芒太,后来,又更名为波士顿,与位于英格兰林肯郡的波士顿同名。

1629年,由约翰·温斯罗普率领的清教徒们签署了《剑桥条约》,确立了波士顿及马萨诸塞湾殖民地的自治权。这支基督教的分支以其宗教献身精神而闻名,对早期波士顿的历史产生了显著的影响。据说当时,波士顿市被认为与上帝有着特殊的关系,"山巅之城"的美称就是指其与天堂的亲近。17世纪30年代,波士顿成为马萨诸塞湾殖民地的首府,只有清教徒才有权选举或行使行政职能。

清教徒控制的波士顿是一个严格但稳定的社会,教育受到重视,美国的第一所学校,波士顿拉丁语学校,就是1635年在这里建立的,第二年,又诞生了哈佛学院。波士顿的学校是现代教育的典范,该市最终也成为美国教育的核心地区之一。

18世纪时,波士顿市迅速成长,并逐渐废除了大多数严格的清教徒法律。然而,18世纪70年代,由于当时的英国政府试图对其美洲殖民地实行直接控制并大量征税,导致波士顿与英国政府发生冲突。

接下来还有许多事件,包括独立战争的一部分都发生在波士顿:例如,波士顿大屠杀,波士顿倾茶事件,保罗·里维尔的半夜骑马报信,彭加山的早期革命战役,莱克星顿和康科德,波士顿的围攻等等。

美国独立战争之后,伴随对外贸易的发展,波士顿的经济迅速繁荣起来。到了19世纪中期,加工制造业已经占据了经济的主导地位。此外,波士顿还以文学、艺术及废奴主义中心而著称。

到了19、20世纪之交,波士顿一度繁荣的工业开始显示出老态,就业机会开始大幅减少。到了20世纪70年代,城市的更新改造为波士顿新城奠定了基础。到了20世纪80年代,这个城市因抵制用公共汽车接送学生及学校合并引起全美关注。新型的商业服务行业取代了古老的加工制造业成为其经济的基础,波士顿再次成为一个在经济上充满活力的城市。最近,波士顿刚刚完成了一项工程浩大的公共建设项目,一项旨在缓解交通拥堵的隧道工程,波士顿人将此项工程戏称为"大开挖"。

声光景点

波士顿国家历史公园位于市中心,其中包括象征美国独立战争时期的杰出建筑和区域。全长3英里的"自由步道"经过许多旧址,还经过波士顿公园和波士顿公共花园。冬天,当地居民喜欢在位于波士顿公园的"青蛙池"溜冰。"散步大道"是一个深受市民喜爱的公园,位于查尔斯河沿岸。

Landmarks in Boston's Back Bay district include the Boston Public Library, Copley Square, and Newbury Street. The historic John Hancock Building still stands today, although the company's offices are currently located in an adjacent modern building.

Notable museums in the city are the Museum of Fine Arts, the Gardner Museum, and the Museum of Science. The University of Massachusetts is a short distance away and has a children's museum, aquarium, and zoo, as well as the Boston Athenaeum, one of the oldest independent libraries in the country.

Bostonians love their sports, and sporting events always draw large crowds. The Boston Bruins of the National Hockey League and the Boston Celtics of the National Basketball Association share their home at TD Banknorth Garden. Historic Fenway Park, which opened in 1912, is the home of the Boston Red Sox. Fenway is home to the imposing Green Monster, the 37-foot-tall left field wall that has confounded heavy hitters for decades. The New England Patriots of the National Football League play in the Boston suburb of Foxboro.

The Trivia

Fact: Boston was a center of literary activity in the 1800s; many literary giants lived in the city, including Louisa May Alcott, Ralph Waldo Emerson, Nathaniel Hawthorne, and Henry Wadsworth Longfellow.

Fact: Boston Common is the oldest public park in the United States, covering 50 acres amid the city's downtown area. Until 1817 the Common was the site of public hangings.

Why Boston is a 50 plus one City

Boston is respected not only for its prominent place in American history, but also for its reputation as an exciting, livable city that emphasizes education, art and architecture. A visit to Beantown is a must for history buffs and those interested in the best of American culture.

地处后湾区的地标建筑包括波士顿公共图书馆、科普利广场和纽伯里大街。具有历史意义的约翰-汉考克大厦至今依然矗立在那里，尽管公司的办公地点已经搬到了与此紧邻的一幢摩登大厦内。

市区内著名的博物馆有波士顿美术馆、加德纳博物馆和科学博物馆。离此不远的马萨诸塞大学拥有一个儿童博物馆、水族馆和动物园。波士顿图书馆是美国历史上最为悠久的独立图书馆之一。

波士顿人热爱体育运动，体育赛事总是能吸引大群的观众。隶属全美冰上曲棍球联盟的波士顿布伦斯队以及国家篮球协会的波士顿凯尔特人队，其本部都设在北岸花园。具有纪念意义的芬威球场建于1912年，是波士顿红袜棒球队的老家，芬威球场内巨大的"绿色怪兽"是一面高37英尺的左外场墙，在数十年里它给那些费力的击球手们带来了不小的麻烦。全美橄榄球联盟的新英格兰爱国者队在位于波士顿郊外的福克斯波罗体育场比赛。

奇闻轶事

之一：19世纪时，波士顿曾是文学活动的中心，许多文学巨匠都生活在这座城市里，其中包括路易莎·梅·爱尔考特，拉尔夫·沃尔夫·爱默生，纳撒尼尔·霍桑和亨利·华兹华斯·朗法罗。

之二：波士顿公园是美国最为古老的公共园林，在市中心地区，占地50英亩，在1817年之前，这里一直是绞刑的公开执行地。

为什么波士顿入选50 + 1个城市？

波士顿之所以广受尊崇，不仅因为它在美国历史上拥有极其杰出的地位，而且因为它是一座以教育、艺术、建筑为核心的既动人又宜居的城市，无论你是一个历史迷，还是一个想了解美国文化精华的人，"豆城"都是你的必游之地。

Eleven

Brussels, Belgium

The Basic Facts

Brussels is the capital of Belgium and the unofficial capital of the European Union. Over the past several years, the city's economy has grown substantially, so much so that the city struggles to preserve its historic treasures.

Geography

Brussels lies at 50 degrees 51 minutes north latitude and 4 degrees 21 minutes east longitude. The city is located in central Belgium and is the largest municipality of the Brussels-Capital Region. The city's population is estimated at only 140,000, but the metropolitan area's population is roughly two million.

Climate

Brussels has a temperate climate with warm summers and mild winters. Annual temperatures range from the lower 40s Fahrenheit in winter to the lower 70s Fahrenheit in summer. It can rain at any time of the year in Brussels, but snow is infrequent even in winter.

Government

The Brussels-Capital Region is divided into 19 regions or communes. Each commune elects representatives to the 89-member Regional Parliament in proportion to its population. The Parliament appoints regional administrators and approves the annual regional budget.

Demographics

Most residents are native-born Belgians or descended from the French. Brussels' population includes immigrants from other countries in Europe, the Middle East, and Africa. Dutch and French are the official languages of Brussels, although French is the usual language spoken by the people of Brussels.

Economy

Brussels is Belgium's center for the banking, insurance and transportation industries. Small industries manufacture ceramics, chemicals, drugs, processed foods, paper and textiles. The headquarters of several international organizations are located in Brussels including the European Union (EU) and the North Atlantic Treaty Organization (NATO); these organizations employ many local residents. Brussels is a hub for Europe's highway system and railroad network. City commuters use the Brussels Metro subway and an extensive tram and bus network. International travelers arrive at Brussels National Airport.

The History

The name Brussels comes from Old Dutch meaning marsh or home on the marsh, depending on the translation. In the late 10th century, Carl of France built a castrum (fortress) on an island in the Zenne. A new city wall was constructed in 1379, as the city had outgrown its original area (the wall is now known as the pentagon or inner ring). In the late 17th century Brussels was attacked by the French; more than 4,000 homes and

---

11

比利时布鲁塞尔

概况

布鲁塞尔是比利时的首都,是欧盟的非官方总部。在过去的几年里,这座城市的经济取得了实质性的增长,由于增长过快,以至于市政府不得不为那些历史文物的保护而煞费脑筋。

一、地理

布鲁塞尔位于北纬50°51′,东经4°21′。地处比利时中部,是布鲁塞尔首都区最大的行政区。尽管市区人口大约只有14万,但是大市范围的人口约有200万。

二、气候

布鲁塞尔气候宜人,冬暖夏凉。年均气温在冬季的华氏41~43度到夏季的华氏71~73度之间变化。在布鲁塞尔,一年中随时都可能下雨,但是即使在冬季也很少降雪。

三、政府

布鲁塞尔首都地区被划分为19个区域或社区。每个社区根据其人口比例选举产生地区议会89个席位的代表。议会任命区域行政官员并通过每年的区域预算。

四、人口

大部分布鲁塞尔居民是土生土长的比利时人或法国后裔。城市人口包括来自欧洲其他国家、中东地区以及非洲的移民。荷兰语和法语是布鲁塞尔的官方语言,不过,布鲁塞尔人通常都讲法语。

五、经济

布鲁塞尔是比利时银行、保险以及交通业的中心。一些小型工业企业主要生产陶瓷、化学制品、药品、加工食品、纸张及纺织品。若干个国际组织的总部都设在布鲁塞尔,其中包括欧盟及北大西洋公约组织,这些组织为许多当地居民解决了就业问题。布鲁塞尔是欧洲公路系统及铁路网的枢纽。市内交通可以依靠布鲁塞尔地铁、分布范围很广的电车及公交网络。来访的国际旅客抵达的是布鲁塞尔国家机场。

光影流金

布鲁塞尔的名字源自古代荷兰语,翻译过来意思就是沼泽或沼泽上的家。10世纪晚期,法国国王查理在塞纳河的一个岛上修建了一座坎城古堡(要塞)。1379年,随着城市

medieval buildings destroyed by fire, but the famous city hall survived.

Brussels became the capital of Belgium when the first Belgian king, Léopold I, ascended to the throne in 1831. Brussels suffered greatly during both World Wars, especially in 1940 when the German army bombed the city relentlessly. Brussels gradually recovered in the post-war era, and its economy is thriving in the present day.

The Sights and Sounds

Brussels is a heart-shaped city divided into two sections. The Lower Section is the older part of the city and includes the Grand'Place (the main square of Brussels) and many historic buildings, some of which date to the 17th century. Most buildings in the Upper City, including the royal palace, parliament, and other government buildings are 100 to 200 years old. Around the Grand'Place are the Baroque guild houses, topped with golden statues and heroes which seem to have a life of their own. The Grand'Place is said to be one of the finest open spaces in Europe and has many cafes, shops and taverns, along with the popular Brewery Museum. The Town Hall also located here, is known for its statue of St. Michael crushing the devil; the building also displays a collection of historical tapestries, some of which date to the 16th century.

A must-see is the Grand Sablon, an expansive shopping and dining area with all its charm and sophistication. The Church of Notre Dame du Sablon and the Church of Notre Dame de la Chapelle are among the finest Gothic churches in all of Northern Europe.

Many impressive museums beckon visitors, including the Fine Arts Museum with its collection of art by the Flemish and Dutch Old Masters. The Museum of Modern Art, in contrast, is as fascinating for its architecture as for the artworks displayed within. The museum is built eight stories into the ground around a natural light well. Music lovers will enjoy the Musical Instrument Museum, with some 7,000 instruments from as early as the Bronze Age. The saxophone, which was invented in Belgium, naturally has one of the larger displays.

Brussels' royal palace was rebuilt in the early 20th century to the specifications of King Léopold II, who was known for his expensive tastes. The palace has an especially grand stairway that leads to the throne room. Today the royal family does not live in the palace, but state affairs are frequently held there.

No one starves in Brussels, as the city has more than 3,000 restaurants and a host of cafés and eateries. Thirsty travelers can visit one of the many pubs for a draught of Belgium's renowned beers. Dance clubs open late and remain open into the wee hours of the morning. Brussels is an exciting city both day and night.

The Trivia

Fact: The Belgian Comic Strip Center is an entertaining museum dedicated to the fine art of cartooning.

Fact: The Belgian Constitution of 1971 attempted to quell the conflicts among French-speaking and Dutch-speaking Belgians. As a result, the country essentially divided itself in terms of linguistics; Brussels, however, remained bilingual.

Fact: Brussels is known as Bruxelles in French.

Why Brussels Is a 50 plus one City

International visitors will be awed by Brussels' historical grandeur and contemporary vitality. It is a European city with a burgeoning economy and a growing global importance: truly a city on the move.

在原有区域基础上不断扩大,人们又修建了新的城墙(如今这座城墙被称为"五边形"或"内环")。17世纪后期,布鲁塞尔遭到法国人袭击,4 000多间房屋及中世纪建筑毁于大火,但是著名的市政厅却幸免于难。

当比利时王国的首位国王利奥波德一世于1831年登基时,布鲁塞尔成为比利时的首都。在两次世界大战期间,布鲁塞尔受难深重,尤其是1940年,当时德国军队对城市进行了残酷的轰炸。战争结束之后,布鲁塞尔逐渐从创伤中恢复过来,如今,其经济又焕发出勃勃生机。

声光景点

整个布鲁塞尔市形似心形,分为两个部分,下城区是城市中较为古老的部分,包括"大广场"(即布鲁塞尔的主要广场)和许多有纪念意义的建筑,其中有些可以追溯到17世纪。上城区的大多数建筑,包括皇宫、国会及其他政府建筑都有100到200年的历史。大广场周围是巴洛克风格的行业公会会馆,顶端装饰着金色的塑像,那些行业英雄看上去栩栩如生。据说大广场是欧洲最棒的露天广场之一,拥有许多咖啡屋、商铺和小酒店,此外,这里还有深受游客喜爱的啤酒博物馆。以圣马克压垮魔鬼的雕塑而著称的市政厅同样坐落在这里,市政厅大厦内收藏了大量手工挂毯,其中部分挂毯历史之久足以追溯到16世纪。

布鲁塞尔的一处必游之地是"大萨布隆",这是一个宽广的购物及餐饮地区,成熟而又迷人。萨布隆圣母教堂和沙佩勒圣母教堂属于所有北欧教堂当中最完美的哥特式风格。

布鲁塞尔有许多令人难忘的博物馆,它们都在敞开双臂迎接着四面八方的游客。其中古典美术馆收藏了大批佛兰芒人和荷兰古代大师们的艺术作品。与之形成鲜明对照的是现代美术馆,其中展示的艺术品同其建筑本身一样令人叹为观止。音乐爱好者们肯定会陶醉于乐器博物馆,这里有大约7 000件各类乐器,最早的产于青铜器时代,由比利时人发明的萨克斯自然在这里拥有最大的馆藏。

布鲁塞尔皇宫是20世纪早期根据利奥波德国王二世的详细建筑说明而重建的,这位国王因其兴趣爱好广泛而出名。整座皇宫内的阶梯异常宏伟气派,且一直延伸至觐见室。如今,虽然王室成员已经不住在皇宫里了,但是一些国家事务仍然经常在此举行。

在布鲁塞尔没有人会忍饥挨饿,因为城里有超过3 000家餐馆和大量的咖啡屋、小吃店。游客如果口渴,不妨到众多的酒馆中挑选一家小憩一下,享受一杯比利时著名的鲜啤酒。舞厅夜总会很晚关门,通常要营业到凌晨时分,无论白天还是夜晚,布鲁塞尔都是一个激动人心的城市。

奇闻轶事

之一:"比利时连环漫画中心"是一家针对卡通艺术的娱乐博物馆。

之二:1971年的《比利时宪法》试图消除说法语与讲荷兰语的比利时人之间的矛盾冲突,但结果却造成这个国家实质上按照语言分裂为两个部分。不过,布鲁塞尔至今依然保持着双语并用的状态。

之三:布鲁塞尔在法语中称为"布鲁与塞尔(Bruxelles)"。

为什么布鲁塞尔入选50＋1个城市?

无论来自何方,世界各地的游客都会仰慕布鲁塞尔历史上的辉煌,赞叹其当今社会的活力,这是一座欧洲城市,一座经济欣欣向荣、全球地位日趋重要的欧洲城市,一座真真切切处在发展中的城市。

Budapest, Hungary

The Basic Facts

Budapest is the capital of Hungary and is a major center for politics, culture, transportation, and industry. It is among the most picturesque of Eastern European cities and is a popular tourist destination.

Geography

Budapest lies at 47 degrees 30 minutes north latitude and 19 degrees 5 minutes east longitude. The city is located along the banks of the Danube River in northern Hungary. Eight bridges span the Danube to connect the east and west sides of the city.

Climate

Budapest's climate is influenced by the Alps to the west and the Great Plain to the east. The city accordingly has humid, warm summers and short, cold winters. Average temperatures range from the mid-30s Fahrenheit in winter to the lower 80s Fahrenheit in summer. Rain occurs throughout the year.

Government

Budapest consists of 23 districts each with its own government, mayor, and council. The city government is headed by the city mayor, deputy mayors, chief clerk, and a 67-member general assembly. Twenty-eight departments within the mayor's office administer various municipal services.

Demographics

The majority of Budapest residents are native Hungarians. Most are Roman Catholic, although there are significant numbers of Calvinists and Lutherans. The official language is known as Magyar. The city's population is roughly 1.7 million.

Economy

Budapest was once a city of craftsmen who engaged in a variety of small industries, but World War II brought significant economic change to the city. Today large industries produce chemical products, textiles, transportation equipment, building materials, electrical equipment, and processed foods. Hungary's banking and finance industries are located in Budapest, as well as the primary hubs for the country's airlines, highways and railroads. Several ports along the Danube make Budapest an important trade center as well.

The History

The Romans built the town of Aquincum in the 1st century A.D. on the site of present-day Budapest. The invading Huns expelled the Romans in the 5th century. Over the next 4 centuries, the area was controlled by the Huns and other regional tribes. The Magyars, the ancestors of modern Hungarians, founded the Kingdom of Hungary in the early 11th century; the kingdom's realm eventually grew to encompass the cities of Buda, Pest, and óbuda. Buda was home to the royal court and was an important city during the Italian Renaissance. Turks invaded the kingdom in the 16th century and retained control until they were ousted by the powerful Austrian Habsburgs. In the 19th century Pest became a center of Hungarian nationalism and culture.

匈牙利布达佩斯

概况

布达佩斯是匈牙利的首都，是匈牙利一个主要的政治、文化、交通和工业中心。在东欧各城市当中，布达佩斯是风景最美、最受游客欢迎的旅游目的地之一。

一、地理

布达佩斯位于北纬47°30′，东经19°5′，地处匈牙利北部多瑙河沿岸，八座横跨多瑙河的大桥将城市的东西两岸连接起来。

二、气候

布达佩斯的气候受到西面阿尔卑斯山以及东部大平原的共同影响，夏季潮湿温暖，冬季短暂寒冷。平均气温在冬季的华氏35度左右到夏季的华氏81~83度变化，全年均有降水。

三、政府

布达佩斯由23个区组成，每个区有自己的政府、区长及委员会，市政府由市长、副市长、首席文员以及一个包括67名成员的城市众议院组成，市长办公室所属的28个部门行使不同的市政服务功能。

四、人口

布达佩斯的多数人口是地道的匈牙利人，大部分信仰罗马天主教，也有相当数量的加尔文信徒及路德教徒。官方语言为匈牙利语。城市人口大约有170万。

五、经济

布达佩斯过去曾经是一个工匠云集的城市，这些工匠从事着各类小型的工业。然而，第二次世界大战使得城市的经济结构发生了明显变化，如今，布达佩斯拥有生产诸如化学制品、纺织、交通设备、建筑材料、电动工具和加工食品等的大型工业企业。匈牙利的银行及金融行业都集中在布达佩斯，此外，布达佩斯还是这个国家空中航线、公路及铁路的第一枢纽。多瑙河沿线的几个港口也使得布达佩斯成为重要的贸易中心。

光影流金

公元1世纪时，罗马人在位于今天布达佩斯市所在地区修建了阿奎肯镇。5世纪时，匈奴人赶走了罗马人。在以后的四个世纪里，这一地区始终处于匈奴人和其他一些区域部落的掌控之中。11世纪早期，马扎尔人，即当今匈牙利人的祖先，建立了匈牙利王国，王国的疆土最终扩大到包括布达、佩斯和老布达的地方，布达是皇家法庭所在地，也是意大利

Modern Budapest was formed in 1873 by uniting the three cities of the former kingdom. World War Ⅱ was a particularly dark time for the city, as most of Budapest's Jews were eradicated by the Nazis.

The Sights and Sounds

The area known as Buda Castle was almost completely destroyed during World War Ⅱ, and the area's original brilliance is slowly returning to the area by way of a lengthy reconstruction process. The Royal Palace is in this area of Budapest; this is not the original palace, although the museums located there today are built on its site.

The Ludwig Museum is the city's museum of international contemporary art, and the Hungarian National Gallery is devoted exclusively to the works of national artists. The Budapest History Museum displays information of the history of the city, from its liberation from the Turks in 1686 to the present day.

Matthias Church reflects the changing fortunes and religions of Budapest. The church was originally built in the 13th century as a mosque. The structure was destroyed and rebuilt in the 19th century, then destroyed again during World War Ⅱ, and rebuilt once more. The church was the site of Habsburg coronations during their Hungarian rule.

Pest is the heart of the city, where visitors can see splendid examples of Budapest's history and architecture. The Hungarian State Opera House has been restored to its 19th century splendor; two marble sphinxes grace its entrance. The Hungarian National Museum opened in 1847 and is the home of the Hungarian Holy Crown and the coronation jewels. Its two permanent exhibitions span the whole of Hungarian history, and there is a contemporary exhibit that commemorates the end of Communism and the Russian troops' departure from Budapest.

The Great Synagogue, one of Europe's largest, was completed in 1859. Its grand organ is one of the finest of its kind and attracts classical musicians from around the world. Although the synagogue was virtually destroyed by the Nazis, restoration of the building is now complete.

The Parliament building stands along the Danube and is one of the most impressive landmarks of Budapest. The Holy Crown of St. Stephen, the country's first king, is prominently displayed in the building for all to appreciate. For a grand view of the city, ride to the top of the cupola at St. Stephen's Basilica, a massive 19th century neoclassical building. Heroes' Square and City Park offer a wealth of entertainment including a zoo, state circus, an amusement park, and mineral baths. Budapest has gained a fine reputation as a hotspot for dining and nightlife; many bars, cafés and restaurants have opened in recent years.

The Trivia

Fact: Buda is home to most of the city's historic churches and older homes. The Royal Palace (including the ruins of an ancient fort) dominates Castle Hill in the middle of the city.

Fact: Pest is the larger population center of the city and is built on a series of plateaus. Pest also includes the city's government offices and House of Parliament.

Why Budapest Is a 50 plus one City

Despite centuries of war, religious persecution, and political strife, Budapest prospers today as a center of industry and culture in Eastern Europe.Increasing numbers of tourists flock to Budapest each year to delight in its historical treasures.

文艺复兴时期的一个重要城市。16世纪时，土耳其人入侵匈牙利，并控制了这一地区，直到他们后来被强大的奥地利哈布斯堡王朝驱逐出去。到了19世纪，佩斯成为匈牙利民族主义和文化的中心。

如今的布达佩斯是1873年由原来王国的三个城市合并而成的。第二次世界大战对于布达佩斯来说是一段特别黑暗的日子，大部分生活在布达佩斯的犹太人惨遭屠杀。

声光景点

被称为"布达城堡"的地区在第二次世界大战期间几乎全部毁于炮火，借助于一个长期的重建过程，这一地区得以缓慢地再现昔日的辉煌。皇宫就位于布达佩斯这一区域，这已不是最初的皇宫，不过，今天在这一旧址上还建起了几个博物馆。

路德维格博物馆是这座城市的国际当代艺术博物馆。匈牙利国家博物馆专门收藏本国艺术家的作品。布达佩斯历史博物馆为展示这座城市的历史提供信息，从1686年自土耳其人手中获得解放直到今天。

马提亚斯教堂是布达佩斯多变的命运和宗教的反映，这座教堂最早是13世纪时作为清真寺而修建的，后来由于建筑被毁坏，于19世纪时重建。然而，第二次世界大战期间，教堂再遭劫难，于是又经历了二次重建。在奥匈帝国统治时期，这座教堂曾是哈布斯堡王朝举行加冕典礼的地方。

佩斯是城市的心脏，在那里游客可以看到反映布达佩斯历史及建筑的辉煌代表。匈牙利国家歌剧院大楼已然再现了其19世纪时期的宏伟壮观，两座大理石的斯芬克斯像守护在大门两旁。匈牙利国家博物馆1847年开馆，收藏有匈牙利国王的王冠及加冕仪式上的珠宝，馆内两处永久性的展区跨越了整个匈牙利的历史。此外，这里还有一处当代展区，用来纪念匈牙利共产党的结束，以及俄国军队离开布达佩斯。

大犹太教堂，作为欧洲最大的犹太教堂之一，建成于1859年。教堂里的大风琴是此类风琴中的极品之一，吸引着来自世界各地的古典音乐家们。虽然，事实上原有的犹太教堂早已被纳粹所毁坏，但是，现在教堂的重建工作已经全部竣工。

议会大厦矗立于多瑙河畔，是布达佩斯最为醒目的地标之一。在大厦里有匈牙利首位国王圣·史蒂芬的神圣王冠供所有人观赏。如果想要体验布达佩斯全城的美景，不妨登上圣·史蒂芬大教堂的圆顶，这是一座19世纪时修建的新古典风格的宏伟建筑。英雄广场和城市公园为游客提供了丰富的娱乐项目，其中包括动物园、马戏表演、游乐园及矿物浴疗等。布达佩斯的美食和夜生活为它赢得了广泛赞誉，近些年来，众多的酒吧、咖啡屋和餐馆相继开张营业。

奇闻轶事

之一：布达佩斯大多数有纪念意义的教堂和较为古老的住宅都位于布达，皇宫（包括一处古代城堡的遗址）占据着城市中心城堡山的显著位置。

之二：佩斯是布达佩斯市人口较多的地区，它建在连绵的高原之上，是该市政府办公及议会大厦的所在地。

为什么布达佩斯入选50 + 1个城市?

尽管历经了数个世纪的战乱纷争、宗教迫害和政治斗争，今天的布达佩斯依然是一座繁荣的城市，是东欧工业及文化的中心，每年，有越来越多的游客涌入布达佩斯，体验那些历史宝藏带给他们的乐趣。

Thirteen

Buenos Aires, Argentina

The Basic Facts

Buenos Aires is the capital and largest city of Argentina, the country's main port and its industrial center. Nearly one-third of all Argentines live in Buenos Aires.Although Buenos Aires is considered one of the most beautiful and modern South American cities, it continues to struggle with housing and transportation problems.

Geography

Buenos Aires lies at 34 degrees 20 minutes south latitude and 58 degrees 30 minutes west longitude. The city is located along a broad, funnel-shaped bay called the Rio de la Plata in eastern Argentina, near the Atlantic Ocean. Buenos Aires itself is only 77 square miles in size, but the metropolitan area covers roughly 1,400 square miles.

Climate

Buenos Aires has a temperate climate that is influenced by the Atlantic Ocean.Annual temperatures range from the upper 50s Fahrenheit in winter to the upper 80s Fahrenheit in summer. Because Buenos Aires is located south of the equator, the winter and summer months are opposite from those in the northern hemisphere; winter occurs between June and August and summer occurs between December and February. Summers are quite warm and humid, making spring and fall the most pleasant seasons in which to visit. The city is rainy throughout the year, with the heaviest rains during the winter months.

Government

Buenos Aires is divided into administrative areas known as barrios (neighborhoods), based on the city's original Roman Catholic parishes. Each barrio has its own junta (city council) to handle local issues. The city government is administered by a mayor, appointed by the president of Argentina, and the city council, elected by the citizens. The scope of the city's municipal authority is limited by the country's government, located in the Buenos Aires federal district.By law, the president of Argentina controls the municipality of Buenos Aires and the National Congress enacts most legislation that governs the city.

Demographics

Residents of Buenos Aires primarily speak Spanish and are referred to as portenos (port dwellers). Nearly three-quarters of the city's population is of Spanish or Italian ancestry; other ethnic groups represented are French, German, Lebanese,Polish, Russian, and Syrians. The barrios are generally integrated, unlike other large world cities. The population of Buenos Aires is estimated at 2.9 million.Buenos Aires is a city of stark class distinctions. Elite upper-class families live either in suburban mansions or homes in the central city, while millions of lower-class families live in wooden shacks in the city's

阿根廷布宜诺斯艾利斯

概况

　　布宜诺斯艾利斯是阿根廷的首都和最大的城市,也是这个国家主要的港口和工业中心。阿根廷几乎1/3的人口都居住在布宜诺斯艾利斯。虽然,布宜诺斯艾利斯被认为是南美城市中最美丽、最现代化的城市之一,但是,住房和交通问题却始终困扰着这个城市。

一、地理

　　布宜诺斯艾利斯位于南纬34°20′,西经58°30′,地处阿根廷东部,靠近大西洋的拉普拉塔河沿岸,事实上,拉普拉塔河是一个宽阔的、呈漏斗形的海湾。布宜诺斯艾利斯本身的面积只有77平方英里,但是,其大市范围的面积却达1400平方英里左右。

二、气候

　　受大西洋的影响,布宜诺斯艾利斯气候温和,年均气温在冬季的华氏57~59度到夏季的华氏87~89度。因为布宜诺斯艾利斯位于赤道以南,冬夏两季的月份与北半球的国家相反,冬天出现在6月~8月,夏天则为12月~2月。由于夏季非常温暖潮湿,所以,春秋两季是最适宜旅游的季节。布宜诺斯艾利斯全年多雨,而且冬天是降雨最多的季节。

三、政府

　　布宜诺斯艾利斯市在最初罗马天主教教区的基础上,被划分为不同的行政区域,名曰"巴瑞欧"(居民区),每个"巴瑞欧"有自己的"扎恩塔"(市政委员会)来处理当地事务。城市政府由一个市长管理,市长由阿根廷总统任命,市政委员会则由居民选举产生。市政当局的权限受到阿根廷政府的限制,而阿根廷政府就设在布宜诺斯艾利斯的联邦区。根据法律,阿根廷总统控制布宜诺斯艾利斯行政区,国家议会则颁布并执行大部分管理城市的法律。

四、人口

　　布宜诺斯艾利斯市的居民主要讲西班牙语,他们被称为"珀提诺"(港口居民),近3/4的城市人口为西班牙或意大利后裔,其他有代表性的民族还有法国人、德国人、黎巴嫩人、波兰人、俄罗斯人和叙利亚人。各个"巴瑞欧"相互融合,这一点与世界上其他城市不同。布宜诺斯艾利斯市的人口有大约290万。布宜诺斯艾利斯是一个阶级界限分明的城市,精英的上层社会家庭要么住在郊区的大宅子里,要么住在市中心的豪宅里,而成千上

suburban slums.

Economy

Trade is the driving force in the economy of Buenos Aires; more than 80 percent of Argentina's foreign trade passes through the city's port. Agriculture, especially in the rich farmlands outside Buenos Aires, is also a vital component of the city's economic profile. Leading industries here include food processing, meat packing,and the manufacture of textiles, rubber products and electrical equipment.

Commuters to the city avoid traffic congestion by traveling on the oldest subway system in South America. Colectivos are another public transportation choice;these small buses carry some 20 passengers at a time. Ministro Pistarini International is the city's main airport; Aeroparque Jorge Newbery serves domestic air travelers.

The History

Buenos Aires was founded in 1536 by Pedro de Mendoza, the leader of a Spanish expedition on a quest for gold in the Americas. These settlers were repeatedly attacked by the indigenous peoples and escaped to Asunción, today the capital of Paraguay. In 1580 the Spanish conquistador Juan de Garay established a permanent settlement in Buenos Aires. In the 17th century the area was frequently raided by French, Portuguese and Danish settlers.

In 1776, the province separated from the Viceroy of Peru and became the capital of a new viceroyalty of the Rio de la Plata; this included much of present-day Argentina as well as Uruguay, Paraguay and Bolivia. During the Napoleonic Wars,settlers expelled British soldiers who occupied the province. This victory spurred an independence movement, and in 1810 an armed group succeeded in removing the viceroy and establishing their own provisional representative government.

Conflict raged in the ensuing years between those in favor of a strong central government and those in favor of local control. In 1880 the city was federalized and left the province, and La Plata became the new provisional capital. Railroad construction in the late 19th century brought tremendous economic growth and a large influx of immigrants. Shanty towns cropped up around the city, housing the burgeoning poor population unable to find jobs in local industries.

The dictator Juan Perón ascended to power in the 1950s, beginning an era of coups, brutal military dictatorships, and economic chaos. Tremendous inflation devastated the middle class and plunged the poor into greater poverty. The government initiated drastic economic reform in the 1980s when it aligned the Argentinean peso to the U.S. dollar, a move that had a significant negative impact on the local economy. Throngs of protesters poured into the streets of Buenos Aires as a succession of governments formed and fell in a matter of days.

The Sights and Sounds

There is a lively warmth and excitement in this very European city. Begin at the Museum of Modern Art of Buenos Aires; the collection includes works by both modern masters and emerging artists from Argentina and beyond. The National History Museum, housed in a family mansion, covers Argentina's history from the 16th through the 20th

万的贫困家庭都住在市郊贫民窟地区简陋的木屋里。

五、经济

贸易在布宜诺斯艾利斯市的经济中起着推动作用,阿根廷80%以上的对外贸易都要通过布宜诺斯艾利斯市港进出。农业,尤其是布宜诺斯艾利斯市郊外富饶的农田,也是该市经济框架中重要的组成部分。这里的主导工业包括食品加工、肉类加工、纺织生产、橡胶产品和电动设备等。

为了避开城市的交通拥堵,来往城区的上下班人员会选择乘坐布宜诺斯艾利斯市最古老的地铁。"克莱克提弗"是公共交通的另一选择,这些小型巴士每次运送20名乘客。埃塞萨国际机场是该市的主要机场,而阿罗帕克机场则为国内旅客提供服务。

光影流金

布宜诺斯艾利斯市创建于1536年,当时佩德罗·门得萨率领一支西班牙探险队为寻找黄金来到美洲。由于不断遭到土著居民的袭击,这些殖民者逃到了亚松森,即今天巴拉圭的首都。1580年,西班牙征服者胡安·德卡拉伊在布宜诺斯艾利斯地区建立了一个永久殖民地。17世纪时,这一地区频繁地遭到法国人、葡萄牙人及丹麦人的袭击。

1776年,该地区的殖民地脱离秘鲁总督,成为新的拉普拉塔总督管辖区的首府,这一区域包括今天阿根廷的大部分地区以及乌拉圭、巴拉圭和玻利维亚。在拿破仑战争期间,殖民者们赶走了占领该殖民地的英国军队,这一胜利引发了一场独立解放运动。1810年,一支武装团队成功地废除了总督,并建立了属于他们自己的临时性代表政府。

在接下来的几年间,那些主张建立一个强有力中央政府的人与那些坚持地方自治的派别发生了激烈的冲突。1880年,布宜诺斯艾利斯市实行了联邦制,摆脱了其殖民地地位,拉普拉塔成为新的临时首都。19世纪后期,铁路的修建带动了经济的飞速发展,大批移民开始涌入城市。市区周边出现了大量的棚屋区,里面住着那些无法在当地企业找到工作的不断增多的贫困人口。

20世纪50年代,独裁者胡安·庇隆登基,开始了一段政变频发、残酷军事独裁和经济混乱的时期。恶性的通货膨胀使得那些中产阶级家庭遭到沉重的打击,而那些穷人更是跌入了贫困的深渊。20世纪80年代,政府开始实行重大的经济改革,将阿根廷比索调整为美元,这一变化为当地经济带来了明显的负面影响。成群结队的抗议者涌上布宜诺斯艾利斯市的街头,一任又一任的政府组建成立,又在几天之内垮台。

声光景点

在这座非常欧洲化的城市里,有着一种活泼的温馨和动人。从布宜诺斯艾利斯市的现代艺术博物馆出发,游客能够首先欣赏到当代艺术大师以及来自阿根廷或其他国家的一些崭露头角的艺术家们的作品。阿根廷国家历史博物馆原是一栋宏大的私人住宅,如今馆内展示的内容贯穿了阿根廷从16~20世纪的历史。在展厅显眼的位置摆放着1810

century. Artifacts from the 1810 War of Independence are prominently displayed, as are several paintings of battles during the 1870 War of Triple Alliances. La Boca Fine Arts Museum of Argentine Artists is a small facility,ideal for those interested in local art.

The Plaza de Mayo is a popular tourist attraction with a variety of sights and sounds: the National Bank of Argentina, a picturesque building with a vaulted dome; the Convent and Basilica of St. Francis, built in the 18th century and restored after being damaged during the Perón years; the Town Hall, an important site during the May revolution of 1810; and the Pink House, which houses the executive branch of government. The Metropolitan Cathedral, St. Ignatius of Loyola Parish Church, and St. Dominick Convent are dramatically beautiful examples of historic architecture.

The busy and pulsating area of el Centro gives Buenos Aires its reputation as a cosmopolitan city. Businesses, restaurants, and shops offer all sorts of entertainment for tourists. The nearby Military Circle, with its 220-foot-tall Obelisk, is a monument to Argentina's officer class.

The Colòn Theatre is among the world's finest opera houses, and has hosted every major opera star since it opened in 1908. Tours of the theatre are available, even if tickets to a performance are not. In the la Recoleta district, shopping, hotels, cafés and boutiques coexist in a delightful and comfortable area. La Recoleta Cemetery's 13 acres of above-ground vaults and crypts date to 1822. Two notable museums are nearby: the National Museum of Fine Arts, with some 11,000 works ranging from medieval to contemporary; and the National Museum of Decorative Art,which contains a vast collection of period furniture and art objects.

Nightlife in Buenos Aires does not even begin until 9 or 10 p.m., and clubs are open until the very wee hours. Buenos Aires is known as a café society in which locals frequently stop to enjoy coffee in a pleasant environment. The city has few skyscrapers, and so the many plazas, parks and broad avenues give the city an open, peaceful feel.

The Trivia

Fact: Eva Perón, one of history's more .amboyant characters, dominated Buenos Aires and Argentina politics as the wife of president Juan Perón. She died of cancer at an early age and became a beloved national icon. Her tomb is located at La Recoleta.

Fact: The name Buenos Aires is Spanish for fair winds. Early Spanish sailors named the broad harbor for Nuestra Senora Santa Maria del Buen Aire, the patron saint of fair winds.

Fact: In an attempt to curb traffic congestion, the city bans private vehicles from the downtown financial district during the day.

Why Buenos Aires Is a 50 plus one City

Buenos Aires is a city of Argentines who think and act like Europeans. Life is easy here. The city is a rich blend of history and modern culture; truly a grand place to visit.

年独立战争期间的手工艺品,此外,还有几幅创作于1870年有关三国同盟战争期间著名战役的绘画作品。集中反映阿根廷艺术家成就的拉博卡美术馆是一家小型展馆,非常适合那些对当地艺术感兴趣的人。

五月广场是一个受人欢迎的充满不同声光色彩的旅游景点:这里有阿根廷国家银行,是一座漂亮的带有圆拱形穹顶的建筑;有修建于18世纪的圣弗朗西斯女子修道院和天主教堂,这座修道院在庇隆时期遭到毁坏,后经过重修;市政厅是1810年5月革命的重要遗址;"玫瑰宫"实际是政府行政部门办公的场所;此外,大都会大教堂、罗耀拉的圣依格纳提斯教区教堂、圣多米尼克女子修道院等不仅都是颇具纪念意义的建筑,而且其外观都异常漂亮醒目。

繁忙律动的市中心地区为布宜诺斯艾利斯市赢得了大都会的美誉,这里的商业、餐馆和商铺为游客提供着各种各样的娱乐享受。离此不远的环形军事区里,有一座高220英尺的方形尖塔,是阿根廷军官阶层的纪念碑。

科隆大剧院是世界上顶尖的歌剧院,自从1908年开业以来,这里为每一位重要的歌剧明星都举办过专场演出。大剧院随时都允许参观,尽管要看演出可能会买不到票。瑞克莱塔区,是一个集购物、酒店、咖啡屋和时装店于一身的休闲娱乐场所。瑞克莱塔公墓的13英亩地上墓园及地下墓室,其历史最早可以追溯到1822年。公墓附近有两座博物馆值得一提:一个是国家美术馆,里面收藏的11 000件作品从中世纪一直到当代应有尽有;另一个是国家装饰艺术博物馆,里面收藏了大量某个历史时期的家具及艺术陈设品。

在布宜诺斯艾利斯,夜生活要到晚上九十点钟才算开始,夜总会的营业时间一直持续到第二天清晨。布宜诺斯艾利斯市素有"咖啡屋社会"之称,当地人常常会选择一个宜人的环境停下来享受咖啡。布宜诺斯艾利斯市几乎没有高楼,因此众多的广场、公园及宽阔的街道赋予了这座城市开放而平和的气息。

奇闻轶事

之一:作为总统胡安·贝隆的妻子,尹娃·贝隆在历史上的光彩和知名度绝不亚于她的丈夫,她曾一度掌控着布宜诺斯艾利斯市乃至阿根廷全国的政治。然而,由于癌症,她英年早逝,死后成为一位受人爱戴的民族偶像,她的坟墓就位于瑞克莱塔。

之二:布宜诺斯艾利斯市的名称来自于西班牙语的"和风",早期西班牙的航海者将这一片广阔的海港取名为"圣玛丽亚夫人的布宜诺斯艾利",意思就是"和风的神圣保护者"。

之三:为了缓解交通拥堵现象,布宜诺斯艾利斯市白天禁止私家车辆进入市中心的商业区。

为什么布宜诺斯艾利斯市入选50 + 1个城市?

布宜诺斯艾利斯是一座拥有欧洲人思想和行为的阿根廷城市,这里生活安逸舒适,历史与现代交相辉映,不同的文化融会贯通,是一个伟大的地方,一个你真正值得一去的地方。

Cape Town, South Africa

The Basic Facts

Cape Town is the legislative capital of South Africa and has the country's third-largest population. After decades of international opposition and internal violence as a result of apartheid, the city has reinvented itself as a regional manufacturing center and popular tourist destination.

Geography

Cape Town lies at 33 degrees 48 minutes south latitude and 18 degrees 29 minutes east longitude. The city is located on the Cape Peninsula, also known as the Cape of Good Hope, and extends south from Table Mountain to the Atlantic Ocean. Cape Town is roughly 964 square miles in size. Surrounding communities that were segregated during apartheid have been merged into modern Cape Town.

Climate

Cape Town has a Mediterranean climate highlighted by warm, dry summers and cooler, rainy winters. Annual temperatures range from the mid-60s Fahrenheit in winter to the upper 70s Fahrenheit in summer. Because Cape Town is located south of the equator, the winter and summer months are opposite from those in the northern hemisphere; winter occurs between June and August and summer occurs between December and February. The Cape Doctor, a strong southeasterly wind, occurs frequently and is so named for its tendency to clear away air pollution.

Government

Cape Town is one of South Africa's six metropolitan municipalities and is divided into 105 municipal districts. Each district elects one representative to the city council. An additional 105 members are elected by a system of party-list proportional representation. The city council appoints the city mayor.

Demographics

Cape Town is a multicultural city including native Africans and European settlers. The majority of the population is Colored (of mixed African and European and Asian descent); other ethnic groups include Black Africans (most from the Xhosa tribe), Whites, and Asians. Cape Town residents primarily speak Afrikaans, Xhosa and English. The city's population is estimated at three million.

Economy

Historically Cape Town was the gateway to southern Africa, and today it is the second largest port in the country. Trade is a major part of the economy, and the city's harbor

南非开普敦

概况

开普敦是南非的立法首都,是这个国家中人口排名第三的地区。在经过种族隔离所带来的数十年的国际对抗及国内动乱之后,这座城市已经重新确立了其作为区域生产中心和著名旅游胜地的位置。

一、地理

开普敦位于南纬33°48′,东经18°29′,地处开普半岛,也称好望角,从桌山向南一直延伸到大西洋。开普敦的

面积大约有964平方英里。种族隔离期间被分割开的周边社区如今已经并入开普敦市。

二、气候

开普敦具有地中海气候特征,夏季温暖干燥,冬季凉爽多雨。年均气温在冬季的华氏65度到夏季的华氏77~79度。因为开普敦位于赤道以南,冬夏两季的月份与北半球地区正好相反,冬天出现在6月~8月,夏天则集中在12月~2月。"开普医生"是一种很强的东南风,经常出现在这一地区,之所以这样命名是因为大风过后,该地区的空气污染往往被刮得无影无踪。

三、政府

开普敦是南非六大直辖市之一,开普敦分为105个区,每个区为市政委员会选举一位代表,另有105位成员是根据各党派的人数比例推选出来的。市政委员会任命城市的市长。

四、人口

开普敦是一个文化多元的城市,既有土生土长的非洲人,又有欧洲殖民者的后裔。人口的绝大多数属于有色人种(即非洲和欧洲或亚洲人混合的后代)。其余少数民族还包括黑非洲人(大部分来自科萨族部落)、白人及亚洲人。开普敦居民大多讲南非荷兰、科萨语和英语。城市人口大约有300万。

五、经济

在历史上,开普敦是通往南部非洲的门户,今天它则是南非第二大港口。贸易是开普敦经济的主要组成部分,港口为往来的商业船只提供维修、燃料和及装货等服务。开普敦

repairs, fuels and loads commercial shipping vessels. Goods manufactured in Cape Town include chemicals, clothing, processed foods,furniture, leather, automobiles and petroleum. Many Cape Town residents work in the thriving tourist industry.

The History

Abundant fossil and artifact evidence indicates that the Cape Peninsula was inhabited more than 600,000 years ago. The San were hunter-gatherers who settled in the area and relied on the sea for most of their food. Two thousand years ago, the Khoikhoi migrated from the north and displaced the San. The Khoikhoi,farmers and livestock owners, were the dominant tribe on the Cape until the mid-17th century.

The navigable Cape was a vital trade link that enabled ships to sail between the Atlantic and Indian Oceans. Vasco da Gama, a Portuguese explorer who reached India in 1497, was the first to round the Cape. In 1652 the Dutch arrived, under the command of Jan van Roebuck, and established a stopover on the Cape for their sailing ships. They soon constructed a fort at the base of Table Mountain; the settlement that grew around the fort became known as Cape Town.

By 1657, the Dutch East India Company allowed its employees to establish their own farms on the Cape; these people became known as Boers (farmers). The Khoikhoi and San populations gradually diminished, their people either killed by the settlers or by smallpox. Those that survived became servants of the Boers, who later aggressively took land from the Xhosa tribes. Their actions prompted a series of bloody wars that continued over the next century.

The Dutch relinquished the Cape to Britain after the Napoleonic Wars, and just as the Boers before them, the incoming British settlers took additional Xhosa land.The Boers chafed under British rule, and skirmishes between the two groups led to the Boer War between 1899 and 1902. Apartheid, the legal separation of whites and blacks, was a direct result of the Afrikaner nationalism movement of the early 20th century.

The Sights and Sounds

Cape Town blends old and new South Africa in a naturally beautiful environment unparalleled in a modern metropolis. Table Mountain looms over the city; those who reach the summit—either by cable car or by hiking its well-traveled paths—are rewarded with a spectacular view of the city and its environs. Cape Peninsula National Park is a short drive from Cape Town. This national treasure along the seashore contains a wide variety of South African flora and fauna. Hiking is a popular pastime in the park, but so too is sitting near the beach to watch the surf roll in.

Just seven miles offshore is Robben Island. The museum here was formerly the penitentiary where South Africa's political prisoners were held. Among its former inmates is Nelson Mandela, who was imprisoned here for 27 years and who later became the first democratically-elected president of South Africa. Tours are conducted by former prisoners, who are well-equipped to provide visitors with firsthand knowledge of the conditions in which they languished for many years.

The South African National Gallery is undergoing a renaissance, essentially rewriting the country's history to reflect the important contributions of Black Africans and other ethnic groups. The gallery prominently presents the works of South African artists, and

所生产的商品主要有化学制品、服装、加工食品、家具、皮革、汽车和汽油。而许多开普敦居民都在为其繁荣的旅游业而忙碌工作。

光影流金

大量的化石及手工艺品表明，早在60万年以前，开普半岛地区就已经有人类居住了，桑族人是一些狩猎的群居者，靠大海获取大部分食物。大约2000年前，科伊科伊人从北方迁移到这里从而取代了桑族人。科伊科伊人从事农业及畜牧业，到17世纪中期之前，他们一直是好望角地区的头号部落。

可以通航的好望角是连接大西洋与印度洋航行船只的贸易命脉。瓦斯科·达·伽马，一位曾于1497年到达印度的葡萄牙探险家，是第一位绕过好望角的人。1652年，荷兰人在简·凡·罗巴克的率领下来到这里，并为他的帆船建立了一个中途停留站。不久，他们又在桌山脚下修建了一个要塞，围绕这一要塞建立起来的殖民地后被称作开普敦。

1657年，荷兰的印度公司允许其员工在好望角地区建立自己的农场，这些人被称作布尔人(农民)。由于被杀或者死于天花，科伊科伊人和桑族人口逐年减少，那些幸存下来的人也都成了布尔人的奴仆。后来，因为布尔人从科萨族人手中大肆掠夺土地，他们的行为引起了一连串血腥的战争，并且这样的战争在接下来的几个世纪里一直在延续。

拿破仑战争后，荷兰人将好望角交给了英国，正如之前的布尔人一样，踏上这片土地的英国殖民者又从科萨族人手中抢夺了大量的土地。由于布尔人不满于英国的统治，双方之间小规模的冲突终于导致1899年~1902年布尔战争的爆发。种族隔离制度，这种将白人与黑人从法律上分割开来的制度，是20世纪初南非白人民族主义运动的直接产物。

声光景点

开普敦将新旧南非融汇在美丽的自然环境中，在当今世界城市当中可谓一枝独秀。影影绰绰的桌山俯视着整个城市，无论是乘坐缆车抑或徒步沿着人流密集的山道登山，一旦登临山顶，人们无不为山下城市及周边地区的美景所折服。开普半岛国家公园距离开普敦只有很短的车程，这座沿着海滨修建的国家珍宝馆，容纳了极为丰富的南非特有的动植物群。尽管徒步走在公园里就是一种非常惬意的享受，但是坐在海滩边观看海浪滚滚而来也是一种不错的选择。

距离海边大约7英里远的地方有座罗本岛，岛上的博物馆原先是用来关押南非政治犯的监狱。在所有曾被关押的犯人当中就有纳尔逊·曼德拉，他在这里被关押了27年，出狱后，他成为南非通过民主方式选举出的第一任总统。岛上的导游都是先前的犯人，因为曾经在此遭受过数年的磨难，他们有足够的能力为游客提供关于监狱情况的第一手信息。

南非国家美术馆正在经历一场复兴运动，即改写历史以反映黑人及其他种族团体对于这个国家所作出的重要贡献，这样做无疑是非常有必要的。在美术馆显著的位置展出的是南非艺术家的作品，并以此来证明这个国家从态度及艺术方式上铲除文化偏见的决

describes itself as debunking cultural biases regarding attitudes and approaches to art.

Kirstenbosch Botanical Gardens always has something beautiful in bloom, for South Africa is home to some 9,000 native floral species. During the summer months, the Gardens host evening concerts. Groot Constantia Manor House is one of the oldest wineries in South Africa. Its Wine Museum serves to educate the public with social commentary and information on the lives of slaves who served there. The museum also includes a beautiful collection of furniture, textiles, and other objets d'art from the 19th and 20th centuries.

The Trivia

Fact: In 1867, fortune-seekers flocked to the area around present-day Kimberly after a rich diamond field was discovered on the site. The British quickly capitalized on the discovery, and in 1871 annexed the site as an addition to the Cape Colony.

Fact: In 1836, after years of resentment toward British rule, a group of Boers loaded their belongings onto ox carts and began heading inland, a historic journey that would come to be known as the Great Trek.

Why Cape Town Is a 50 plus one City

Cape Town is a city of uncompromising physical beauty. It is also a city that lives with its past sins, unable to escape the realities of the bygone apartheid era and the ever-expanding AIDS epidemic in South Africa. But sorrow and shame give way to hope and a new future in this city dedicated to uniting all the peoples of South Africa.

心。

　　克斯坦博西植物园内一年四季都有鲜花盛开，因为南非拥有大约9 000种本地特有的花卉品种。在夏季的月份里，植物园里会举办音乐会。大康斯坦夏庄园大厦是南非最古老的葡萄酒厂之一，它的葡萄酒博物馆主要为公众提供教育服务，通过社会现场报道向人们介绍那些曾经在此工作过的奴隶们的生活状况。此外，这所博物馆里还收藏有许多19~20世纪的漂亮家具、纺织品及其他物品。

奇闻轶事

　　之一：1867年，在今天被称为金伯利的地区，人们发现了一座储量丰富的钻石矿，因此，大批渴望发财致富的人蜂拥来到这里。而当时的英国政府在对矿藏迅速做出评估鉴定之后，于1871年宣布将该地区添加并入其开普殖民地。

　　之二：1836年，由于对殖民地的英国统治积怨已深，一批布尔人将他们的财物装上牛车，开始向内陆地区开拔，这一具有历史意义的旅程后来被称作"大迁徙"。

为什么开普敦入选50 + 1个城市？

　　开普敦既是一座拥有毋庸置疑的天然美景的城市，同时也是一座身负着往昔罪恶的城市，从始至终，这座城市都难以摆脱过去种族隔离以及今天在南非不断蔓延的艾滋病的阴影。然而，随着南非各族人民的团结努力，痛苦与耻辱终将过去，希望和一个崭新的未来正在这座城市中悄然显现。

Fifteen

Caracas, Venezuela

The Basic Facts

Caracas is the capital of Venezuela and is the country's largest city. Caracas was transformed in the oil boom of the 20th century as its population expanded and experienced greater social mobility.

Geography

Caracas lies at 10 degrees 30 minutes north latitude and 66 degrees 58 minutes west longitude. The city is located in a beautiful valley framed by the waters of the River Guaire and the coastal mountains, and lies close to the Caribbean Sea.

Climate

Caracas boasts a lush tropical climate that is consistently mild and spring-like throughout the year. Annual temperatures range from the upper 70s Fahrenheit in winter to the low 80s Fahrenheit in summer.

Government

Venezuela's executive, legislative, and judicial branches are all located within Caracas. The city is also the capital of the Distrito Federal (federal district);the district governor is appointed by the Venezuelan president. Caracas itself is governed by a democratically-elected mayor and city council.

Demographics

The multicultural population of Caracas re.ects the population of the entire country. Caraquenians, as they are known, range from indigenous peoples to Western Europeans and Africans. The city has a well-defined class structure with a wide economic and cultural gap between rich and poor. Castilian Spanish is the official language of Caracas, but several indigenous languages are spoken as well.The population of the metropolitan area is estimated at 3.3 million.

Economy

Most Caraquenians work in the federal, provincial or local government; nearly 40 percent of Venezuela's government workforce lives in the city. The governmentowned oil industry employs large numbers of residents. A small industrial base produces beer, cement, paper, and textiles. Caracas, like many rapidly growing cities, suffers from ongoing traffic congestion and air pollution. In an attempt to alleviate these problems, the city now has a modern subway system, the first section of which was opened in 1983. The city's airport, Maiquetia International, is located in the nearby suburb of Maiquetia.

The History

Caracas began as a Spanish settlement in 1567, when an expedition led by Diego de Losada discovered the beautiful valley and coastal range that framed the area. The indigenous peoples fiercely resisted the invaders, but Losada's landing party eventually defeated them. Losada publicly claimed the lands for the King of Spain, and in so doing founded the city of Caracas. In 1577 the city became the administrative seat of the Province of Venezuela; it was selected for its proximity to the sea, its rich land, and its ability to defend itself against pirate raids.

委内瑞拉加拉加斯

概况

加拉加斯是委内瑞拉的首都和最大的城市，随着20世纪对石油需求的增长，加拉加斯发生了翻天覆地的变化，人口迅速膨胀，社会流动性日益加大。

一、地理

加拉加斯位于北纬10°30′，西经66°58′，地处瓜伊尔河和沿岸山脉环绕之下的一处美丽的谷地，靠近加勒比海。

二、气候

加拉加斯拥有浓郁的热带气候，常年温和，四季如春。年均气温在冬季的华氏77~79度至夏季的华氏81~83度。

三、政府

委内瑞拉的行政、立法及司法机构都位于加拉加斯，同时，加拉加斯还是联邦行政区的首府，行政区的总督由委内瑞拉总统任命。加拉加斯市由一位民主选举产生的市长及市政委员会管理。

四、人口

加拉加斯人口的多元文化也是委内瑞拉全国人口特征的反映，被称为"加拉奎人"的加拉加斯人实际上包括了原住民、西方的欧洲人和非洲人。这个城市有着阶级界限分明的社会结构，富人与穷人之间存在着巨大的经济与文化鸿沟。卡斯蒂利亚(标准西班牙)语是加拉加斯的官方语言，但是另有若干土著语言也在使用。大市范围的人口有330万左右。

五、经济

大多数加拉奎人在联邦、省级或地方政府部门工作，委内瑞拉近40%的政府工作人员都住在城里。国有的石油工业也解决了大量当地居民的就业问题，一些小型工业基础主要生产啤酒、水泥、纸张和纺织品。正如许多快速发展的城市一样，加拉加斯市也面临着交通堵塞和空气污染的问题，为了努力减轻这些问题，该市尝试建立一个现代化的地铁交通系统，目前地铁的一期工程已经于1983年投入运营。加拉加斯的麦奎尔国际机场，位于城市近郊的麦奎尔地区。

光影流金

加拉加斯的雏形是1567年西班牙的一个殖民地，当时，一支由迪戈·德·罗萨达率领的探险队发现了这个美丽的山谷和其周边的海域。尽管土著居民强烈抵制这些入侵者，但是罗萨德的这支登陆部队最终还是打败了他们。罗萨达公开宣称这些领土为西班牙国王所有，并以此为由建立起了加拉加斯市。1577年，加拉加斯被选定为委内瑞拉省的省府行政中心，原因是它靠近大海，靠近富饶的大陆，有能力抵御海盗的袭击。

The city flourished over the next 200 years, but in 1812 was devastated by an earthquake. Some priests believed that the disaster was divine punishment for the citizens' growing revolt against Spanish rule. As a result, Simón Bolívar, himself a Caraquenian, led citizens in a successful attempt to reclaim Caracas for themselves. He became a hero in his native Venezuela, and earned the moniker el Libertador (the Liberator).

Caracas became one of the most prosperous Spanish colonial communities in South America, and grew steadily during the next 2 centuries. In the 1950s, Venezuelan dictator Marcos Peréz Jimenéz converted Caracas into a city with state-of-the-art, aesthetically pleasing buildings; funds for construction came from money raised during the oil boom.

The Sights and Sounds

Some may say that Caracas' improved cityscape has ruined this historic South American city. It has a functional, hurried style rather than charming and warm. Caracas lacks a central downtown, and as a result, the city's sights and sounds are scattered among various districts. El Centro is the oldest part of the city, where Caracas was originally founded. The Plaza Bolívar is a large open space in the city, surrounded by the best of old Caracas.

The National Capitol is a two-building compound founded on the site of a 17th century convent. The original buildings were dismantled in 1874 when religious orders were banned; new federal and legislative buildings were built on the site.

Casa Natal de Bolívar is the former home of el Liberador. Although the building is largely devoid of personal or historical memorabilia, it is nevertheless an excellent example of a colonial Venezuelan house.

Two churches in the area are worth noting. The Metropolitan Cathedral was built at the end of the 17th century and is home to the Bolívar family chapel. One of the best examples of colonial architecture in Caracas is the 16th century Church of San Francisco. It was the place where Bolívar declared Venezuela's independence; after his death his state funeral was held there.

The National Art Gallery has literally thousands of works of Venezuelan origin. The gallery shares space with the Museo de Bellas Artes, which has a broader international collection. Most major exhibits and cultural events are held at Bellas Artes. The Museum of Contemporary Art, with its extensive collection of modern works, is just off Central Park—which is not a park at all, but rather a concrete block of high-rise flats.

The night comes alive late in the evening—a problem for unsuspecting tourists in a city with a high crime rate. Follow the Caraquenians' example and do not venture into neighborhoods after dark unless you have a cab waiting.

The Trivia

Fact: The city of Caracas was originally named Santiago de León de Caracas: Santiago for the patron saint of Spain; León for the governor of the day; and Caracas in honor of the indigenous tribe that inhabited the coastal mountain range.

Fact: In the 19th century the Venezuelan ruler Antonio Guzmán Blanco was determined to transform Caracas into a South American version of Paris. He commissioned the construction of a series of buildings to reflect the designs of Parisian buildings.

Why Caracas Is a 50 plus one City

Visitors to Caracas may view its class distinctions as being rather extreme, but the city is among the greatest in South America, and continually strives to take its proper place in history, art and architecture.

在其后的200年间,加拉加斯日渐繁荣。然而,1812年时,一场地震将这座城市化为废墟,有些牧师相信这场灾难是神的惩罚,目的是帮助市民反抗西班牙的统治。后来,出身加拉奎人的西蒙·玻利瓦尔领导市民成功地确立了加拉加斯的独立地位,在他的家乡委内瑞拉,西蒙·玻利瓦尔成了一名英雄,并且获得了民族独立英雄的美称。

加拉加斯成为南美最为繁荣的西班牙殖民地之一,并且在以后的两个世纪里始终保持着稳定的发展。20世纪50年代,委内瑞拉的独裁者马科斯·佩雷茨·希梅内斯将加拉加斯改建成了一座时髦的新城,修建了许多赏心悦目的建筑,而建设基金都源自石油需求增长所带来的丰厚利润。

声光景点

在有些人看来,加拉加斯对城市景观的改造,破坏了其南美城市的历史风貌,在拥有功能与浮躁的同时,城市失去了其原有的魅力与温馨。加拉加斯缺少一个中心城区,因此,城中的景点散落于各个不同的区域。"中城"是加拉加斯最古老的部分,是城市最初建立的地方。玻利瓦尔广场是城中一处巨大的露天广场,四周环绕着古老的加拉加斯建筑的精华。

国会大厦是一个由两栋建筑组合而成的复合体,建在一处17世纪女子修道院的遗址上,原有的建筑在1874年时,由于宗教建筑柱型被禁止而遭到拆除,于是在此基础上人们修建了新的联邦和立法大楼。

玻利瓦尔故居是这位民族英雄以前的家,虽然房子里已经基本找不到玻利瓦尔本人的东西或历史纪念物,但是,这座建筑仍不失为一幢殖民地时期委内瑞拉房屋的最佳范例。

这里还有两座教堂值得一提,大都会大教堂建于17世纪末,玻利瓦尔家族所在的礼拜堂就位于其中。加拉加斯殖民地教堂的另一优秀代表,是16世纪修建的圣弗朗西斯科教堂,正是在这里,玻利瓦尔宣布了委内瑞拉的独立,在他死后,其隆重的国葬也是在这座教堂举行的。

委内瑞拉国家美术馆拥有至少上千件本国艺术家的原创作品,该美术馆与贝拉美术馆共用展厅,后者收藏了大量来自全球的艺术品,大多数重要的展览及文化活动都在贝拉美术馆举行。以大量现代艺术作品著称的当代美术博物馆,距离中央公园不远,中央公园其实根本不是公园,而是一处由高层公寓大厦构成的钢筋混凝土的丛林。

随着夜幕的降临,这座城市也开始变得生动起来 —— 然而,对于那些毫不设防的游客来说,要警惕这个城市犯罪率高发的问题。不妨效法加拉奎人的做法,在天黑之后,不要冒险进入那些居民区,除非你是要等出租车。

奇闻轶事

之一:加拉加斯市最初的名字是"圣地亚哥·德·莱昂·德·加拉加斯":圣地亚哥代表西班牙的神圣保护者,莱昂代表白昼的主司,加拉加斯则代表那支定居于沿海山区的土著部落。

之二:19世纪时,委内瑞拉的统治者安东尼奥·古斯曼·布兰科,下决心将加拉加斯改造成南美洲的巴黎,在他的授权之下,一系列反映巴黎建筑风格的大楼拔地而起。

为什么加拉加斯入选50+1个城市?

或许来到加拉加斯的人不会认同这座城市里非常极端的阶级划分,但是,他们不会否认这座城市作为南美最伟大城市之一的事实。如今,加拉加斯依然在为自己的历史、艺术以及建筑努力争取一个更加合理的地位。

Chicago, United States

The Basics

Chicago is the third most populous city in the United States and the country's largest inland city. Among its many nicknames, the Windy City is the one best known throughout the world. Chicagoland is the name given to the city and its surrounding suburbs.

Geography

Chicago lies at 41 degrees 49 minutes north latitude and 87 degrees 37 minutes west longitude. It is located in the Midwest United States in the state of Illinois, where the Chicago River meets the southwestern shore of Lake Michigan. It is far and away the largest city in the Midwest.

Climate

Chicago is widely perceived to have bitter cold winters, although the average winter temperature is relatively mild for the Midwest. Annual temperatures range from the low 30s Fahrenheit in winter to the low 80s Fahrenheit in summer. Chicagoans are quick to mention, however, that the temperature can dip below zero in January and February and exceed 90 degrees in summer. As a rule, Lake Michigan has a moderating effect on temperatures in the city, making the lakeshore cooler in summer and warmer in winter; this phenomenon leads to the popular summertime expression, cooler by the lake.

Government

Chicago has a mayor-city council form of government. The mayor is the chief executive and is elected to a 4-year term. The city council is the legislative body and consists of 50 aldermen (currently, one-third of whom are women), one from each city ward. In the mid-20th century, corruption was rife among the ward bosses, giving rise to the expression, vote early, vote often.

Demographics

Chicago and its inner-ring suburbs have experienced a steady population decrease over the past 20 years as residents have sought more space in the outlying areas. The city's population is roughly 2.9 million, while that of the entire metropolitan area is 9.8 million. Chicago's population is the 14th largest in the world.

Economy

Chicagoland has a manufacturing base that is unparalleled in the United States; traditional manufacturing industries employ 15 percent of the total workforce. The area economy is now widely diversified, especially in financial services, education, publishing, and business services.

美国芝加哥

概况

芝加哥是美国第三大人口众多的城市，也是美国最大的内陆城市。芝加哥有许多别名，"风之城"是其中享誉世界的一个，"芝加哥大陆"则被用来指代这座城市及其周边。

一、地理

芝加哥位于北纬41°49′，西经87°37′，地处美国中西部地区的伊利诺斯州，芝加哥河与密歇根湖西南岸在此交汇。芝加哥无疑是中西部地区最大的城市。

二、气候

许多人都知道芝加哥的冬天异常寒冷，尽管这里冬季的气温在中西部地区还是属于相对温和的。年均气温在冬季的华氏31~33度至夏季的华氏81~83度，不过，芝加哥人很快会告诉你，这里1月、2月的气温能降到冰点以下，而夏季则可能超过华氏90度。通常说来，密歇根湖对城市里的温度起着温和的调节作用，使得沿湖地区夏季凉爽，冬季温暖，这一现象也造就夏令时节的流行语：湖畔空调。

三、政府

芝加哥市政府是市长负责的市政委员会形式，市长是主要行政长官，任期4年，市政委员会是立法机构，由50位立法委员（目前，1/3委员为女性）组成，每一位委员来自城市的一个区。20世纪中期，由于各选区领导内部腐败现象猖獗，因此，曾有这样一种说法："早早投（票），常常投（票）"。

四、人口

在过去的20年中，由于城市居民向城市外围寻找更广阔的空间，芝加哥市及其内环线地区的人口逐年下降，全市人口大约有290万，不过，整个大市范围的人口在980万左右，芝加哥的人口在世界上排名第14位。

五、经济

芝加哥大陆作为生产加工基地，其地位在全美首屈一指。在传统的加工制造行业工作的人口占劳动力总数的15%。如今，这一地区的经济更趋多样化，特别是在金融服务、教育、出版和商业服务领域。

The History

The area around present-day Chicago has been inhabited by indigenous peoples for more than 5,000 years. The Potawatomi tribe is known to have lived in the area by the mid-17th century, for it was they who warmly welcomed the French-Canadian explorer Louis Jolliet and the French Jesuit priest Jacques Marquette as they canoed along the Chicago River.

In the 1770s, a Haitian fur trader named Jean Baptiste Point du Sable migrated from New Orleans to the Chicago area and established a trading post on the north bank of the Chicago River. A permanent settlement later formed on this site. In 1803, the United States built the first military post, Fort Dearborn, was built on the river's south bank. Illinois became a state in 1818 and granted a city charter to Chicago settlement in 1837.

Chicago became a major railroad hub in the Midwest, and stockyards were built to take advantage of the city's transportation potential. Chicago was also a prime lumber processing center at the time, and virtually all buildings in the entire city were constructed of wood. This is one reason that The Great Chicago Fire of 1871 was so devastating to the city. A small fire that began on the near south side quickly grew into a conflagration that raged through the helpless city for 2 days in October. The disaster burned 2,000 acres of property, wiped out well over $200 million worth of property, killed 300 people, and left some 100,000 others homeless. In the aftermath of the fire, city government enacted strict building codes in favor of masonry construction. Chicago reinvented itself in short order and became an architectural gem. Visitors to the 1893 World's Columbian Expedition stood in awe of the transformed city.

The decade of the 1920s was an infamous period in Chicago's history. Prohibition spurred the rise of several mob factions that warred with each other for control of the city's illicit liquor market. Riots followed the April 1968 assassination of Martin Luther King, Jr. and the Democratic National Convention that August. Chicago lived through these events to claim its place as a world-class city and center of architecture, culture and music.

The Sights and Sounds

Many visitors to the United States travel either to the East Coast or the West Coasts and overlook the Midwest. They therefore miss the opportunity to see Chicago, with its pristine lakefront, outstanding museums, and its lively culture.

The core structure of Chicago was built according to the Burnham Plan, named for the famous architect Daniel Burnham. Central to the Burnham Plan was the inclusion of green spaces and public areas: expansive lakeside parks, including Lincoln to the north and Grant to the south; free and accessible beaches; and marinas that hug the shoreline.

One of the best ways to learn about Chicago and its history is to take a river and lake tour. Architecture is what Chicago is all about, and the skyline is best seen from well out on Lake Michigan. Once the world's tallest office building, the Sears Tower is a definite must-see; ironically, Sears, Roebuck and Company, for which the building is named, moved its headquarters to the suburbs years ago.

Michigan Avenue is a fabulous upscale shopping area and a favorite with tourists. Nearby are the John Hancock Center, the historic Drake Hotel, and the former Palmolive Building, once home to Playboy Magazine. The Mies van der Rohe apartments hug the inner edge of Lake Shore Drive a short distance away. Go around the bend of the Drive to

光影流金

早在5 000多年前，在今天的芝加哥地区就已经有了原始的土著居民，目前已知的是，帕塔瓦多米部落在这一地区生活到17世纪中期，因为，正是这些印第安人，在看到法裔加拿大探险家路易斯·若利埃和法国传教士雅克·马奎特划着独木舟出现在芝加哥河沿岸时，将他们热情迎接上岸的。

18世纪70年代，一位名为让·巴蒂斯特·泊恩特·杜·萨布勒的海地皮毛商人，从新奥尔良来到芝加哥，在芝加哥河北岸建立了一处贸易驿站，后来，在此基础上一个永久的殖民地逐步形成。1803年，美国又在河的南岸地区建立了第一个军事要塞——迪尔伯恩要塞。1818年，伊利诺斯成为美国的一个州，1837年，该州授予芝加哥殖民地一部城市宪章。

芝加哥成为中西部地区主要的铁路枢纽，为了充分发挥城市的交通潜力，人们在这里建立了大量的牲畜围场。此外，芝加哥还是当时木材加工的首要中心，城里几乎所有的建筑都是木质结构，正因为如此，1871年的芝加哥大火才对这座城市造成了毁灭性的打击。10月的一天，一场起于城南的小火迅速蔓延成熊熊烈焰，人们眼睁睁看着它肆虐了整整两天，这场灾难将2 000英亩的城区化为灰烬，价值超过2亿美元的财产毁于一旦，300人葬身火海，大约10万人流离失所。火灾过后，市政府制定了严格的房屋建设条例，鼓励建造砖石建筑，芝加哥旋即进入了一场彻底改造，并且造就了一颗建筑史上的明珠。那些来到1893年为纪念哥伦布探险而修建的世博会遗址参观的游客，无不为这座城市翻天覆地的变化而赞叹不已。

20世纪20年代的10年间，在芝加哥的历史上是一段不太光彩的日子。禁酒令引发了若干暴乱组织之间为了争夺该市非法酒类市场的控制权而彼此火拼。骚乱过后，1968年3月，马丁·路德·金遇刺身亡，同年8月，民主党召开全国大会。历经上述种种事件，芝加哥并没有消亡，相反，它却逐步确立了自己作为一座世界级城市，以及建筑、文化、音乐中心的地位。

声光景点

许多到访美国的人都会选择东部或西部沿海地区而忽略了中西部，因此，他们也就错过了来芝加哥看一看的机会，看一看这里原始的湖泊平地、著名的博物馆藏以及鲜明的文化特色。

芝加哥的核心建筑是根据伯恩罕计划建造的，而该计划则是以著名建筑师丹尼尔·伯恩罕的名字命名的，伯恩罕计划的核心包括绿地和公园：例如，由北面的林肯公园和南面的格兰特公园共同组成的占地宽广的湖畔公园；可以随意出入的免费的海滩；还有紧靠海滨沿线的游艇停靠区。

了解芝加哥及其历史的一个最好的方法是来一次泛湖之旅。建筑是芝加哥的灵魂，而欣赏其空中轮廓线的最佳方式来自于密歇根湖的远眺。希尔斯大厦曾经是世界上最高的办公大楼，无疑是你必定要看的，颇具讽刺意味的是，几年前，希尔斯-罗巴克公司已经将它的总部搬到市郊地区，而这座大厦恰恰是以这家公司的名字命名的。

密歇根大街是一个绝佳的高档购物区，也是游客们的最爱。附近可以看到约翰－汉考克中心、历史上著名的翠壳酒店以及曾经是《花花公子》杂志总部的帕尔莫里夫大厦。离此不远，被湖滨大道的内侧边缘环绕的是密斯－凡德罗公寓楼群，来到大道的拐弯处，能

see the vintage condos overlooking Oak Street Beach.

The Art Institute is one of the finest multi-level museums in the world; but do not pass up the opportunity to see Chicago's many other gems: the Oriental Institute at the University of Chicago; the Museum of Contemporary Art; the Field Museum of Natural History; the Museum of Science and Industry; the Shedd Aquarium;Lincoln Park Zoo; and the wildly popular urban playgrounds Millennium Park and Navy Pier.

The Trivia

Fact: Chicago's nickname the Windy City does not refer to the weather—although the downtown area gets more than its share of blustery winds. A New York columnist coined the phrase when Chicago was competing rather loudly with New York for the 1893 World's Columbian Exposition.

Fact: The nuclear age began in Chicago when the first sustained nuclear chain reaction was accomplished at the University of Chicago on December 2, 1942.

Fact: The Chicago Water Tower, constructed of dolomite limestone, was one of the few buildings in the city to survive the Great Chicago Fire.

Fact: Chicago was the site of two deadly tragedies attributed to human error. The 1903 Iroquois Theater fire claimed more than 600 lives, and in 1915 the Eastland passenger ship capsized in the Chicago River, killing more than 800 people.

Fact: Chicago has also been called Hog Butcher to the World (after its enormous stockyards), Second City (until the 1980s it was second only to New York City in terms of its population), and The City of Big Shoulders (so named by the Illinoisborn poet Carl Sandburg).

Fact: Chicago's motto is Urbs in horto (Latin for City in a Garden).

Why Chicago Is a 50 plus one City

No American city has transformed itself over the last 50 years as much as Chicago. Once a gritty industrial town known for stockyards and steel, today's Chicago is a clean, sophisticated and artistic city. Chicago is the home of Encouragement Press, LLC.

够感受到古老的公寓大楼俯视下面橡树街海滩的景象。

艺术学院是世界上最完美的多层博物馆之一。除此之外,千万不要错过参观一下芝加哥大量其他建筑精华的机会:譬如,芝加哥大学的东方学院,当代艺术博物馆,菲尔德自然历史博物馆,科学工业博物馆,谢特水族馆,林肯公园动物园,广受欢迎的市区游乐场千禧公园和海军码头等。

奇闻轶事

之一:"风之城"作为芝加哥的别名其实并不是指天气 —— 尽管市中心的风力的确比其他地方要大一些。事实上,是一位纽约的专栏作家杜撰了这么个名称,为的是在芝加哥和纽约竞争1893年世博会主办权时能够击败对手。

之二:核武器时代开始于芝加哥,因为1942年12月,第一个持续的核链式反应就是在芝加哥大学完成的。

之三:芝加哥水塔因其建筑材料为白云灰岩,而成为在芝加哥大火中幸存下来的极少数建筑之一。

之四:在芝加哥曾经发生过2起由于人为失误造成的致命悲剧。一次是1903年艾罗果伊斯剧院的火灾,有600多个生命消逝在这场大火之中。另一次是1915年,伊斯特兰客轮在芝加哥河倾覆,造成了800多名旅客丧生。

之五:芝加哥也被称为"世界生猪屠夫(因其众多的畜牧围场而得名)","第二大市(就人口而言,直到20世纪80年代之前,芝加哥都是仅次于纽约排名第二的城市)","巨肩之城(此名得于伊利诺斯出生的诗人卡尔·桑德伯格)"。

之六:芝加哥的城市格言是"鄂伯斯因郝特"(这句拉丁语的意思是"一座花园中的城市")。

为什么芝加哥入选50 + 1个城市?

在过去的50年间,没有任何一座美国城市的变化能够像芝加哥市一样巨大,一个曾经以畜牧围栏和钢铁制造而出名的不起眼的小镇,如今已经幻化成为一座干净整洁、成熟发达、精致艺术的大都会,芝加哥还是出版本书的"励志出版社"的所在地。

Seventeen

Cologne, Germany

The Basic Facts

Cologne is Germany's oldest city and is the country's center of industry, commerce and culture. Cologne was devastated by Allied bombing during World War II ;about 90 percent of the city center was destroyed, and the population decreased significantly due to the bombing and evacuation. But in Cologne fashion, the city bounced back strongly after the war. The city center was rebuilt, new infrastructure helped spur development, and Cologne's industries returned to full strength. The city has regained its status as one of Germany's most vital cities, and there is a rich and fascinating history to explore.

Geography

Cologne lies at 50 degrees 56 minutes north latitude and 6 degrees 57 minutes east longitude. The city is located in the German Federal State of North Rhine-Westphalia, in a larger region known as the Rhineland. Cologne covers about 156 square miles on both sides of the Rhine River. Industry is centered along the east bank and commercial and residential areas are located chiefly along the west bank.

The city's inner boundaries are delineated by the Ringstrassen, a network of semicircular roads that replaced the walls of the old city's medieval fortresses.

Climate

Cologne is within the North-West German lowlands and the climate is in.uenced by the Atlantic Ocean and the North Sea. Cologne has a mild climate with moderate precipitation, high humidity, and cloudy skies. Average temperatures range from the mid-40s Fahrenheit in the winter to the lower 70s in the summer.

Government

The city's administration is led by a lord mayor and two deputy mayors. The lord mayor and the 90-member city council are elected by the city residents.

Demographics

Cologne's residents are primarily German-born, and include Rhinelanders, Polish Germans (formerly Prussians) and German Turks. Many foreign immigrants come from Spain and Poland, and there is a large Japanese community in nearby Düsseldorf. The metropolitan area of Cologne includes more than 12 million inhabitants.

Economy

Cologne, as well as the surrounding Rhineland, is a chief industrial center in Germany. The city's manufacturing industries include metals, automobiles, beers,chemicals, pharmaceuticals and petrochemicals. Electrical power generation is also an important

德国科隆

概况

科隆是德国最古老的城市,也是这个国家的工业、商业和文化中心。在第二次世界大战期间,盟军的炸弹几乎将科隆化为废墟,市中心大约90%的地区遭到了破坏,而由于轰炸和撤离,城市人口显著下降。不过,当战争结束之后,科隆以自己特有的方式强有力地反弹,迅速重建了市中心,新的基础设施促进了城市的发展,科隆的工业再次焕发出充沛的活力。如今,这座城市已经重新确立了其作为德国最重要城市之一的地位,并且正以其丰富而神奇的历史期待着你的光临。

一、地理

科隆位于北纬50°56′,东经6°57′,属于德国被称为"莱茵兰"区的北莱茵-威斯特法伦联邦州。科隆市位于莱茵河两岸,占地面积大约156平方英里。城市的工业主要集中在莱茵河的东岸,而商业和住宅区则主要位于西岸地区。

环城林荫大道是在旧城的中世纪城堡围墙遗址上建造起来一个半圆形公路网,它勾勒出了城市的内环区域轮廓。

二、气候

科隆位于德国西北部的低洼地带,气候受到大西洋和北海的共同影响。科隆气候温和,降水量平均,湿度较高,天空多云。平均气温在冬季的华氏45度至夏季的华氏71~73度。

三、政府

科隆的行政管理由市长大人和两名副市长负责,市长大人及包括90名成员的市政委员会都由当地居民选举产生。

四、人口

科隆居民以德国出生的人为主,还包括莱茵兰人、波兰裔德国人(即先前的普鲁士人)以及德裔土耳其人。许多外国移民来自西班牙和波兰,此外,在杜塞尔多夫附近还有一个庞大的日本人社区。科隆大市范围居住的人口超过了1 200万。

五、经济

科隆以及周边的莱茵兰地区是德国首要的工业中心,其加工工业涉及金属、汽车、啤

industry here.

Cologne is an important river port and rail center, connecting the city to the rest of Europe. Germany's insurance businesses are largely headquartered in the city.Cologne is known for its famous *Eau de Cologne*, which is now manufactured in the city and elsewhere.

The History

Cologne began as a Roman settlement in 50 A.D.. The Romans displaced the Ubil,an ancient Germanic people who had lived there for centuries. The Romans eventually established Christianity as the official religion of Cologne.

Charlemagne founded the Archbishopric of Cologne in 785; the archbishop became one of the most powerful figures in the Holy Roman Empire. The Middle Ages was a golden era for Cologne, unlike many cities in the area. At the time the largest city north of the Alps, Cologne was a member of the Hanseatic League and was more important commercially than the well-established commercial centers of London and Paris.

Cologne soon became one of the most populous in German-speaking Europe. The first municipal university in Europe was established there in 1338; and the city maintained its status as an economic and educational center for the next several hundred years. In 1475 Cologne officially became an Imperial Free City, meaning that the city was formerly responsible only to the Holy Roman Emperor.

Nineteenth-century industrialization was a boon for the city, which had quickly seized on the opportunities of new industries. Cologne's industrial output was hindered during World War I , but the city came back after the war. World War II ,however, had a far greater negative effect on the city, as Nazi Germany engaged in widespread religious persecution. Four important synagogues were destroyed and many Jews were either imprisoned or murdered.

The Sights and Sounds

The Rhineland, including Cologne, is certainly one of the finest and most beautiful areas in all of Germany. As the Rhine meanders through the countryside, it passes vineyards, farming communities, and cities large and small.

Much of Cologne's early 1950s architecture and its associated blocky forms still exist today. However, the reconstruction following World War II yielded a significant change in the city's appearance. These architectural improvements have made Cologne one of the great cities of Germany and of Europe.

One of the reasons visitors flock to Cologne is to see the Old Town and its major attraction, the Cologne Cathedral (Köner Dom), which is dedicated to St. Peter and the Virgin Mary. The cathedral was completed in the late 19th century, more than 600 years after construction began in 1248. Once completed, the Dom became the world's second-tallest Gothic structure. The cathedral's spires are a lofty 515 feet tall, and the height of its interior vault is nearly 139 feet. Like so many churches and cathedrals throughout the rest of Germany and Europe, the Cologne Cathedral was built to house relics of the Magi, who are said to have visited the baby Jesus. The 13th century gold and silver reliquary alone is worth a visit, as it is a glorious tribute to faith and church. Great nobles and bishops are buried within the cathedral.

酒、化学品、制药和石油化学制品等。此外，发电设备也是科隆重要的工业之一。

科隆除了是一个重要的港口城市以外，还是连接该地与欧洲其他城市的铁路网中心。德国的保险业总部大多设在科隆。科隆还以"古龙水"闻名世界，如今这种香水的生产不仅在科隆，而且在其他很多地方都可以找到。

光影流金

公元50年，科隆作为罗马人的殖民地开始创建，罗马人赶走了已经在那里生活了几个世纪的名为乌比尔的日耳曼人部落，并最终将基督教定为科隆的正式宗教。

785年，查理曼创建了科隆大主教管辖区，在整个神圣罗马帝国内，大主教管辖区成为最有权势的地区之一。不同于这一地区的其他城市，中世纪对于科隆来说是一段黄金岁月，当时作为阿尔卑斯山以北最大的城市，科隆不仅属于汉萨同盟的成员之一，而且拥有比伦敦和巴黎这些老牌商业中心更为重要的地位。

在德语为主的欧洲地区，科隆很快成为人口最多的城市之一。1338年，欧洲第一所地方性大学在科隆建立，并且，在接下来的数百年间，科隆始终保持着其经济和教育中心的地位。1475年，科隆正式成为一座"皇家自由城市"，意思就是说这座城市那时只对神圣罗马皇帝负责。

19世纪的工业化革命进一步推动了这座城市的发展，科隆迅速抓住了新型工业的契机。虽然，第一次世界大战阻碍了城市的生产，然而，战后这座城市便重新焕发了活力。遗憾的是，第二次世界大战为科隆带来了更为严重的负面影响，由于纳粹德国大肆进行种族迫害，城内四座重要的犹太教堂遭到破坏，众多的犹太人被关押或杀害。

声光景点

包括科隆在内的莱茵兰地区无疑是整个德国最精致、最美丽的地区之一，莱茵河蜿蜒流过这片土地，两岸是碧绿的葡萄园、农业社区以及大大小小的市镇。

在科隆，大部分建于20世纪50年代早期的建筑以及由这些建筑联合形成的块状区域至今依然存在，然而，二战之后的重建很大程度上改变了这座城市的面貌。这些建筑上的修缮提高使得科隆成为德国乃至欧洲最伟大的城市之一。

科隆之所以游客如织，原因之一在于它的旧城，而旧城内的主要景点就是科隆大教堂(科隆圆顶)，这座教堂是为圣彼得和圣母玛丽亚而修建的，工程开始于1248年，而全部完成却到了600多年后的19世纪晚期。一经完工，立刻成为世界上高度第二的哥特式建筑。教堂的尖塔高达515英尺，内部的穹顶高度也达到了139英尺。和遍布德国以及欧洲的众多大小教堂一样，科隆大教堂的修建为的也是供奉东方三博士的神圣遗骨，据说他们曾在基督诞生时前来拜访。仅仅那件13世纪时的金银制成的圣骨盒就值得一看，因为它是一件奉献给信仰和教会的荣耀贡品。那些名门贵族和主教们去世后也都葬在这座大教堂里。

The Germano-Roman Museum lies next to Cologne Cathedral. A fully-preserved mosaic floor was discovered on the site in 1941 as the government built an underground air-raid shelter to protect citizens from Allied bombers. Two other notable museums in Cologne are the Museum Ludwig, with its collection of 20th century artworks, and the Wallraf-Richartz Museum, which holds an extensive collection of art from the 13th through 19th centuries. Together, the three museums represent some 2,000 years of German and European art.

The Old Town Hall dates to Roman times as the center of Cologne's government and administration. Some of its statuary and embellishments are as much as 900 years old. One of the building's particularly interesting sites is a religious bath from the city's old Jewish quarter.

St. Martin's Square (Martinsviertel) surrounds the Great St. Martin's church, is a Romanesque treasure in an old section of the city that barely survived World War II. During reconstruction, efforts were made to replicate the original medieval architecture. Schnutgen Museum, which houses a good deal of medieval art from the region, is a common tourist attraction.

The Trivia

Fact: Cologne was named by Agrippina, the wife of the Roman Emperor Claudius. Agrippina was born in the area and proclaimed the settlement Colonia. Agrippina was one of the most powerful women in Roman history and was the mother of the future emperor Nero. Interestingly, Nero ordered his own mother's murder soon after he gained power.

Fact: Roman influences are everywhere in Cologne. Remnants of the original city walls and first water pipes are evident. A section of the Roman road that connected Cologne to the Roman road network is now called the Hohe Strasse, and it is the most popular shopping district in the city.

Why Cologne Is a 50 plus one City

Cologne is a fine city to visit. Travel the Rhine and take in the city's sights and sounds from various points of view. Cologne Cathedral alone is worth the trip. While many rave about the famous churches of Europe, it is certainly one of the most magnificent. The city is Germany at its best. Stroll and enjoy Cologne, a jewel of the Rhineland.

日耳曼—罗马博物馆紧邻科隆大教堂，博物馆内保存完好的马赛克镶拼的地面是1941被发现的，当时，德国政府正在为保护市民免遭盟军飞机的轰炸而修建一个地下防空洞。此外，还有两个著名的博物馆，一个是收藏了大量20世纪艺术品的路德维希博物馆，另一个则是以拥有大量13~19世纪艺术品而闻名的瓦尔拉夫·理查尔茨博物馆。这三座博物馆共同成为德国以及欧洲2000年历史的代表。

作为科隆政府和行政的中心，老市政厅的历史可以追溯到罗马人统治的时代，市政厅里的一些雕像和装饰已经有约900岁了，其中特别有趣的一处遗址是来自科隆老犹太区的一个教会用的浴缸。

圣马丁广场以伟大的圣马丁教堂为中心，是位于科隆老城区的一处罗马风格的宝贵地区，险些毁于二战的炮火。在重建期间，建设者们曾力图恢复其原有的中世纪建筑风貌。施纽特根博物馆是广场上一处著名旅游景点，里面收藏了许多在这一地区发现的中世纪艺术品。

奇闻轶事

之一：科隆这个名字源于罗马皇帝克劳狄的妻子阿格丽派娜，阿格丽派娜出生在这一地区，并宣布这一殖民地为"科隆尼亚"。在罗马历史上，阿格丽派娜是权力最大的女性之一，并且是后来罗马皇帝尼禄的母亲。有意思的是，尼禄在夺取权力之后，亲自下令谋杀了自己的母亲。

之二：在科隆，罗马的影响无处不在，原始城墙的遗址和第一条输水管线就是证明。那条连接科隆与罗马路网的罗马街道的部分路段，如今被称为雷赫大街，是城里最繁华的商业区。

为什么科隆入选50＋1个城市？

科隆是旅游的好去处，泛舟莱茵河上，可以从不同的角度欣赏到城市的声光景色。仅科隆大教堂一地就会令你不虚此行，当许多人流连于欧洲各式各样著名的教堂时，别忘了这座大教堂是其中最辉煌的一个。科隆是德国最完美的代表，来科隆漫步享受一下吧，这颗莱茵兰上的宝石！

Eighteen

Copenhagen, Denmark

The Basic Facts

Copenhagen is the capital of Denmark and the nation's largest city. It is a major port and the center of Denmark's economy, politics and culture. Denmark is a constitutional democracy, and the royalty calls Copenhagen home. The city is a popular tourist attraction, as it is considered one of the world's major centers of culture and the arts.

Geography

Copenhagen lies at 55 degrees 43 minutes north latitude and 12 degrees 27 minutes east longitude. The city is located on both the eastern side of the Zealand,an island in the North Sea, and the nearby island of Amager. Copenhagen harbor,with its world-famous statue of The Little Mermaid (based on the story by Hans Christian Andersen), dominates the city. Town Hall Square forms the city center,and Copenhagen's main streets and highways extend out from the square.

Climate

Copenhagen's weather is mild throughout the year, with winter temperatures averaging in the upper 30s and summer temperatures averaging in the upper 60s. Rain and cloudy skies are common year round, but the climate is typically moderate.

Government

Copenhagen's local government is run by a committee system, as are most Danish municipalities. The government consists of a finance committee and six standing committees; each committee has its own area of responsibility and each is led by a separate adminstrator and mayor. The city's main political body is the City Council,which consists of 55 members who are elected for 4-year terms. The City Council directs the actions of the various committees.

Demographics

Copenhagen is divided into 15 city districts, and demographics vary among these areas. In general, Copenhagen residents are younger than those living elsewhere in Denmark. Native-born Danes comprise the vast majority of Copenhagen's population; however, immigration is on the rise from other European countries,primarily Scandinavia. The municipality of Copenhagen has some 500,000 residents, but the metropolitan area's population is more than twice this size.

Economy

As Copenhagen is Denmark's major port, international trade is a key source of employment for Copenhagen residents. The city is Denmark's industrial center and

丹麦哥本哈根

概况

　　哥本哈根是丹麦的首都和最大的城市,也是丹麦主要的港口及经济、政治和文化中心。丹麦实行的是民主立宪制,王室成员称哥本哈根为他们的家。作为世界上主要的文化和艺术中心之一,哥本哈根也是著名的旅游城市。

一、地理

　　哥本哈根位于北纬55°43′,东经12°27′,地处北海中的西兰岛以及附近的阿玛格岛的东岸。哥本哈根港在城市中占据了重要位置,港口处的小美人鱼像(根据汉斯·克里斯蒂安·安徒生的童话故事而创作)全球闻名。市政厅广场构成哥本哈根的中心,主要街道以及公路都从广场向外延伸。

二、气候

　　哥本哈根一年四季气候温和,冬季平均气温在华氏37~39度,夏季平均维持在华氏67~69度。尽管一年当中下雨和多云的天气非常普遍,但是,总的说来,气候相当宜人。

三、政府

　　哥本哈根地方政府由一个委员会组织进行管理, 这一点和丹麦大多数自治区域相同。政府由一个财政委员会和六个固定委员会组成,每个委员会分管一个地区,有自己独立的行政长官和区长。哥本哈根的主要政治团体是市政委员会,包括55名成员,他们由选举产生,任期4年,市政委员会指导其他各类委员会的工作。

四、人口

　　哥本哈根市被划分成15个区,不同的区人口也各不相同。总的说来,哥本哈根的居民较之丹麦其他地方的居民要年轻,土生土长的丹麦人构成了城市人口的大多数,然而,来自欧洲其他国家,尤其是斯堪的纳维亚国家的移民正逐年增多。哥本哈根市区的人口大约只有50万,但是大市范围的人口却是它的两倍以上。

五、经济

　　由于哥本哈根是丹麦的主要港口,国际贸易就成为城市居民就业的重要渠道。此外,这座城市还是丹麦的工业中心,生产加工啤酒、柴油发动机、家具和陶瓷等。同几乎所有

manufactures beer, diesel engines, furniture and porcelain. Like almost every major European city, tourism is a large part of the local economy. The city attracts many visitors each year, primarily from Europe and North America. Government services, in addition to industry, are a driving force of Copenhagen's economy.

The History

Copenhagen began as a small fishing village in the early 11th century. In 1167 a small fortress was constructed on the banks of the harbor to discourage raids by German tribes. The fortress was eventually destroyed by invaders, and Copenhagen Castle was constructed on the site.

Copenhagen became the capital of Denmark after 1416, when the reigning monarch King Eric of Pomerania moved into the Copenhagen Castle. In fact, during the 15th century Denmark also ruled Norway and Sweden, so at the time Copenhagen was the capital of three countries. Copenhagen grew rapidly in size and population over the next several centuries, but tragedy struck early in the 18th century. Bubonic plague would kill one-third of the population and two major fires would devastate the city's infrastructure.

During the Second Battle of Copenhagen in 1807, the British navy fiercely bombarded the city in an attempt to prevent the Danes from handing over its naval fleet to Napoléon. After Denmark became a democracy in 1849, the country experienced a period of relative peace and managed to maintain neutral status in World War I. During World War II, however, the Nazis occupied the city for 5 years.

The Sights and Sounds

Copenhagen is a city dominated by water; the presence of the sea and the various canals lends a maritime aura to the city. Although it is the largest city in Scandinavia—which includes Denmark, Sweden, Finland and Norway—Denmark's capital has a quaint, comfortable feel which invites visitors to walk the streets and bridges to see the sights.

Amalienborg Palace has been the home of the royal family since 1784. Tourists often visit the Amalienborg Museum within the palace, which presents a variety of royal family memorabilia as well as information about the history of Denmark and the art and artifacts of Copenhagen. A centerpiece of the exhibit is a formidable Viking ship.

The Botanical Garden certainly is one of the finest in Northern Europe, with special exhibits for tropical palms, orchids and cactus. In 1167 Bishop Absalon built the city's first walls and protection against raiders; in its place today is Christianborg Castle, built at the beginning of the 20th century as the Parliament House and Royal Reception Chambers.

There are many wonderful museums in Copenhagen. Of particular interest to visitors is the Hirschsprung Collection of art from the 19th century, Denmark's golden age. The Museum of Decorative Art has a large collection of handicrafts, silver and other artifacts from around the world. The National Museum, of course, contains the largest collection of art from all eras in Denmark's history, as well as fine displays of Egyptian, Greek and Roman artifacts and antiquities.

Do not miss the National Art Gallery, a 100-year old building that houses many 19th century Impressionist works. Also, the New Carlsberg Sculpture Museum displays a wonderful collection of Greek and Roman sculpture and art.

No one can visit Copenhagen without strolling through Tivoli Gardens, an amusement

的欧洲城市一样,旅游业构成当地经济的主体,每年,哥本哈根都会吸引大批的游客,他们主要来自欧洲和北美地区。市政服务,外加工业生产,成为哥本哈根经济的推动力量。

光影流金

哥本哈根始于11世纪早期一个小小的渔村。1167年,人们在港口沿岸修建了一个很小的要塞以防御日耳曼人部落的袭击,这个要塞最终被入侵者摧毁,之后,人们又在原址上修建了哥本哈根城堡。

1416年后,当时在位的波美拉尼亚国王埃瑞克搬进了哥本哈根城堡,哥本哈根成为丹麦的首都。事实上,在15世纪时期,丹麦还统治着挪威和瑞典,因此,当时哥本哈根实际上是这三个国家的首都。虽然在此后的几个世纪里,哥本哈根市的面积和人口都迅速增长,但是,悲剧却于18世纪初降临到这座城市头上。腺鼠疫夺去了大约1/3人口的生命,两场大火则吞噬了城市的基础设施。

在1807年第二次哥本哈根海战期间,英国海军对这座城市进行了猛烈的轰炸,以阻止丹麦人将其海军舰队移交给拿破仑。1849年,当丹麦实行了民主政体之后,这个国家经历了一段相对和平的时期。在第一次世界大战期间,丹麦设法保持了中立,然而,在第二次世界大战期间,纳粹却占领了哥本哈根长达五年之久。

声光景点

哥本哈根是一座以水为主的城市,邻近的大海以及纵横交错的运河赋予这座城市一种海上气息。尽管丹麦的首都是斯堪的纳维亚地区 —— 包括丹麦、瑞典、芬兰和挪威 —— 最大的城市,但它却以一种古雅而舒适的感觉吸引着八方来客踏上它的街道、穿过它的小桥,去欣赏城中的美景。

自1784年以来,阿美琳堡王宫一直是丹麦王室的住所,游客经常参观的是位于城堡内的阿美琳堡博物馆,里面展示的除了各种各样的王室纪念品之外,还有关于丹麦历史的信息以及哥本哈根的美术与手工艺品,其中一件核心展品是一艘令人望而生畏的北欧海盗船。

哥本哈根植物园无疑属于北欧地区最漂亮的植物园之一,这里有热带棕榈树、兰花和仙人掌的特殊展区。1167年,阿布萨隆主教修建了哥本哈根的第一堵城墙以抵御袭击者。今天,伫立在城墙旧址上的是克里斯蒂安堡城堡,它同议会大厦以及皇家礼宾室一样都修建于20世纪初期。

在哥本哈根有许多出色的博物馆,其中令游客特别感兴趣的有希施斯普隆美术馆,里面的藏品来自于19世纪丹麦的黄金时期;装饰艺术博物馆汇集了大量来自世界各地的手工艺品和银器等;当然,丹麦国家博物馆无疑拥有馆藏最大的来自丹麦不同历史时期的艺术品,以及相当数量的埃及、希腊和罗马时期的手工艺品及古玩。

千万不要错过丹麦国家美术馆,在这座已有100年历史的建筑内,摆放着许多19世纪印象派画家的作品。此外,新卡尔斯伯格雕塑博物馆展出的则是精美的希腊和罗马时期的雕塑与美术作品。

凡是来到哥本哈根的游客,谁也不会放弃到蒂沃利花园漫步的机会。这座1843年修

park dating from 1843.   It is far more than the average amusement park!   There are theatres, dance halls, beer gardens, rides, marching bands,upscale restaurants and concerts of all genres during the summer months. At night, the Chinese Pagoda, fountain and trees are illuminated with 100,000 white lights, and fireworks add to the festivities.

City Hall Square,   dominated by the Town Hall building,   is the business center of Copenhagen.   The lookout at the top of the Town Hall's 350-foot-tower provides a marvelous bird's-eye view of Copenhagen.   And the monument honoring Bishop Absalon, the city's founder, is prominently on display in Høbro Plads for all to admire.

If the view from the Town Hall is not good enough, try the top of the 600-foot Round Tower, originally built as an observatory in 1642 by Christian IV. There is an art museum halfway up the steps if you need a break from climbing! Also,you must include at least one church in your itinerary.   The Church of Our Lady,Copenhagen's main cathedral since 1924,   is built upon the site of the original church that was completed in the late 16th century.

New Harbor is the center of Copenhagen's social scene.   The area features restaurants, shops, bars and other attractions where one might enjoy a summer evening of drinking and fun.   Old sailing ships in the harbor and delightful 18th century buildings provide a splendid backdrop for the area.

The Trivia

Fact: In the 19th century Copenhagen was a major center of culture. The philosopher Søen Kierkegaard,   the theologian Nikolaj Grundtvig,   and the artist Wilhelm Eckersberg (founder of the Danish School of Art) called Copenhagen home.

Fact: The writer most often associated with Copenhagen is Hans Christian Andersen. Andersen created some of the most beloved fairy tales of all time,   and enjoyed great popularity in his lifetime and through to the present day.   One of Copenhagen's most famous landmarks is The Little Mermaid statue in the city's harbor. The statue is based on a character from one of Andersen's stories.

Fact: Many of Copenhagen's most famous buildings were built during the Renaissance, including the Rundetarn (Round Tower), built as an observatory and still used for that purpose.

Fact: The Golden Age of Copenhagen in the late 1800s yielded great writers, architecture,   and sculpture.   Several grand neoclassical sculptures by artist Bertel Thorvaldsen were donated to the city during this time and survive to this day.

Fact: Many residents take advantage of the city's extensive system of bike paths and its bike-rental services. Not surprisingly, Copenhagen is sometimes referred to as the city of bicycles.

Why Copenhagen Is a 50 plus one City

Copenhagen is a 50 plus one City for its natural beauty,   its rich history and the ease with which visitors can enjoy the city. Visitors flock to Copenhagen, if for no other reason than to see and enjoy the Tivoli Gardens—a place where greatness is displayed on a human scale.

建的游乐园绝对不是普通游乐园所能比拟的！这里有剧院、舞厅、啤酒园，有游乐设施、行进的乐队和高档餐厅。每到夏季，园内还会举办各种形式的音乐会。当华灯初上，园内的中国塔、喷泉和树木被10万只左右的白色灯光所点亮，五彩的焰火将节日的气氛推向高潮。

以市政大厦为主的市政厅广场是哥本哈根的商务中心，站在市政大厦350英尺高的塔楼顶上向四周鸟瞰，哥本哈根的美景一览无余。为纪念城市的缔造者阿布萨隆主教而修建的纪念铜像醒目地矗立在高桥广场中供所有人瞻仰。

假如从市政大厦远眺还不足以令你尽兴，那么你还可以尝试登上600英尺高的"园塔"塔顶，这座园塔最初是作为天文台于1642年由克里斯钦四世修建的。在塔的中部有一个美术馆，正好可以让你在登塔的过程中休息一下！另外，在你的行程当中，应该包括至少一座教堂，圣母大教堂自1924年以来就是哥本哈根主要的大教堂，它是在16世纪晚期建成的教堂基础上修建的。

"新港"是集中反映哥本哈根社会生活的地方，这里有餐馆、商店、酒吧，有能够让游客在享受美酒和娱乐的同时度过一个美妙夏日黄昏的特色景点。港口内古老的帆船以及赏心悦目的18世纪建筑，构成了一幅绝妙的背景图画。

奇闻轶事

之一：19世纪时，哥本哈根是一个主要的文化中心，哲学家索伦·齐克果，神学家尼古拉·格伦特维以及画家维尔汉姆·埃克斯伯格（丹麦美术学校的创始人）都把这里当成自己的家。

之二：最常与哥本哈根联系在一起的作家当属汉斯·克里斯蒂安·安徒生。安徒生创作了许多脍炙人口的童话故事，不仅在他生前，而且直到今天他的作品依然有众多读者。哥本哈根最著名的地标之一就是位于港口的小美人鱼雕像，这座雕像是根据安徒生所写的其中一个故事中的人物创作的。

之三：在哥本哈根最著名的建筑当中，有许多都修建于文艺复兴时期，其中包括作为天文台修建的"园塔"，它至今仍发挥着天文台的作用。

之四：19世纪晚期哥本哈根的"黄金时期"造就了许多伟大的作家、建筑家和雕塑家，当时由美术家博特尔·托瓦尔德森创作的几件新古典风格的雕塑作品，也被捐献给了这座城市，并有幸保存至今。

之五：许多哥本哈根的当地居民都常利用城市中大量的自行车道及自行车租赁服务，因此，哥本哈根有时被称作"自行车城"也就不足为奇了。

为什么哥本哈根入选50+1个城市？

哥本哈根之所以能够入选50＋1个城市，是因为它的自然之美，它的丰富历史，它的适宜游历。蜂拥而至的游客，或许不为别的，就只为了亲眼目睹、亲身体验一下哥本哈根的蒂沃利花园 —— 一个展现人类伟大创造的地方。

Hong Kong, China

The Basic Facts

Hong Kong is one of the largest cities in the world. It is a Special Administrative Region (SAR) of China. China leased Hong Kong to the British in 1898, and under the terms of this lease, the city and region returned to Chinese control in 1997.China had declared that the relationship between the central government and the city would be one country, two systems. This led to the creation of the framework for Hong Kong's administration, known as the Basic Law. According to the law's provisions, Hong Kong retains its own executive, legislative and judicial systems.It remains a free port, issues its own currency and maintains its own police force.Defense and foreign policy matters remain under Chinese central government control.Hong Kong has become a major world center for tourism.

Geography

Hong Kong lies at 21 degrees 45 minutes north latitude and 115 degrees east longitude. The city is located on the southern coast of China near the mouth of the Zhu Jiang (Pearl River). The city comprises a peninsula from the Chinese mainland and with 236 islands. The peninsula consists of the New Territories in the north and Kowloon to the south. Hong Kong Island, the main island, is south of the peninsula.

Hong Kong and Kowloon are the major cities in the Hong Kong SAR and are located on opposite sides of Victoria Harbour. Kowloon is the largest city, yet Hong Kong is the government seat and financial center. Tai Ping Shan (also known as Victoria Peak) towers over the city of Hong Kong, and various other mountains and rolling hills cover the region.

Climate

Hong Kong winters are cool and relatively dry with temperatures averaging in the mid-60s Fahrenheit. Summers are often warm and humid with average temperatures in the high 80s Fahrenheit.

Heavy rains typically occur in the summer and early fall, which lead to mudslides and Flooding.

Government

Hong Kong's government follows the Basic Law. This system took effect on July 1, 1997 when control of Hong Kong was formally transferred from the British to the Chinese. The law established the one country, two systems policy,giving the Hong Kong region a high degree of autonomy.

The Hong Kong region is governed by a chief executive chosen by an 800-member election committee. The chief executive serves for 5 years, and committee members come from various socioeconomic classes and individual governmental bodies. The chief executive

---

中国香港

概况

香港是世界上最大的城市之一,是中国的一个特别行政区。1898年中国将香港租借给英国。根据租借条款,香港的城市和地区于1997年回归中国政府,中国宣布中央政府与香港的关系是一个国家、两种制度,这就是香港行政框架的创立,成为香港基本法。根据该法律条文,香港拥有自主的行政、立法和司法系统,仍然保持其自由港的地位,发行自己的货币,拥有自己的警察队伍。而其防卫及外交事务则由中央政府管理。香港已经成为世界上一个重要的旅游中心。

一、地理

香港位于北纬21°45′,东经115°,地处珠江口附近的中国南部沿海地区。香港由一个从中国大陆延伸出来的半岛及236个小岛组成,这个半岛包括北面的新界和南面的九龙,香港岛,即主岛,位于半岛的南部。

香港和九龙是香港特别行政区的主要城市区,分别位于维多利亚港的两岸,虽然九龙是城区面积最大的,但香港却是政府所在地和金融中心。太平山(也称维多利亚峰)是香港市区的制高点,此外,还有一些山脉及起伏的丘陵遍布整个港岛。

二、气候

香港冬季凉爽,相对干燥,气温平均在华氏65度左右,夏季经常温暖湿润,平均气温在华氏87~89度。在夏季和初秋季节,时常会下大雨,造成泥石流和洪水。

三、政府

香港政府遵循基本法原则,这一体系于1997年7月1日起施行,也就是当香港的统治权被正式由英国政府移交给中国政府的时候。这一法律确立了"一国两制"的政策,赋予香港地区高度的自治。

香港地区由一位主要的行政长官统领,这一行政长官是经过由800名成员组成的选举委员会选出的。行政长官任期5年,委员会成员来自社会经济各个阶层以及独立的政府机构,行政长官负责任命行政委员会的委员,而行政委员会负责行使政府的各项职能。香

appoints members to an Executive Council, which performs the duties of the government. Hong Kong's principal legislative body is a 60-member Legislative Council. Hong Kong residents elect half of the council's members, and professional and special interest groups, called functional constituencies, elect the remainder.

Demographics

Almost all Hong Kong residents are native Chinese, including many immigrants from southern China. The non-Chinese minority consists of people from Australia, the United Kingdom, India, Japan, the United States and Vietnam. Over six million people live in the region.

Hong Kong's two official languages are Chinese (primarily Cantonese) and English, although most Hong Kong residents cannot speak or understand English. Urban areas are crowded, but recent settlements outside of the cities are attracting new residents. Small farming villages are responsible for the region's agriculture, which includes livestock and crops.

Economy

Hong Kong is an international center of trade, finance and tourism. It is a free port, meaning that there are no levies on incoming goods. Because of this, most goods sold in Hong Kong are inexpensive.

Most Hong Kong residents work in the service industry. A thriving industrial base generates textiles, clothing, electronics, plastics, watches and clocks.

The History

People have lived in Hong Kong for thousands of years. During the 1800s, British merchants openly smuggled opium into China. Disputes between these merchants and the Chinese government led to the First Opium War (1840 to 1842). After the merchants prevailed, the Chinese ceded control of Hong Kong and surrounding area to Britain. In 1898 the Chinese leased the region to the British for a period of 99 years.

The population of Hong Kong grew quickly with a wave of immigration in the early 1900s. During this period, the Republic of China was born when nationalist revolutionaries overthrew the Manchu Dynasty. In the 1950s Hong Kong began to develop into a center of international trade, finance and industry.

The Sights and Sounds

Hong Kong is a bright, vibrant city with the soul of the East and the amenities of the West. You can find tailor-made suits, cheap electronics and fabulous food almost anywhere you look. The buildings are new, state-of-the-art and flashy. Hong Kong is also full of natural beauty, as it has a beautiful coast and has reclaimed much land by filling in coastal areas. Victoria Peak overlooks the city, and the rich and powerful live on the mountainside.

Victoria Peak is one of the key sights in the city. Locals suggest that first-time visitors ride the Peak Tramway to the summit, where the view is breathtaking. Most will tell you to go at night, so you can experience the grandeur of the illuminated buildings below. Every night at 8 p.m., Hong Kong's skyscrapers blossom with light in a show called the Symphony of Lights. A local radio station broadcasts music to accompany the show, and

港的主要立法机构是一个由60人组成的立法委员会,香港居民选举产生该委员会的一半成员,剩下的成员则由一些被称为功能选区的职业及特殊利益集团推选产生。

四、人口

几乎所有的香港居民都是土生土长的中国人,其中包括许多来自中国南方的移民。非华裔的少数居民来自澳大利亚、英国、印度、日本、美国和越南等国。共有600多万人生活在这个地区。

香港的两大官方语言是汉语(最初为粤语)和英语,不过,大多数香港居民不会说、也听不懂英语。虽然香港市区非常拥挤,但是近年来城市外围的居民区吸引了许多新来的移民。小型农业村庄承担着香港的农业生产,包括家禽饲养及庄稼种植。

五、经济

香港是国际贸易、金融及旅游的中心,也是一个自由港,换句话说,就是对进口货物不征收关税。正因为如此,在香港出售的大多数商品价格都很便宜。

大多数香港居民都在服务行业工作,蓬勃的工业基础造就了纺织、服装、电子、塑料和钟表等产品。

光影流金

香港地区有人类居住的历史已经有数千年了。19世纪时期,英国商人将鸦片公开走私进中国,这些商人与中国政府的争端导致第一次鸦片战争(1840~1842)的爆发。当这些英国商人占据上风之后,中国将香港及其周边地区的控制权转让给了英国,1898年,中国又将这一地区以99年的租期租借给了英国。

20世纪初,随着移民潮的涌入,香港的人口迅速增长,这一时期,正是中华民国诞生,中国民族主义革命家推翻清朝统治之时。20世纪50年代,香港开始发展成为一个国际贸易、金融及工业的中心。

声光景点

香港是一个欣欣向荣、充满生机的城市,它融东方的灵魂与西方的外表于一身。在这里,你既可以发现手工制作套装的裁缝,又可以看到便宜的电子产品,以及几乎无处不在的美味佳肴。这里的建筑崭新时髦、熠熠生辉。当然,香港也不乏自然美景,因为这里有美丽的海滨,通过填海改造的陆地。维多利亚峰傲视全城,香港有钱有势的人都住在这座山的山腰地区。

维多利亚峰是这座城市的重要景点之一,当地居民会建议初来香港的游客乘坐登山电车直达山顶,那里的景色令人心旷神怡。大多数人还会告诉你最好晚上去,那样你就可以欣赏到山下一副由灯光映衬下的建筑所构成的美轮美奂的图画。每晚8点,香港的摩天大楼在灯光中绽放,一场名为"幻彩咏香江"的表演正式开始。在灯光演出的同时,一家当

tourist attractions throughout the city carry this music as well. The different colors and types of light fascinate locals and foreigners alike.

The ferry route from Hong Kong to Kowloon offers unbelievable views of the area. Many experienced travelers to Hong Kong suggest that tourists ride the ferry twice during their visit. Go during the day to see the magical view of the water and coastline. Go again at night to see the skyscrapers lit up and to watch the light reflecting off the harbor.

In addition to the modern buildings and trendy houses, Hong Kong is also home to fascinating Chinese architecture, including various interesting temples that dot the city. Two of the most captivating temples are Man Mo Temple and Wong Tai Sin Temple; the buildings, statuary and incense that wafts through the air make a visit here well worth the trip.

Yuen Yuen Institute is an example of old-world Chinese architecture; its buildings are as beautiful inside as they are outside. The Institute is composed of monasteries and temples that represent Taoism, Confucianism and Buddhism.

In a city of imposing skyscrapers, the Bank of China Tower is in a class of its own. Designed by I. M. Pei, the 70-story structure is 1,209 feet tall and resembles a blue glass needle. There is an observation deck on the 43rd floor, which provides panoramic views of Hong Kong's skyline and coastline.

The Hong Kong Museum of History is the best place to learn more about the city. This museum is rather small considering Hong Kong's 6,000-year history;however, the museum has a fascinating exhibit on the history of the city.

The Hong Kong Museum of Art, with more than 12,000 pieces of Chinese art,houses one of the largest collections in China. For a small fee, you can view the museum's collections of calligraphy, silks, pottery and paintings.

The Hong Kong Space Museum is one of the largest planetariums in Asia. The museum opened in 1980 and features museum space as well as a theatre with engaging programs for planetarium visitors.

The Trivia

Fact: Hong Kong is both a region and a city, much like New York in the United States. Locals usually refer to the entire region as Hong Kong.

Fact: The name hong kong means fragrant harbor. The region surrounds Victoria Harbour, with Hong Kong on the northern part of Hong Kong Island and Kowloon on the southern part of the mainland.

Fact: The only time the population of Hong Kong decreased was during the Japanese occupation in World War II. The occupation was cruel and many Hong Kong residents fled to the relative safety of China—to return after the war.

Why Hong Kong Is a 50 plus one City

No visitor to Asia can pass up Hong Kong: it is exotic, crowded, sophisticated and modern, all at the same time. It is difficult to imagine how this region grew from a small port into the economic engine and cultural icon it is today. Hong Kong is a blend of East and West that is unmatched anywhere in the world.

地的电台还会播放音乐,全城的旅游景点将这一音乐传遍大街小巷,绚烂的色彩、变幻的灯光令中外游客叹为观止。

在从香港到九龙的渡轮沿线,游客同样能够欣赏到令人难以置信的美景。许多到过香港的有经验的游客都会建议你乘两次渡轮,一次选在白天,因为你可以看到奇幻曼妙的海浪和海岸线,一次选在晚上,因为你可以观赏摩天大楼点亮之后的效果以及港口灯光在水中的倒影。

除了现代化的大厦及时髦的房屋之外,香港也同样拥有许多神奇的中国建筑,其中包括点缀于城中的各式各样有趣的寺庙。两座香火最旺的寺庙是文武庙和黄大仙祠,里面的建筑、佛像及漂浮于空气中的香火,都令游客感到不虚此行。

香港圆玄学院是古代中国建筑的代表,建筑的内部和外部同样漂亮,学院整体由代表道教、儒教和佛教的寺院及庙宇组合而成。

在一座高楼林立的城市里,中银大厦的塔楼可谓独领风骚,由贝聿铭设计的这座共70层高1 209英尺的建筑,看上去很像一根蓝色的玻璃针,在大厦第43层有观景台,可以俯瞰香港城市的轮廓及海岸线的全景。

想要更好地了解这座城市,香港历史博物馆无疑是个好去处。相对于这座城市6 000年的历史来说,这个博物馆实在是很小,然而,博物馆内对于城市历史的介绍却引人入胜。

香港艺术博物馆拥有超过12 000件中国的艺术作品,是中国最大的展馆之一,只需一点点门票钱,你就可以欣赏到博物馆内大量的书法作品、丝绸、陶器以及绘画作品。

香港太空馆是亚洲最大的天文馆之一,1980年开馆至今,以其宽敞的展厅以及太空剧院上演的精彩节目而吸引了大量游客。

奇闻轶事

之一:香港既是一个地区,又是一座城市,这一点很像美国的纽约。当地人通常用香港来指整个地区。

之二:香港名称的含义是"芳香的港口",环绕维多利亚港,香港岛的北部是香港,南部是九龙。

之三:香港人口唯一一次减少是在第二次世界大战期间,日本军队占领了香港,其残酷统治迫使许多香港居民逃亡到相对安全的中国内地 —— 直到战争结束之后才重返香港。

为什么香港入选50 + 1个城市?

无论是谁,来到亚洲,必到香港:它的异域风情、它的熙来攘往、它的成熟复杂、它的现代时尚,凡此种种,皆在同一时间展现在你的面前。很难想象这个地区是如何从一个小小的港口发展成为今天这样一座经济快车和文化象征式的城市。这就是香港,一个东方和西方无与伦比的混合体。

Tenty

Istanbul, Turkey

The Basic Facts
Istanbul has been one of the world's most important cities for centuries, serving at various times as the capital of the Roman, Byzantine and Ottoman Empires. Kemal Atatürk made Turkey a republic in 1923 and moved the capital from Istanbul to Ankara. Istanbul grew rapidly throughout the 20th century and the city underwent a series of civic improvements, including bridges across the Bosporus and slums and factories replaced with parks and playgrounds.

Geography
Istanbul lies at 41.02 north latitude and 29 degrees east longitude. The city is located at the south end of the Bosporus, a strait in northwestern Turkey that connects the Black Sea and the Sea of Marmara. Istanbul is unique in that it is the only metropolitan area on two continents, Europe and Asia.

Istanbul covers 769 square miles; the European side of the city is larger than the Asian side, and has a higher population. The European part of Istanbul is further divided by the Golden Horn, an inlet of the Bosporus; the northern section is more modern than the old section.

Climate
Istanbul's climate ranges from hot and humid in the summer to cold, rainy and even snowy in the winter. Temperatures average from the upper 40s in winter to the mid-80s in summer. Although summer is the driest season, there are usually no summer droughts, unlike other Mediterranean cities. The city is also quite windy with average winds of 11 mph.

Government
The mayor of Istanbul is appointed by the president of the republic, and is prefect of Istanbul city and governor of Istanbul il (province). The Emperor Constantine divided the city into 14 districts to emulate the divisions in Rome. Today, Istanbul is divided into 12 circumscriptions (kazas), each governed by a kaymakam.

Demographics
Muslim Turks comprise the vast majority of Istanbul's residents; Jews, Greeks and Armenian Christians largely constitute the city's minority. In the late 1960s, the population grew sharply, and by 1990 the population was roughly nine times what it had been in 1935. Half the city's residents are either native to Istanbul or from rural areas in Turkey. The metropolitan area's population numbers roughly 10 million.

Economy
Istanbul has been Turkey's cultural center for hundreds of years. City universities generate a good portion of the economy, but Istanbul's location also makes it a major trade center. It is also a major tourist attraction due to its rich variety of museums, mosques, Byzantine churches, palaces and bazaars.

20

土耳其伊斯坦布尔

概况

几个世纪以来，伊斯坦布尔都是世界上最重要的城市之一。在不同的历史时期，这里曾经是罗马帝国、拜占庭帝国和奥斯曼帝国的首都。1923年，基马尔将土耳其变成了共和国，并将首都从伊斯坦布尔迁到了安卡拉。在20世纪期间，伊斯坦布尔迅速发展，城市经历了一系列的市政方面的改造和提升，包括修建了横跨博斯普鲁斯海峡的大桥，以及将贫民窟和工厂改造成为公园或游乐场等。

一、地理

伊斯坦布尔位于北纬41.02°，东经29°，地处土耳其西北部连接黑海和马尔马拉海的博斯普鲁斯海峡南端。伊斯坦布尔是唯一一个地跨欧洲和亚洲两大洲的大都会，其地理位置非常独特。

伊斯坦布尔占地面积768平方英里，城市位于欧洲的部分不仅面积大于其亚洲的部分，而且人口也较多。伊斯坦布尔的欧洲部分又被金角，即波斯普鲁斯海峡的入口，进一步划分为两部分，北边部分比老城区更为现代。

二、气候

伊斯坦布尔的气候夏季炎热潮湿，冬季寒冷多雨甚至多雪，平均气温在冬季的华氏47~49度到夏季的华氏85度左右，尽管夏季是最干燥的季节，但是与其他地中海城市不同的是，通常情况下这里却没有旱灾。此外，城市的风也很大，平均风速达到每小时11英里。

三、政府

伊斯坦布尔市的市长由土耳其共和国总统任命，并兼任伊斯坦布尔市行政长官和土耳其省的省长职务。康斯坦丁国王效仿罗马帝国将城市划分为14个区，如今，伊斯坦布尔市分为12个区，每个区由一个"卡马坎"负责。

四、人口

伊斯坦布尔居民大多是信仰伊斯兰教的土耳其人，其他还有少数犹太人、希腊人以及信仰基督教的美国人。20世纪60年代，该市人口迅速增长，到了1990年，全市人口大约已是1935年的9倍。有半数的伊斯坦布尔居民都是本地出生或者来自土耳其农村。伊斯坦布尔大市范围的人口数量在1000万左右。

五、经济

伊斯坦布尔作为土耳其的文化中心，其历史已经有好几百年了。虽然该市的大学在其经济生活中起着很重要的作用，但是，这座城市特殊的地理位置却使它成为主要的贸易中心。此外，由于拥有大量的博物馆、清真寺、拜占庭教堂、宫殿以及集市，伊斯坦布尔还是一处重要的旅游度假的胜地。

Istanbul is the largest center of industry in Turkey. Its factories produce cement,drugs, electrical appliances, glassware, leather goods, machinery, plastics,processed foods, and automobiles and trucks. The shipyards on the Bosporus also maintain a lively business.

The History

The Asian part of Istanbul has been occupied perhaps as early as 3,000 years ago. In 667 B.C., Greek colonists founded the city of Byzantium on the site of what would become Istanbul. The city was absorbed into the Roman Empire, and in 330 A.D. the Roman emperor Constantine I declared Byzantium the imperial capital. After Constantine's death, the city was renamed Constantinople (literally,Constantine's city).

Sixty years later the Roman empire was split into two parts. Barbarians conquered the Western Roman Empire in the 5th century, while Constantinople remained the capital of the Eastern Roman or Byzantium Empire. Over the next several hundred years Constantinople would be attacked and conquered several more times.Ottoman forces conquered Constantinople in 1453, the city became the capital of the Ottoman Empire, and was renamed Istanbul. By the middle of the 16th century, following military campaigns into Europe and the Middle East, Istanbul had become a major center of politics, culture and commerce. After a period of decline in the 17th and 18th centuries, the sultans implemented various reforms to modernize the empire, including European style schools and other Western ideas.

The Ottoman Empire was defeated in World War I by the Allies, who occupied Istanbul from 1918 to 1923. In 1922 Kemal Atatürk, the father of modern Turkey,abolished the sultanate, made Turkey a republic, and moved the capital to Ankara.

The Sights and Sounds

The city of Istanbul is an amalgam of East and West, Christian and Muslim, Asian and European. There are two Istanbuls, in essence: Asian Istanbul, with Western housing and suburbs, and European Istanbul, the older and more historically significant area. The bridges that span the Golden Horn connect these two portions of the city.

The Old City is roughly the size of the original city as laid out by Constantine.It contains most of the city's treasures, including the Hagia Sophia, the Church of the Divine Wisdom, and is no longer a church or a mosque, but a museum.The original church was completed in 360, but the building and its successor were destroyed by fire. The current building was finished in 537 under Emperor Justinian I, and it remained the center of Eastern Rite Orthodoxy until it was converted into a mosque in 1453. In 1935 Kemal Atatürk established the Ayasofya Museum within the building. That Hagia Sophia survived at all is a miracle; neither earthquakes nor invaders destroyed the building or defaced its beauty.

While Hagia Sophia captures the city's history and culture, visitors frequently begin their tour of Istanbul at Topkapi Palace. Between the 15th and 19th centuries,the palace was the home of sultans and their harems. This important historical site includes such wonders as Hagia Eirene, the Court of the Janissaries (the royal guards), and the Gate of Salutation. Beautiful gardens and reflecting pools surround the palace's exterior. Remember to visit the harem, a popular attraction having nearly 400 rooms and apartments built around the sultan's quarters.

No visit to Istanbul would be complete without a visit to a bazaar. The largest of its kind in the city is the Grand Bazaar, a covered market with an estimated 4,000 shops and

◄ Istanbul, Turkey ►

伊斯坦布尔是土耳其最大的工业中心，其工厂主要生产水泥、药品、电器、玻璃器皿、皮革产品、机械、塑料、加工食品以及汽车、卡车等，位于博斯普鲁斯海峡的造船厂也始终保持着旺盛的生产力。

光影流金

早在3 000多年前，伊斯坦布尔的亚洲部分就已经有了人类居住。公元前667年，希腊殖民者在后来成为伊斯坦布尔的地方建立起了拜占庭城，这座城市后来被罗马帝国吞并。公元330年，罗马皇帝君士坦丁大帝宣布拜占庭为其王国首都，君士坦丁死后，这座城市便更名为君士坦丁堡(意思是"君士坦丁的城市")。

60年后，罗马帝国一分为二。5世纪时，一些非基督教徒占领了西罗马帝国，而君士坦丁堡仍然是东罗马帝国或称拜占庭帝国的都城。在接下来的数百年里，君士坦丁堡曾数次遭受袭击或被攻克。1453年，奥斯曼军队攻入了君士坦丁堡，这座城市随之成为奥斯曼帝国的首都，并被更名为伊斯坦布尔。16世纪中期，随着军事运动进入欧洲以及中东地区，伊斯坦布尔成为一个政治、文化和商业的中心。经过17、18世纪的衰退之后，苏丹王推行了各项不同的改革以促进王国的现代化，其中包括建立欧洲风格的学校以及遵循其他一些西方思想。

第一次世界大战期间，奥斯曼帝国被盟军打败，从1918年到1923年间，伊斯坦布尔一直被盟军占领。1922年，基马尔·阿塔丘克 —— 现代土耳其之父 —— 废除了苏丹统治，建立了土耳其共和国，并将首都迁往了安卡拉。

声光景点

伊斯坦布尔这座城市是东方和西方、基督教和伊斯兰教、亚洲和欧洲完美的结合体。从本质上来说，这个世界上有两座伊斯坦布尔：一座是拥有西方建筑和城郊的亚洲伊斯坦布尔，一座是更为古老的、更具历史意义的欧洲伊斯坦布尔，而将这两座伊斯坦布尔连接起来的就是那些横跨金角的大小桥梁。

伊斯坦布尔古城的面积大约就是原来君士坦丁大帝规划的大小，这座城市大多数的宝藏都在这里，其中就有圣索菲亚大教堂，或称神圣智慧教堂，如今它既不是教堂，也不是清真寺，而是一座博物馆。最初的教堂建成于360年，但是，那座教堂连同之后的数座建筑都毁于大火。今天的建筑是537年在拜占庭皇帝查士丁尼一世的命令下修建的，在很长一段时间里它是东正教的礼拜堂和活动中心，直到1453年，才被改成了清真寺。1935年，基马尔·阿塔丘克在这座建筑里又建起了阿亚索非亚博物馆。圣索非亚大教堂能够保存到今天堪称一个奇迹，无论是地震还是外敌入侵都没能将它摧毁，至今依然美丽如初。

如果说圣索菲亚大教堂承载着伊斯坦布尔的历史和文化，那么，托普卡普宫殿则通常是游客旅程的第一站。在15~19世纪，这座宫殿是苏丹及其妻妾的住所，在这座宫殿里，可以看到圣伊莲娜教堂、禁卫军(皇家保安)法庭以及朝圣门之类颇具历史意义的景点。环绕在宫殿外部的是美丽的花园以及倒影清澈的池塘。别忘了去皇室寝宫转一下，那里以苏丹住所为中心建有近400间卧室和套房，是深受游客喜爱的场所。

来到伊斯坦布尔不能不去参观一下这里的集市，城里最大的集市就叫"大市集"，这座拥有顶棚的集市里大约有4 000家商铺和餐馆，"大市集"创建于大约1450年，至今仍

restaurants. The bazaar was built around 1450 and operates much the same as it has for hundreds of years. In addition, vendors at the nearby Egyptian (or Spice) Bazaar, built in the 17th century, sell a variety of foods from fruit to nuts.

The city of Istanbul contains some 1,000 mosques, and visitors favor two in particular. The Suleiman Mosque, named for the sultan Suleiman I, dates from the mid-16th century; this mosque is famous not only for its grandeur but also for the tombs of Suleiman I and his family. The Sultan Ahmed (or Blue) Mosque, is named for the sultan Ahmed I and is still a place of worship. This mosque, with its beautiful stained glass windows, was intentionally built opposite Hagia Sophia to rival the latter's architecture. Its original blue tiling gave the mosque its common Western name, although this tiling is now being replaced as inconsistent with the building's original appearance.

At one time, Istanbul had a stadium where horse races and other public events were held. The Hippodrome of Constantinople was a massive structure with seats for 100,000 spectators. Today only fragments of the Hippodrome remain, and the area has been converted into a square known as the Sultanahmet Meydani.

Yerebatan Sarayi (the Sunken Palace) is a cistern that dates to the 4th century during the reign of Constantine I. The Dolmabahç Palace, so named for its surrounding gardens, is in the western part of the city and combines a variety of architectural styles and cultural aspects. Careful observers will note Hindu, Turkish and European in.uences on the building and its interior. The palace was built in 1853 as the residence of the last sultans of the Ottoman Empire. Notable features of this palace include the Crystal Staircase, decorated with Baccarat crystal, the 88-foot clock tower, and Kemal Atatürk's room in which he lived shortly before his death. Visit at night when the building is illuminated.

Nightlife in Istanbul is seemingly never-ending. At dawn, as devout Muslims face Mecca for morning prayers, revelers arrive to patronize the city's cafes, bars and nightclubs. The city also has a thriving theatre district.

The Trivia

Fact: At 3,000 years old, Istanbul is one of the oldest cities of the world and the only major city in the world that is situated on two continents.

Fact: Orthodox Christianity and Islam have had a tumultuous relationship in Istanbul, but for the most part the two religions coexist. The city has 25 Byzantine churches and more than 1,000 mosques.

Fact: Until 1930 the city was known colloquially as both Istanbul and Constantinople. In that year the Turkish government declared Istanbul the official name of the city.

Fact: Most of Istanbul's Greek population emigrated from the city in 1955 after the Istanbul Pogrom. Greeks now constitute a tiny minority of the city.

Why Istanbul Is a 50 plus one City

Istanbul is the gateway to the Middle East and the geographic terminus of modern Europe. Straddling two worlds, it reflects myriad cultures, languages, customs and religions, all of which make this an exotic, culturally rich and entertaining city. The sights and sounds of this ancient city delight visitors.

然保留着几百年前的经营模式。除此以外,在不远处还有一家创建于17世纪的埃及(或称香料)市场,那里你可以买到从水果到坚果等各类食品。

伊斯坦布尔市内有大约1 000座清真寺,其中两座最受游客青睐,一座是苏莱曼清真寺,它以苏丹苏莱曼一世的名字命名,其历史可以追溯到16世纪中期,这座清真寺之所以出名,不仅因为其宏大的建筑,而且因为苏莱曼一世和其家人死后就埋葬在这里。另一座是苏丹艾哈迈德(又称蓝色)清真寺,它是根据苏丹艾哈迈德一世的名字命名的,至今依然香火甚旺。这座拥有漂亮的彩色玻璃窗的大清真寺,最初修建时是为了和对面的圣索菲亚大教堂的建筑相抗衡,它独特的蓝色盖瓦为其赢得了那个在西方广为流传的名字。可是,如今这些屋顶瓦正逐步被替换掉,理由是它们与建筑的原有风貌不符。

过去,伊斯坦布尔曾经拥有一座体育馆,赛马或其他一些公共活动都在那里举行,君士坦丁堡古竞技场曾经是一个宏大的建筑,可以容纳10万观众,今天这座古竞技场只剩下断垣残壁,这一地区已经被改造成了一个广场,取名为"苏丹艾哈迈特-梅达尼"。

耶雷巴坦-萨拉伊(地下宫殿)是一个地下蓄水池,修建于4世纪君士坦丁大帝在位期间。朵玛巴恰宫因其四周的花园而得名,它位于城市的西面,融合了不同风格的建筑与多元文化的特征,细心的游客能够在建筑内外发现印度、土耳其和欧洲等元素的影响。这座奥斯曼帝国末代苏丹所居住的皇宫修建于1853年,皇宫内非常有特色的东西包括由巴卡拉水晶玻璃装饰的水晶楼梯,88英尺高的钟楼,以及基马尔死前住过的房间。建议大家最好安排一次夜游,你会发现灯光映衬下的朵玛巴恰宫别有一番韵味。

伊斯坦布尔的夜生活似乎永无止境,黎明时分,当虔诚的穆斯林们面向麦加作晨祷的时候,狂欢的人们正光顾着城里的咖啡屋、酒吧和夜总会,市区的影剧院区也总是生意兴隆。

奇闻轶事

之一:3 000年的历史使得伊斯坦布尔成为世界上最古老的城市之一,同时,它也是世界上唯一横跨两大洲的重要城市。

之二:虽然东正教和伊斯兰教在伊斯坦布尔的关系总是吵吵闹闹,但是两大宗教在很大程度上却是同生共存的,这座城市拥有25座拜占庭教堂和1 000多座清真寺。

之三:以前在民间,这座城市既被称为伊斯坦布尔,又被叫做君士坦丁堡。直到1930年,土耳其政府才宣布伊斯坦布尔为这座城市的官方名称。

之四:1955年,伊斯坦布尔大屠杀之后,大部分住在伊斯坦布尔的希腊人离开了这座城市,如今,希腊人只占该市人口的很小一部分。

为什么伊斯坦布尔入选50 + 1个城市?

伊斯坦布尔既是进入中东地区的门户,同时在地理上又是现代欧洲的终点站,由于横跨两个大陆,它所反映的文化、语言、风俗和宗教异彩纷呈,所有这一切都赋予这座城市独特的异域风情、丰富的文化内涵以及迷人的风光景致。这座古老而充满魅力的城市正吸引着来自世界各地的游客。

Twenty-one

Jakarta, Indonesia

The Basic Facts

Jakarta is Indonesia's capital and largest city, as well as the country's economic powerhouse.

Geography

Jakarta lies at 6 degrees 17 minutes south latitude and 106 degrees 45 minutes east longitude. The city is located on the northwest coast of the Indonesian island of Java on the Ciliwung River. The city is mostly flat and dominates the island.

Climate

Jakarta is a tropical city featuring an annual rainfall of more than 67 inches and typical relative humidity between 75 percent and 85 percent. The climate is consistently warm; average annual temperatures range in the 80s Fahrenheit, although the high humidity often makes it feel much warmer. Because Jakarta is located south of the equator, the winter and summer months are opposite from those in the northern hemisphere; winter occurs between June and August and summer occurs between December and February.

Government

Jakarta is officially considered a province of Indonesia, not a city. Thus, a governor heads the provincial government. The province is divided into five city municipalities (kotamadaya), each headed by its own mayor (walikota) and regent (bupati).

Demographics

Jakarta is the economic and political capital of Indonesia, and as such the city attracts immigrants from the rest of Indonesia and from other countries. As a result, Jakarta has a rich culture and a cosmopolitan feel. Immigrants from other areas of Java speak a mixture of dialects of the Javanese and Sundanese languages, and they have brought traditional foods and customs to the city. The Orang Betawi Indonesian ethnic group is descended from residents of the surrounding area of Batavia, who came to the region to meet labor needs. These immigrants, with their distinct languages and culture, are rather different than the Jakarta Sundanese and Javanese. The city currently has more than 8.8 million residents.

Economy

The Indonesian economy is centered in Jakarta, and the Port of Tanjung Priok is the hub of much of the nation's foreign trade. Jakarta's factories manufacture motor vehicles, processed foods, chemicals, electronics, paper and printed material, and textiles.

The national and provincial government is a major employer, and employment in

21

印度尼西亚雅加达

概况

雅加达是印度尼西亚的首都和最大的城市,也是这个国家经济的能源中心。

一、地理

雅加达位于南纬6°17′,东经106°45′,地处印度尼西亚西北部吉利翁河中的爪哇岛上,整个城市大部分地势平坦,且占据了爪哇岛的主体。

二、气候

雅加达是一座热带城市,年均降雨量超过67英尺,相对湿度在75%~85%。气候四季温暖,年均气温在华氏80度上下。不过,由于湿度很大,常常使人感觉温度比实际的要高。因为雅加达位于赤道以南,冬夏两季的月份与北半球正好相反,冬天出现在6月~8月,夏天则为12月~2月。

三、政府

雅加达在印度尼西亚官方被认为是一个省,而不是一座城市,因此,管理地方政府的是一位省长,而雅加达省划分为五个自治市(考塔马达亚),每个自治市有自己的市长(瓦利考塔)和地区长官(布帕提)。

四、人口

雅加达是印度尼西亚经济和政治核心,正因如此,这座城市吸引了来自印尼其他地区以及世界各地的移民,这也赋予了雅加达丰富的文化和大都会的气质。来自爪哇岛其他地区的移民讲一种混合了潠他语和爪哇语的方言,他们为这座城市带来了传统的食品和风俗习惯。奥朗-巴达维印尼人是来自周边巴达维亚地区的居民后代,这些少数民族的到来不仅满足了城市对劳动力的需求,同时,这些移民以其特有的语言和文化区别于雅加达的潠他人和爪哇人。今天,这座城市拥有超过880万居民。

五、经济

印度尼西亚的经济以雅加达为中心,这个国家大部分对外贸易则以丹戎不碌港为枢纽。雅加达的工厂生产机动车辆、加工食品、化学品、电子产品、纸张、印刷品以及纺织品。

印尼国家政府和雅加达省政府是这些企业的主要法人,而近些年来,私人工厂正迅

private industry has grown rapidly in recent years.

The History

The area around present-day Jakarta was settled by native peoples as early as the 5th century. Later, the area became part of the Hindu dynasty of Pajajaran, the last Hindu kingdom of West Java until the Portuguese arrived in 1522 to use the port for their burgeoning spice trade. The Muslim leader and Saint Sunan Gunungjati drove the Portuguese from the area, and renamed the city Jayakarta (victorious and prosperous).

The Europeans returned to the area in the early 17th century, when trade centers were established by Dutch and British merchants. Merchants battled for control of the region's trade, and the Dutch triumphed. The area became a Dutch colony, and would remain so until the Japanese invasion of Java in World War II.

After the war, nationalist leader Sukarno established the Republic of Indonesia, but the Dutch soon returned to take control of the area. A bloody civil war erupted in which nationalist Indonesians fought the Dutch and the British, who were aligned with the Dutch in support of trade in the region. Jakarta escaped most destruction during the war, although Sukarno briefly moved the capital from Jakarta to Yogyakarta to avoid Dutch repression. International pressure eventually forced the Dutch to withdraw, and in 1949 control of the country reverted to the nationalists.

Under Sukarno, Jakarta became a modern city and its infrastructure was much improved. Jakarta saw street combat in the 1960s as Sukarno battled his military leaders for control.

The Sights and Sounds

Jakarta is the largest city in Indonesia, and 60 percent of the population lives here. Amid skyscrapers, modern buildings and apartment houses, there are small houses made of bamboo and a fascinating local culture. The Indonesians are known for their shadow puppetry (Wayang), batik fabric and their orchestras known as gamelans.

National Monument (MONAS) celebrates the independence of Indonesia from the Dutch. It is 450 feet tall, with an observation deck that visitors can reach by elevator. The monument provides panoramic views of Jakarta and also contains an exhibit on the history of Indonesia.

The Jakarta Arts Center features live theater and dance programs; the gamelan, an Indonesia folk orchestra, often accompanies these events. Gamelans include a variety of metal and stringed instruments. The sound is interesting and uncommon to foreign visitors.

The Jakarta Museum in Fatahillah Square is housed in an ornate Dutch building from Jakarta's colonial period. It is a history museum with period furniture, arts and crafts, and significant information about Indonesia's Dutch colonial occupation.

Wayang Museum is dedicated to the shadow puppetry native to Indonesia. The puppets are flat and frequently made from buffalo hide. Performers move them against a screen that is illuminated from behind, so that the puppets look like shadows moving across the stage. Shows are based on folk tales and are often accompanied by music; shows are held most days. The museum also contains an impressive collection of puppets old and new.

Ragunan Zoo supports a wide variety of animals from Indonesia such as tapirs, komodo

速发展崛起。

光影流金

早在5世纪时,位于今天雅加达地区就已经有了原住居民,后来,这一地区成为印度教巴查查兰王国,也就是西爪哇的最后一个印度教王国的一部分。1522年,葡萄牙人来到这里,利用港口进行当时盛行的香料贸易。伊斯兰教领袖圣·苏南·古龙贾帝将葡萄牙人赶出了这一地区,并将这座城市更名为查雅加达(胜利与繁荣)。

17世纪初,欧洲人再次回到这一地区,来自荷兰和英国的商人还在此建立了贸易中心。商人们为了争夺对这一地区贸易的控制权而彼此争斗,最终荷兰人取得了胜利,这个地区成为荷兰的一个殖民地,这种状态一直持续到第二次世界大战,当日本人入侵爪哇岛时才宣告结束。

二战结束之后,印尼民族主义领袖苏加诺成立了印度尼西亚共和国。然而不久,荷兰人又再次将该地区占为己有,一场血腥的内战就此爆发,印尼民族主义者们与荷兰殖民者以及为了支持该地区贸易而与荷兰人结盟的英国人展开了斗争。战争期间,雅加达躲过了大部分炮火的破坏,不过,为避免荷兰人的镇压,苏加诺曾一度将首都从雅加达迁往日惹。最终,迫于国际社会的压力,荷兰人不得不撤出了该地区,1949年,这个国家的所有权重新回到印尼人的手中。

在苏加诺的领导下,雅加达发展成了一座现代化的城市,其基础设施得到了极大的改善。20世纪60年代,在苏加诺与其他军队领导争夺军事控制权时,雅加达市的街头曾出现过械斗。

声光景点

雅加达是印度尼西亚最大的城市,印尼60%的人口都居住在这里。在高耸的摩天大楼、摩登大厦以及公寓住宅之间,还有一些低矮的小竹楼,散发出诱人的地方文化色彩,那里有印度尼西亚著名的皮影(瓦仰),蜡纺印花织物以及名为"给姆兰"的木琴乐队。

民族纪念碑是为纪念印度尼西亚从荷兰殖民者手中取得独立而修建的,它高450英尺,游客可以乘电梯直达顶端的观景台,在观景台上,既可以俯瞰雅加达市的全貌,也可以参观设在那里的展览,了解一下印尼的历史。

在雅加达艺术中心,可以欣赏到剧院的现场歌舞表演节目。"给姆兰",作为印尼传统的民族乐团,经常在此演出,"给姆兰"包括各种各样的金属及弦乐,对于外国游客来说,那种声音非常有趣而独特。

位于法塔西拉广场的雅加达博物馆,是一座修建于殖民地时期的华丽的荷兰风格的建筑,这座历史博物馆里陈设有那一时期的家具、手工艺品,以及关于荷兰殖民者统治印尼时的各类有价值的信息。

瓦仰博物馆是专为印尼所特有的皮影戏而修建的,这些木偶都是扁平的,一般用牛

dragons and gibbons. The attached Schmutzer Primate Center is laid out so that the animals have room to move about in large enclosures. This state-of-the-art primate facility offers an opportunity to view gorillas and other primates in an area similar to their original habitat.

The National Museum includes thousands of artifacts from throughout Indonesia and Asia; its statues are particularly impressive. The galleries are large and clearly marked for tourists

Some of the most impressive orchids in the world are grown in Indonesia, and the many varieties are displayed at the Orchid Gardens. Many local greenhouses also allow visitors to view their flowers. The variety of colors and sizes of these exotic blooms is truly amazing.

The Trivia

Fact: Wealthy city residents once lived in a former Dutch section of Jakarta called Menteng; they now live in fashionable areas south of the city. Many Jakartans live in wood or bamboo structures called kampongs; sadly, these houses are typically found in slums with poor sanitation and a lack of potable water.

Fact: Chinese immigrants to Jakarta faced major repression in the 18th century.

Fact: British forces allied with the Dutch launched a bloody attack in Jakarta on November 10, 1945. This day is now called Heroes Day and commemorates a galvanizing event in Indonesia's struggle for independence.

Fact: Like most densely populated cities, Jakarta suffers from significant air and noise pollution.

Why Jakarta Is a 50 plus one City

A visit to Jakarta is a visit to the exotic East, where a melding of cultures has produced a fascinating and often complicated city. Teeming with people, it is a complex meld of old and new, East and West. The city has survived wars and political strife, yet still stands as a testament to the greatness of Indonesia.

皮制成。表演者躲在一块用灯光照亮的幕布后面，将木偶抵住幕布来回移动进行表演，所以看上去这些木偶就像是在舞台上移动的影子。表演的内容都是根据民间故事改编的，并且常常有音乐伴奏，这样的表演全天大部分时间都在进行。此外，博物馆里还收藏了大量或新或旧的木偶。

拉古南动物园里有大量来自印度尼西亚本地的珍禽异兽，例如：貘，巨蜥和长臂猿。园内的史姆泽灵长类动物中心，是一处开放的区域，动物们能够在更大的范围内活动。这一最新的灵长类动物放养形式，使得游客有机会在一种类似于野生的环境下看见大猩猩。

印尼国家博物馆收藏有来自印尼本国以及亚洲地区的成千上万件艺术品，这里的雕塑作品尤其令人印象深刻，宽敞的陈列室都设有明显的标志以方便游客参观欣赏。

世界上一些最美丽的兰花品种在印尼都有种植，而要欣赏这些珍稀的兰花最好去"兰花园"，当然，许多当地的暖房也是允许游客参观赏花的，五彩缤纷、形状各异的花朵绝对予人一种奇妙的体验。

奇闻轶事

之一：过去，有钱的城里人都住在雅加达一处叫做"门腾区"的原荷兰人居住区内，然而，如今他们大都选择城南的时髦区域。许多雅加达人住在被称作"坎蓬"的木制或竹制的房子里，遗憾的是，这些房子大都处在贫民区，卫生条件极差，且缺乏饮用水。

之二：18世纪时，雅加达的华人移民曾面临种族迫害。

之三：1945年11月10日，英国军队联合荷兰人在雅加达发动了一场流血袭击，这一天如今被称为"英雄日"，用以纪念印度尼西亚在争取独立的过程中所发生的这一令人震惊的事件。

之四：和其他人口稠密的城市一样，雅加达也面临着严重的空气和噪音污染问题。

为什么雅加达入选50＋1个城市？

来到雅加达，你就来到了充满异域风情的东方，来到了一座由于多种文化混合而显得既奇妙又复杂的城市。在人头攒动的都市里，古老与崭新、东方与西方交融汇集。在经历了无数的战乱和政治纷争之后，雅加达并没有垮掉，相反，它成为印度尼西亚顽强与伟大的佐证。

Twenty-two

Jerusalem, Israel

The Basic Facts

Jerusalem is the capital of Israel, one of the world's oldest cities, and the spiritual center of the Christian, Jewish and Muslim faiths. Britain took control of Jerusalem in World War I and administered it until 1947, when the United Nations voted to divide Palestine into Jewish and Arab states, with Jerusalem being an international city. This touched off violence and warfare between Jews and Palestinian Arabs that continues to this day.

Geography

Jerusalem lies at 31 degrees 46 minutes north latitude and 35 degrees 14 minutes east longitude. The city is located in the Judean Hills in Israel, about 40 miles east of the Mediterranean Sea, and consists of the Old City, West Jerusalem (also called the New City) and East Jerusalem. The West Bank, a highly disputed area inhabited by both Israelis and Palestinians, surrounds the city on three sides.

The Old City is the historical heart of Jerusalem and is enclosed by 40-foot stone walls. West Jerusalem is the most modern part of the city, and East Jerusalem is home to much of the city's Arab population.

Climate

Jerusalem is warm and dry, but winters can bring cold weather thanks to the city's altitude (roughly 2,500 feet). Temperatures average in the mid-50s Fahrenheit in winter and in the upper 80s Fahrenheit in summer. Jerusalem is rare among large world cities in that it has little air pollution.

Government

Jerusalem was deemed a single city under the Israeli government administration when East and West Jerusalem were united in 1967. The city is governed by a 31-member Municipal Council, elected to 5-year terms, and a mayor elected for a 4-year term.

Demographics

Jews comprise nearly three-quarters of Jerusalem's population, and Arabs primarily constitute the minority. Only about 50 percent of Jerusalem Jews were born in Israel; the remainder emigrated from Europe, the Middle East and northern Africa. Most Jews live in West Jerusalem, and most Palestinians live in East Jerusalem, although in recent years some Jews have moved into new East Jerusalem neighborhoods. Jerusalem's population numbers more than 700,000.

Economy

Tourism is the main driving force in Jerusalem's economy; visitors come to see the

以色列耶路撒冷

概况

耶路撒冷是以色列的首都，是世界上最古老的城市之一，也是基督教、犹太教和伊斯兰教的精神中心。第一次世界大战期间，英国人曾占领了耶路撒冷，并控制了这一地区。直到1947年，当时的联合国投票将巴勒斯坦划分为犹太和阿拉伯两部分，耶路撒冷变成了一座国际化城市，这一决定引发了犹太人和巴勒斯坦地区阿拉伯人之间的暴力及武装冲突，并且此类冲突一直延续至今。

一、地理

耶路撒冷位于北纬31°46′，东经35°14′，地处以色列境内的朱迪亚丘陵地带，距离地中海以东大约40英里，由古城、西耶路撒冷（又称"新城"）和东耶路撒冷三部分组成。西岸地区是一片广受争议的地区，它从三面环绕着耶路撒冷市，这里居住的既有以色列人，也有巴勒斯坦人。

二、气候

耶路撒冷的气候温暖而干燥，由于城市的海拔较高（大约2 500英尺），冬季异常寒冷。冬季的平均气温在华氏55度左右，夏季则在华氏87~89度。耶路撒冷几乎没有空气污染，这一点在全球的大城市里非常罕见。

三、政府

1967年，当东西耶路撒冷统一以后，耶路撒冷就被认为只有一个，由以色列政府负责行政管理，市政委员会由31名成员组成，他们通过选举产生，任期5年，而同样由选举产生的市长任期为4年。

四、人口

犹太人占耶路撒冷人口的近3/4，阿拉伯人则属于少数，而耶路撒冷的犹太人只有大约50%出生于以色列，其余都是来自于欧洲、中东和北非地区的移民。大多数犹太人住在西耶路撒冷，而阿拉伯人则主要生活在东耶路撒冷，不过，近些年来，一些犹太人也搬到了新建的东耶路撒冷居民区。耶路撒冷的人口数量总计在70万以上。

五、经济

旅游业是耶路撒冷经济的主要推动力，来到耶路撒冷的游客都是为了看一看这里具

historic and religious sites that dominate the city's architecture.   The population of Jerusalem boomed after Israel became independent in 1948, and construction has become an important part of the city's economy.

There is no heavy industry in Jerusalem,   but there are small factories in West Jerusalem that manufacture chemicals, clothing, machinery, plastics, printing and foods. The city's many handicraft businesses produce pottery, glassware, silver,embroidery and carvings.

The city is accessible by highway and rail lines.   Commuters typically travel by bus,and there are plans for constructing a light-rail system in the future.   Ben Gurion International Airport, named for the first Prime Minister of Israel, is located southeast of nearby Tel Aviv and is the country's largest airport.

The History

Jerusalem has existed in various forms for more than 5,000 years.   In about 1,000 B.C., David conquered the city and declared it the capital of the Kingdom of Israel.Later, after the death of King Solomon,   tribal tensions led to the creation of two separate kingdoms: the northern kingdom of Israel and the southern kingdom called Judah. Jerusalem remained the capital of Judah.

Throughout the centuries, Judah was invaded and conquered by Babylon, Persia and Alexander the Great.   In 63 B.C. the kingdom of Judah became a clientkingdom of the Roman Empire and was renamed Judea.   Rome maintained control of the area for more than 100 years, but in 66 A.D. a group known as the Zealots revolted against Roman rule and seized Judah and Jerusalem. Four years later the Romans, under Titus, destroyed most of the city.   Jerusalem remained uninhabited until 130, when the Romans rebuilt the city and constructed temples to Roman gods.

Christianity became the official religion of the Roman Empire in 325,   and under Emperor Constantine these temples were replaced by Christian churches.   Muslim Arabs took control of Jerusalem in 638 and held it until 1099,   when the First Crusaders conquered the city and decimated its Muslim population.   In 1517, the Ottoman Empire conquered Jerusalem; it would remain under Ottoman control for 400 years.

Jews returned to the city during this period,   and by 1870 constituted the majority population.   Britain took control of Jerusalem during World War I and administered it until 1947,   when the 1947 UN Partition Plan divided Israeli territory into Jewish and Arab states.

The Sights and Sounds

Jerusalem is one of the oldest cities in the world,   and you cannot walk the narrow cobbled streets of the Old City without imagining the scene during biblical times.The rest of Jerusalem,   however,   is modern and utilitarian.   In some areas,   ancient and modern structures lie next to one another on the same street.   The city's main industry is tourism, and tourists from all over the world flock to the holy sites of Islam, Christianity and Judaism.

The Old City is roughly a third of a mile square and perfect for walking.   In fact,the narrow streets make most automobile travel impossible.   The Old City Gates are of particular interest,   as well as the area's four major neighborhoods: Muslim,Jewish, Christian and Armenian.

有历史意义和宗教色彩的建筑。1948年,以色列独立之后,耶路撒冷的人口迅速增长,因此,城市建设成为经济生活的一个重要组成部分。

虽然在耶路撒冷没有重工业,但是在西耶路撒冷地区,有一些小型工厂加工生产化学制品、服装、机械、塑料、印刷和食品等。城里的许多手工艺商行生产陶器、玻璃器皿、银器、刺绣和雕刻品等。

耶路撒冷的交通主要靠公路和铁路,城里人上下班一般是乘坐公交车,未来城市建设规划是建设轻轨交通系统。本—古里安国际机场是根据以色列第一位总理的名字命名的,机场位于城市附近的特拉维夫港东南,是以色列最大的机场。

光影流金

耶路撒冷已经以不同的形式存在于这个地球上超过5 000年了。在公元前大约1 000年时,大卫征服了这座城市,并宣布它为以色列王国的首都。之后,在所罗门国王死后,部落矛盾导致这一地区分裂为两个独立的王国:以色列北部王国和被称为"犹大"的以色列南部王国,耶路撒冷仍然是犹大王国的都城。

在接下来的几个世纪里,犹大王国先后被入侵的巴比伦、波斯以及亚历山大大帝所征服占领。公元前63年,犹大王国成为受罗马帝国保护的一个王国,并更名为朱迪亚。罗马人对这一地区的控制持续了100多年。公元66年,一群名为吉拉德的宗教狂热分子反抗罗马统治,占领了犹大和耶路撒冷。4年后,罗马人在提图斯的率领下,摧毁了城市的大部分地区,此后,耶路撒冷变成了无人居住区。公元130年,罗马人重建了这座城市,盖起了供奉罗马诸神的庙宇。

325年,基督教成为罗马帝国的正式宗教,在国王君士坦丁统治时期,这些庙宇变成了基督教的教堂。638年信奉伊斯兰教的阿拉伯人取得了对耶路撒冷的控制权,并将这种权力保持到1099年,那一年,第一批十字军攻占了这座城市,并屠杀了大批伊斯兰教信徒。1517年,奥斯曼帝国征服了耶路撒冷,并统治了这一地区长达400年。

在奥斯曼帝国统治期间,犹太人重新回到这座城市。到了1870年,犹太人已经成为城市人口的绝大多数。第一次世界大战时期,英国人控制了耶路撒冷,直到1947年之前,掌管该地区的始终是英国人。1947年,联合国颁布的分割计划将以色列的领土划分成犹太和阿拉伯两部分,进而宣告了英国统治的结束。

声光景点

耶路撒冷是世界上最古老的城市之一,当你走在古城区狭窄的用大卵石铺成的街道上时,不可能不联想到那些圣经时代的故事。然而,耶路撒冷其余的部分却是现代而功利的。在有些地区,古代与现代的建筑会肩并肩出现在同一条街道上。耶路撒冷的主要经济行业是旅游业,每年,成群结队的游客从世界各地来到这座伊斯兰教、基督教和犹太教的圣地。

耶路撒冷古城区的面积在0.33平方英里左右,非常适合步行,事实上,大多数汽车在这些狭窄的街道上也根本无法通行。许多人对古城的大门都特别感兴趣,此外,这里还有四个主要的街区:分别隶属于伊斯兰教徒、犹太人、基督教徒和亚美尼亚人。

The Western Wall, also called the Wailing Wall, it is the only surviving section of the Second Temple. The wall is a holy place for Jews, who visit the wall to mourn the loss of their sacred shrine. The Church of the Holy Sepulchre is regarded by biblical scholars as the site of Golgotha, where Jesus is believed to have been crucified.

The Temple Mount is an area of the Old City sacred both to Jews and Muslims.Jews believe that ancient temples were built here, and Muslims believe that Muhammad ascended to heaven at the site of the Dome of the Rock.

The Mount of Olives is believed to be the site at which Jesus last saw his disciples before ascending to heaven. Another common pilgrimage site is the Via Dolorosa,a street in the Old City through which Jesus is thought to have carried the cross.The Via Dolorosa ends at Golgotha (the Place of the Skull, or Calvary), where Jesus is said to have been crucified.

While in Jerusalem, many tourists visit Yad Vashem, Israel's memorial to the victims of the Holocaust and the largest museum of its kind in the world. The Citadel (Tower of David) Museum is something of a misnomer. This site is believed to be a former palace of King David, but this is probably not the case. Nevertheless,the museum contains an extensive collection detailing the history of Jerusalem.

The Garden of Gethsemane is the site where biblical scholars believe Jesus was betrayed by Judas. There is a church here, as well as olive trees that date back thousands of years.

The Trivia

Fact: Jerusalem is a holy city Jews, Christians and Muslims. These groups,especially the Jews and Muslims, have vied for control of the Temple Mount and continue to do so.

Fact: Jerusalem is a union of several ancient cities: the Old City, which occupies most of Biblical Jerusalem; West Jerusalem, which is the most modern part of the city; and East Jerusalem, where most of Jerusalem's Arabs reside.

Fact: According to tradition the Prophet Muhammad selected Jerusalem as the qibla, towards which the Muslims should face during prayer. Muhammad later declared Mecca the focus of prayer so as to symbolize the independence of Islam.

Fact: Jewish immigration to Jerusalem increased rapidly in the 1920s and 1930s, fueled both by Nazi persecution in Europe and by a growing Zionist movement that aimed to create a Jewish homeland in Palestine. It was during this time that many Jewish neighborhoods were established, primarily in West Jerusalem.

Why Jerusalem Is a 50 plus one City

If there is any city that is complicated by history, politics and religion, it is Jerusalem. That said, this is the very reason why the city is one of the greatest in the world. Although other large cities have more modern, sophisticated sights and sounds, people visit Jerusalem for the rich cultural and religious heritage that is its lifeblood.

西墙,又被称为"哭墙",是第二神殿唯一残存下来的部分。对于犹太人来说,这堵墙是一处圣地,人们来到此墙为他们失去的圣所而哀悼。圣墓大教堂被圣经学者们认为是"各各他"的遗址,也就是耶稣被钉死在十字架上的地方。

神殿山是位于古城区的一个地方,对于犹太人和穆斯林来说都是神圣之所,犹太人相信古代的神庙都建在这里,而穆斯林信徒则相信穆罕默德就是在磐石圆顶清真寺升天的。

橄榄山据称是耶稣在升入天堂之前,最后一次会见他的门徒的地方。另外一处公共朝圣的地方名叫"苦路",这是位于古城区的一条街,据说耶稣就是背负着十字架经过这里的,"苦路"的尽头就是"各各他"(骷髅地或髑髅地),据称耶稣就是在这里殉难的。

在耶路撒冷,许多游客还会参观犹太大屠杀纪念馆,即以色列为大屠杀遇难者所建立的纪念馆,也是世界上此类博物馆中最大的一个。城堡(大卫之塔)博物馆有一点名不副实,虽然,有人相信这里曾是国王大卫以前的一个皇宫,但或许这并不符合事实,但不管怎样,这座博物馆里收藏了大量关于耶路撒冷历史的详细资料。

一些圣经学者相信,客西马尼(蒙难地)花园是耶稣被犹大出卖的地方,这里有一座教堂,还有树龄已达上千年的橄榄树。

奇闻轶事

之一:耶路撒冷无论对犹太人、基督徒还是穆斯林来说都是一座圣城,这些持不同信仰的人们,尤其是犹太人和穆斯林,为了拥有对神殿山的控制权而长期争斗,直至今天。

之二:耶路撒冷是几座古代城池的联合体,其中,古城部分承载着圣经中关于耶路撒冷的大部分内容,西耶路撒冷展示的是城市最现代化的部分,东耶路撒冷则是大多数阿拉伯人居住的地方。

之三:根据伊斯兰教的传统,先知穆罕默德选择耶路撒冷作为教徒礼拜的方向,也就是说,穆斯林教徒在祈祷时应该面对的方向,后来,穆罕默德宣布麦加为朝圣的中心,用以象征伊斯兰教的独立。

之四:20世纪20年代至30年代间,迁往耶路撒冷的犹太人数量迅速增长,这一方面是由于纳粹在欧洲对犹太人的迫害,另一方面则是因为当时发展迅速的犹太复国主义运动,其目的主要是在耶路撒冷创建一个犹太人的家园,正是在这一时期,许多犹太人社区建立起来,其中大部分都位于西耶路撒冷。

为什么耶路撒冷入选50 + 1个城市?

如果说世界上有一座城市,因其历史、政治和宗教而异常复杂,那一定是耶路撒冷。而这,也正是为什么它能够成为世界上最伟大的城市之一的原因。尽管其他大城市的景点可能更为现代、更为发达,但是,耶路撒冷吸引游客的是其丰富的文化和宗教遗产,这些才是耶路撒冷的生命血脉。

Twenty-three

Johannesburg, South Africa

The Basic Facts

Johannesburg is the largest city in South Africa and the capital Gauteng Province. Some of the earliest human fossils were discovered in this region. Following the demise of the apartheid government in 1994, Johannesburg has been moving toward a new era of racial tolerance.

Geography

Johannesburg lies at 26 degrees 8 minutes south latitude and 27 degrees 54 minutes east longitude. The city is located in Gauteng Province in northeastern South Africa. Johannesburg lies within the Witwatersrand, a 60-mile-long mountain range that runs through Gauteng. The Johannesburg metropolitan area includes the communities of Midrand, Randburg, Roodepoort, Sandton, Alexandra, Ennerdale, Lenasia and Soweto.

Climate

Johannesburg lies roughly 5,700 feet above sea level. The climate is sunny, mild and dry. Annual temperatures range from the mid-60s Fahrenheit in winter to the upper 70s Fahrenheit during the summer. Note that because South Africa lies south of the equator, the winter and summer months are opposite from those in the northern hemisphere. Thus, winter occurs between June and August and summer occurs between December and February.

Government

Johannesburg's first post-apartheid City Council, established in 1995, subdivided the city into four regions. Each region's authorities have substantial autonomous authority, yet the City Council is governed by a central metropolitan council.

Johannesburg's financial situation had fallen into disarray by 1999; in that year a city manager was appointed to reorganize the city's finances. This manager, together with the Municipal Council, coordinated plans for Igoli 2002, a blueprint to bring Johannesburg out of insolvency and into financial surplus.

Demographics

Black Africans are the majority group in Johannesburg, comprising 73 percent of the population; Caucasians, Colored South Africans (i.e., mixed racial) and Asians make up the remainder. Residents primarily speak Nguni or Sotho; one-quarter speak either English or Afrikaans (a derivation of Dutch). More than 3.2 million residents live in Johannesburg.

Economy

Johannesburg is South Africa's financial hub and the country's economic center. Although gold mining was once the city's main industry, the mines are no longer in operation. Even so, the headquarters of many mining companies are still located here.

南非约翰内斯堡

概况

约翰内斯堡是南非最大的城市，是豪登省的省府。在这一地区，人们发现了人类最早期的化石。1994年，伴随着种族隔离制度的消亡，约翰内斯堡已经迈入了一段民族互谅互让的崭新时期。

一、地理

约翰内斯堡位于南纬26°8′，东经27°54′，地处南非东北部的豪登省境内，同时，约翰内斯堡还处在连绵60英里的威特沃特斯兰德山脉地区。约翰内斯堡大市范围包括梅德兰、兰德堡、路德堡、山德顿、亚历山德拉、恩内德尔、里纳沙和索韦托8个自治区。

二、气候

约翰内斯堡的海拔高度在5 700英尺左右，日照充足，气候温和干燥。年均气温在冬季的华氏65度至夏季的华氏77~79度。值得注意的是，约翰内斯堡位于赤道以南，因此冬夏两季的月份与北半球地区正好相反，冬季出现在6月~8月，夏季则出现在12月~2月。

三、政府

成立于1995年的约翰内斯堡首个后种族隔离时期的市政委员会，将城市进一步划分为4个区。虽然每个区的地方当局享有相当大的自治权利，但是市政委员会由一个大市中央委员会统一管理。

到了1999年，约翰内斯堡的财政状况陷入混乱，于是，当年市政当局任命了一名财务总管来重新整合政府的财政，这位总管和市政委员会一起整理出了2002年"艾格利"调整计划，这是一份引导约翰内斯堡走出资不抵债的困境，进而走向财政结余的蓝图。

四、人口

在约翰内斯堡，非洲黑人占了人口的大多数，约为73%，其余为白人、有色人种(混血人种)以及亚洲人。居民主要讲努尼语或索托语，有1/4的人口讲英语或南非荷兰语(荷兰语的派生语)，生活在约翰内斯堡的居民总数超过320万。

五、经济

约翰内斯堡是南非的金融枢纽和经济中心，虽然金矿曾是这座城市的主要工业，但是现在这些金矿已经停止生产。即便如此，许多采矿公司的总部仍然设在约翰内斯堡，黄金、铀矿、白银和钻石始终是约翰内斯堡经济的重要组成部分。此外，其他工业还包括钢

Gold, uranium, silver and diamonds remain an important part of Johannesburg's economy; however; other industries include steel and cement manufacturing.

Despite the city's economic advances, nearly 40 percent of Johannesburg's residents are chronically unemployed.

The History

In the 1820s the Ndebele leader Mzilikazi invaded the region surrounding Johannesburg. Mzilikazi was defeated in 1837, allowing Boers (white farmers from the Cape region) to establish settlements in the region.

After the Boer War of 1880, the British, who had annexed the Transvaal, allowed the settlers more independence. The region's fortunes changed dramatically in 1886, when one of the world's largest gold deposits was discovered on the Witwatersrand. Johannesburg was founded that year as a result of the gold rush and became a free-wheeling mining town. The city was named after Johann Rissik,the city's first surveyor-general, and Christiaan Johannes Joubert, the original vice president of the Transvaal republic.

An influx of enterprising foreigners and nearby black laborers caused the area's population to grow rapidly after the discovery of the Witwatersrand gold deposit.Over time Johannesburg evolved into a center of commerce and government.

Apartheid, South Africa's legalized form of segregation, was established in 1948 and continued into the early 1990s. Johannesburg became the flashpoint for resistance among Black and Colored Africans, who rebelled against the disparity inherent in the system. Many countries throughout the world also objected to apartheid and imposed economic sanctions on South Africa.

Johannesburg continued to thrive, but change was inevitable, especially after the 1990 release of anti-apartheid activist Nelson Mandela from prison. Mandela became the first president of South Africa after the abolition of apartheid in 1994. Since that time, South Africa's economy and international reputation have significantly improved.

The Sights and Sounds

Johannesburg is a modern city with a long history. Now that the specter of apartheid is behind it, the city is set for new growth and endless potential. Tourists come to Johannesburg to see its host of museums, art galleries, clubs, restaurants and nightlife.

The Apartheid Museum offers a multimedia glimpse into the city's apartheid era.This museum, which opened in 2001, contains a number of audio and video exhibits created by a series of South African filmmakers, historians and designers.

Visit the Origins Centre for a fascinating history of humanity as well as an exhibit on genetic testing and ancestral research. The collection houses excellent examples of early human skeletons; you can also visit the archeological digs currently underway in South Africa.

The Mandela Family Museum is located in Soweto, a poor neighboring township of Johannesburg. The modest former home of Nelson Mandela, the museum's collection tells the story of Mandela's life and imprisonment, as well as the history of apartheid.

Constitution Hill is a former prison containing multimedia exhibits describing the treatment of once-incarcerated criminals. The museum is one of Johannesburg's newest historical landmarks and is near the city courts, where visitors may watch trials and other court proceedings.

Johannesburg Art Gallery is the largest of its kind in sub-Saharan Africa. The collection

铁和水泥生产。

尽管约翰内斯堡的经济发展良好,但是有近40%的居民长期处于失业状态。

光影流金

19世纪20年代,恩德比利族领袖兹利卡兹入侵了约翰内斯堡附近地区,1837年兹利卡兹战败,布尔人(来自开普地区的白人农民)得到允许,在这一地区建立了殖民地。

1880年布尔战争之后,吞并了德兰士瓦省的英国人赋予了殖民者更大的自由。1886年,当世界上最大的金矿之一在威特沃特斯兰德被发现以后,这一地区的财富急剧增加,而淘金热的结果就是在这一年建立了约翰内斯堡市,并且这里还成为不受约束的采矿大镇。这座城市的名字来源于它的第一任总监督官约翰·内斯克,以及德兰士瓦省的原副省长克里斯蒂安·约翰·儒贝尔的名字。

在威特沃特斯兰德金矿储备被发现之后,大批的外国企业家和附近的黑人劳工涌入这一地区,从而造成人口的迅速增长,在此期间,约翰内斯堡市也逐步发展成为一个商业和政府的中心。

种族隔离制度,作为南非合法化的分裂形式,是1948年建立起来的,并且一直持续到20世纪90年代早期。由于不满于此种制度所固有的不平等,约翰内斯堡市的黑人及有色非洲人的反抗运动一触即发。此外,世界各地的许多国家也纷纷反对这种种族隔离制度,并对南非实行了经济制裁。

尽管约翰内斯堡仍在繁荣发展,但是,变化也是不可避免的,尤其是1990年,反对种族隔离制的激进分子纳尔逊·曼德拉被释放出狱,并于1994年成为种族隔离制废除后南非的第一任总统。从那以后,南非的经济以及国际声誉显著提高。

声光景点

约翰内斯堡是一座历史悠久的现代化城市,如今,甩掉了种族隔离的阴影,这座城市正进入新的成长时期,并且显示出无穷的潜力。来到约翰内斯堡,游客要么希望参观一下这里大量的博物馆和美术馆,要么希望享受一下这里的夜总会、餐厅和夜生活。

种族隔离博物馆以多媒体的方式为游客提供了种族隔离时期这座城市的缩影,这座开放于2001年的博物馆拥有许多由南非电影工作者、历史学家以及设计师所创作的系列视听展品。

参观一下人类起源中心吧,这里既可以学到关于人类历史的精彩知识,还可以看到基因测试以及血统研究方面的展览,这里的展品包括大量完美的早期人类的骨骼标本,除此以外,你还可以参观目前南非正在进行中的考古挖掘。

曼德拉家族博物馆位于索韦托,这是约翰内斯堡市内一处贫穷的居民区,作为纳尔逊·曼德拉曾经生活过的家,这座简陋的博物馆里收藏的东西,向我们讲述的也是关于曼德拉的家庭、狱中生活以及种族隔离制度历史的故事。

宪法山是过去的一个监狱,里面借助声光效果向游客介绍曾经在此关押的犯人所遭受的待遇,这座博物馆是约翰内斯堡最新的地标之一,位于城市法庭附近,因此,游客还可以到法庭旁听审判,或者了解其他一些法律程序。

约翰内斯堡美术馆是沙哈拉以南非洲地区最大的美术馆,其藏品不仅包括南非本土

not only includes South African works of art, but also those of international artists such as Picasso, Monet and Degas. The three-story building has 15 exhibit halls and sculpture gardens in adjoining Joubert Park.

AECI Dynamite Factory Museum exhibits the history of explosives used in Johannesburg's mining industry. Mining companies use dynamite to penetrate the rock that covered the rich diamond lodes in the Johannesburg area.

A trip to South Africa would be incomplete without a trip to one of the wild game reserves that surround the city. Visitors can hike and picnic in certain areas, and can ride trucks through the park. Common sights include gazelles, lions, hippos and wild dogs.

Johannesburg's current mining operations center on diamond extraction; however,the natural resource originally mined here was gold. Gold Reef City is a theme park with exhibits on the discovery, mining, and use of this important metallic element. The park recreates Johannesburg as it looked when gold was discovered there.

Soweto—a name derived from South Western Townships—is the site of primarily Black African ghettos near Johannesburg. Residents of these townships engaged in uprisings that eventually led to the demise of apartheid. Experts strongly recommend that visitors to this area take guided tours.

Erikson's Diamond Centre houses exhibits on the art of diamond cutting, as well as shops where visitors may purchase diamonds and have them made into jewelry.

The Trivia

Fact: South Africa recognizes 11 official languages. Most Johannesburg locals do speak English, but they have their own idiomatic expressions that may perplex tourists.

Fact: There are more than six million trees in the metropolitan area of Johannesburg. The summer and winter months are reversed due to South Africa's location south of the equator. Although the area is usually dry, frequent rainstorms occur in summer; visitors are advised to bring raingear.

Fact: Guateng, the province in which Johannesburg lies, literally means Place of Gold. Guateng is an apt name for this area in which a significant gold deposit was discovered in the 19th century.

Fact: The Johannesburg Fort, built shortly after the city's founding in 1886, was constructed not as a defense against invaders, but as a means to control the area's early mining population. The fort became a prison after the Anglo-Boer War of 1899 to 1902. The prison is now closed, and the site is being converted into the new home of South Africa's Constitutional Court.

Fact: Johannesburg's boundaries expanded after apartheid to include surrounding communities of poor Black Africans under the old system these areas were separately administered. The city's current boundaries were finalized in 2000.

Fact: South Africa is the largest diamond producer in the world and is the home of the DeBeers diamond empire.

Why Johannesburg Is a 50 plus one City

Despite a troubled past, Johannesburg is a city of multiple cultures. European and African cultures now exist side by side, and that fact alone has made Johannesburg a city with great cultural importance.

的艺术品，还包括诸如毕加索、莫奈和德加等国际大师的作品。这座三层楼的建筑内拥有15个展厅，在毗邻的儒贝尔公园内还有几个雕塑园。

AECI炸药工厂博物馆展示的是约翰内斯堡采矿业所使用过的爆炸物的历史，采矿公司利用甘油炸药来穿透岩石，以找到那些被岩石所包裹的约翰内斯堡地区丰富的钻石矿藏。

来到约翰内斯堡，如果不去参观一下城市周边的某个野生动物保护区，你的行程就不算完美，在某些区域，游客可以步行或野餐，还可以乘坐卡车在公园内转一圈，常见的野生动物包括瞪羚、狮子、河马和野犬等。

尽管目前约翰内斯堡的采矿工业以钻石提取为主，但是，最初这里开采的自然资源却是黄金，"金礁城"是一个主题公园，主要展示这一重要金属元素的发现、开采和使用过程，公园将黄金发现以后约翰内斯堡的淘金热潮重新展现在人们面前。

索韦托 —— 一个源于西南部黑人居住区的名字 —— 最初是约翰内斯堡附近非洲黑人的聚居区，正是由于这一地区居民的反抗暴乱，才最终导致了种族隔离制度的灭亡。旅行专家强烈建议大家，到这一地区参观时必须有导游引导。

艾里克森的钻石中心主要向游客介绍钻石的切割工艺，此外，游客还可以在这里的商店购买钻石，并现场加工成首饰。

奇闻轶事

之一：在南非，已获认可的官方语言达11种之多，虽然大多数约翰内斯堡的居民都讲英语，但是他们所特有的一些表达方式却可能令游客迷惑不解。

之二：在约翰内斯堡大市范围，有600多万种树木。由于南非位于赤道以南，冬夏两季的月份与北半球相反，虽然气候通常来说比较干燥，但是在夏季常会出现暴雨，因此建议游客要带好雨具。

之三：约翰内斯堡所属的豪登省，其字面意思是"黄金之地"，19世纪时，在这里发现了一个储量相当大的金矿，因此，"豪登"这个名字也就非常贴切了。

之四：约翰内斯堡要塞修建于这座城市建立不久之后的1886年，它的修建并非为了抵御外敌入侵，而是早期为了控制淘金人口所采取的手段。英国人与布尔人之间于1899~1902年所进行的战争结束之后，这座要塞变成了监狱。如今，监狱也关闭了，这里正被改造成为新的南非宪法法庭所在地。

之五：种族隔离制度废除后，约翰内斯堡市扩大了城市的范围，将周边贫困的原先在旧制度下行政独立的黑非洲人社区也包括了进来，城市目前的区划是于2000年最终确定的。

之六：南非是世界上最大的钻石生产者，是德比尔斯钻石王国的总部。

为什么约翰内斯堡入选50＋1个城市？

尽管有着不堪的过去，约翰内斯堡仍是一座拥有多元文化的城市，今天，欧洲文化与非洲文化在此交融并存，仅这一点就足以令它成为一座伟大的文化重镇。

Twenty-four

Las Vegas, United States

The Basic Facts

Las Vegas is famously known as Sin City; gambling, resorts, shows and other activities have given the city an anything goes reputation. It is also fast becoming a popular convention center. The city lost some of its luster in the 1970s and early 1980s, but was reborn in the 1990s as luxurious mega-resorts were constructed and the city recast itself as a family tourist center. The city's current rapid growth contributes to problems such as high water usage, crowded schools and urban sprawl. Most visitors, however, are not aware of these problems as they crowd the Las Vegas casinos, showplaces and wedding chapels.

Geography

Las Vegas lies at 36 degrees 12 minutes north latitude and 115 degrees 10 minutes west longitude. This was a grassland area when the city was incorporated in 1911—its name is derived from vegas, or meadows in Spanish—although it is in now in the midst of the Mojave Desert.

Las Vegas is the county seat of Clark County, and the metropolitan area includes Nye County in Nevada and Mohave County in Arizona. Nearly half of the urban area referred to as Las Vegas (including Fremont Street and the Las Vegas Strip) lie outside the actual city limits.

Climate

For most of the year, Las Vegas has a warm and dry climate; any significant rainfall occurs in the winter months. Winter temperatures average in the lower 60s Fahrenheit, but summer temperatures often exceed 100 degrees Fahrenheit.Many say that it is not the heat; it is the humidity. Indeed, Las Vegas' low humidity makes the brutally hot summers somewhat more bearable than less arid portions of the country.

Government

Las Vegas is run by a city council and city manager. The mayor and six council members are elected to 6-year terms and appoint a city manager to administer policies and city operations. Clark County is governed by seven commissioners who are elected to 4-year terms, and they appoint a county manager with similar administrative duties.

Demographics

Nearly 70 percent of Las Vegas residents are Caucasian; the remainder are African-Americans, Latinos, Native Americans and Asians. The city has more than 500,000 residents, although the population has been growing rapidly since the mid-1990s.

Most Las Vegas residents are not native to the area, but come from throughout the country and around the world. The city's recent economic boom is responsible for its significant population growth.

美国拉斯维加斯

概况

拉斯维加斯以"罪恶之城"而著称,赌博、度假、表演以及其他一些活动,使得这座城市有了一个"干什么都行"的名声。此外,它正迅速成为一个受人欢迎的会议中心。尽管20世纪70年代和80年代初,这座城市一度失去一些光彩,但是到了90年代,随着豪华超大型度假村的修建,以及城市作为家庭度假中心地位的确立,拉斯维加斯又重新焕发青春。目前,城市由于发展迅速,也产生了一些问题,例如,用水量过大、学校人数过多、城市扩张过乱等。不过,当游客涌入拉斯维加斯的赌场、表演场以及婚礼小教堂时,他们中的大多数并不会意识到这些问题。

一、地理

拉斯维加斯位于北纬36°12′,西经115°10′。1911年,当这座城市并入美国时,这里还是一片草原地区 —— 它的名字来源于"维加斯",即西班牙语中的"低湿草地"的意思 —— 尽管今天它是处于莫哈维沙漠的中部地区。

拉斯维加斯是克拉克县政府所在地,大市范围包括内华达州的奈县和亚利桑那州的莫哈维县。事实上,占城市面积近一半的被称为拉斯维加斯的地方(包括弗里蒙特大街和拉斯维加斯大道)是位于城市范围之外的。

二、气候

一年中的大部分时间,拉斯维加斯的气候都是温暖而干燥的,下雨多集中在冬季月份。虽然冬天气温平均在华氏61~63度,但是夏季气温经常达到华氏100度以上。许多人认为温度并不重要,湿度才是关键的,的确,拉斯维加斯的低湿度使得其酷热的夏天比起美国其他一些潮湿的地区来说,相对更容易忍受。

三、政府

拉斯维加斯政府由一个市政委员会和一个市政执行官负责管理,市长及6个市政委员会成员通过选举产生,任期6年,同时,由他们任命一位市政执行官来负责各项政策的执行以及市政管理。克拉克县由7位选举产生的委员负责,他们任期4年,并负责推选一位市政执行官来承担类似的行政职责。

四、人口

拉斯维加斯近70%的居民属于白种人,其余为非洲裔美国人、拉丁美洲人、印第安人及亚洲人。全市共有50多万人口,不过,自从20世纪90年代以来,城市人口一直在快速增长。

大多数拉斯维加斯居民并不是土生土长的当地人,而是来自世界各地或者美国其他地区,而近些年来,城市经济的迅速增长正是造成人口显著增多的原因。

Economy

Las Vegas' economy is driven primarily by tourism and conventions. The Las Vegas Convention Center is the largest single-level convention center in the United States, and more than three million people attend conventions in Las Vegas every year.

While most Las Vegas residents are employed in the service industry, the federal government is also a major employer. Nellis Air Force Base and Range are located nearby, and the Nevada Test Site is located 65 miles northwest of the city.

The History

In 1855 Mormons settled the surrounding area to serve as a stopover for travelers between Salt Lake City and San Bernardino. The city was established in 1905, when the San Pedro, Los Angeles and Salt Lake Railroad company auctioned off its lands. The town's population grew to 1,000 in 1910, and was incorporated as a city in 1911. Nevada legalized gambling in 1931, but in 1935 construction began on a federal project that would transform the region. Hoover Dam, a 726-foot-high concrete arch-gravity dam on the Colorado River, was built over 5 years by more than 21,000 workers. These workers flocked to Las Vegas in their off hours and money began to pour in to the city's coffers. The Flamingo Hotel, the first large casino, opened in 1946 and a steady succession of others followed.

Fremont Street and the Strip became the city's two major recreational areas. The city developed rapidly during the 1950s and 1960s and organized crime held sway over many of the casino hotels. Today, Las Vegas is a tourist mecca and has recreated itself—for the most part—as a family-oriented attraction.

The Sights and Sounds

The sights and sounds of Las Vegas cannot be described in a few words. Unlike other world cities, the history, architecture and fine arts do not attract visitors;tourists come for fun, gambling, live shows, dining, and just about every other possible recreation. There is something for everyone in Las Vegas.

Although Las Vegas is a relatively small city, distances are deceptive on Fremont Street and the Strip because the hotels and casinos are simply enormous. A stroll to the next building often takes 10 or 15 minutes. The Strip is more popular than the downtown area, but several points of interest continue to attract visitors to the latter. The most famous of these is the Fremont Street Experience, a pedestrian mall that is enclosed by a huge awning illuminated by millions of lights. The Experience is said to be the most brightly-lit area in the world. Another attraction is the Viva Vision, a 90-foot-tall video display—the largest in the world—that screens state-of-the art audiovisual shows nightly. The Viva Vision cost $17 million to build,and its nightly operating cost must be immeasurable.

One of the classic casinos downtown is the Golden Nugget, named for the 60-pound gold nugget on display in the hotel lobby. The property opened in 1946 and is currently undergoing renovations to attract visitors otherwise drawn to the Strip.

Only Las Vegas would house the Neon Museum, whose mission is to preserve and display neon signs from the 1940s to the present. The museum runs an outdoor walking tour of some of its pieces that have been restored as public art. The Museum opened its doors in 1996 when the world-famous Hacienda Horse and Rider sign was installed at the

五、经济

拉斯维加斯的经济主要由旅游业和会议业来推动，拉斯维加斯会议中心是美国最大的单层会议中心，每年有300多万人来到拉斯维加斯参加各种会议。

拉斯维加斯的大多数居民从事服务行业，同时，联邦政府也是一个大的雇主。内利斯空军基地和试射场就位于城市附近，而内华达测试基地则在距离城市西北大约65英里的地方。

光影流金

1855年，摩门教教徒在今天拉斯维加斯附近地区建立起了殖民地，作为旅行者在盐湖城和圣贝纳迪诺市之间的中途停留地。1905年，当圣皮得罗、洛杉矶和盐湖铁路公司通过拍卖处理掉其所有的土地之后，拉斯维加斯正式建立。1910年，城镇人口增加到1 000人，并于1911年合并建立城市。尽管内华达州于1931年就已经将赌博合法化，但是，1935年开始动工的一项工程最终彻底改变了这一地区，这项名为"胡佛水坝"的联邦建设工程，是在卡罗拉多河上建造一座高达726英尺的混凝土拱形重力坝，该工程耗时5年，共有21 000多名工人参与了建设，而这些工人在闲暇之余纷纷涌入拉斯维加斯市，与此同时，金钱也便源源不断地涌入这座城市的金库。佛拉明戈（火烈鸟）酒店作为拉斯维加斯第一家大型赌场于1946年开业，以后，其他类似的赌场也相继出现。

弗里蒙特大街和"长街"（拉斯维加斯大道）是这座城市里两大主要的娱乐区。20世纪五六十年代，在城市迅速发展的同时，一些有组织的犯罪团体曾控制了许多赌场酒店。今天，拉斯维加斯不仅是一个旅游胜地，而且，在很大程度上，还是居家旅游的理想之所。

声光景点

拉斯维加斯的景点是很难用几个字描述清楚的，与世界上其他城市不同的是，这座城市吸引游客的并不是它的历史、建筑和艺术，游客们来此就是为了玩、为了赌博、为了现场表演、为了美食，为了其他任何可能的娱乐活动。在拉斯维加斯，无论是谁，都能找到他所喜欢的东西。

虽然拉斯维加斯是个相对比较小的城市，但是，在弗里蒙特大街和"长街"却很容易迷路，因为这里的酒店和赌场实在是太大了，从一幢大厦走到另一栋大楼常常需要10或15分钟。尽管"长街"（拉斯维加斯大道）比起市中心地区更受游客喜爱，但是，在后一地区还是有几处吸引人的景点。其中最著名的就是"弗里蒙特街大体验"，这是一个由巨大的顶棚围合起来的步行街，里面华灯璀璨。据说，这处体验区是世界上灯光最为明亮的步行街。另外一处景点名为"万岁！视觉！"，是一个高90英尺的影像展示——全球最大——屏幕上每晚上映最新的视听节目，这一声光秀的建成耗资1 700万美元，而每晚放映所需的费用无疑更是难以计算。

市中心最经典的赌场之一是金块酒店，这一名称源自酒店大堂所陈列的重达60磅的金块，这家1946年开张的赌场目前正在整修，以唤回那些可能被"长街"所吸引走的顾客。

只有拉斯维加斯才会拥有霓虹博物馆，它的使命就是保存并展出从20世纪40年代至今的霓虹灯箱，博物馆经营着一项户外步行游项目，引导游客参观一些业已修复好的公众艺术品，这家博物馆是1996年对外开放的，当时正巧世界著名的哈先达赛马及骑手

corner of Fremont Street Experience and Las Vegas Boulevard.

The Stratosphere Tower, at 1,149 feet, is the tallest building west of the Mississippi River. Visitors can get a terrific view of the surrounding area from the tower's observation deck. The Top of the World restaurant, 800 feet up, revolves in a complete circle in 80 minutes. The tower's three thrill rides, however, are the main attraction. These rides, at the very top of the tower, are definitely not for the faint of heart.

Nothing says Las Vegas more than the four-mile stretch of Las Vegas Boulevard known as the Strip. This remarkable area regularly reinvents itself to change with the times. Casino Hotels are razed and rebuilt when they are no longer large enough, fancy enough, or popular enough to appeal to visitors. Among the bestknown properties are:

·Bellagio—the second largest casino in Las Vegas;
·Caesar's Palace—an opulent Roman-themed casino;
·Circus Circus—a vintage casino hotel with a circus motif;
·Flamingo—built in 1946 by the infamous gangster Bugsy Siegel;
·Luxor—with visions of ancient Egypt;
·MGM Grand—a property with a Hollywood flavor;
·Mirage—with a South Seas atmosphere; and
·Tropicana—a lush, tropical oasis with a popular swimming pool.

No visit to the city is complete without a side trip to Hoover Dam and Lake Mead. The Hoover Dam tamed the Colorado River to harvest hydro-electric power. The dam's construction resulted in Lake Mead, the largest man-made lake in the western hemisphere and a playground for boaters, fishing enthusiasts and swimmers from around the world.

The Trivia

Fact: Ironically, the area that became Sin City was originally settled by Mormons.

Fact: The wealthy eccentric Howard Hughes came to Las Vegas in 1966 and purchased several casino hotels; transactions that effectively ended mob control over the area. While living in Las Vegas, Hughes was a recluse who never left his residence on the ninth floor of the Desert Inn.

Fact: The city's economy is partly driven by the United States government. Before the Nuclear Test Ban Treaty was implemented, Las Vegas residents would regularly see mushroom clouds rise from the desert.

Fact: There are no clocks in casinos, an intentional decision designed to encourage gamblers and other patrons to stay and spend their money.

Why Las Vegas Is a 50 plus one City

Las Vegas is a modern marvel, exuding excess like no other place in the world. The city is fun and entertaining: the sinful capital of the world. Most everyone wants to visit Las Vegas at least once, and for good reason.

的灯箱广告被安装在弗里蒙特体验街和拉斯维加斯林荫大道的拐角。

高1149英尺的云霄塔是密西西比河以西地区最高的建筑,从塔顶的观景台望下去,四周景致一览无余。位于云霄塔800英尺处的"世界之巅"餐厅每80分钟旋转一圈。不过,塔上的3个惊险刺激的游乐设施才是真正吸引人的地方,这些设在云霄塔顶的项目肯定不是为那些心脏脆弱的人准备的。

什么都不如"长街"这条绵延4英里的拉斯维加斯林荫大道更能说明这座城市的了,这条诱人的大街随着岁月的流逝会定期地进行改造,每当一些赌场酒店显得不够宽敞、不够漂亮、不够诱人的时候,它们就会被拆除重建,其中最著名的赌场酒店有以下这些:

- 百乐宫 —— 拉斯维加斯第二大赌场
- 恺撒宫 —— 一座奢华的罗马风格的赌场
- 马戏马戏 —— 一家以马戏团基调为主的老式赌场酒店
- 弗拉明戈(火烈鸟) —— 1946年由臭名昭著的黑帮分子毕斯·西格尔修建
- 卢克索(金字塔) —— 古埃及的景致
- 大米高梅 —— 好莱坞风格的酒店
- 海市蜃楼 —— 拥有南太平洋的氛围
- 热带风情 —— 建有一个漂亮泳池的葱翠的热带绿洲

来到赌城,不去一下周边的胡佛水坝和米德湖是很遗憾的。驯服了科罗拉多河水的胡佛水坝不仅能够提供大量的水力发电,同时水坝建设还造就了米德湖这一西半球最大的人工湖泊,造就了一处游船、钓鱼和游泳爱好者的乐园。

奇闻轶事

之一:颇具讽刺意味的是,这个成为"罪恶之城"的地方最初却是摩门教徒建立起来的。

之二:1966年,富有的怪人霍华德·休斯来到拉斯维加斯,买下了好几座赌场酒店,这些交易有效地结束了黑帮集团对这一地区的控制。在拉斯维加斯生活期间,休斯深居简出,从未离开过他位于"沙漠客栈"九楼的住所。

之三:拉斯维加斯的经济部分得益于美国政府的支持,在禁止核试验条约实施之前,这里的居民会定期看到从沙漠地区升腾起的蘑菇云。

之四:在拉斯维加斯的赌场,你看不到钟表,这是一项国际约定,专为鼓励赌徒及其他光临赌场的人留下来花钱而设计的。

为什么拉斯维加斯入选50＋1个城市?

拉斯维加斯是一个现代奇迹,它所散发出的光芒无与伦比。这座城市是娱乐的、开心的,也是世界罪恶之都。几乎人人都想在有生之年去一次拉斯维加斯,至少一次,并且他们总能找到充分的理由。

Twenty-five

Lima, Peru

The Basic Facts

Lima is the capital and largest city of Peru, and the country's center for commerce, industry and culture. The city grew in a chaotic fashion during the 20th century, due to an influx of rural Peruvians. Lima's architecture blends 16th century mansions with modern buildings in its business district. There is a rigid class structure in Lima based on race and ethnicity, but for the visitor Lima is a striking example of one of South America's first capital cities.

Geography

Lima lies at 12 degrees 6 minutes south latitude and 76 degrees 55 minutes west longitude. The city is located in west-central Peru, less than 10 miles from the Pacific Ocean, in the lowlands to the west of the Andes Mountains.

Climate

Lima's climate is relatively moderate due to its proximity to the Andes Mountains and the Pacific Ocean. The cold Humboldt current helps add to the ocean's moderating effects. Average temperatures range from the upper 60s Fahrenheit in winter to the lower 80s in summer. Because Lima is located south of the equator, the winter and summer months are opposite from those in the northern hemisphere; winter occurs between June and August and summer occurs between December and February. The climate can also be rather humid, and Lima is prone to heavy fogs from May through November.

Government

The Peruvian government is comprised of 12 regions and 24 departments, which are subdivided into provinces and districts within provinces. Lima, a province in itself, has 30 districts. A mayor and the Metropolitan Lima Municipal Council have authority over the city's districts.

Demographics

As one of South America's largest cities, Lima is ethnically diverse. Mestizos, those of mixed Spanish and American Indian descent, historically dominated the Lima population. In the late 20th century, however, political and economic instability spurred the immigration of Campesinos (full-blooded American Indians) from the Andean highlands. The Campesinos, most of whom live in poverty-stricken shantytowns, speak native languages of Quechua and Aymara.

Lima's population also includes residents with Spanish, Italian, German, and African ancestry (Afro-Peruvians are descendants of Africans brought to Peru by the Conquistadors). Interestingly, Lima has one of South America's largest concentrations of Japanese and

秘鲁利马

概况

　　利马是秘鲁的首都和最大的城市，也是秘鲁商业、工业及文化的中心。在20世纪里，由于秘鲁农村人口的大量涌入，这座城市以一种混乱的方式在发展。在利马的商业区，你既可以看到16世纪的豪宅，也可以看到现代的建筑。虽然在利马，根据民族和种族渊源整个社会有着严格的阶级界限，但是对于游客来说，利马只是南美第一大都城的典范之一。

一、地理

　　利马位于南纬12°6′，西经76°55′，地处秘鲁中西部地区，距离太平洋不到10英里，在安第斯山脉以西的低地内部。

二、气候

　　由于距离安第斯山脉和太平洋都很近，利马的气候相对温和，寒冷的洪堡海流进一步促进了海洋的温和效应。利马的气温在冬季的华氏67~69度至夏季的华氏81~83度。由于利马位于赤道以南，冬夏两季的月份与北半球地区正好相反，冬天出现在6月~8月，夏天则在12月~2月。此外，利马的气候有时相当潮湿，从5月一直到11月，都有可能出现大雾天气。

三、政府

　　秘鲁政府由12个地区和24个部门组成，这些地区和部门再进一步划分为省份和省属地区。利马本身是一个省，包括13个区。一位市长和利马大市的市政委员会具有对城市所有地区的管辖权。

四、人口

　　作为南美洲最大的城市之一，利马民族繁多，梅斯蒂索人，是那些西班牙人和美洲印第安人混血儿的后代，在历史上他们是利马人口的主体。然而，20世纪后期，政治和经济的动荡引发了来自安第斯高原地区的坎佩西诺（纯血统的南美印第安人）移民的涌入，这些坎佩西诺人大多居住在贫困的棚户区，他们讲本族的盖丘亚语和埃马拉语。

　　利马的人口还包括祖先为西班牙、意大利、德国及非洲人（非洲秘鲁人就是被西班牙征服者带到秘鲁的非洲人的后代）的居民。有意思的是，利马还是南美最大的日本及中国

Chinese immigrants.

Economy

Lima's economy is primarily national government-based. Lima is also Peru's manufacturing center, with industries producing textiles, paper, paint and food products. Retail business has grown rapidly in the past 2 decades and shopping malls have sprung up throughout the city. Museums and cultural features also attract significant numbers of tourists, which contributes to economic growth.

The History

The earliest residents of Peru were likely North American Indians who migrated to the area approximately 12,000 years ago. Lima is built on an area where civilizations built monuments and settlements as early as 2800 B.C.. Between 1100 and 1300 A.D., the Incas founded a kingdom in Peru; Incans were skilled architects and builders, and they created many of Peru's greatest historical treasures.

By the early 1500s, before the Spanish Conquistadors arrived, the Incan empire that included the present-day countries of Peru, Colombia, Ecuador, Chile and Argentina. In 1532 a Spanish expedition led by Francisco Pizaro arrived in Peru seeking purported treasures of silver and gold. Pizarro remained in the region and founded Ciudad de los Reyes in 1535 on the site of what would become Lima.

During the Spanish Colonial era, viceroys from the Hapsburg court in Spain ruled the country. In the early 1800s Peruvians rebelled against Spanish control with the help of armed forces from neighboring countries. The rebels were successful, and in 1821 Peru became an independent nation. Lima would witness several skirmishes for power in the next few decades, along with a succession of governments, but the city continued to flourish. Lima was sacked during a lengthy war with Chile and Bolivia that began in 1879. Post-war reconstruction essentially transformed Lima into a new city.

The Sights and Sounds

Visitors can explore a good deal of historical and colonial Lima by focusing on the city center around the Plaza Mayor, an enormous 16th century square. The museums are not centrally located, so careful planning is suggested. The plaza's most striking feature is its bronze fountain with the statute of the Angel of Fame.The Plaza de Armas commemorates Peruvian independence.

The Lima Cathedral, completed in 1538, combines Baroque and neo-classical styles. Twin towers were added to the entrance in the 1790s. Francisco Pizarro himself placed the cathedral's first stone; not surprisingly, he is buried there in a chapel.

The most frequented church in Lima is the Church of Saint Francis of Assisi, built around 1674. The richly ornamented Baroque style was very popular when this and other buildings in Peru were built. The church has vast catacombs where an estimated 75,000 people are buried. There are so many bones in the burial area that they are stacked up like inventory in a macabre warehouse.

The Inquisition Museum is housed in a former mansion of the founding families of Lima; the mansion became the home of the Spanish Inquisition in Peru. While the museum is architecturally beautiful, it contains original jails and torture chambers in which heretics

移民聚居地之一。

五、经济

利马的经济主要是国有经济，利马还是秘鲁加工生产的中心，其工业包括纺织、造纸、涂料、食品等。在过去的20年间，零售业发展迅速，购物中心在全市如雨后春笋般出现，博物馆和各类文化设施在为经济发展作贡献的同时，也吸引了相当数量的游客。

光影流金

秘鲁最早的居民有可能是北美的印第安人，他们在近1.2万年前迁移到这一地区。早在公元前2800年，利马地区就有了人类文明，他们建起了纪念馆和居留地，而利马正是在此基础上建立的。公元1100年至1300年间，印加人在秘鲁建立了王国，印加人是出色的建筑师和工匠，秘鲁的许多最伟大的历史宝藏都是由他们所创造的。

16世纪早期，在西班牙征服者到来之前，印加帝国包括今天的秘鲁、哥伦比亚、智利和阿根廷等国家。1532年，一支由弗朗西斯科·皮萨罗率领的西班牙探险队到达秘鲁，寻找梦想中的金银财宝。皮萨罗在这一地区留了下来，并于1535年在后来成为利马的地方创建了"国王城"。

在西班牙殖民统治期间，来自西班牙哈布斯堡法庭的总督统治着这个国家。19世纪初，在邻国武装组织的帮助下，秘鲁人开始反抗西班牙的统治，反抗者最终取得了胜利，1821年，秘鲁成为独立的国家。在接下来的几十年里，虽然利马见证了几次小规模的权利争斗和政府更迭，但是城市的繁荣发展并没有因此而停歇。然而，1879年开始的秘鲁与智利及玻利维亚之间的长期战争却将利马洗劫一空。因此，战后城市的重建非常有必要，并且利马也被彻底改造成了一座新城。

声光景点

想要探寻历史的以及殖民地时期的利马，游客不妨以环绕马约尔广场的市中心地区为重点。马约尔广场是一个16世纪时修建的宏大广场，四周博物馆的位置并非井然有序，因此，最好在出发前好好计划一下。广场内最醒目的标志就是以"名誉天使"雕塑为核心的铜喷泉。武器广场是为纪念秘鲁独立而修建的。

利马大教堂建成于1538年，融合了巴洛克和新古典主义的建筑风格。18世纪90年代时，在其入口处增建了双子塔，弗朗西斯科·皮萨罗为大教堂安放了第一块奠基石，而他死后被埋葬在其中的一个小教堂内也就不足为奇了。

在利马最受欢迎的教堂当数修建于大约1674年的阿西西圣弗朗西斯教堂，在修建这座教堂以及秘鲁其他一些教堂的时候，极尽装饰的巴洛克风格正值盛行。据估计有7.5万人埋葬在这里，因此，教堂内墓室众多。在墓葬区，由于尸骨太多而不得不一个个编号叠放起来，看上去如同一个骷髅仓库。

宗教法庭博物馆设在利马创建者家族先前住过的一幢大宅子里，这栋豪宅成为秘鲁的西班牙宗教法庭所在地，博物馆不仅建筑华丽，而且里面保存着最初异教徒们遭受折

were tortured.

The National Museum of Art, built around 1872, exhibits a fine collection from pre-Columbian artifacts to Spanish colonial art. An important exhibit displays 2,000-year old weavings that were discovered in the area.

San Martín Plaza was inaugurated in 1921 to commemorate the 100th anniversary of Peruvian independence. Notable features include the statue of the general José de San Martín and the former hotel Bolivar, once the most fashionable in Lima. Visitors delight in the orange-colored facades of the surrounding buildings—somewhat unusual for Lima.

The Trivia

Fact: Pizarro referred to the city of Lima as the City of Kings. Early maps display both names, but Lima prevailed as the more common name.

Fact: Air pollution is a serious health issue in this ever-expanding city. Leaded gasoline is still used, and no restrictions are placed on either the age or condition of motorized vehicles.

Fact: The viceroy was the single most important person in Lima during the period of Spanish control; his authority equaled that of the Spanish kings. There is a legend that when a new viceroy first entered the city of Lima, the streets would be paved with silver bars, from the doors of the city to the viceroy's new home.

Fact: Lima and Peru went through a golden period in the late 1800s, curiously called the age of Guano. This natural fertilizer found on the Pacific coast became a lucrative export, mainly to Europe. The money generated during this era helped finance a series of civic improvements in Lima.

Fact: Lima is arranged in the manner of ancient Roman settlements, with 117 blocks surrounding the main square. Colonial institutions were built along the square's perimeter, including Pizarro's residence, restored in the 20th century and currently the seat of Peru's executive branch.

Fact: The Spanish established a strict class system in Peru, which endures in some form today. Under this system, an elite white upper class controlled the large native Indian lower class. In the early 1900s a middle class of whites and mestizos began to emerge.

Why Lima Is a 50 plus one City

Lima represents both the grandeur and the suffering of its colonial past. Few cities in the world are so tied to the Spanish Empire. The city reflects the convergence of Spanish and Peruvian history and culture. At times chaotic and challenging, Lima is nevertheless a bastion of cultural and artistic greatness.

磨的监狱和刑讯室。

国家美术博物馆大约建于1872年，收藏有大量从早年哥伦比亚时期的手工艺品直到西班牙殖民时期的艺术品，其中一个重要展厅内陈列的是在这一地区发现的，已有2 000年历史的纺织品。

圣马丁广场于1921年正式落成，用以纪念秘鲁独立100周年。广场上著名的景点有何塞·德·圣马丁将军的雕塑以及原来的玻利瓦尔饭店，它曾经是利马最时髦的建筑。游客徜徉在四周橙色的建筑之中，体会着利马的独特魅力，定会有一种心旷神怡的感觉。

奇闻轶事

之一：皮萨罗将利马市称为"国王之城"，虽然早期的城市地图上两个名字都有，但是利马逐渐成为更为常见的名称。

之二：在这个不断扩张的城市里，空气污染是影响健康的重要因素，含铅汽油至今仍在使用，并且城市对于机动车辆的使用年限或使用状况没有任何限制。

之三：在西班牙统治时期，总督是利马唯一最重要的人物，他的权力与西班牙国王一样大，传说那时每当新任总督进入利马市的时候，从城门一直到总督府的街道都铺满了银条。

之四：十九世纪末，利马和秘鲁都经历了一段黄金期，有趣的是，这段时期被称为"鸟粪时代"，在太平洋沿岸随处可见的这种天然肥料变成了能够赚钱的商品，主要向欧洲出口，而从中获得的利润则被政府财政用来改善利马的市政设施。

之五：利马市的布局是以古罗马城市格局设计的，围绕主广场建有117个街区，那些殖民地机构沿广场周边依次排开，其中包括20世纪时重新修复的皮萨罗的住所，现为秘鲁行政部门所在地。

之六：西班牙人在秘鲁建立了严格的等级制度，直到今天其影响依然存在。在这种制度之下，上流社会的白人精英分子控制着处于社会下层的印第安人。20世纪早期，一些属于中产阶级的白人和梅斯蒂索人开始出现。

为什么利马入选50 + 1个城市？

利马同时代表了其殖民地过去的辉煌及痛苦，世界上没有任何一座城市能够与西班牙王国联系得如此紧密，这座城市是西班牙和秘鲁两国历史及文化的交汇点，尽管有时它显得比较混乱和富有挑战，但是利马仍不失为一座文化和艺术的伟大堡垒。

Twenty-six

Lisbon, Portugal

The Basic Facts

Lisbon is the capital and largest city in Portugal. Almost a fifth of the country's people live in and around the city. After decades of economic instability, Lisbon has become a thriving center of Portugal's economy with a revitalized urban landscape.

Geography

Lisbon lies at 38 degrees 42 minutes north latitude and 9 degrees 5 minutes west longitude. The city a major European port, located in southwestern Portugal where the Tagus River empties into the Atlantic Ocean. Lisbon covers 32 square miles and is composed of many public squares, avenues and parks. Most areas of the city are hilly, with many streets too steep for automobiles, but the downtown area (the Baixa) near the harbor is flat.

Climate

Lisbon's climate is one of the warmest of any European city, thanks to the infiuence of the Gulf Stream. Average temperatures range from the upper 50s Fahrenheit in winter to the lower 80s Fahrenheit in summer. Spring and summer in Lisbon are usually sunny; autumn and winter are often quite rainy and windy.

Government

Portugal is divided into 22 districts, each with an elected governor and legislature. Cities and towns within each district also have their own local governments. A civil governor, appointed by the central government, is responsible for the district of Lisbon. The district is subdivided into municipalities, wards, and parishes. Parish representatives are elected locally and then elect the parish committee. Lisbon's Municipal Assembly, the legislative branch of the local government, includes parish committee representatives and those directly elected by the local citizens. The chamber is headed by a president appointed by the district governor.

Demographics

Lisbon is Portugal's largest and fastest-growing region. The area's first inhabitants were the Iberians, who settled more than 3,000 years ago. The population later expanded with an influx of peoples from eastern Europe, the Mediterranean and former African colonies. The current population includes all of these groups.

Economy

Trade is a major part of Lisbon's economy; ships travel through the Tagus estuary, one of Europe's most important natural harbors. Shipbuilding is a major industry in Lisbon, as

葡萄牙里斯本

概况

里斯本是葡萄牙的首都和最大的城市,葡萄牙几乎五分之一的人口都住在这座城市及其周边地区。在历经了数十年的经济动荡之后,如今,里斯本以其焕然一新的城市景观,成为葡萄牙一个繁荣的经济中心。

一、地理

里斯本位于北纬38°42′,西经9°5′,地处葡萄牙西南塔霍河流入大西洋的入口处,是欧洲的主要港口之一。里斯本市占地面积32平方英里,由众多的公共广场、街道和公园组成。城市的大部分地方起伏不平,许多街道由于坡度太大而无法行车,不过,市中心区域(巴夏)还是非常平坦的。

二、气候

得益于湾流的影响,在所有的欧洲城市当中,里斯本的气候是最温暖的之一,平均气温在冬季的华氏57~59度至夏季的华氏81~83度。在春夏两季,里斯本通常是阳光明媚的,而秋冬季节则经常下雨、刮风。

三、政府

葡萄牙分为22个区,每个区有自己选举产生的行政长官和立法机构,各区内的城镇也有自己的地方政府。里斯本区由一名经中央政府任命的行政长官负责,该区进一步划分为若干分区、街区和教区。教区的代表由当地选举产生,之后再选举产生教区委员会。里斯本的市政议会是当地政府的立法机构,由教区委员会的代表以及那些由市民直接推选的人员组成。议会办公室是由一名经地区行政长官任命的议长主管的。

四、人口

里斯本是葡萄牙最大、也是发展最快的地区,该地区的原始居民是古伊比利亚人,他们早在3 000多年前就定居于这里,后来,随着来自东欧、地中海以及原非洲殖民地地区人口的大量涌入,里斯本的人口迅速膨胀,目前城市人口的构成也以这些人为主。

五、经济

贸易是里斯本经济的主体,塔霍河口作为欧洲最重要的自然港之一,经常有船舶来往穿梭。同加工制造业一样,造船业也是里斯本的主要工业,此外,这座城市还是葡萄牙

is manufacturing. The city is also the center of Portugal's banking and commercial sectors.

The History

The earliest inhabitants of the area surrounding present-day Lisbon were the Iberians. The Celts invaded about 1000 B.C.and intermarried with the Iberians.Most scholars believe that Lisbon dates to pre-Roman days and that it was a constant battleground between the Phoenicians, Greeks and Carthaginians. Lisbon was the most important city in the western Iberian region during the time of Roman rule, which began in 205 B.C.. After the Roman Empire collapsed, the area was ransacked by a series of northern European tribes until the area was seized by the Moors in 714 A.D..

In 1147, Christian forces led by Alfonso I wrested the city of Lisbon from Moorish control, and Alfonso I became Portugal's first king; Lisbon became the country's capital in 1255. Portugal's golden era of exploration began in the 15th century;one of the most famous Portuguese discoveries was that of Vasco da Gama, who navigated the first sea route to India.

Felipe II of Spain became king in 1580, and reigned for 60 years until nationalist Portuguese seized power. During that time, Brazil was a Portuguese territory; gold was discovered there in the 17th century and Lisbon enjoyed a brief economic boom. Some 60,000 to 90,000 people perished in 1755, when a major earthquake devastated the city.

Napoleon occupied the city briefly at the start of the 19th century. Following his defeat and withdrawal, the city and country spiraled into a lengthy period of political chaos. In 1926 António de Oliveira Salazar became prime minister of Portugal; he led an authoritarian regime until his overthrow in 1974. Lisbon and Portugal rose out of the squalor following Salazar's regime. With the help of the European Union, Lisbon has rebounded to become a thriving center of Portugal's economy.

The Sights and Sounds

Lisbon is small in comparison to other major European cities. Touring the city can be a challenge because the city is built on a series of hills. Distances can be deceptive because landmarks and sites are at different heights. Funicular railways and street elevators help visitors navigate the steep hills.

St. George Castle, a majestic structure in the heart of Lisbon, is architecturally significant for its Roman, Visigoth and Moorish influences. Beautiful gardens surround the structure. It is an ideal location from which to view the city from afar; travel nearby and explore the Alfama district.

Alfama surrounds St. George Castle in an area that roughly parallels that of the city's original Moorish settlement. Visitors find the district's white-washed houses and red-tiled roofs rather charming.

The Baixa is the city center; also called the lower town, it is an area home to crafts and trades including artists, street performers and metal smiths. The neighborhood reflects this tradition with a variety of shops selling traditional Portuguese wares. Cafes and restaurants line the area to ensure that everyone is well fed while wandering the Baixa.

The Calouste Gulbenkian Foundation displays classical paintings, fine porcelain,jewelry and other antiquities. Several specialty museums in Lisbon include the Puppet Museum, the Port Wine Institute—yes, samplings are provided—and the National Tile Museum.

银行及商业的中心。

光影流金

　　最早在今天里斯本周边地区定居下来的是古伊比利亚人,大约在公元前1 000年,凯尔特人入侵这一地区,并和伊比利亚人有了通婚。大多数学者相信里斯本的历史可以追溯到罗马帝国出现之前,他们还相信这一地区经常成为腓尼基人、希腊人及迦太基人之间的战场。从公元前205年起,罗马人开始统治这一地区,里斯本是当时西伊比利亚地区最重要的城市。罗马帝国垮台之后,这一地区遭到了一系列来自北方的欧洲部落的劫掠,直到公元714年,摩尔人夺取这一地区后,这种混乱的状况才得以结束。

　　1147年,由阿方索一世率领的基督教势力从摩尔人手中夺取了里斯本市的控制权,阿方索一世成为葡萄牙的第一位国王,1255年,里斯本成为葡萄牙的首都。15世纪时,葡萄牙开始了其探险的黄金时代,这期间最著名的发现之一当数由瓦斯科·德·伽马首辟的到达印度的海上航线。

　　1580年西班牙的菲利普二世国王登基,并且开始了对这一地区长达60年的统治,直至葡萄牙民族主义分子取得政权。在那段时间里,巴西是属于葡萄牙的领土,17世纪时,由于在巴西发现了黄金,所以,里斯本的经济得以在短时间内快速增长。1755年一场大地震降临这座城市,夺去了6 000~9 000人的生命。

　　19世纪初,拿破仑的军队曾一度占领里斯本,伴随着他的失败和撤出,这座城市以及它所在的国家进入了一段持续很长时间的政治混乱及动荡期。1926年,安东尼奥·德·奥利维拉·萨拉查当选葡萄牙的总理,并且开始了其长期的独裁管制。1974年,萨拉查被推翻,里斯本和葡萄牙从专制统治的泥潭中站立起来,借助于欧盟的帮助,里斯本市的经济迅速反弹,并且发展成为葡萄牙繁荣的经济中心。

声光景点

　　相比其他主要的欧洲城市,里斯本显得很小。由于城市建在连绵的山丘之上,因此,在市区观光可以说是一种挑战。同时,由于各种地标和景点处在不同的高度,所以,判断距离变得非常困难。轨道缆车和沿街电梯成为游客在陡峭的山丘间游览的好帮手。

　　位于里斯本市心脏地带的圣乔治城堡是一座宏伟的建筑,从中可以看到罗马、西哥特及摩尔建筑的多重影响,美丽的花园环绕城堡四周,这里是远距离欣赏里斯本的理想场所。城堡附近的阿尔法玛区也值得一去。

　　围绕圣乔治城堡的阿尔法玛区,其面积大约相当于原摩尔人居住区的大小,许多来访的游客都会深深爱上这里白墙红瓦的房子。

　　巴夏区是市中心,又被称为下城区,以手工艺及贸易为主,是艺术家、街头艺人和金属工匠的聚居区。作为此种传统的反映,这里的居民区有各类出售传统葡萄牙物品的商店,遍布该区的咖啡屋和餐馆保证了光顾这里的每位游客能够吃饱玩好。

　　卡鲁斯特-古班卡恩基金大厦展出的有古典绘画、精美陶瓷和珠宝古玩等。若干里斯本所特有的博物馆包括木偶博物馆、波尔图葡萄酒研究所 —— 没错,这里可以提供葡萄酒样品 —— 还有国家瓷砖博物馆。

A museum devoted exclusively to Portuguese art is the National Museum of Art. Housed in a grand 17th century palace, the collection emphasizes the finest art of Portugal from the 15th to 19th centuries.

Belém is an old quarter of Lisbon near the seacoast. Visitors come here to view the neighborhood's Gothic architecture, including the the Jerónimos Monastery.This historic structure was built in the 16th century over a period of 50 years, and commemorates Vasco da Gama's voyage to India. Also here is the Bélem Tower,which was built during the same period to defend the monastery and the nearby port of Bélem.

The Trivia

— *Fact:*   Although most historians believe Lisbon was founded by the Phoenicians,a popular legend has it that the city was founded by Ulysses, the famous Greek explorer. After the Romans gained control of the city, it was briefly named Felicitas Julia in honor of Julius Caesar.

Fact: Lisbon was a neutral city during World War II and was a safe haven for Europeans (especially Jews) seeking passage to America. The classic movie *Casablanca* focuses on a flight to Lisbon to escape Nazism and the government of Vichy France.

Fact: The Roman Catholic Church was effectively part of the Portuguese government until the two entities separated in 1911; nevertheless, Catholicism remains the predominate religion in Portugal. Devout pilgrims travel to the small town of Fátima each year to visit the Sanctuary of Fátima, where the Virgin Mary reportedly appeared to three peasant children in 1917.

Fact: In 1290 King Denis I founded the first university in Lisbon.

Fact: The westernmost point of continental Europe is located at Cabo da Roca, a cape overlooking the Atlantic Ocean west of Lisbon.

Fact: Fado is a Portuguese music genre reminiscent of the blues, expressing longing, lost lovers and sadness. Restaurants that feature this traditional music are generally upscale and the shows typically begin after 10 p.m..

Fact: Trams and funicular railways are Lisbon's primary modes of public transportation. The Tagus River is spanned by the 25th of April Bridge, one of the world's longest suspension bridges, and the Vasco de Gama Bridge, the longest bridge in Europe.

Why Lisbon Is a 50 plus one City

Lisbon is a popular tourist destination for those interested in its colonial past, its history of exploration, and its cultural influences. Lisbon may be a relatively small city, but it is charming and delightful, and proudly displays its rich heritage.

　　专门为葡萄牙艺术开设的博物馆是国家美术馆,它位于一座17世纪修建的宏伟宫殿内,其藏品着重强调从15世纪到19世纪葡萄牙最精美的艺术。

　　贝伦区是里斯本市靠近海滨的一处古城区,游客来到这里只为欣赏居民区内的哥特式建筑,其中包括杰洛尼莫斯修道院。这座具有纪念意义的建筑从16世纪时开始修建,历时50年方才完工,用来纪念瓦斯科·德·伽马航行到达印度。此外,这里还有修建于同一时期的贝伦塔,用以保护修道院及附近的港口。

奇闻轶事

　　之一:虽然大多数历史学家相信里斯本是由腓尼基人创立的,但是一则流传很广的传说,讲的是希腊著名的探险家尤利西斯建立了这座城市。在罗马人取得城市的控制权之后,曾一度将该市更名为菲利希塔斯—尤利亚以纪念尤利乌斯·凯撒大帝。

　　之二:第二次世界大战期间,里斯本属于中立城市,对于那些寻求机会去美洲的欧洲人(尤其是犹太人)来说,这里是一个安全的港湾。经典影片《卡萨布兰卡》就集中讲述了为逃避纳粹统治和法国维希政府,一群人逃往里斯本的故事。

　　之三:天主教会曾经是葡萄牙政府中一个颇具影响力的组成部分,直到1911年,这两个实体分离,此种影响才宣告结束。然而,在葡萄牙天主教始终是占主导地位的宗教。每年虔诚的清教徒们都要到法蒂玛小镇去参观那里的法蒂玛圣所。有报道称,1917年时,圣母玛丽亚曾出现在3个农民孩子的面前。

　　之四:1290年,国王丹尼斯一世在里斯本创建了第一所综合性大学。

　　之五:欧洲大陆的最西端位于罗卡角,这是里斯本以西俯视大西洋的一个海岬。

　　之六:"命运歌"是葡萄牙所特有的一种音乐形式,通常以忧伤的怀旧内容,用以表达渴望、失去的爱以及悲伤等主题,以这种传统音乐为特色的餐馆一般是迎合高层次消费的,表演通常在晚上10点以后开始。

　　之七:有轨电车和轨道缆车是里斯本主要的公共交通方式,横跨塔霍河的4月25日大桥,是世界上最长的悬索桥之一,瓦斯科·德·伽马大桥则是欧洲最长的大桥。

为什么里斯本入选50 + 1个城市?

　　里斯本是一个深受游客喜爱的旅游目的地,人们感兴趣的是它的殖民地过去、它的探险历史、它的文化影响。虽然,里斯本是一座相对较小的城市,但是,这座小城却是如此迷人、如此快乐,它以自身丰富的文化遗产傲立于世界大都会之林。

Twenty-seven

London, England

The Basic Facts

London is the capital of the United Kingdom, which includes England, Wales and Northern Ireland. It is the largest city in the UK and one of the world's greatest cities, with an amazing mix of culture, commerce, and historic architecture and sites. London is also one of the world's oldest cities, and was originally a trading post for the Roman Empire around 43 A.D.. The city was devastated during bombing raids in World War II, but reconstruction began soon afterward, giving the London skyline new and brilliant skyscrapers. The city hosts thousands of visitors every year, but still must deal with the problems of traffic congestion and pollution.

Geography

London lies at 51 degrees 30 minutes north latitude and 0 degrees 7 minutes west longitude. The city is located in the southeast of England and the Thames River flows through its center. The Thames connects London to the North Sea, enabling access to worldwide shipping routes.

The entire city covers 614 square miles and is divided into specific areas: the City Section, which includes London's financial center; the West End, which includes stores, nightlife, and the UK government center; and South Bank, a center of London culture with many art galleries, museums and theaters.

Residential areas, small offices and factories surround Central London, beyond which are less-crowded areas known to Londoners as the suburbs.

Climate

Although London is a northern city, it has a temperate climate thanks to the North Atlantic Drift of the Gulf Stream. Severe cold and warmth are uncommon; average winter temperatures are in the mid-40s Fahrenheit and summers average in the upper 60s to lower 70s Fahrenheit.

Contrary to popular belief, London's climate is not extraordinarily rainy or foggy.Rain is moderate throughout the year, and the demise of 19th century industry has eliminated the thick fogs for which London is famous (or infamous).

Government

London consists of 32 boroughs and the City of London. Each has its own council and mayor elected every 4 years. With the exception of police and fire departments and public transport, the borough councils control most aspects of their local government services.

The Greater London Authority controls citywide services, including police, fire and public transport. The authority is composed of a 25-member assembly and a mayor elected for 4 years.

英国伦敦

概况

　　伦敦是英国的首都，即由英格兰、威尔士和北爱尔兰组成的联合王国的首都，它是英国最大的城市，也是世界上最大的城市之一，是一个融合了文化、商业、古建筑和遗址等多重元素的神奇混合体。此外，伦敦还是世界上最古老的城市之一，在公元43年左右，它曾是罗马帝国一个贸易驿站。第二次世界大战期间，伦敦遭到轰炸几乎变为废墟，然而，之后不久，这座城市便开始了重建，漂亮的摩天大楼拔地而起，城市的轮廓焕然一新。如今，伦敦每年都要接待成千上万的游客，同时，城市也必须面对交通拥堵和污染等问题。

一、地理

　　伦敦位于北纬51°30′，西经0°7′，地处英格兰的东南部，泰晤士河穿城而过，同时也将伦敦和北海连接了起来，使得船舶可以与世界各地的航道相连。

　　整座伦敦市占地614平方英里，被分为几个特色区域：主城区包括伦敦的金融中心，西端主要为商店、夜生活馆和英国政府所在地，南岸是伦敦的文化中心，包括许多的美术馆、博物馆、剧院等。

　　居民区、小型写字楼和工厂都集中在中心伦敦区，该区以外就是人口密度相对较小的被伦敦人称为郊区的地区。

二、气候

　　虽然伦敦是一座北方城市，但是，由于受北大西洋暖流的影响，气候温和、极少出现极端寒冷或炎热的天气，冬季的平均气温在华氏45度左右，夏季则在华氏67~73度。

　　与人们通常的想法相反，伦敦并非多雨或多雾，全年降水比较平均，19世纪工业的消亡已经将伦敦出名(或臭名昭著)的浓雾大大地减少了。

三、政府

　　伦敦由32个区以及伦敦城组成，每个地区有自己的委员会和每四年选举一次的区长。除警察、消防以及公交部门以外，区委员会负责管理当地市政服务的大多数部门。

　　大伦敦管理局掌控着全城的服务行业，包括公安、消防和公交系统。管理局由包括25名成员和任期4年的局长共同管理。

The Court of Common Counsel governs the City Section, and consists of elected alderman, 100 non-elected council members and the Lord Mayor of London.

Demographics

Each borough has its own identity, and most Londoners identify themselves by the specific borough in which they live. By popular tradition, the only real residents of London are Cockneys, those born within earshot of the bells of St. Mary-le-Bow. London's present population, like many of the world's large cities, is a melting pot, drawing people from other parts of the UK and from around the world. Nearly seven million people call London home.

Economy

London is the driving force behind the UK's economy, with residents working in finance, government, trade, and national or local government. Major London industries include printing and publishing, clothing and textiles, electronics, food and pharmaceuticals. Even though London's trade has moved mostly from its ports to container shipping elsewhere, the city is the major conduit of trade from the nearby port city of Tilbury.

London is home to some of the world's greatest financial and insurance institutions. Tourism is a major industry for the city. London is also the base for most of England's communications industry, including the BBC.

The History

In the 5th century, the Romans left Britain to defend Rome from a Barbarian invasion. London quickly declined as most other inhabitants abandoned the city at this time. In the mid-1000s the city's population rebounded after Edward the Confessor built a palace and a monastery church on the Thames about two miles southwest of London. The modern city of Westminster is located around this site. During the Middle Ages, many of London's most famous landmarks were created, including London Bridge and Old St. Paul's Cathedral. London became selfgoverning during this period. The city grew rapidly during the 16th and 17th centuries, especially under the rule of Henry VIII and Elizabeth I. In America's early years, London became an important trade center, a development that helped England assert its colonial control throughout the world.

The Great Plague and the Great Fire of London ravaged the city in the late 1600s. Puritans led by Oliver Cromwell seized power from King Charles I during this period and ruled both England and London. But by the 1800s, London was the largest city in the world, due largely to the advent of the Industrial Revolution. Many Londoners then moved to the suburbs that were growing in the outlying areas.

London experienced sporadic bomb damage during World War I, yet during World War II the city was devastated in an attack known as the Blitz. German bombers rained bombs on the city in an attempt to weaken Londoners' resolve. Much to Germany's chagrin, the Blitz empowered the city to rebuild.

The Sights and Sounds

To explore London is a massive undertaking, so you will need ample time to enjoy the city's sights and sounds. Although most of the art and architecture of London is

市议会庭管理主城区，其构成包括选举产生的高级市政官、100名非选举产生的市政成员以及伦敦市长大人。

四、人口

伦敦的每个区都有自己的身份，大多数伦敦人以自己所居住的特色区为识别的标志，通常的做法是，只有真正的伦敦居民才被称为"伦敦佬"，也就是那些在听得到圣玛利勒堡教堂钟声的范围内出生的人。和世界上其他大城市一样，伦敦现有人口的构成就是一个大熔炉，包括来自英国各地以及世界各地的人们，有近700万人把伦敦当做自己的家。

五、经济

伦敦是英国经济的推动力，居民主要在金融、贸易以及国家或地方政府部门工作，伦敦的主要工业包括印刷出版、服装纺织、电子产品、食品以及制药等。尽管伦敦的贸易主要是通过港口的集装箱把货物运往世界各地，但是这座城市仍是附近提尔伯里港镇的主要贸易口岸。

伦敦是世界上一些最大的金融及保险公司的总部，旅游业是伦敦的主要产业，此外，伦敦还是包括英国广播公司在内的英格兰的通讯行业的基地。

光影流金

五世纪时，罗马人为了抵御入侵罗马的异族人而离开了不列颠岛，当时，由于大部分其他居民也弃城而去，伦敦迅速衰落。11世纪中期，爱德华—忏悔者在伦敦西南大约两英里的地方，修建了一座宫殿和一座修道院，之后，城市人口快速增长。这一地区就是当今威斯敏斯特镇所在地。中世纪时，许多伦敦最著名的地标被创造出来，其中包括伦敦大桥和老的圣保罗大教堂。那时的伦敦是一座自治城市。16和17世纪时，这座城市快速发展，特别是在亨利八世和伊莎白一世统治时期。在美洲早期开发年间，伦敦成为重要的贸易中心，并且当时的发展促使英国在世界范围内维持了其殖民统治。

17世纪后期，伦敦大瘟疫和伦敦大火一度肆虐整个城市。这一时期，清教徒们在奥立佛·克伦威尔的领导下从国王查尔斯一世手中夺取了政权，并且统治了英格兰和伦敦。然而，伦敦之所以能在19世纪成为世界上最大的城市，很大程度上得益于工业革命的来临。于是，许多伦敦人把家搬到了城市外围的郊区地区。

第一次世界大战期间，伦敦仅仅经历了零星炮火的袭击，然而，在第二次世界大战中，这座城市却遭受了被称为"闪电战"的毁灭性空袭，德国的轰炸机在城市上空投下了如雨般的炸弹试图削弱伦敦人的决心，可是，令他们大为恼火的是，闪电空袭反而给了这座城市重建的力量。

声光景点

探寻伦敦可谓一项浩大的工程，你需要有充裕的时间才能尽情享受它的声光景色。

concentrated in the city's two main sections (Westminster and the City of London),the geographic area is quite extensive. Government is centered in Westminster, and the City of London is the home of commerce, banking and business. If time and energy permit, visitors may want to include Covent Garden, Hyde Park, Kensington Gardens and the South Kensington museum district in their itinerary.

Buckingham Palace surely rates as one of the greatest sites in London. Many,however, consider the building's architecture to be rather average; one would expect the palace's exterior to be more opulent, as it is the home of the royal family. The monarchy and its administration are in residence for most of the year, and as a result, only parts of the palace are open for viewing during the summer months.

The Houses of Parliament stand in tribute to the British tradition of representative government. Visitors will enjoy the nearby Palace of Westminster; regrettably,however, the only parts of the original building still standing are the Jewel Tower (built around 1365) and Westminster Hall. The remainder of the building,including the chambers and committee rooms of Parliament, was rebuilt after a fire in 1834. Victoria Tower and St. Stephen's Tower flank the building on either end. The latter is formally known as the Clock Tower, and houses the famous bell affectionately known as Big Ben.

No. 10 and 11 Downing Street are famous addresses for British government and for the world at large. No. 10 is the official residence of the Prime Minister,and No. 11 contains the offices of the financial minister, the Chancellor of the Exchequer.

British monarchs are by tradition crowned in the most important church in all England: Westminster Abbey. This church, which dates from the 11th century,contains the Henry VII Chapel, one of the finest in Europe. Poets Corner, another historic part of the building, is the resting place of literary greats including Chaucer, Hardy, Dickens, Tennyson and Browning.

History buffs will enjoy a visit to the Cabinet War Rooms, perhaps not a popular spot on a London tour, but a fascinating one nevertheless. This underground bunker behind the Foreign Office was the nerve center for the British Empire during World War II . Winston Churchill and his cabinet met here to direct the war effort and were protected from the ravages of the Blitz. Today, the room appears as though the Prime Minister and his cabinet were about to arrive; time has left the room untouched and ready for action.

The British Museum is renowned for its collection of historically significant antiquities, including the priceless Elgin Marbles and the Rosetta Stone. No other museum in the world comes close to rivaling its collections. The Egyptian, Greek and Roman collections are without equal, and the Renaissance collection of art and artifacts is outstanding. The British Museum is enormous, requiring several visits to see all the exhibits. Another notable London museum is the National Gallery in Trafalgar Square, which houses countless important works of art between the 14th and 19th centuries.

St. Paul's Cathedral, completed around 1710, is the heart and soul of London.The famous architect, Christopher Wren, designed this imposing structure—he is buried there in tribute—and its impressive dome attracts visitors time and time again. The cathedral survived the Blitz as a memorial to faith, to the city of London,and to Christopher Wren. St. Paul's American Chapel pays tribute to the 28,000 U.S. servicemen who lost their lives in World War II .

The Tower of London, built in the 11th century, is perhaps the strangest building in all

虽然伦敦大部分的艺术和建筑都集中在两个主要地区(威斯敏斯特和伦敦城),但是整个地理面积还是相当大的。英国的内阁以威斯敏斯特为中心,而伦敦城则是商业、银行和贸易的家园。假如你有足够的时间和精力,可以将科文特加登广场、海德公园、肯星顿花园以及南肯星顿博物馆地区列入旅行计划。

白金汉宫无疑位列伦敦最伟大的景点之一,不过,许多人都觉得这座建筑相当普通,因为它是皇家成员的居住地,所以,人们自然期望看到一座外观更为豪华的宫殿。一年大多数时间,皇室和内阁成员都住在这里,因此,在夏季白金汉宫只有部分是对外开放的。

议会大厦作为英国传统的代议政体的象征矗立在那里,游客可以游览近旁的威斯敏斯特宫,不过,令人遗憾的是,如今只有宝石塔(大约建于1365年)和威斯敏斯特大厅属于原有建筑,而其余部分,包括议会的会议厅及委员会办公室,都是在1834年一场大火之后重建的。维多利亚塔和圣史蒂芬塔分别位于宫殿两侧,后者先前被称为"钟塔",因为塔上的钟非常有名,人们亲切地称之为"大本钟"。

唐宁街10号和11号无论是对英国政府来说,还是在全世界都是著名的地址,10号是首相官邸,11号则是财政部长,也就是财政大臣的办公处。

根据传统,英国皇室在全英格兰最重要的教堂 —— 威斯敏斯特大教堂 —— 举行加冕仪式。这座修建于11世纪的教堂内有国王亨利七世的祷告室,是欧洲最完美的祈祷室之一。"诗人角"是教堂内另一处有纪念意义的地方,英国的文坛巨匠,如乔叟、哈代、狄更斯、丁尼生和勃朗宁,都曾把这里作为休息场所。

历史爱好者们将会有兴趣参观一下内阁战争室,或许这里并不是伦敦游线路的热门景点,但是它会是一个令人兴奋的地方。这个位于外交部大楼后面的地下掩体,在第二次世界大战期间,曾是大英帝国的神经中枢,温斯顿·丘吉尔和他的内阁成员正是在这里开会,指挥战役,并躲避纳粹的闪电空袭的。今天,房间的布置一如当初,仿佛首相和他的内阁即将来临,时间并没有给这间屋子留下任何痕迹,它依然在随时待命。

大英博物馆以其收藏的大量具有历史意义的古董而闻名于世,其中包括无价之宝埃尔金大理石雕和罗塞塔石碑。全世界没有任何博物馆的收藏可以与之匹敌,埃及、希腊和罗马的藏品独一无二,文艺复兴时期的美术及手工艺品精美绝伦,大英博物馆庞大的展品需要你数次光临才可能领略其全貌。伦敦另一处有名的博物馆是位于特拉法尔加广场内的国家美术馆,这里收藏了无数14和19世纪重要的艺术作品。

建成于1710年的圣保罗大教堂是伦敦的心脏和灵魂。著名建筑大师克里斯托弗·雷恩设计了这座雄伟的建筑 —— 为了对他表示感谢,他死后就被葬在了这里 —— 教堂那醒目的穹顶吸引着八方游客一次次来到这里。在纳粹的闪电空袭中,大教堂幸免于难,从而成为对信仰、对伦敦城、对克里斯托弗·雷恩的一种纪念。圣保罗美国礼拜堂是为纪念在第二次世界大战中牺牲的2.8万名美国军人而修建的。

建于11世纪的伦敦塔或许是整个英格兰最奇特的建筑了,虽然现在这里存放着王冠

England. Today the tower houses the Crown Jewels, but it formerly served as a fortress and a palace. Visitors, however, flock to the tower for its historical significance as a prison and a place of execution. The area around the tower is a complex of buildings that comprised the old medieval palace.

Trivia

Fact: During the 1950s, Londoners dealt with deadly smog caused by coal smoke from homes and private industry. Four thousand Londoners died in 1952 during a particularly deadly smog event, after which Parliament passed clean air acts limiting coal-smoke emissions in the city.

Fact: Until 1750, London's only link with its South Bank was the original London Bridge. Westminster Bridge was completed in 1750 and many other bridges were built in later years.

Fact: The London theater scene, which is still thriving today, began during the reign of Elizabeth I, a noted patron of the arts. The theaters attracted such unruly crowds that they were actually located outside the city walls. One of the most famous theaters was the Globe, where many of William Shakespeare's plays debuted. The original Globe Theatre was demolished in 1644, but a replica located near the original site opened in 1997 to great acclaim.

Why London Is a 50 plus one City

London was a Roman city that has become a seat of government and a major world financial center. It is truly one of the most impressive cities, known for its size, its vitality, and its marvelous historical significance. London was and remains a city of the world for all to enjoy.

钻石,但是过去却是作为城堡和宫殿来使用的。不过,蜂拥而来的游客则是为了看一下这座曾经的监狱和刑场。伦敦塔的周围是由古老的中世纪宫殿构成的一个复杂的建筑群。

奇闻轶事

之一:20世纪50年代期间,伦敦人遭受着着来自居民和私人工厂煤烟所引起的致命烟雾的侵害。1952年,一次特别致命的烟雾事件夺取了4000伦敦人的生命,从那以后,议会通过了清洁空气的法案来限制城市中的煤烟排放。

之二:1750年之前,伦敦城与南岸区的唯一联系就是伦敦大桥,1750年,当威斯敏斯特大桥建成通车以后,许多其他的大桥陆续出现。

之三:至今依然兴旺的伦敦演剧业开始于伊丽莎白一世在位期间,因为女王本人就是剧院的常客。当时,这些剧院甚至吸引了大批住在城墙以外地区的不安分人群。其中一所最著名的剧院名为环球剧院,威廉·莎士比亚的许多戏剧就是在此首演的,最初的环球剧院于1644年被拆除,1997年,一座在原址附近修建的复制品正式落成,并且赢得了广泛的赞誉。

为什么伦敦入选50 + 1个城市?

伦敦是一座已经成为内阁所在地和世界主要金融中心的罗马风格的城市,它肯定是最令人难忘的城市之一,它的规模、它的活力、它辉煌的历史意义举世闻名。伦敦过去是,现在依然是令所有人喜爱的世界大都市。

Twenty-eight

Madrid, Spain

The Basic Facts

Madrid is the capital of Spain and the country's largest city. The city was founded by the Moors in the 9th century. After the fall of the Spanish fascist government in the late 1900s, Madrid underwent rapid growth helped by developing industries and extensive building programs.

Geography

Madrid lies at 40 degrees 26 minutes north latitude and 3 degrees 42 minutes west longitude. The city is located on a high plateau near the geographic center of Spain. At an altitude of 2,150 feet, it is one of the highest European capitals.In the 1950s Madrid experienced a population boom, and since then has expanded to include residential and industrial suburbs. Madrid covers almost 234 square miles.

Climate

Madrid has a Mediterranean climate. Average temperatures range from the mid-40s Fahrenheit in winter to the upper 80s Fahrenheit in summer. Rainfall is limited throughout the year and summers tend to be very dry.

Government

Spain is divided into autonomous communities that have authority over the government services within those communities. Madrid is the capital of the Autonomous Community of Madrid and consists of a single province.

The city of Madrid has an elected city council and mayor. Each member of the city council also serves as an administrator for a particular part of the city government.The Autonomous Community of Madrid has an elected regional parliament, which elects a president to lead the regional government. The president is assisted by ministers who oversee the community's administrative services.

Demographics

Madrid residents are officially known as Madrilenos, but they are colloquially called gatos (cats). Madrilenos speak Castilian Spanish, the official language of Spain. Most residents live in apartments, and the city is rather crowded.

In the late 20th century, the city's actual population decreased due to suburban flight; recent immigration has reversed that trend. The current population numbers about three million people. Major immigrant groups include Ecuadorians, Peruvians, Colombians, Moroccans, Chinese, Guineans,Romanians and Filipinos.

Economy

Madrid's economy has historically focused on the national government. In the 1900s,

西班牙马德里

概况

马德里是西班牙的首都和最大的城市,这座城市是19世纪由摩尔人建造的。20世纪后期,西班牙法西斯政府倒台之后,由于不断发展工业和扩大建设项目,马德里市迅速发展壮大起来。

一、地理

马德里位于北纬40°26′,西经3°42′,地处靠近西班牙中部地区的高原。海拔2 150英尺,是欧洲最高的首都之一。20世纪50年代,马德里经历了一段人口暴涨期,从那时起,城市也逐步扩张到包括城郊的住宅及工厂地区。马德里的面积有近234平方英里。

二、气候

马德里拥有地中海气候,平均气温在冬季的华氏45度到夏季的华氏87~89度之间变化,全年的降水比较有限,因此,夏季一般非常干燥。

三、政府

西班牙全国被划分为自治社区,每个社区有权管理本区内的政府事务,马德里是马德里自治社区的首府,属于单一的行政区。

马德里市由一个选举出的市政委员会和一个市长管理,同时,市政委员会的每个成员还分管市政府的某一部门。马德里自治社区拥有选举产生的地区议会,议会再选出议长来领导地区政府。议长则由各部长协助工作,部长们负责监督社区的行政事务。

四、人口

马德里的居民被正式称为马德里人,但是民间俗称"卡多人"(猫)。马德里人讲卡斯蒂利亚西班牙语,即西班牙官方语。大多数居民住在公寓里,且城市相当拥挤。

20世纪后期,由于人们向城郊迁移,实际上市区人口在不断下降,而近些年来,移民的涌入改变了这一趋势,目前城市的人口数量大约为300万,其中主要的移民群体包括厄瓜多尔人、秘鲁人、哥伦比亚人、摩洛哥人、中国人、几内亚人、罗马尼亚人和菲律宾人。

五、经济

历史上,马德里的经济始终围绕着国家政府管理,到了20世纪,国家努力增加马德里

an effort was made to increase Madrid's industrial base, and today the city is second only to Barcelona in terms of manufacturing. Major industries include automobiles, chemicals, clothing and electronics. A significant portion of the economy depends on tourism; Madrid is one of the most popular tourist attractions in Europe.

The History

The Moors built a fortress called Majerit on the site that would eventually become the city of Madrid. King Alfonso VI of Leon and Castile ousted the Moors from the area in 1085, but Madrid remained a small town until 1561, when Philip II moved the court to Madrid, essentially making it the capital of Spain.

In the 15th and 16th centuries, as the Spanish Empire grew in power and Spain's explorers discovered treasures in the Americas, Madrid flourished and became one of western Europe's great cities. Although the city was home to rich aristocrats and powerful royal officials, most of the city residents lived in poverty. At the time, Madrid was not considered a safe city due to frequent epidemics and a skyrocketing crime rate. The government took steps to clean up the city in the 1700s; conditions substantially improved for the population as a whole.

Napoleon occupied the city from 1808 to 1813 until a growing Spanish resistance movement drove the French from Spain. Madrid did not join the Industrial Revolution of the late 18th and early 19th centuries. As a result, Madrid's population decreased at a time when industrialized cities in Europe experienced a population boom. Madrid languished until the 1930s when the city became pivotal in the Spanish Civil War. The government-supporting Spanish Republicans moved the capital from Madrid to Valencia and then to Barcelona, but when the fascists under General Francisco Franco won the war in 1939, Madrid was re-established as the nation's capital. After the war, industrial growth helped to improve Madrid's economic situation. Spain was officially a neutral country during World War II.

The Sights and Sounds

The Royal Palace is an excellent first destination. It is said that Philip V, the first Bourbon King of Spain, designed the building in the manner of the gardens and buildings of Versailles. No expense was spared in the construction of this magnificent 2,800 room palace. The palace was built between 1738 and 1755 on the site of a former Moorish fortress named Antiguo Alcázar. Spanish monarchs lived in the palace from from 1764 to 1931. The sheer size of the palace, its lavish decorations, and its elaborate Rococo splendor make this one of Madrid's finest tourist sites. The adjoining gardens, not surprisingly, are some of the best in Madrid. The palace is no longer the residence of the king, but is used for state functions and diplomatic receptions.

The Queen Sophia Arts Centre, which opened in 1986, is one of the most recent additions to the already impressive Madrid arts scene. One of the most famous works here is Picasso's Guernica. This painting, which captures the brutality and despair of war, depicts the Nazi bombing of the Basque city of Guernica. The center also includes important works by the Spanish painters Joan Miró and Salvador Dalí. The permanent collection is divided between the second and fourth floors of the museum. The division intentionally separates works created before and after 1939, the end of the Spanish Civil War.

的工业基础,如今,这座城市的加工制造业在全国排名第二,仅次于巴塞罗那。主要工业包括汽车、化学品、服装和电子产品。经济的相当一部分依赖于旅游,马德里是欧洲最热门的旅游目的地之一。

光影流金

摩尔人在后来成为马德里市的地方首先修建了一座要塞,称为"马格利特"。1085年,莱昂和卡斯蒂利亚王国的国王阿方索六世将摩尔人从这一地区驱逐了出去。不过,之后马德里一直是一座小镇,直到1561年,腓力二世把王宫迁到马德里,这里才真正成为西班牙的首都。

15和16世纪里,随着西班牙帝国权力的加强,加之西班牙探险者在美洲发现的财宝,马德里的繁荣达到顶峰,并成为西欧最伟大的城市之一。尽管有钱的贵族和有权的皇室官员都住在城里,但是大多数城市居民生活在贫困之中。当时的马德里并不是一座安全的城市,经常有流行病爆发,犯罪率猛涨。进入18世纪后,政府采取措施清除了城市内的犯罪分子,对于整个城市人口来说,居住环境才得以真正改善。

从1808年到1813年,拿破仑占领了这座城市,直到不断高涨的西班牙反抗势力将这些法国人赶出西班牙。马德里并没有加入18世纪后期到19世纪初的工业革命,因此,当欧洲工业化的城市正经历人口暴涨的时候,马德里的人口却在一段时间内呈下降趋势。马德里逐渐失去了原有的活力,直到20世纪30年代,当这座城市成为西班牙内战的轴心,其重要性才重新被人们认识。虽然由政府支持的西班牙共和党人将首都从马德里迁到瓦伦西亚,之后又从瓦伦西亚迁往巴塞罗那,但是,1939年,当弗朗西斯科·佛朗哥将军率领的法西斯分子赢得内战以后,马德里被重新确立为国家的首都。战争结束之后,工业的发展改善了马德里的经济环境。在第二次世界大战期间,西班牙属于官方中立国家。

声光景点

皇宫是马德里旅游绝佳的首选站点。据说,波旁家族的第一位西班牙国王腓力五世,仿照凡尔赛宫的花园和建筑设计了这座宫殿,这座包括2 800间房屋的恢宏宫殿在建筑期间,没有花费任何代价,皇宫是在原来摩尔人的一处名为安提瓜宫的城堡基础上建造的,建设周期从1738年一直持续到1755年。1764年~1931年,西班牙王室成员都住在这里。无论是宫殿庞大的面积、极尽铺张的装饰,还是复杂精美的洛可可式华彩都使它成为马德里最完美的旅游胜地之一,毫无疑问,与皇宫毗连的花园在整个西班牙也是首屈一指的。如今,皇宫已经不再是国王的住所,而是用来作为国宴和外交接待的场所。

1986年开张的索菲亚王妃艺术中心可谓是马德里出色艺术风景的锦上添花之作,这里最著名的作品之一是毕加索的《格尔尼卡》,这幅以战争暴力和绝望为主题的油画作品描绘的是纳粹轰炸格尔尼卡的巴斯克城的景象。此外,艺术中心其他重量级的展品还包括西班牙画家胡安·米罗以及萨尔瓦多·达利的作品。在博物馆的2层和4层之间还被划分出永久性收藏馆,有意识地将1939年,即西班牙内战之前和之后的作品分开展示。

The Convent of the Royal Barefoot Nuns, which remains active to this day, dates to the time of Charles V, a Holy Roman Emperor and King of Spain in the 16th century. The nuns who entered this convent were royals from the courts of Spain and its empire. For this reason, the convent holds a treasure-trove of art, paintings, religious artifacts and tapestries, most of which are on display to the public.

The Prado Museum is considered one of the finest museums of its kind in the world, housing a virtual history of Spanish art and culture. Magnificent works from Goya and El Greco are just the beginning. It is difficult to see all the museum has to offer, even in a day or two. There are some 8,600 paintings alone, along with many sculptures, drawings and other art.

If there is anything missing from the Prado collection, visitors will find it at the Thyssen Bornemisza Museum of Art, a collection of some 800 paintings from the 13th through the 20th century. This collection was acquired by Spain from a Swiss baron; the museum is named in his honor.

Visitors and locals alike love the Sunday morning market at El Rastro Flea Market. The market has been in business for nearly 5 centuries. Vendors sell all kinds of goods and there are many excellent tapas restaurants nearby.

One of the most magnificent buildings in Madrid is the Palace of Bibliotecas y Museos. It was built in 1892 to celebrate the 400th anniversary of Columbus's discovery of America and to honor his Spanish patron, Queen Isabella II. It now houses the Archaeological Museum as well as the National Library and Art Galleries.

Madrid's Great Square is an architecture marvel and gathering place. King Philip III established the square in 1619; in tribute to him, there is a statue of Philip III on horseback in the middle of the square. Throughout history this place has been the site of canonizations, hangings, riots, bullfights and just about every other social gathering.

Madrid, and all of Spain for that matter, is especially known for bullfighting and flamenco dancing. Bullfighting takes place at the Plaza La Ventas, usually on Sundays between March and October. Traditional flamenco dancers, graceful and expressive, frequently perform in the city's nightclubs.

The Trivia

Fact: The Madrilenos, residents of Madrid, have a leisurely lifestyle. Many offices and stores open at 9 a.m. and close at 1:30 p.m. for lunch. Businesses usually reopen at 5 p.m. and close again around 8 p.m..

Fact: Football (known as soccer in America) is Spain's national passion. Real Madrid is the local football team and one of the most beloved world teams.

Fact: Visitors may be surprised to note that dinner typically does not start until around 10 p.m.. In fact, traffic jams are a common occurrence in the early morning, when revelers return home from a night of fun.

Why Madrid Is a 50 plus one City

Imagine a city with nearly 500 years of wealth accumulated from far-flung and culturally rich colonies. This is Madrid in a nutshell, defined by its artistic, religious, architectural and cultural heritage. Visitors come to this fine European city to be both entertained and educated.

直到今天依然活跃的皇家赤足女修院,其历史可以追溯到查理五世,一位16世纪时的神圣罗马皇帝和西班牙国王在位时期。进入该修道院的修女都是来自西班牙皇宫和帝国的皇亲国戚。正因为如此,修道院里收藏了许多珍贵的艺术宝物,如油画、宗教手工艺品和挂毯等,其中大多数都面向公众开放。

普拉多博物馆被公认为世界上此类博物馆中最完美的一座,涵盖了整个西班牙艺术和文化的历史,戈雅和艾尔·格列柯的恢弘作品仅仅是开始,要欣赏完博物馆里所有的展品有些困难,即使花费一两天时间也不一定能做到。这里单单油画就有8 600件,此外,还有许多雕塑作品、素描及其他艺术品。

假如游客在普拉多博物馆错过了一些展品的话,在提森–波那米萨美术馆可以得到弥补。这里收藏有大约800件13~20世纪的绘画作品,而这些藏品是西班牙政府从一位瑞士男爵那里得到的,因此,该博物馆也就以他的名字命名。

无论是游客还是当地人都同样喜欢光顾周日早上开放的艾尔拉斯特洛跳蚤市场,这个交易市场已经存在了近五个世纪了,小贩们兜售各类商品,附近还有许多很棒的餐前小吃馆。

图书馆和博物馆大宫是马德里最富丽堂皇的建筑之一,这座修建于1892年的建筑当时是为了纪念哥伦布发现美洲大陆400周年,同时也为了纪念他的西班牙赞助者女王伊丽莎白二世。现在这座建筑成为西班牙考古博物馆、国家图书馆以及美术馆的所在地。

马德里大广场是一处考古奇迹和集会场所,1619年国王腓力三世修建了这个广场,为了纪念他,人们在广场中央矗立起了一座腓力三世在马背上的雕像。在西班牙历史上,这个广场曾被作为死者追封地、绞刑场、暴乱地、斗牛场以及几乎所有可能的社会活动集会地。

马德里以及西班牙所有地区都以斗牛和弗拉门戈舞而著名,斗牛通常都在3月到10月期间的星期日于凡塔斯广场举行。传统的弗拉门戈舞优雅且富有表现力,常常在市区的夜总会进行演出。

奇闻轶事

之一:马德里人,即马德里的居民,过着一种悠闲的生活,许多办公场所和商店上午九点开门,到下午一点半关门吃午饭,通常下午五点再次开门,然后到八点左右再次关门。

之二:足球(在美国称为英式足球)是西班牙全民族的爱好,皇家马德里队是当地的足球队,也是最受宠爱的世界级球队之一。

之三:来到马德里的游客可能会惊讶地发现,当地人直到晚上十点才吃晚饭,事实上,凌晨的交通堵塞在马德里是一个非常普遍的现象,因为,这时正是那些狂欢人员一夜享乐后回家的时间。

为什么马德里入选50 + 1个城市?

设想一下,有这样一座城市,它拥有在近500年的历史长河中,从其广为延伸的、文化丰厚的殖民地积累起来的财富,这就是马德里。概括地说,这是一座拥有丰富的艺术、宗教、建筑和文化遗产的城市。游客们来到这座美丽的欧洲城市既得到了快乐,也受到了熏陶。

Twenty-nine

Mecca, Saudi Arabia

The Basic Facts

Mecca is the holiest city of Islam and the birthplace of the prophet Muhammad. One of the Five Pillars of Islam requires that every Muslim who is physically and financially able must make a pilgrimage to Mecca (known as the hajj) at least once.

Geography

Mecca lies at 21 degrees 27 minutes north latitude and 39 degrees 45 minutes east longitude. The city is located in western Saudi Arabia in a barren valley surrounded by hills and mountains. The heart of Mecca is the Kaaba within the Sacred Mosque. The Kaaba is a black granite structure, one of the most sacred sites in Islam; Muslims throughout the world face the direction of the Kaaba during their daily prayers.

In the 1950s, modern housing was built in the city for permanent residents and hotels for hajj pilgrims. Suburbs sprang up around the city for wealthier residents.

Climate

Mecca's climate is similar to the rest of Saudi Arabia: arid and quite warm throughout the year. Average temperatures range from the mid-80s Fahrenheit in winter to the upper 90s Fahrenheit in summer.

Government

Saudi Arabia is ruled by a king with the assistance of appointed ministers. The country is divided into 13 regions. Each region has a regional governor in charge of government services. The governor reports directly to the Saudi Arabian Minister of the Interior.

Demographics

The population of Mecca is almost entirely Middle Eastern and numbers about 1.1 million people. Many residents are employed year-round solely to prepare for and manage the activities of the annual hajj, which attracts millions of Muslims from around the world. During the hajj, roadblocks are set up to keep non-Muslims from entering Mecca. In fact, non-Muslims are prohibited from entering the city at any time. This has not prevented some non-Muslims from secretly participating in the hajj and writing about their experiences.

Economy

Mecca's economy depends almost entirely on the money spent by hajj pilgrims. The Saudi Arabian government invests millions of dollars every year to help the city provide adequate security, health care and other services. There are small industries located in Mecca, but the city itself has not been a significant contributor to the Saudi Arabian economy since the 1940s.

沙特阿拉伯麦加

概况

麦加是伊斯兰教最神圣的城市,是先知穆罕默德出生的地方。作为伊斯兰教的"五功"之一,每一位穆斯林在身体和经济能够承受的情况下,都必须去麦加朝觐(被称作哈吉)至少一次。

一、地理

麦加位于北纬21°27′,东经39°45′,地处沙特阿拉伯西部一个荒芜的山谷里,四周被丘陵和山脉包围。麦加的心脏是位于神圣大清真寺内的"克尔白"(天房)。天房是一座黑色的建筑,是伊斯兰世界最为神圣的地方之一,每天,世界各地的穆斯林们都要在祷告时面向天房的方向。

20世纪50年代,现代建筑出现在麦加城内,作为那些永久性居民的住宅以及来朝觐的教徒居住的旅馆。城市郊区也开始发展成为有钱人的居住区。

二、气候

麦加的气候与沙特阿拉伯其他地区一样:全年干旱,而且温暖异常。平均气温在冬季的华氏85度至夏季的华氏97~99度。

三、政府

沙特阿拉伯由一位国王统治,国王任命的大臣辅助其工作,全国划分为13个地区,每个区都有一个地区行政长官负责地方政府的管理。而行政长官直接向沙特阿拉伯内务部长汇报。

四、人口

麦加的人口构成几乎全都是中东地区的人,总数大约在110万。许多居民一年到头的工作就是为每年一次的哈吉做准备和安排活动,因为哈吉期间,会有来自世界各地数百万的朝圣者,所以为了防止非穆斯林教徒进入麦加,人们会设置路障。其实任何时候,非穆斯林教徒都被禁止进入城市的,即便如此,一些非穆斯林教徒还是会偷偷溜进去参加哈吉,并将他们的经历写出来公之于众。

五、经济

麦加的经济几乎全部依赖于朝觐教徒所赐,沙特阿拉伯政府每年投入数百万美元帮助城市提供安全保障、医疗服务以及其他服务项目。尽管麦加也有一些小型工业,但是自从20世纪40年代以来,城市本身对于国家经济的贡献并不明显。

The Madinah al-Munawarah Highway is the principal road serving Mecca. Rail travel is almost nonexistent in Saudi Arabia. The King Abdul Aziz International Airport in nearby Jiddah is the principal airport for international pilgrims making the hajj.

The History

Abraham, the patriarch of the Israelites, is said to have arrived in Mecca as early as 3000 B.C.. According to Islamic tradition, Abraham left Mecca on God's command, leaving his wife and son there to die. Abraham later returned and according to tradition, God commanded him to create the Kabaa.

Mecca began as a trading center in about 500 A.D.. The residents gradually moved away from the monotheism practiced by Abraham and became monotheistic; they worshipped their idols at the Kaaba. The prophet Muhammad was born in Mecca in 570, but was driven from the city in 622 after its people rejected his teachings.In 630 AD, Muhammad and his followers returned to take Mecca by force. They destroyed the pagan idols, but left the shrine of the Kabaa intact. Shortly after his return, Muhammad instituted the ritual of the hajj and declared the city the center of Islam.

Although Mecca remained a holy city, its political influence in the Middle East declined rapidly in the 7th century. Mecca was ruled until 1924 by the descendants of Muhammad known as Sharifs. In that year, the Arab leader, Abd al-Aziz ibn Saud conquered the city and it became part of the Kingdom of Saudi. The city grew rapidly in the latter half of the 20th century and attracts thousands of the world's Muslims during the annual hajj.

The Sights and Sounds

Pilgrims end their hajj at the Sacred Mosque (Masjid al-Haram), where they recite prayers and perform various rituals over a period of several days. One of these rituals involves circling the Kaaba seven times.

Kaaba is the holy shrine at Mecca that houses a sacred religious relic. Muslims believe that this shrine was built by Abraham and his son Ishmael. It is thought to be the first place created on the planet and a place so sacred that God's power directly touches the Earth at this point.

The Well of Zamzam is another holy site in Mecca. The water from this well is believed to have healing properties. Most Muslim visitors bring a large bottle of this holy water back home with them.

Pilgrims also visit a village close to Mecca called Mina. There they perform another sacred ritual called stoning the devil. To symbolize this ritual, Mina has a number of stone columns in the village. After visiting the village of Mina, pilgrims walk up a hill called the Mount Arafat to pray. This site was where the prophet Muhammad delivered his final sermon.

Medina, near Mecca, is also off-limits to non-Muslims. Medina is the second holiest city of Islam because it is the former home of Muhammad and also where he died. The first Islamic mosque is also located in Medina. Pilgrims who visit Mecca also visit Medina during the hajj.

The Trivia

Fact: Saudi Arabia is an Islamic country and has strict rules regarding the manner in

马迪娜–阿姆纳瓦拉公路是通往麦加的主要道路,在沙特阿拉伯,铁路交通几乎不存在,位于麦加附近吉达港的国王阿卜杜勒·阿齐兹国际机场,是为全世界来参加哈吉的朝圣者提供服务的主要机场。

光影流金

据说,犹太人的始祖亚伯拉罕早在公元前3 000年就到达了麦加,根据伊斯兰教的传说,亚伯拉罕在上帝的命令下离开了麦加,而他的妻子和儿子则被留在那里一直到死。传说后来亚伯拉罕又回到了麦加,并根据上帝的指令创建了天房。

公元500年左右麦加开始成为贸易中心,居民们逐渐脱离了亚伯拉罕信奉的一神教,开始了对不同神的崇拜,他们在天房祭祀自己心目中的神。570年,先知穆罕默德在麦加出生,然而,622年由于人们拒绝接受他的教义,他被赶出了麦加。630年,穆罕默德和他的追随者们通过武力重返麦加,他们捣毁了异教徒的神像,但是却将天房的圣坛完好地保留了下来。不久,穆罕默德建立了宗教哈吉仪式,并宣布麦加为伊斯兰教的中心。

虽然麦加依然是一座圣城,但是,7世纪时它在中东地区的政治影响却迅速下降。麦加一直处在被称作沙里夫的穆罕默德的后代统治之下,直到1924年,阿拉伯领袖阿卜杜勒·阿齐兹·伊本·沙特征服了这座城市,麦加也成为沙特阿拉伯王国的一部分。20世纪后半期这座城市发展迅速,在每年的哈吉期间,麦加都要吸引成千上万来自世界各地的穆斯林。

声光景点

麦加的神圣大清真寺(马吉德–阿哈拉姆)是朝圣者们完成哈吉的地方,他们在这里诵咏祷文,进行各类宗教仪式,整个过程要持续几天。其中一项仪式就是绕着天房转七圈。

天房是位于麦加的圣坛,供奉着一件神圣的宗教遗物,穆斯林们相信这座圣坛是由亚伯拉罕和他的儿子以实玛利建造的,他们还认为这里是这座星球上第一个被创造出来的地方,它是如此神圣,以至于在这里可以直接感到上帝施加于地球的力量。

"渗渗井"是麦加的另一处圣所,人们相信这口井的水有治疗功效,大多数来访的穆斯林在回家时都要带上一大瓶这口井里的圣水。

此外,朝圣者们还要拜访麦加附近的一个名叫米纳的村子,在那里,他们举行另一项神圣的宗教仪式,称作"射石驱魔",作为这项仪式的象征,在米纳村里有许多石柱。拜访完米纳村之后,朝圣者们会步行登上一座名为阿拉法特的山做祈祷,这里是先知穆罕默德作最后一次布道的地方。

离麦加不远的麦地那也是禁止非伊斯兰教徒入内的,麦地那是伊斯兰教的第二大圣城,因为这里是原来穆罕默德的家,也是他死去的地方。第一座伊斯兰教清真寺也坐落在麦地那。在哈吉期间,来麦加朝圣的人们也会光临麦地那。

奇闻轶事

之一:沙特阿拉伯是一个伊斯兰教国家,因此,在妇女着装和行为方面有着严格的规

which women can dress and behave. Female visitors are advised to dress modestly in long shirts, long skirts and headscarves. Passersby often comment raucously if they see an improperly-dressed woman.

Fact: Experts advise that a woman should travel to Mecca—and elsewhere in Saudi Arabia, for that matter—with her husband or another male relative, in order to spare themselves from unnecessary trouble with locals. Women are also strongly recommended never to walk unattended.

Fact: The Kaaba stands within the Sacred Mosque and contains the Black Stone, which Muslims believe was sent from heaven by Allah and discovered by Muhammad.

Fact: According to Arab tradition, after they were cast out from Eden, Adam and Eve eventually came to Mount Arafat, near Mecca. Adam prayed to God to let him build a shrine in Mecca. According to legend, Adam is buried in Mecca and Eve is buried in nearby Jiddah.

Fact: The pilgrimage of the hajj is one of five fundamental Islamic practices known as the Five Pillars of Islam. Before commencing the hajj, the pilgrim must redress all wrongs, pay off all debts, and have enough money both for the journey and to support his or her family while away.

Why Mecca Is a 50 plus one City

Mecca's greatness results not from its tourism, and certainly not for its nightlife.Mecca is a great city because it a holy city, the holiest in all Islam. Most westerners simply cannot comprehend the significance of this city for worldwide Muslims.During the hajj the city is chaotic and crowded, but for the devout it is a religious experience that cannot be equaled.

定,建议女性游客穿着要端庄,以长衬衫、长裙和头巾为主,假如路人看见一位妇女穿着不得体,他们常会指指点点。

之二:旅行专家建议到麦加以及沙特阿拉伯其他地区旅行的妇女,应当和丈夫或别的男性亲属同行,以避免与当地人可能产生的不必要的麻烦。同时,强烈建议妇女不要单独在街上行走。

之三:天房位于神圣大清真寺内,里面供奉着黑石,穆斯林们相信这块石头是安拉从天堂送来并被穆罕默德发现的。

之四:根据阿拉伯传说,当亚当和夏娃被上帝逐出伊甸园后,他们最终落脚到麦加附近的阿拉法特山。亚当向上帝祷告,允许他在麦加建造一座圣坛。根据传说,亚当就被埋在麦加,而夏娃则被埋在附近的吉达。

之五:哈吉朝觐是被称为伊斯兰教"五功"的五项最基本的伊斯兰教仪式中的一项,在开始哈吉之前,朝圣者必须纠正一切错误,偿清一切债务,为旅程备足盘缠,也为他的家人预留下足够的家用。

为什么麦加入选50 + 1个城市?

麦加的伟大并非源自于旅游,肯定也和夜生活毫无关系,麦加之所以伟大是因为它是一座圣城,是所有伊斯兰教徒心中最神圣的地方,大多数西方人根本无法理解这座城市对于全世界穆斯林的意义,在哈吉期间,麦加城混乱而拥挤,然而,对于那些虔诚的教徒来说,这却是一次无法比拟的宗教经历。

Thirty

Mexico City, Mexico

The Basic Facts

Mexico City, the capital of Mexico, is one of the largest cities in the world. The city experienced an economic boom from the 1940s to 1970, which caused an influx of immigrants and contributed to the overcrowding problems the city experiences today.

Geography

Mexico City lies at 19 degrees 28 minutes north latitude and 99 degrees 9 minutes west longitude. Mexico City is built on ground that used to be the lake bed of Lake Texcoco in central Mexico, roughly halfway between the Gulf of Mexico and the Pacific Ocean. The city sits in a natural basin almost 1.5 miles above sea level. The city covers roughly 600 square miles and the metropolitan area, including parts of the state of Mexico to the north.

Climate

Mexico City is 7,349 feet above sea level. This altitude makes Mexico City much cooler than the nearby coastal areas. However, visitors to Mexico City may initially be short of breath until they grow accustomed to the thinner air. Temperatures are moderate and consistent throughout the year; average temperatures range from the upper 60s in winter to the mid-70s in summer. Mexico City is mostly dry during the year, but there can be unexpected afternoon showers in the summer. Apart from the thin air, visitors to Mexico City should be aware of another aspect of its climate: the high level of air pollution and smog resulting from the city's overcrowding and traf.c congestion.

Government

Mexico City has the same official boundaries as the Federal District (Distrito Federal, or D.F.) of Mexico, which is a separate political area governed similarly to the United States' District of Columbia.

Mexico City's mayor (whose official title is Jefe de Gobierno, or head of government) is the chief official of the D.F.. The mayor is elected to a 6-year term and is considered second in power only to the president of Mexico.

Voters also elect a legislative assembly of 66 deputies representing city wards, as well as senators and deputies from the D.F. to serve in Mexico's General Congress.

Demographics

The majority of Mexico City residents are mestizos, descendants of the native Indians and the Spanish settlers who arrived in the 1500s. Almost all residents are Spanish-speaking; roughly 2 percent also speak an Indian language. The promise of good paying jobs and economic opportunities has drawn many rural Mexicans to Mexico City. Recent European, Middle Eastern, and Asian immigration has given the city an international flavor. Roman Catholicism is the dominant religion. The population numbers more than 8.7 million, but the entire metropolitan area's population is over 19 million, making it one of

墨西哥墨西哥城

概况

墨西哥的首都墨西哥城是世界上最大的城市之一。从20世纪40年代到70年代，这座城市经历了一次经济的快速增长，同时，也吸引了大批的外来移民，造成今天墨西哥城过度拥挤的问题。

一、地理

墨西哥城位于北纬19°28′，西经99°9′，城市建在墨西哥中部原塔克斯科克湖湖底之上，大致处在墨西哥湾和太平洋之间，并且坐落于海平面以上1.5英里的一个自然盆地内。墨西哥城主要范围的面积约为600平方英里，包括北面的墨西哥州。

二、气候

墨西哥城海拔7 349英尺，高纬度使得墨西哥城较之周边沿海地区更为凉爽，但是，来到墨西哥城的游客一开始可能会喘不上气，除非他们逐渐适应了这里相对稀薄的空气。墨西哥城全年气候温和、变化不大，平均气温在冬季的华氏67~69度到夏季的华氏75度。虽然墨西哥城一年大部分时间都很干燥，但是夏天午后有可能出现雷阵雨。除了稀薄的空气以外，来到墨西哥城的游客还应该意识到这里气候的另一面：由于人口过剩及交通堵塞而引起的重度的空气污染和烟雾。

三、政府

墨西哥城和墨西哥联邦行政区有着同样的行政区划，而墨西哥联邦行政区是一个独立的政治地区，其管理类似于美国的哥伦比亚特区。

墨西哥城市长（官方头衔为政府首脑）是墨西哥联邦行政区的主要官员，由选举产生，任期6年，被认为是权力仅次于墨西哥总统的人物。

此外，选民还选举产生一个立法会，立法会包括66名代表各自选区的成员、参议员以及来自墨西哥联邦行政区的为墨西哥国家议会服务的代表。

四、人口

墨西哥城的大多数居民都是梅斯蒂索混血儿，也就是美洲印第安人与16世纪来到这里的西班牙殖民者的后代。几乎所有的居民都讲西班牙语，此外，还有大约2%的人讲印第安语。

由于在城里有可能找到薪水较高的工作且有更多的就业机会，许多农村人都被吸引进墨西哥城，近年来，大批来自欧洲、中东和亚洲的移民赋予了这座城市国际大都市的味道。天主教是当地主要的宗教。尽管市区人口是870万，但是整个大市范围的人口却达到

the largest metropolitan areas in the world.

Economy

Almost half of Mexico's manufacturing industry is located in or around Mexico City. Many workers also work in the petroleum, mineral relining and construction industries. The city and the federal government are also major employers. Mexico City is the country's center for finance and telecommunications. An interesting media fact is that 14 newspapers are published daily in the city—more per capita than any other world city.

The History

The Aztec city of Tenochtitlán was founded in 1325 on the site that would become Mexico City. Emperor Montezuma welcomed the Spanish explorer Hernándo Cortés into the city in 1519, believing him to be a representative of the Aztec god Quetzalcoatl. Cortés promptly took control of the city, but was forced out a year later. He returned with a larger force in 1521, reclaimed the city and destroyed it. Cortés then directed the construction of Mexico City on the site, and declared it the capital of New Spain. The city soon became the largest city in the Western Hemisphere. After a disastrous flood in 1629, the Spanish created canal and dike systems to drain Lake Texcoco.

In 1810 Mexico declared independence from Spain, and Mexico City remained the capital. In 1847, during the Mexican-American War, U.S. troops invaded and besieged Mexico City until 1848. France conquered Mexico City in 1863 and Maximilian—of the Austrian Habsburg family—became emperor of Mexico.Maximilian was deposed by General Porfirio Díaz, who became the country's president in 1876 and ruled as a dictator. Discontent grew, however, and Díaz was jailed in 1910, an event that brought about the Mexican Revolution. Many groups would fight for control of the city over the next several decades.

The Sights and Sounds

The heart of the historical and traditional section of Mexico City is the Centro Histórico. Several important museums in this area are frequent stops for visitors,including the Antiguo Colegio de San Ildefonso, built originally as a Catholic college in the 18th century. The museum features exhibits of regional artists. In addition, Museo de la Ciudad de México, the city museum, houses a fine collection devoted almost exclusively to the history of Mexico City. Visitors also enjoy the Museo Cuevas, which honors the work of José Luis Cuevas and other modern artists from around the world.

The Church of Santo Domingo, built in the 18th century, is a fine example of the Baroque style so popular at the time the church and other buildings were constructed. Alameda Central is nearby: a large and scenic park filled with fountains, lush landscaping, and often crowded with locals and visitors alike. This area had once been an Aztec market.

Mexico City's Zócalo, or the main square, is a huge space devoted largely to spectacular events: Independence Day celebrations, festivals and political rallies.This area was once the ceremonial center of the Aztec empire; later, the Spanish constructed marvelous buildings in this area.

The Cathedral Metropolitan took nearly 3 centuries to complete; like most cathedrals completed over so many years, it re.ects the various styles of architecture of many different eras. The church is filled with art, artifacts and altars—an amazing collection, among the finest in the Spanish Empire. Concern for the structural integrity of the church recently

了1 900万,使之名副其实地成为世界上最大的城市之一。

五、经济

墨西哥几乎近一半的加工工业都位于墨西哥城内或周边地区,此外,还有许多工人从事石油、矿石提炼以及建筑行业。市政府和联邦政府是主要的雇主。墨西哥城是国家财政和电讯行业的中心。在传媒方面有一个有趣的现象,那就是这座城市里每天出版的报纸多达14家 —— 是世界上人均报刊最多的城市。

历史

1325年,阿兹特克人在后来成为墨西哥城的地方建立了特诺奇提特兰市。1519年,阿兹特克皇帝蒙提祖马,因为相信西班牙探险家费尔南多·科尔特斯是阿兹特克羽蛇神的化身而将他迎入城中,然而,科尔特斯立刻夺取了城市的控制权,可惜,好景不长,一年后他就被赶出了这座城市。1521年,科尔特斯率领更多人重新夺取了城市,并对它进行了彻底破坏。之后,在科尔特斯的指导下,在城市原址上重新建立起了墨西哥城,并被宣布为新西班牙的首都。这座城市很快成为西半球最大的城市。1629年一场灾难性的洪水之后,西班牙人修建了运河和堤坝系统来输导塔克斯科克湖水。

1810年,墨西哥宣布从西班牙统治中获得独立,墨西哥城仍为国家首都。1847年,墨西哥和美国战争期间,美军部队入侵并围攻墨西哥城长达一年。1863年,法国征服墨西哥城,麦克米连 —— 他属于奥匈帝国的哈布斯堡家族 —— 成为墨西哥皇帝。1876年,麦克米连被波菲里奥·迪亚兹废黜,后者成为墨西哥总统并开始了其独裁统治。然而,随着国内不满情绪的增长,1910年,迪亚兹被关进监狱,这一事件被称为墨西哥革命。在接下来的几十年间,许多组织都曾试图夺取对城市的控制权。

声光景点

墨西哥城传统和历史的核心部分就是"历史中心",这一区域的几座重要的博物馆是游客经常光顾的地方,其中包括古老的圣伊德凡索学院,最初是18世纪时作为天主教堂修建的,该博物馆展出的是大量当地艺术家的作品。此外,墨西哥城博物馆,即城市博物馆内精美的收藏几乎都是关于墨西哥城历史的。令游客感兴趣的还有奎瓦斯博物馆,因收藏了约瑟·路易斯·奎瓦斯以及其他来自世界各地的现代艺术家的作品而颇受关注。

圣多明戈教堂修建于18世纪,是那个时代教堂及其他建筑流行的巴洛克风格的完美代表。附近的阿拉米达(林荫散步)中央公园是一座大型景观公园,里面有各式各样的喷泉、繁茂成荫的绿地,无论是当地人还是外来客都会经常在此聚集,这里曾经还是阿兹特克人的一个市场。

墨西哥城的"萨卡罗"或主广场是一个面积很大的广场,主要为举行一些大型的公共活动服务,例如,独立日庆典、节日及政治集会等。这一区域过去是阿兹特克皇帝举行典礼仪式的中心,后来,西班牙人在这里修建了许多令人不可思议的建筑。

大都会大教堂的建成花费了近三个世纪的时间,正如大多数耗时多年的教堂一样,这座教堂同样反映了不同时代建筑的多样风格。教堂内随处都是美术品、手工艺品和祭坛 —— 其精美程度在整个西班牙帝国都可谓首屈一指。近年来,由于不堪自身重负,教

spurred rehabilitative efforts; it was sinking under its own weight.

The Palacio National is at the site of Montezuma's former castle. This palace was built under the direction of Hernándo Cortés in the 17th century; additions were constructed in the 20th century. It is the seat of government and houses the famous liberty bell, first rung by Miguel Hidalgo in 1810 to proclaim Mexico's independence. Murals painted by the famous Mexican artist Diego Rivera dominate the palace; these murals depict more than 200 years of Mexican history,and took more than 15 years to complete.

Museo de Templo Mayor is a large museum built on the former location of the Great Temple of Tenochtitlán. A notable feature is the temple dedicated to the ancient Aztec gods Huitzilopochtli and Tlaloc, representing death and rain,respectively. Thousands of people are said to have been sacrificed to the gods at this spot. The adjacent museum contains thousands of historical artifacts (including skulls, carvings, and ceramic) that were discovered here and at other central Mexican ruins. The museum's pièce de résistance is the Coyolxauhqui Stone, an eight-ton carving named for the Moon goddess who was beheaded for slaughtering hundreds of her people. Cheery group, these Aztecs!

The Museo Nacional de Antropología is considered one of the world's greatest anthropological museums, with its outstanding collection of Aztec and Mayan art as well as artifacts of other Mexican cultures. The museum is in Chapultepec Park,along with others including the Museum of Modern Art and the Tamayo Museum of Contemporary Art.

The Trivia

Fact: Most of historical Mexico City was built by native Mexicans. Rubble from the original Aztec city was used to construct much of the city.

Fact: A major earthquake struck Mexico City in September 1985. The earthquake and its aftershocks destroyed more than 100,000 dwellings. The damage was so extensive due to the underlying soft clay. Survivors described the buildings as shaking like jelly. Following the earthquake, city officials instituted major reforms of city building codes and other safety measures. Official reports declared that 5,000 people were killed; unofficially, however, the death toll was estimated at nearly 50,000. As many as 90,000 people were rendered homeless.

Fact: Mexico City was besieged by U.S. troops in the Mexican-American War after the Battle of Chapultepec. In 1847 six military students jumped to their deaths from Chapultepec Castle to avoid having to surrender. The Monumento a los Niños(Monument to the Young Heroes) stands in their honor in Chapultepec Park.

Fact: Residents do not refer to the city as Mexico City. Rather, they call it either Mexico or D.F., the latter as an abbreviation for Distrito Federal.

Fact: Mexico City suffers greatly from air pollution due to population density,traffic congestion, and it location in a natural basin. The skies are often overcast with a thick brown smog, at which time the government officially declares dangerous pollution levels.

Why Mexico City Is a 50 plus one City

Mexico City's expanse can be intimidating for visitors, but that feeling can be overcome by taking ample time to explore the city's sights and sounds. One cannot help to be impressed by the rich history, culture and vitality of this marvelous North American city. Viva la Ciudad!

堂正在下沉,因此,为了保持教堂建筑的完整性,人们开始了修缮工作。

国家宫是在原来蒙提祖马城堡旧址上修建的,宫殿建造于17世纪,是在费尔南多·科尔特斯指导下进行的。20世纪时,宫殿又经过了扩建。如今,这里是政府办公场所。宫殿内著名的自由大钟,其第一声是1810年由米格尔·伊达尔戈撞响的,用来宣告墨西哥独立。由墨西哥著名的画家迭戈·里维拉创作的壁画占据了宫殿的主体,这些壁画描绘了墨西哥城200多年的历史,并且是画家超过15年心血的结晶。

大神庙博物馆是在特诺奇提特兰大寺庙的旧址上修建的,其中著名的景观是供奉古代阿兹特克人的主神威济洛波特利和特拉洛克的神庙,这两个神分别代表死亡和降雨。据说在这里成千上万的人曾被作为献给诸神的祭品。与此毗邻的博物馆里有数千件历史上在该地或墨西哥其他主要的废墟内发掘出的手工艺品(包括骷髅画、雕刻品和陶瓷等)。镇馆之宝是科约尔斯考奎石,这块重达8吨的石刻是以月亮女神的名字命名的,而这位女神由于杀人如麻而被砍头。瞧这些阿兹特克人,他们是多么活泼乐观的一群!

墨西哥国家人类学博物馆被认为是世界上最伟大的人类学博物馆之一,首届一指的是馆内阿兹特克和玛雅艺术品,以及其他属于墨西哥文化的手工艺品。博物馆位于查普特佩坎公园内,与它同样位于这座公园的还有现代艺术博物馆和塔马约当代艺术博物馆。

奇闻轶事

之一:历史上的墨西哥城大部分是由墨西哥当地人建造的。城市的主体是用早期阿兹特克城的碎石作建筑材料的。

之二:1985年9月,一场大地震袭击了墨西哥城,这场地震和其余震摧毁了超过10万间房屋,地震的破坏性之所以如此巨大主要是因为地下的软泥,幸存者们描述这些建筑就像水母一样地颤动。地震之后,城市官员制定了城市住宅建设标准以及其他一些安全措施。在这次地震当中,官方宣布的死亡数字是5000人,而民间估计死亡人数有近5万人,9万人因地震而无家可归。

之三:查普特佩坎战役之后,墨西哥和美国战争期间,墨西哥城遭到了美军部队的围攻,1847年,6名军校学员为了不当俘虏纵身跳下城堡,为了纪念他们,人们在查普特佩坎公园内矗立起了一座洛尼诺斯纪念碑(青年英雄纪念碑)。

之四:当地居民并不以墨西哥城来称呼他们的城市,他们要么称之为墨西哥,要么称之为D. F.,后者是联邦区的缩写。

之五:墨西哥城由于人口稠密、交通拥挤,且位于自然盆地内,因而城市污染严重,城市的天空常常被浓重的褐色烟雾所笼罩,而每当这时,政府就会正式宣布污染的危险指数。

为什么墨西哥城入选50＋1个城市?

虽然,墨西哥城大到足以令游客望而生畏的地步,然而,当你有充足的时间去探寻这座城市的声光景致的时候,那种恐惧感便会逐渐消失,你会禁不住为这座北美城市神奇的历史、丰富的文化、热情的活力而深深吸引,万岁,墨西哥城!

Thirty-one

Montreal, Canada

The Basic Facts

Montreal is one of the world's largest French-speaking cities. It is also largest city in the province of Quebec and the second largest city in Canada. In the late 20th century high-tech industries came to dominate Montreal's economy.

Geography

Montreal lies at 45 degrees 30 minutes north latitude and 73 degrees 35 minutes west longitude. Montreal is located on the triangular Island of Montreal in southwestern Quebec, at the confluence of the St. Lawrence and Ottawa Rivers. The city is named after Mount Royal—actually a large hill, being roughly 700 feet tall—which lies due north of the city center. The Greater Montreal Area includes the city itself, Laval, Longueuil, and smaller neighboring cities.

Both the St. Lawrence River and Lachine Canal have served Montreal as important commercial and industrial corridors. The canal once served as a detour around the St. Lawrence's Lachine Rapids, but is no longer used for commercial shipping.

Climate

Montreal lies at the nexus of several climactic regions, so the weather can vary greatly day by day and even during the course of a single day. Montreal receives almost seven feet of snow during the winter and is rainy throughout the year. Due to its far northern location, winters in Montreal can be very cold with temperatures averaging in the lower 20s Fahrenheit. Summer is usually sunny, with temperatures averaging in the mid-70s Fahrenheit.

Government

In 2002 the Quebec provincial legislature enacted a law to combine Montreal with several surrounding municipalities; the city of Montreal now has 27 boroughs. The city is led by a mayor and a city council, whose members are elected from each borough. Elected officials serve 4-year terms.

Demographics

French is the dominant language of Montrealers; nearly 70 percent of residents speak French as a first language. Most street signs, therefore, are in French. Almost half of Montreal residents speak French and English, 35 percent speak only French, and 10 percent speak only English. Over 50 percent of Montrealers claim French ancestry. The city's population is roughly 1.5 million, and the population of the Greater Montreal Area is more than 3.5 million.

加拿大蒙特利尔

概况

　　蒙特利尔是世界上最大的讲法语的城市之一,也是加拿大第二大城市以及魁北克省最大的城市。20世纪后期,高科技产业占据了蒙特利尔经济的主导地位。

一、地理

　　蒙特利尔位于北纬45°30′,西经73°35′,地处魁北克省西南部圣劳伦斯河与渥太华河交汇处,呈三角形状的蒙特利尔岛上,这座城市因位于市中心正北方向的皇家山而得名——事实上皇家山是一个大约700英尺高的巨大的丘陵。大蒙特利尔区包括城市本身、拉法尔、隆戈尔以及周边一些较小的城镇。

　　圣劳伦斯河和拉辛运河都是为蒙特利尔商业及工业服务的重要通道,虽然这条运河曾经一度作为环绕圣劳伦斯河拉辛快速航线的迂回线路,但是现在已经不再有商业船只经过这里。

二、气候

　　由于蒙特利尔位于数个气候区的汇合处,因此,每天的天气可能差异很大,即使在一天之内,天气也可能瞬息万变。蒙特利尔全年都可能降水,在冬季的降雪几乎能够达到七英尺厚。由于地理位置偏北,冬季往往非常寒冷,平均气温可以降到华氏21~23度,夏季通常阳光明媚,平均气温在华氏75度左右。

三、政府

　　2002年,魁北克省立法委员会通过了一项法案,将蒙特利尔与周边几个行政区进行了合并,如今蒙特利尔市有27个区。城市由一位市长及一个市政委员会管理,市政委员会成员由各区选举产生,任期4年。

四、人口

　　法语是蒙特利尔的主要语言,近70%的居民以法语为母语。因此,大部分的街道路牌都是用法语书写的。蒙特利尔有几乎一半的居民讲法语和英语两种语言,35%的人只讲法语,10%的人只讲英语。超过50%的蒙特利尔居民声称自己是法国人后裔。市区人口大约有150万,而大蒙特利尔区的人口则超过了350万。

Economy

Montreal is a major hub for Canadian transportation, finance and manufacturing industries. Agriculture is important in the surrounding area, and thus food processing is an important component of Montreal's economy. Manufacturing industries are numerous, including aircraft and aircraft parts, telecommunications equipment, pharmaceuticals and other chemicals, clothing, and tobacco products. Montreal's high-tech industry has grown significantly in recent years.

The History

The Huron, Algonquin and Iroquois lived here for thousands of years—well before 1535, when the French explorer Jacques Cartier arrived. Samuel de Champlain established a fur trading post on the island in 1611, which was attacked repeatedly by the Iroquois. The Iroquois fiercely defended their land until 1701, when they signed a peace treaty with the French colonists. By the early 1700s, the city became known as Montreal and was the heart of France's North American empire. The British captured the city during the French and Indian War.

In 1763 the Treaty of Paris ended the war and Canada became a British colony. The city grew through the 18th and 19th century, largely due to British migration. Montreal also served as the capital of the United Province of Canada from 1844 to 1849.

The Sights and Sounds

Montreal is an old city in a new skin. Visitors can wander narrow cobblestone streets in Vieux-Montréal (the Old City) or enjoy the latest in haute couture downtown on Rue Steet Catherine. The city has much to offer year-round. The Underground City, an amazingly large collection of walkways, shops and restaurants, is a temperature-controlled option for winter visitors. Mount Royal affords four season sports including downhill and cross-country skiing, skating, biking and hiking.

Vieux Montréal contains most of the oldest structures and most romantic restaurants in the city. Cobblestone streets are lined with interesting antique shops, restaurants and cafes. In the summer, couples sip wine outside and watch the passing crowd. It is not uncommon to see street performers in this section of the city.

Visitors marvel at how far they feel from the city when in Mount Royal Park, which surrounds its namesake. The park, which covers about 490 acres, offers beautiful views of the cityscape. A 100-foot iron cross is lighted at night and provides a beautiful view from below.

Le Jardin Botanique de Montréal is the second largest botanical garden in the world, after London's Kew Gardens. Thousands of varieties of flowers and plants from around the world are showcased here. One highlight is the Chinese Garden featuring ponds, statues and plantings common to authentic gardens in China. The Insectarium de Montréal displays collections that include thousands of insects. Visit the delightful Butterflies Go Free Exhibit, where patrons can interact with thousands of wild butterflies in a simulated natural habitat.

Of all the Gothic churches in Montreal, the Notre-Dame de Montréal Basilica is a must-see. The architecture hearkens back to the centuries-old cathedrals of Europe, and its grand interior blends ornamentation with color in a dazzling display. Its stained-glass windows represent the city's rich history. Stars made of gold adorn the rich blue ceiling,

五、经济

蒙特利尔是加拿大交通、金融和加工制造业的中心,在城市周边地区农业则是非常重要的,因此,食品加工业也是蒙特利尔经济的一个重要组成部分。生产制造业种类繁多,其中包括飞机、航空零部件、电讯产品、药品和化学品生产、服装以及烟草产品等。近年来,蒙特利尔的高科技产业也取得了显著发展。

光影流金

1535年之前,在蒙特利尔地区,休伦族人、阿尔冈昆人,以及易洛魁人已经居住了数千年,法国探险家雅克·卡蒂埃的到来打破了这里的宁静。1611年,塞缪尔·尚普兰在岛上建立了一个毛皮交易站,这个交易站遭到了易洛魁人的反复袭击,易洛魁人为捍卫自己的土地而进行的这种激烈抗争一直持续到1701年,那一年他们与法国殖民者签订了一项和平条约。18世纪初,这座城市正式定名为蒙特利尔,并且成为法属北美帝国的核心。在法印战争期间,英国人一度占领了这座城市。

1763年,《巴黎条约》的签订标志着战争的结束,加拿大成为英国的一个殖民地。18到19世纪期间,主要由于英国移民的涌入,这座城市迅速发展。在1844年~1849年,蒙特利尔还曾作为加拿大联合省的省府。

声光景点

蒙特利尔是一座新皮包裹下的旧城,游客可以在老城区狭窄的卵石铺成的街道上漫步,也可以到圣凯瑟琳大街的高级女装店欣赏最新的时装。这座城市可以为你提供全年的享受,地下城是一座专为冬季来访的游客设计的有温度控制的神奇的大型购物场所,里面有众多的人行道、商铺和餐馆。皇家山可以为游客提供一年四季的运动项目,如高山和越野滑雪、溜冰、自行车、徒步旅行等。

这座城市里最古老的建筑和最浪漫的餐厅大都位于老城区,卵石铺成的街道两边是一家家很有特色的商店、餐馆及咖啡屋。夏季,情侣们坐在户外一边呷着葡萄酒,一边注视着过往的行人,在蒙特利尔的这一区域,如果出现个把街头表演艺人你也不必感到奇怪。

身处与皇家山同名的皇家山公园,游客会惊讶地发现他们似乎距离城市那么遥远,这座面积大约490英亩的公园风景如画,美丽宜人,当夜晚来临之时,100英尺高的铁质十字架被灯光照亮,抬头望去,犹如仙境。

蒙特利尔植物园是世界上第二大植物园,仅次于伦敦的克幽花园,园内展出的有世界各地成千上万的花卉和植物品种。一个值得推荐的去处是中国花园,内有地道的中国园林常见的池塘、雕塑和栽培植物。蒙特利尔昆虫馆展出的昆虫种类多达数千种,你还可以到蝴蝶自由观赏区欣赏美丽的蝴蝶,在模拟的自然环境内和成千上万的野生蝴蝶来一次亲密的接触。

在蒙特利尔所有的哥特式教堂里,圣母大教堂是必游之地,这座建筑会让你仿佛回到数个世纪以前的欧洲,教堂内部的五颜六色的装饰令人眼花缭乱,彩色的玻璃窗代表

and visitors often imagine stars shining in the heavens. The enormous organ contains nearly 7,000 pipes!

Summer is festival season in Montreal. In July the city hosts some of the best jazz musicians in the world at the International Jazz Festival. The World Film Festival screens great movies from around the globe in July and August. The Just For Laughs Comedy Festival and museum offers a unique insight into the definition of humor and how culture helps determine what is considered funny.

Montreal is home to the world-famous Cirque de Soleil, a modern humansonly circus. Its amazing and entertaining shows feature acrobats who contort themselves into unbelievable poses. The circus attracts tourists and locals alike.

The Stewart Museum, located on Île Sainte-Hélène near Montreal, provides an interesting glimpse into colonial life in the area. Permanent collections include the History Gallery, the Gunsmith's Gallery, and the 18th Century Physics Cabinet. Summer activities include a re-enactment of colonial life, 18th century military drills, and the Noonday Gun Salute.

Le Centre Canadien d'Architecture contains a variety of interactive exhibits on Canadian architecture, as well as multimedia presentations on architecture unique to Montreal. The building itself is unique in its design and structure.

The Trivia

Fact: A local ordinance requires that all companies having more than 50 employees must use French as their official business language.

Fact: Montreal was briefiy occupied by American forces during the Revolutionary War. Despite the repeated efforts of Benjamin Franklin and other American diplomats to join the war against the British, French Canadians refused to do so,seeing the war as just a quarrel between Britain and her colonies.

Fact: One of the world's most unusual apartment developments is in Montreal.Called Habitat 67, it contains 158 apartments arranged like a stack of concrete boxes, with one apartment's roof serving as the terrace of another apartment. The complex was built for the 1967 World Fair.

Why Montreal Is a 50 plus one City

Montreal has an old-world feel unlike most other North American cities. Its French influences and its French-speaking population may seem out of step with other Canadian cities, but that is part of its charm. Visitors enjoy exploring its art,architecture, nightlife, and colonial history.

了城市丰厚的历史,金质的繁星点缀着精致华丽的蓝色屋顶,游客常常感觉那些星星是在天空中闪烁。教堂内的管风琴有近7 000根音管。

夏季是蒙特利尔的喜庆季节。每年7月蒙特利尔都会主办国际爵士音乐节,全世界最好的爵士乐家汇聚这里。7月~8月举办的蒙特利尔国际电影节上,全球电影大师的作品构成银幕盛宴。"只为你笑"喜剧节及其展览,是对幽默一词进行的一次独特的诠释,同时也唤起我们重新认识文化是如何帮助我们决定什么是滑稽可笑。

蒙特利尔是世界著名的太阳马戏团的所在地,这是一个只有人做演员的马戏团,他们的表演令人惊叹、使人开心,其中最具特色的节目就是杂技演员把自己扭曲成令人难以置信的姿势,这家马戏团的观众既有外地游客也有当地居民。

位于蒙特利尔附近圣海伦岛上的斯图尔特博物馆,为我们提供了这一地区殖民地时期生活的一瞥,其中的永久性馆藏包括历史美术馆、枪炮工匠美术馆和18世纪物理学陈列馆。夏季,这里会举办再现殖民地生活的系列活动、18世纪时的军事训练以及正午的鸣炮礼。

加拿大建筑中心有各种关于加拿大建筑的互动式展览,以及关于蒙特利尔特有建筑形式的多媒体演示,而该中心大楼建筑本身在设计和建造上也非常独特。

奇闻轶事

之一:蒙特利尔当地的一条法令规定,所有雇员超过50人的公司都必须以法语为正式的贸易语言。

之二:在美国独立战争期间,蒙特利尔曾被美军短时间占领,尽管本杰明·弗兰克林与其他美国外交官,反复劝说这些法属加拿大人加入那场针对英国人的战争,但是最终加拿大人还是拒绝了美国人的请求,因为在他们看来,这场战争只不过是英国人与其殖民地的一次争吵而已。

之三:世界上最奇特的公寓开发项目之一就位于蒙特利尔,这片名为67号住宅区的建设项目包括158套公寓,犹如一个个混凝土盒子被整齐地累放起来,一套公寓的屋面就是另一套公寓的露台。整个建筑群是为1967年举办的世博会而修建的。

为什么蒙特利尔入选50 + 1个城市?

与大部分北美城市不同的是,蒙特利尔给人一种旧世界的感觉,法国的影响以及这座城市里那些讲法语的居民似乎都与加拿大其他城市的步调不太一致,然而,这恰恰正是这座城市的魅力所在,这种魅力吸引着游客们去探寻蒙特利尔的艺术、建筑、夜生活和它殖民地的历史。

Thirty-two

Moscow, Russia

The Basic Facts

Moscow is the capital of Russia and the former capital of the USSR. The city dominates Russia's government, economy, industry, science and culture.

Geography

Moscow lies at 55 degrees 45 minutes north latitude and 37 degrees 37 minutes east longitude. The city is named after the Moscow River on which it is located, in European west-central Russia. The modern city has a wheel-shaped arrangement,which stems from its early history as a fortified city. Wide boulevards that extend from the center of the city make up the spokes of the wheel, and circular boulevards make up the inner and outer rims of the wheel.

Climate

Moscow's has a continental climate with warm summers and very cold winters. Average temperatures range from the lower 20s Fahrenheit in winter to the lower 70s Fahrenheit in summer.

Government

Moscow is one of two federal cities in Russia (St. Petersburg is the other); as such, the city operates as a region separate from Russian republics and other administrative divisions. Moscow is divided into 10 administrative districts that are subdivided into 125 municipal districts. The city is governed by a mayor, a vice-mayor and a 35-member Duma (city council); all are elected to 4-year terms.The mayor also appoints a first-deputy and deputy mayor, as well as prefects, who administer the 10 administrative districts.

Demographics

Muscovites, the residents of Moscow, speak the Russian language and use a modern form of the Cyrillic alphabet. For example, Moscow is spelled MocBa and pronounced moskva in English. Russians constitute the majority of the city's population; other nationalities represented include Ukraine, Belarus and Armenia.The city has no distinct ethnic neighborhoods. The city government has sought to limit the population in recent years due to a lack of affordable, quality housing. Even so, Moscow is a huge city by any standard: some 10.5 million people live in the city itself.

Economy

Many city residents are employed in the city and federal governments. Since the fall of the Soviet Union, most businesses in Moscow are privately owned,and the number of foreign businesses has risen. Moscow is the core of the Russian economy; industries include

俄罗斯莫斯科

概况

莫斯科是前苏联以及当今俄罗斯的首都，这座城市在俄罗斯的政治、经济、工业、科学和文化方面都占据着主导地位。

一、地理

莫斯科位于北纬55°45′，东经37°37′，地处俄罗斯中西部地区，属欧洲大陆，城市的名字取自于当地的莫斯科河。现代莫斯科城是一个轮盘式布局，这种布局源自历史上早期这里曾作为城防堡垒的原因，宽阔的林荫大道从市中心延伸开去，如同轮盘上的辐条，而环形大道则构成轮盘的内外轮辋。

二、气候

莫斯科属于大陆性气候，夏季温暖，冬季异常寒冷。平均气温在冬季的华氏21~23度至夏季的华氏71~73度。

三、政府

莫斯科是俄罗斯两大联邦城市(另一个为圣彼得堡)之一，因此，莫斯科是独立于俄罗斯共和国及其他行政区的直辖区。莫斯科市被划分为10个行政区，这些行政区进一步划分为125个市政区。城市管理由一位市长、一位副市长和一个包括35名成员的杜马(市政委员会)负责，所有这些人都通过选举产生，任期4年。此外，市长要任命一名首席副市长和副市长，以及其他行政长官，分别负责10个行政区的行政管理。

四、人口

莫斯科居民讲俄罗斯语，使用西里尔字母的一种现代形式，例如，莫斯科的拼写是MocBa，英语发音为"莫斯科瓦"。城市人口的大多数是俄罗斯族人，其他有代表性的民族还包括乌克兰人和亚美尼亚人。市内没有明显的民族居住区域。近些年来，由于高质量经济住宅的匮乏，市政府业已设法减少人口数量，即便如此，莫斯科市无论从哪方面衡量都是一座庞大的城市：大约有1 050万人生活在城市内。

五、经济

莫斯科市的许多居民都为市政府及联邦政府工作，自从苏联解体之后，莫斯科市内大多数贸易企业都变为私有，外资企业数量也开始增加。莫斯科是俄罗斯经济的中心，其工业企业包括轿车、公交车、化学品、乳制品、电动设备、钢铁、纺织和建筑材料。俄罗斯的

automobiles, buses, chemicals, dairy products, electrical equipment, steel, textiles and building materials. Russian communications are centered in Moscow, and the national newspaper Izvestia is headquartered here.

The History

Moscow was first mentioned in Russian chronicles in 1147 as a small town. In 1237 and 1238, invading Mongols killed the inhabitants and demolished the town. By the 14th century, however, the town rebounded and eventually became the capital of the Vladimir-Suzdal principality. The city's growth was attributed to its proximity to important land and water trade routes. In 1380, the Russian army defeated the Mongols in the Battle of Kulikovo. Tatars controlled the city during much of the 15th century, but in 1480 they were forced out by Ivan the Great.

In 1547, at the age of 16, Ivan the Terrible was crowned the first czar of Russia; Moscow became the country's capital. During the next century a succession of czars built the palaces of the Kremlin, mansions, churches and monasteries, thus greatly expanding the city and developing its industry. Although Peter the Great moved the Russian capital to St. Petersburg in 1712, Moscow remained the center of commerce and culture. Muscovites left the city when Napoleon invaded in 1812, but not before burning most of it to the ground. Moscow was quickly rebuilt following Napoleon's retreat that winter.

By the mid-1800s, Moscow regained its status as a transportation and industrial center and the population grew rapidly. Moscow became the capital of Russia once again following the Bolshevik revolution against czarist rule. German bombs heavily damaged Moscow during World War II, but following the war the city more than doubled in size.

The Sights and Sounds

Moscow is an old city with fascinating sights around every corner. From the old Soviet-era décor of the GUM department store to the modern apartment complexes on the edge of the city, Moscow is a city of endless possibilities. Muscovites are generally friendly toward Westerners, and since the dissolution of the USSR Moscow has been a popular tourist destination. Residents are often the best source of information on the city's finest sights and sounds.

No visit to Moscow is complete without a tour of the Kremlin. This massive fortified building, once the seat of supreme czarist power, is now the official residence of the President of the Russian Federation. The Armoury building, located in the northwestern section of the Kremlin, is a museum dedicated to Russian imperial treasures, as well as an impressive collection of priceless Faberge eggs.

St. Basil's Cathedral, or the Cathedral of St. Basil the Blessed, is a Moscow icon. It is recognized the world over, known as the church with the colorful onion domes.

The Kremlin and St. Basil's Cathedral are both located in Red Square, the central square of Moscow and home to annual parades and celebrations. You simply cannot visit Moscow without stopping in Red Square to admire its grandeur. Many visitors frequently line up at Lenin's Mausoleum, where the body of the former Bolshevik leader is still on display.

GUM (pronounced goom) department store is on the east side of Red Square and is the largest of its kind in Russia. Under Communist rule the center was owned by the federal

通讯以莫斯科为中心,国家报刊《消息报》的总部也设在这里。

光影流金

莫斯科最早是1147年作为一个小镇出现在俄罗斯的编年史中的。1237和1238年,入侵的蒙古人杀死了当地居民,并且将这座小镇夷为平地。然而,到了14世纪,这座小镇重获生机,并最终成为弗拉基米尔公国的首府。城市的发展得益于其地理位置距离重要的陆上及水上贸易通道都很近。1380年,俄罗斯军队在同蒙古人的战役中取得胜利。15世纪的大部分时间里,这座城市处在鞑靼人的控制之下,1480年,鞑靼人被伊凡大帝赶出了莫斯科。

1547年,年仅16岁的伊凡暴君加冕成为俄罗斯的第一位沙皇,莫斯科也成为俄罗斯的首都。在接下来的百年间,一代接一代的沙皇修建了克里姆林宫、各种豪宅、教堂和修道院,于是城市面积迅速扩大,城市工业也得到快速发展。尽管1712年,彼得大帝将俄罗斯的首都迁到了圣彼得堡,但是莫斯科仍然是商业和文化的中心。1812年,当拿破仑入侵莫斯科时,莫斯科市民撤离了自己的城市,但是,在离开之前,他们几乎将整座城市都烧为灰烬。同年冬天,拿破仑撤离城市之后,莫斯科人便迅速开始了城市的重建。

到了19世纪中期,莫斯科重新确立了其交通和工业中心的地位,城市人口也迅速增长。随着反对沙皇统治的布尔什维克革命,莫斯科再次成为俄罗斯的首都。在第二次世界大战期间,德国人的炸弹严重毁坏了城市的设施,但是战争结束之后,莫斯科城的面积却翻了一番多。

声光景点

莫斯科是一座古城,城市的每个角落都是迷人的景致。从古老的代表前苏联时期装饰风格的GUM百货公司到城市周边现代化的公寓群,莫斯科是一座拥有无限可能的城市。通常莫斯科人对于西方客人都非常友好,自从前苏联解体之后,莫斯科已经成为一个颇为热门的旅游胜地。莫斯科当地居民常常成为游客了解城市声光景色、获取各类信息的最佳途径。

来到莫斯科不参观克里姆林宫是会遗憾的,这座宏伟的城堡式建筑曾经作为沙皇至高权力的象征,如今这里是俄罗斯联邦政府总统的官邸。宝库大厦位于克里姆林宫西北角,这是一座用来收藏俄罗斯皇家宝物的博物馆,同时值得关注的还有大量价值连城的由法贝热作坊精制的复活节彩蛋。

圣巴西勒大教堂,或称神圣的圣巴西勒大教堂,是莫斯科的标志性建筑。因其彩色的洋葱头形圆顶而被全世界所熟知。

克里姆林宫和圣巴西勒大教堂都坐落于红场,也就是莫斯科的中央广场,每年大型的阅兵和庆祝活动都在这里举行。如果来到莫斯科,却不到红场做短暂停留,欣赏一下这里壮观的景色简直是不可想象的。许多游客还时常会在列宁纪念堂外排队,以便进去瞻仰这位前苏联共产党人领袖的遗容。

GUM(音"古姆")百货公司位于红场东面,是俄罗斯最大的百货公司,共产党领导时期,这一购物中心属于联邦政府所有,但如今却是私有企业。这里大约有150家商铺,其中

government, but today it is privately owned. There are some 150 stores here, including a variety of high- and medium-fashion shops and a café; most Muscovites, however, cannot afford to purchase many of the items on display. The building's architecture and its central fountain are worth a look even if you do not feel like shopping.

One of the most impressive theaters in the world is Moscow's Bolshoi. Best known for its world-famous Bolshoi Ballet, the theatre also stages operas and concerts. The theater's architecture and décor are beautiful, especially at night.

The State Historical Museum is also in Red Square. It is the largest and most extensive Russian historical museum; its exhibitions span prehistory to the present day and include millions of Russian relics and artifacts.

Many Westerners, especially film buffs, are attracted to Gorky Park. This 300-acre amusement park includes cafes, a towering Ferris wheel, children's play areas, thrill rides and entertainment venues. Gorky Park is a fine place to escape the city and take in some people watching.

The Pushkin Museum of Fine Arts is located on Volkhonka Street and is a haven for art lovers. Exhibits run the gamut from ancient civilizations to Post-Impressionism.

Moscow is famous for the Great Moscow State Circus, a five-ring circus located on Tsvetnoi Boulevard. The amphitheatre in this dome-shaped structure is over 100 feet tall and seats 3,400. Visitors enjoy the elaborate shows that stage excellent acrobatics and animal acts.

The Trivia

Fact: Moscow is surrounded by acres of trees and parks known as the Green Belt.

Fact: One of the major pastimes in Moscow is playing chess. Russia's greatest chess champions have come from this city.

Fact: Russians are a very polite people. If you visit a house or apartment, it is customary to bring a small gift such as flowers or a bottle of wine or vodka. If you bring flowers, make sure to bring an odd number. Many Russians are a bit superstitious; even numbers of flowers are only put on graves.

Fact: Moscow was the center of two key battles in the country's history. The Russians ousted Napoleon's forces from the city—a success that inspired Tchaikovsky's 1812 Overture. In 1941 the German army was stopped outside the city, a fact which many historians credit with changing the course of World War II.

Fact: Moscow was the first Russian city to host the Summer Olympics in 1980.

Fact: The Kremlin occupies 68 acres in the city center and is the seat of the Russian government.

Why Moscow Is a 50 plus one City

It is now a popular destination for adventurous tourists. Stand in front of the Kremlin and imagine just for a moment being a part of Moscow's glorious history. Moscow's notable Russian architecture, its resilient people, and its national treasures are a testament to this world-class city.

包括各种各样中高档的服装店和咖啡屋。然而,这里陈列的许多商品,大多数莫斯科人是买不起的。即使你并不想购物,大厦建筑本身以及里面的中央喷泉也值得一看。

世界上最令人难忘的剧院之一当数莫斯科的彼得罗夫大剧院,这里最著名的就是享誉全球的彼得罗夫芭蕾舞团。此外,剧院也上演歌剧及音乐会。剧院的建筑和装潢都非常漂亮,特别是在夜晚时分。

俄罗斯国家历史博物馆也位于红场,这是关于俄罗斯历史的最大、也是覆盖面最广的博物馆。其藏品跨度从史前一直到当今,包括数百万件俄罗斯的珍贵遗产以及手工艺品。

许多西方人,特别是那些电影爱好者,都会被高尔基公园所吸引,这座占地300英亩的主题公园内有众多的咖啡屋、一座巨型弗里斯摩天轮、儿童游乐场以及惊险刺激的游乐设施。高尔基公园是躲避城市喧嚣、欣赏人文风景的好去处。

普希金美术馆位于伏尔科浩加大街,这里为美术爱好者提供了一个安静的角落,这里的展品涵盖了从古代文明到后印象派时期的整个发展历程。

莫斯科之所以著名,还因为这里有蜚声全球的大莫斯科国家马戏团,这座五环形的马戏表演场位于茨维特诺伊(鲜花)大道,整座剧场是一个圆顶形建筑,高100多英尺,内设3 400个座位,大量精彩的杂技和驯兽表演令观众赏心悦目。

奇闻轶事

之一:莫斯科市周围被大量的绿树和公园所环绕,这些地区被称为绿化带。

之二:莫斯科人的主要消遣之一是国际象棋,俄罗斯最伟大的国际象棋大师都来自于这座城市。

之三:俄罗斯人是非常友好的,假如你到某个人家或公寓做客,按照礼节应该带一个小礼物,比如,鲜花或一瓶葡萄酒或伏特加,如果你带的是鲜花,记着一定要是单数的,许多俄罗斯人都有点迷信,双数的鲜花只有在葬礼上才用。

之四:在这个国家的历史上,莫斯科是两次重大战役的中心,一次是俄罗斯人把拿破仑的军队赶出莫斯科 —— 正是这次胜利激发柴可夫斯基创作了他的《1812年序曲》;另一次战役是1941年德国人被挡在莫斯科城外,这一事件被众多历史学家认为具有改变第二次世界大战进程的重大意义。

之五:莫斯科是俄罗斯第一座主办夏季奥林匹克运动会的城市,那是1980年。

之六:克里姆林宫位于莫斯科市中心,占地68英亩,是俄罗斯政府所在地。

为什么莫斯科入选50 + 1个城市?

如今,对于那些爱好冒险的游客来说,莫斯科是一个理想的目的地。站在克里姆林宫前,重温一下莫斯科辉煌的历史,仅仅一小部分,仅仅几秒钟,你也会由衷地发出赞叹。毫无疑问,莫斯科是一座世界级的城市,那些著名的俄罗斯建筑,那些顽强灵活的莫斯科人,还有那些璀璨的民族宝藏都是最好的佐证。

Thirty-three

Nairobi, Kenya

The Basic Facts

Nairobi is the capital of Kenya and one of Africa's most important commercial centers. Nairobi was founded on the site of a water hole called Enkare Nairobi (cold water). The city became the nation's capital in 1963 after the British granted independence to Kenya. Nairobi experienced explosive growth through the end of the 20th century and is now the largest city between Cairo and Johannesburg.

Geography

Nairobi lies at 1 degree 17 minutes south latitude and 36 degrees 49 minutes east longitude. The city is located on a high plateau beside the Rift Valley in south-central Kenya. The valley is ringed by the Ngong Hills to the west, Mount Kenya to the north and Mount Kilimanjaro to the southeast. The Nairobi River flows just north of the city center.

Climate

Nairobi is near the equator, but is more than a mile above sea level. This altitude helps moderate the city's weather throughout the year. Average temperatures are typically in the 70s Fahrenheit. The rainy seasons are spring and autumn, but annual rainfall is relatively moderate.

Government

The Kenyan government is based in Nairobi. The country is divided into eight provinces, one of which is Nairobi province. Nairobi's mayor is elected to serve a 2-year term, although provincial affairs are controlled by the national government.

Demographics

Nairobi's population is estimated at 2.5 million. Most residents are either from Kenya or other African nations that were once British colonies. Nairobi is regarded as a multi-cultural city; residents come from various African ethnic backgrounds and practice widely different religions. Regrettably, the city's crime rate has risen in recent years, largely due to the impoverished majority population. The government constantly struggles to control HIV infection and prevent AIDS-related deaths common to metropolitan areas in Africa.

Economy

Although the well—known Nairobi National Park is a popular tourist attraction, tourism does not significantly contribute to the city's economy. Manufacturing in and around Nairobi includes clothing, textiles, building materials, processed foods, beverages and cigarettes.

Railroads were a critical component of Nairobi's economic growth, and the city

---

肯尼亚内罗毕

概况

内罗毕是肯尼亚的首都,也是非洲最重要的商业中心之一。内罗毕建在一个名为"恩卡尔-内罗毕"(意思是"冷水")的水泉之上。1963年,当英国人准许肯尼亚独立之后,这座城市成为肯尼亚的首都。20世纪末,内罗毕经历了一段快速增长期,现在,它已跻身非洲最大城市的行列,与开罗及约翰内斯堡齐名。

一、地理

内罗毕位于南纬1°17′,东经36°49′,地处肯尼亚中南部地区靠近拉夫特山谷的高原之上,拉夫特山谷西面是尼共山,北面是肯尼亚山,东南则为乞力马扎罗山,内罗毕河就从城市中心以北流过。

二、气候

尽管内罗毕靠近赤道,但是却位于海平面一英里以上,这一高度使得城市的气候全年都很温和,平均气温一般在华氏70度左右,春秋两季属于雨季,不过,每年的降水相对比较适中。

三、政府

肯尼亚政府的核心就位于内罗毕,这个国家分为8个省份,其中一个就是内罗毕省,内罗毕市市长经选举产生,任期两年,不过,省级事务由国家政府控制。

四、人口

据估计,内罗毕的人口在250万左右,大多数居民来自于肯尼亚或非洲其他原属英国殖民地的国家。内罗毕被公认为是一个多元文化的城市,居民来自非洲不同的民族,信仰各自不同的宗教。遗憾的是,近些年来,由于城市内大多数贫困人口的原因,城市的犯罪率明显上升。此外,政府还在不断努力控制艾滋病毒传播,以预防在非洲大城市地区常见的艾滋病类疾病。

五、经济

虽然著名的内罗毕国家公园是非常热门的旅游景点,但是旅游业在这座城市的经济中却并不占主导地位,内罗毕市内及周边地区的加工制造行业包括服装、纺织、建筑材料、加工食品、饮料和卷烟等。

铁路是内罗毕经济发展的重要组成部分,这座城市始终都是货运及客运交通的重要

remains a major hub for freight and passenger traffic.

The History

Nairobi came into existence with the construction of the Mombasa to Uganda railway; the site was a convenient place for railroad workers to rest before heading into the highlands. Nairobi was established in 1899, and in 1905 became the capital of the British East Africa Protectorate.   The influx of white settlers sparked friction with the local tribes, especially the Kikuyu, but these settlers helped the area to prosper through agriculture.

During the 1920s and 1930s the Kikuyu began a political movement to return the country to tribal control. One of the leaders of this movement was Johnstone Kamau, who later changed his name to Jomo Kenyatta (Swahili for Light of Kenya).He was an outspoken leader and is considered the father of the Kenyan Nation. After Kenya declared its independence from Britain—after continued international pressure—Nairobi became the nation's capital and Kenyatta became its first president.

The Sights and Sounds

Nairobi is a modern city in the midst of the African wilderness. The city is surrounded by countless species of exotic animals, and thousands of safari enthusiasts flock to the area each year.   Poaching and habitat destruction over the years have contributed to a sharp increase in the number of endangered species, including the Grevy's Zebra, the northern white rhinoceros, and the African elephant.   A crackdown on poaching and vigorous conservation efforts are attempting to reverse this trend.

Nairobi National Park, a 45-square-mile acre game reserve, is just outside the city.Wild animals roam freely in their natural habitat while expert guides lead tourists on safari—although today's visitors come not to kill but to photograph.

The Giraffe Centre in nearby Karen is a park dedicated to the conservation of the Rothschild giraffe. Visitors to the 140-acre park can see the animals up close and even feed them.   Giraffe Manor within the park is a luxury hotel, but do not be surprised if a giraffe suddenly pokes its head through your window! The manor was originally privately owned, but today both the Centre and the Manor are operated by the African Fund for Endangered Wildlife.

The Danish author Karen Blixen lived in Nairobi from 1913 to 1931.   She wrote several novels under the pseudonym Isak Dinesen, but is best known for her memoir *Out of Africa*. Her former home in nearby Karen is now a museum that features books from her library and exhibits on her life and writing.

The vast Kenya National Museum in Nairobi houses hundreds of tribal cultural artifacts from Kenya and other African nations. Visitors can view fossil displays, human skeletons, and even footprints of Homo erectus, a predecessor of modern humans.

The David Sheldrick Wildlife Trust is a must-see. Sheldrick was a famous naturalist who fought to prevent poachers from killing elephants and other exotic African species. Sheldrick died in 1977, and today his wife operates this wildlife orphanage that houses baby elephants and rhinos. Visitors can view many of the orphaned animals and learn about efforts to reintroduce them into the wild.

枢纽之一。

光影流金

内罗毕市是伴随着蒙巴萨和乌干达之间的铁路建设而诞生的,这块地方是铁路工人在进入高原地带之前进行休息的一处方便之所。1899年,内罗毕正式建立,1905年,内罗毕成为英国东非护国时期的首府。大批涌入非洲的白人殖民者激起当地部落的不满,双方时常发生摩擦,尤其是殖民者与吉库尤人之间的矛盾。然而,正是这些殖民者帮助这一地区通过农业生产逐步繁荣起来。

20世纪20~30年代期间,吉库尤人开始了一项旨在将国家统治收回部落手中的政治运动,此次运动的领袖之一是约翰斯东·卡毛,后来他把自己的名字改为乔莫·肯亚塔(斯瓦希里语的意思是"肯尼亚之光"),他是一位直言不讳的领袖,被公认为肯尼亚民族之父。肯尼亚宣布脱离英国独立之后 —— 在经过长期来自国际社会的压力之后 —— 内罗毕成为国家首都,肯亚塔成为第一任总统。

声光景点

内罗毕是位于非洲荒漠中的一座现代化城市,城市周边地区有数不清的珍稀动物种类,每年成千上万的徒步旅游爱好者聚集到这一地区。许多年来,由于偷猎和对动物栖息地的破坏,造成一些濒危动物的数量急剧下降,其中包括格里维的斑马、北方白犀牛以及非洲大象。目前,肯尼亚政府正试图通过严厉打击偷猎行为以及采取更加有力的保护措施来扭转这种趋势。

内罗毕国家公园就位于城市外围,这是一处面积达45平方英里的动物保护区。在这一自然栖息地内,野生动物们自由自在地漫步,专业导游引导游客进行徒步旅游 —— 不过,如今游客来此的目的不是捕猎而是拍照。

长颈鹿中心位于附近的卡伦区,是一个专为保护罗特希尔德长颈鹿而修建的公园,来到这座有140英亩大的公园,游客能够近距离地观赏到长颈鹿,甚至给它们喂食。公园内的长颈鹿庄园虽是一家豪华宾馆,但是住在这里的游客,如果突然看见有一头长颈鹿把脑袋从房间的窗户伸进来,也不要太过惊讶!虽然这家庄园最初是私人财产,但是今天长颈鹿中心和庄园都由非洲濒危野生动物基金会管理。

丹麦作家凯伦·布里克森曾于1913~1931年住在内罗毕,虽说她以伊萨克·迪内森为笔名创作了几部小说,但是,她最著名的作品却是她的回忆录《走出非洲》。她原来位于卡伦附近的家现在是一家博物馆,里面主要收藏了来自她本人图书馆的书籍以及有关她生平和写作生涯的物品。

位于内罗毕的面积宏大的肯尼亚国家博物馆,收藏了成百上千件来自肯尼亚及非洲其他国家的反映部落文化的手工艺品,在这里游客可以看到化石展示,人类骨架,甚至还有被认为是现代人类祖先的足印。

戴维-谢德里克野生动物托管所是一处不应错过的地方。谢德里克是一位著名的博物学家,终生致力于阻止捕猎者捕杀大象和其他珍稀的非洲物种。1977年谢德里克去世,如今,他的妻子经营着这家拥有许多小象和犀牛的野生动物托管所,游客在这里可以看到大量动物孤儿,还可以了解到有关帮助这些小动物重返自然的方法。

The Trivia

Fact: English is the official language of Kenya, and most middle-class Kenyans speak English. The common spoken language, however, is Swahili.

Fact: Nairobi is the headquarters of the United Nations Environment Programme, which is dedicated to preserving the global environment for future generations.

Fact: The 1985 film Out of Africa, starring Meryl Streep and Robert Redford, is based on Karen Blixen's memoir of the same name.

Fact: The movement for Kenya independence was fueled after World War II ,as returning African soldiers who had been aligned with the Allies rejected the colonial government of their homeland.

Fact: In 1898, as a railway bridge over the Tsavo River was under construction,two maneless male lions attacked and killed nearly 140 railroad workers. The lions terrorized the workers' encampment for months before they were finally killed by the construction engineer. The maneaters became known as the Ghost and the Darkness, and they now reside in a display case at Chicago's Field Museum of Natural History.

Why Nairobi Is a 50 plus one City

The sights and sounds of Nairobi may appear modest by world standards, but the city is central Africa's most populous city and continues to grow. Nairobi represents the growing awareness of Africa and its natural riches, history and culture, and the city reflects the dramatic change from colonial times to the present.

奇闻轶事

之一：英语是肯尼亚的官方语言，大多数中产阶层的肯尼亚人都讲英语，不过，常见的口头交流语却是斯瓦希里语。

之二：内罗毕是联合国环境项目总部所在地，这一项目是专为子孙后代保护全球环境而设立的。

之三：1985年，由梅丽尔·斯特里普与罗伯特·罗德福得主演的电影《走出非洲》就是根据凯伦·布里克森的同名回忆录改编的。

之四：第二次世界大战之后，随着那些曾与同盟国结成联盟的非洲士兵的返家，肯尼亚独立运动进一步高涨。

之五：1898年，在扎瓦河铁路大桥修建期间，两头没有狮鬃的雄狮袭击并咬死了近140名铁路工人，连续数月，铁路工人的宿营地都因这两头狮子而处于极度恐慌之中，直到它们最终被一名建筑工程师杀死。人们把这两头吃人的动物称作"鬼魂"和"黑暗"，现在它们的标本就位于芝加哥自然历史博物馆的展示架内。

为什么内罗毕入选50 + 1个城市？

虽说按照国际标准来衡量，内罗毕的景点很不起眼，然而这座城市却是中非人口最多的城市，并且仍然处在发展之中，内罗毕代表了非洲的不断觉醒，代表了非洲的天然财富，代表了非洲的历史文化，同时，这座城市更反映了非洲从殖民地时代直至今天所发生的巨变。

Thirty-four

New York City, United States

The Basic Facts

New York City is the largest city in the United States and its metropolitan area is one of the largest in the world. In many ways the Big Apple has a tremendous influence on the U.S. and the world, so much so that nearly 40 million tourists visit the city each year. There is so much to see and do that visitors need at least a week to enjoy its remarkable sights and sounds.

Geography

New York City lies at 40 degrees 40 minutes north latitude and 73 degrees 58 minutes west longitude. The city is located in the southeast corner of New York State and comprises five counties, known as boroughs: Manhattan, Brooklyn, The Bronx, Queens and Staten Island. The Hudson River separates Brooklyn from Staten Island, and the East River separates Queens and Brooklyn from Manhattan and The Bronx. Together, the five boroughs cover over 450 square miles. The area of Manhattan is the smallest of the five, but is the most densely populated; Brooklyn has the highest population at roughly 2.5 million. The New York metropolitan area includes parts of northeastern New Jersey, southwestern Connecticut, northeastern Pennsylvania, and southern New York State.

Climate

New York City's weather changes with the seasons; winters are cold and snowy and summers are hot and humid. Average annual temperatures range from the upper 30s Fahrenheit in winter to the lower 80s Fahrenheit in summer. Spring in New York City is usually mild, making this one of the best times to visit the city.

Government

New York City's government is more centralized than most other major U.S. cities. The government is not only responsible for municipal services (e.g., fire, police and public works), also for public education, penal institutions, libraries, and recreational facilities. The mayor and the 51 city council members of the city council are elected to 4–year terms. In addition, each borough elects its own borough president to a 4-year term. Borough presidents act as mayoral advisors occasionally serving on special city committees.

Demographics

New York City is a melting pot of many cultures and ethnic groups. During the 19th and early 20th centuries, the city was the main port of entry for waves of European immigrants, many of whom remained in the area and created their own ethnic enclaves. New Yorkers hail from all parts of the world, but nearly two-thirds of them are of African, Irish, Italian, Jewish and Puerto Rican descent. The population of the city itself is more than

---

202

美国纽约

概况

纽约市是美国最大的城市，就大市范围来说，也是世界上面积最大的城市之一。在许多方面，这个"大苹果"也对美国全国产生着深远的影响，正因为如此，每年有近4 000万游客来到这里，在这座城市，可看可做的事是如此之多，游客需要至少一周的时间才可能真正领略到它迷人的风采。

一、地理

纽约市位于北纬40°40′，西经73°58′，地处纽约州东南角，由五个被称作自治区的县级行政单位组成:曼哈顿、布鲁克林、布朗克斯、昆斯和斯塔腾岛。哈得孙河将布鲁克林与斯塔腾岛分割开来，东河则成为昆斯、布鲁克林与曼哈顿、布朗克斯的分界线。这五个区加起来的面积超过了450平方英里。曼哈顿地区是5个区中最小的一个，却是人口最为稠密的地区，人口最多的布鲁克林区拥有大约250万人。纽约大市范围包括新泽西州东北部，康涅狄格州西南部，宾夕法尼亚州东北部以及纽约州南部部分地区。

二、气候

纽约市的天气随季节而变化，冬季寒冷多雪，夏季炎热潮湿，年均气温在冬季的华氏37~39度至夏季的华氏81~83度,纽约市的春天通常比较温和,因此是来此旅游的最佳季节之一。

三、政府

纽约市市政府较之美国其他大城市来说更加集中,政府不仅负责市政服务(例如消防、警察和市政工程),还掌管公共教育、服刑机构、图书馆、娱乐设施,等等。市长以及51位市政委员会成员都是选举产生,任期四年。此外,每个区选出自己的区内任职4年的长官,区长偶尔为特殊市政委员会服务,相当于市长顾问的角色。

四、人口

纽约市可谓多种文化和民族团体的大熔炉,19世纪~20世纪,这座城市曾是欧洲移民潮进入美国的主要港口,他们中的许多人就留在了这个地方,并创建了自己民族的聚居地。虽然纽约人来自世界各个角落,但是其中近2/3属于非洲人、爱尔兰人、意大利人、

eight million.

Economy

New York City is one of the world's most important centers of industry, trade and finance. These businesses provide nearly seven million jobs for area residents. The city is home to the headquarters of many important U.S. financial institutions. The American Stock Exchange (AMEX) is located here, as is the New York Stock Exchange (NYSE)—the largest in the U.S. and a key exchange for the world economy. Although most people consider New York an urban center, it ranks third in the nation in terms of manufacturing. Among the most important industries are printing, publishing and clothing production.

The History

Native Americans originally settled in the area that would become New York City. The English explorer Henry Hudson discovered Manhattan in 1609. The Hudson River, which now bears his name, is the river on which he sailed north to Albany. The Dutch were the first Europeans to live on Manhattan Island, and built a city that they called New Amsterdam.

In 1664 the British arrived in the harbor at New Amsterdam, conquered the city, and changed its name to the New York. The city was a frequent battleground during the early years of the Revolutionary War, and in 1785 became the temporary capital of the new United States. New York soon surpassed other major American cities such as Boston and Philadelphia in size and importance, due to its large natural harbor and an influx of European immigrants.

In 1883 the completion of the Brooklyn Bridge linked Manhattan and Brooklyn. Other communities became the boroughs of The Bronx, Queens and Staten Island, and in 1898 the newly formed New York City encompassed all five boroughs. At that time the city had more than three million residents. Many Manhattan residents relocated to other boroughs, after other bridges and the subway began to operate; Manhattan, however, remained the most powerful of the boroughs. Several financial crises befell the city during the 20th century, and public strikes were common. New York City successfully endured these hardships and in the 1980s its economy began to improve.

Until 2001, the imposing twin towers of the World Trade Center (WTC) dominated the New York City skyline; they are now a bygone symbol of the city. The WTC suffered two significant terrorist attacks in its history. On February 26, 1993, a car bomb exploded below the North Tower of the World Trade Center, killing six people and injuring more than 1,000. On September 11, 2001, terrorists hijacked two commercial airliners and flew them into the North and South Towers. Both towers collapsed within hours, and more than 2,700 people lost their lives. The tragedy galvanized the city and country to carry on throughout grief and adversity. Plans have been approved to build a memorial to the victims on the site.

The Sights and Sounds

The sights and sounds of New York City are virtually endless. The city's dozens of neighborhoods each have a distinct identity, and some of their names—Chelsea, Greenwich Village, SoHo, and Little Italy, to name a few—are as famous as the city itself.

犹太人和波多黎各人的后裔,市区人口超过了800万。

五、经济

　　纽约市是世界上最重要的工业、贸易和金融中心之一,这些行业为当地居民提供了近700万个就业岗位。这座城市还是许多重要的金融公司的总部所在地。美国证券交易所(AMEX)就位于这里,也就是纽约证券交易所(NYSE)——美国最大的证券交易所,同时,也是世界经济的核心交易场所。尽管大多数人认为纽约市是美国的城市中心,但是,就工业生产来说,它在美国仅排名第三。其中最主要的工业包括印刷、出版及服装制造。

光影流金

　　最早定居于纽约所在地区的是美洲的印第安人。1609年,英国探险家亨利·哈得孙发现了曼哈顿,如今以他的名字命名的哈得孙河,就是当年他向北方奥尔巴尼航行经过的河流。荷兰人是最早定居于曼哈顿的欧洲人,他们建立的城市被称为新阿姆斯特丹。

　　1664年,英国人抵达新阿姆斯特丹港,并占领了这座城市,将其更名为纽约。在美国独立战争头几年,这个城市时常成为战场。1785年,纽约市成为新美国的临时首府,借助于巨大的天然港口,以及大批涌入的欧洲移民,纽约很快便超过了波士顿、费城等大城市,一举成为美国最大、最重要的城市。

　　1883年,布鲁克林大桥建成通车,从而将曼哈顿和布鲁克林连接起来,其他的社区则成为布朗克斯区、昆斯区和斯塔腾岛。1898年,新组成的纽约市涵盖了所有这五个区,那时整个城市的居民有300多万人。随着其他几座大桥的建成以及地铁开始运行,许多曼哈顿居民重新搬迁到了其他区定居,然而,曼哈顿却始终是所有行政区中权利最大的一个。20世纪时,纽约市先后发生了几次财政危机,当时公众罢工成为普遍现象,然而,纽约市成功地渡过了这些难关,到了20世纪80年代,城市经济开始好转。

　　直到2001年之前,气势宏伟的世贸大厦(WTC)双子塔一直是构成纽约市空中轮廓线中主要的风景,然而,现在它们却只是这座城市里一个逝去的象征。历史上世贸大厦遭到过两次严重的恐怖袭击,1993年2月26日,一辆装满炸弹的汽车在世贸中心北塔下爆炸,造成六人死亡,1 000多人受伤。2001年9月11日,恐怖分子劫持了两架商用飞机,分别撞向世贸大厦的北塔和南塔,在数小时之内,两座塔楼分别倒塌,有超过2 700人在这次恐怖袭击中被夺去生命,这场悲剧震惊了纽约市,震惊了美国,它所带来的伤痛和厄运延续至今。目前,纽约市政府已经通过计划,将在世贸大厦旧址上修建一座纪念碑以纪念那些遇难者们。

声光景点

　　纽约市内的景点简直数不胜数,市内数十个街区各自都有其鲜明的个性,其中一些名字——这里只举几个例子:切尔西、格林尼治村、休南区和小意大利——其名气并不亚于城市本身。

Manhattan is the center of this metropolis—the most visited and most recognized area of the city. Nothing says Midtown Manhattan quite like the Rockefeller Center and Radio City Music Hall. Named for the famous philanthropist and oil tycoon,Rockefeller Center is a massive upscale business area that covers some 22 acres of prime real estate. A plaza in the complex becomes an ice-skating rink during the winter, delighting both New Yorkers and tourists. Radio City Music Hall is the largest indoor theatre with nearly 6,000 seats, and is home to the world—famous Rockettes. Fifth Avenue is paradise for those shoppers with deep pockets. St.Patrick's Cathedral is a short distance away at the intersection of 50th Street and Fifth Avenue. This glorious Gothic church, dedicated in 1879, is the largest Roman Catholic cathedral in the U.S. The United Nations is headquartered in Manhattan along the East River.

Times Square is famous—and infamous—for its checkered past as a seedy and dangerous side of town. A major clean-up effort swept away the peep shows and adult movie theaters in favor of attractions more palatable to tourists. Its main intersection at 42nd Street and Broadway is the site for New Year's Eve celebrations, annually attracting nearly one million revelers to party in the streets.Times Square is home to Broadway, a popular spot for theatergoers interested in first-run entertainment. While many tourists appreciate that this area is now safer,cleaner, and more attractive, hard-core New Yorkers feel Times Square has lost its luster.

It is impossible to visit New York City without seeing the Empire State Building.This 102-story office building is a beautiful Art-Deco style skyscraper. When it was completed in 1931, it was the tallest building in the world. Tenants were few in the building's early years, presumably as a result of the economic collapse during the Great Depression. Today, however, the Empire State Building is the city's media center; it is the base for many commercial television and radio stations. An elevator whisks visitors to the outdoor observatory on the 86th floor, from which tourists can take in a fabulous view of the city's skyline.

The museums of New York are world-famous and world-class. The Metropolitan Museum of Art, near Central Park, is a day trip all in itself. Every notable era in art and architecture is represented here. The museum's collection is so large that exhibits must be periodically stored so others may be displayed. The representative exhibits for each period are said to be the best in the world. The Solomon R. Guggenheim Museum, designed by Frank Lloyd Wright, is the city's museum of modern art. Its continuous spiral architecture gives it a futuristic appearance—perfectly suited to the exhibits contained within. The American Museum of Natural History is the largest in the world and perhaps the most significant museum of its kind. Exhibits include everything from ancient skeletons and huge meteorites to the 563-carat Star of India sapphire.

An afternoon spent strolling Greenwich Village is an afternoon well spent. Famous for its writers and artists, it is also gracious is a funky sort of way, with quaint,tree-lined streets. The stores, shops, restaurants and the adjacent Washington Square with its famous Memorial Arch make touring an enjoyable event.

Even the most jaded New Yorker appreciates the ferry ride from Battery Park to Ellis Island, where the 152-foot tall Statue of Liberty looms over New York Harbor. From 1892 to 1954, more than 12 million immigrants were processed at the federal immigration station at Ellis Island. The island is now a national monument and museum. The Statue of

曼哈顿是这座大都会的中心 —— 也是这座城市中游客最多、人们最为熟悉的地区。没有什么能比洛克菲勒中心和无线电城音乐厅更能代表曼哈顿市中心的了,以著名的慈善家和石油大亨所命名的洛克菲勒中心是一处大型高档商业区,总面积约22英亩,是信用等级最高的不动产建筑。这座大型建筑群内的一个广场在冬季会变成一个溜冰场,非常受纽约人和游客的欢迎。无线电城音乐厅是最大的室内剧场,能够容纳6 000观众,它还是世界著名的列队歌舞女演出地。第五大道是购物者的天堂,圣帕特里克大教堂就坐落于离此不远的第50街与第五大道的交叉路口,这座漂亮的哥特式教堂修建于1879年,是美国最大的天主教堂。联合国总部则位于曼哈顿东河沿岸。

时代广场的名气可谓毁誉参半 —— 因为这里曾是城中一处下流而危险的区域,为了吸引更多健康的观光客,市政府下大力气铲除了那些色情表演及成人影剧院。广场与第42大街及百老汇的交汇处是除夕举行庆祝活动的地方,这里的大街小巷每年都会吸引近百万的狂欢者。时代广场也是百老汇的所在地,这里是那些爱好歌舞剧的人们欣赏首轮表演的热门场所。尽管许多游客很高兴看到这里如今变得更安全、更整洁、更有吸引力,但是,一些铁杆纽约人还是感觉时代广场已经失去了它往昔的光彩。

来到纽约市,你不可能不去看一下帝国大厦,这座102层的办公楼是一座漂亮的装饰派艺术风格的摩天大厦。1931年,当这座大厦落成之时,它是世界上最高的建筑。大厦建成最初几年,由于正值经济衰落的大萧条时期,来租房的人少之又少。然而,今天帝国大厦是纽约市的传媒中心,许多商业电视以及广播电台都以此为基地。大厦内的快速电梯可以将游客一直送到位于86层的室外观景台,从那里游客能够欣赏到整座城市天际的绝妙景致。

纽约的博物馆不仅世界闻名,而且世界一流,靠近中央公园的大都会美术馆,本身就足以构成一日游。在这里,你可以找到美术和建筑史上每个时期的代表作,由于博物馆的馆藏太过丰富,因此,许多展品只能展出一段时间,以便为其他展品腾出地方。据说,该博物馆内的代表性展品在全世界都是最棒的。由弗兰克·劳埃德·赖特设计的所罗门-古根海姆博物馆是这座城市的现代艺术博物馆,其呈螺旋式上升的外表赋予这座建筑一种未来主义的风格 —— 也使大厦内外完美地切合统一。美国自然历史博物馆是世界上此类博物馆中最大、或许也是最重要的一个,其展品从远古人类的骨架、巨大的陨石到重达563克拉的"印度之星"蓝宝石,可谓无所不包。

选择一个下午到格林尼治村转一转,你将会不虚此行,这个以作家和艺术家出名的地方不仅街道宽敞时髦,绿树成荫,而且风格独特。这里的商店、餐馆以及毗邻的拥有著名的纪念拱门的华盛顿广场都将令你的行程充满快乐。

即便是最不喜欢凑热闹的纽约人,也会对来往炮台公园与艾利斯岛之间的渡轮情有独钟,高达152英尺的自由女神像,赫然耸立在艾利斯岛上俯视着整个纽约港。从1892年直到1954年,共有1 200多万移民在位于艾利斯岛上的联邦移民局接受入境检查,如今,

Liberty was a gift from France as a gesture of friendship between the two nations. It was dedicated in 1886 to commemorate the United States centennial.

While in Lower Manhattan, take in Fraunces Tavern, best known as the site of General George Washington's farewell address to his officers. The New York Stock Exchange is nearby on Wall Street.

The Trivia

Fact: In 1653, Dutch colonists on Manhattan built a large wall along the northern edge of the town to discourage attacks. The wall was abandoned after it fell down shortly afterward. The colonists chose to build a road in its place, which became known as Wall Street.

Fact: The Erie Canal, completed in 1825, was critical to the growth of New York City's economic importance. The canal linked the city to points west and in effect led to the growth of major cities throughout the Midwest.

Fact: For more than 150 years, Tammany Hall was the name of New York City's Democratic Party machine. The group garnered the immigrant vote by offering jobs, gifts and advice to the new arrivals. William M. (Boss) Tweed was the most notorious of the group's leaders. When he was removed from power in 1872, he was imprisoned and charged with bilking the city of several million dollars.

Why New York City Is a 50 plus one City

Love it or hate it, New York City represents the United States to the world. Crowded, aggressive, dynamic and ever-changing, the city is a symbol of capitalism, great entertainment, celebrities, enormous buildings and a style all of its own. Critics have frequently written off New York City as unworkable and unmanageable, but each time the city proves them wrong.

这个小岛成了国家级文物单位和博物馆。自由女神像是一件来自法国的礼物,以示两国友好,是专为1886年美国建国100周年纪念而制作的。

如果你身处下曼哈顿,不妨参观一下弗朗西斯客栈,这里曾是乔治·华盛顿将军向其手下军官发表告别演说的地方,纽约证券交易所就位于附近的华尔街上。

奇闻轶事

之一:1653年,荷兰殖民者在曼哈顿沿城镇北部边缘,修建了一堵高墙以阻止敌人袭击,这堵墙在倒塌后不久便被废弃,后来,殖民者选择在这个地方修建了一条路,并称之为华尔街。

之二:1825年建成的伊利运河,对于纽约市的经济增长来说至关重要,这条运河将城市与西部站点连接起来,并且促进了中西部地区主要城市的发展。

之三:在150多年里,坦慕尼协会会堂都是纽约市民主党机器的代名词,这个组织通过向新到来的移民介绍工作、发放礼物和提供建议等手段,获取了大量选票,威廉·M(老板)·特威德是这个团体领导者中最臭名昭著的一个。1872年他下台后,被关进监狱,其罪名是侵吞了该市数百万美元的资金。

为什么纽约市入选50 + 1个城市?

爱它也好,恨它也罢,在全世界人眼里,纽约市就代表了美国,喧闹拥挤、争强好胜、活泼生动、气象万千,这座城市是资本主义的象征,这里有最大的娱乐、有众多的名流、有无数的大厦、有自己独特的风格。评论家们曾经撰文贬低纽约市是个无法运转、无法管理的地方,但是,每一次这座城市都能证明他们是错的。

Thirty-five

Prague, Czech Republic

The Basic Facts

Prague is the capital and largest city of the Czech Republic, and is also one of the oldest cities in central Europe. Prague was once the capital of the former Czechoslovakia, but in 1993, following the collapse of the Soviet Union,Czechoslovakia split into two independent countries: the Czech Republic and Slovakia. Prague remained the capital of the Czech Republic.

Geography

Prague lies at 50 degrees 5 minutes north latitude and 14 degrees 26 minutes east longitude. The city is located on both banks of the Vltava River in the central part of the Czech Republic. Many bridges link the two banks of the river, but the most famous is the historic Charles Bridge. Prague covers nearly 2,000 square miles.The city has been called the city of a hundred spires for its many churches.

Climate

Prague's north-central European location lends itself to a climate of extreme weather. Average temperatures range from the lower 30s Fahrenheit in winter to the mid-80s Fahrenheit in summer. Spring and autumn are normally cool and wet.

Government

Prague's main governmental body is the City Assembly, which consists of 70 elected members. The Assembly oversees municipal policies and elects the 11-member City Council. This City Council is charged with implementing city services and includes a mayor, four deputy mayors, and six councilors.

Demographics

Czechs constitute the vast majority of Prague residents. The city had a large German-born population prior to World War II, but Czechoslovakia expelled most Germans after the war. Since the latter half of the 20th century immigration to Prague has been tightly restricted by the government. This policy, combined with a low birth rate among residents, means the city's population has only slightly increased since the end of the war. Many of the city's older buildings have remained in poor condition, a factor that has contributed to a citywide housing shortage.

Economy

Prague is one of the Czech Republic's leading manufacturing centers. Its industries produce aircraft engines, automobiles, beer, chemicals, furniture, machine tools,and processed foods. Over the last few years, many international companies have moved their

35

捷克共和国布拉格

概况

布拉格是捷克共和国的首都和最大的城市,也是中欧最古老的城市之一。虽然布拉格曾经是原来捷克斯洛伐克共和国的首都,但是1993年,随着苏联的解体,捷克斯洛伐克分裂为两个独立的国家:即捷克共和国和斯洛伐克。布拉格仍是捷克共和国的首都。

一、地理

布拉格位于北纬50°5′,东经14°26′,地处捷克共和国中部伏尔塔瓦河两岸,尽管沿河两岸桥梁众多,但是,最著名的还是具有纪念意义的查尔斯大桥。布拉格的面积有近2 000平方英里。由于市内有许多教堂,布拉格被称为"百尖塔之城"。

二、气候

由于地处欧洲中北部,布拉格常会出现极端天气现象,平均气温在冬季的华氏31~33度至夏季的华氏85度,春秋季节通常凉爽而潮湿。

三、政府

布拉格的主要政府机构是城市众议院,包括70名选举产生的议员,他们监督市政方针,并推选出11名市政委员会成员,市政委员会由1名市长、4名副市长和6名顾问组成,负责执行城市的各项服务。

四、人口

捷克人构成布拉格市居民的绝大多数,在第二次世界大战之前,这座城市里居住着许多德国后裔,但是,战后他们中的大多数都遭到驱逐。20世纪后半期以来,捷克政府严格限制进入布拉格的移民,这一政策,加之居民出生率较低,导致战后城市人口只是略微增长。由于城中许多古老的建筑年久失修,因而造成全市居民住房紧张。

五、经济

布拉格是捷克共和国主要的生产中心之一,其工业包括航空发动机、汽车、啤酒、化学品、家具、机械工具和加工食品。在过去几年里,许多全球公司都将其总部搬到了这座城市。在第二次世界大战期间,布拉格相比较而言没有遭到什么破坏,因此,这座城市成

headquarters to the city. Prague was relatively undamaged during World War II, and so the city has become a popular location for films that are set during or before the war.

The History

The city is believed to have been founded in the 9th century. It soon became a major trading center and eventually the residence of the Bohemian kings. Many of the city's most impressive buildings were constructed in the 14th century during the reign of King Charles IV, then ruler of the Holy Roman Empire; he saw Prague as a new Rome. Charles also founded the first university in Prague in 1348.

Prague was the home of the Hussite religious reformation in the 1400s and suffered damage from the religious wars that soon followed. The Thirty Years' War began in Prague in 1618, when Protestant Bohemians rebelled against the Roman Catholic Habsburgs. Their revolt failed, and the Habsburgs ruled the city and surrounding country until after World War I.

In 1918, Prague became the capital of the new country of Czechoslovakia. German troops occupied the city during World War II, and thousands of Czechoslovakians were killed, especially Jews. The Soviet Union then held sway over the city in support of the Czechoslovak Communist Party.

The Sights and Sounds

The beauty of Prague, aside from the obvious art and architecture, is that the city is reasonably compact and easy to explore. Most of historical Prague is within an hour's stroll of the Charles Bridge—and a slow-paced stroll at that, allowing visitors time to take in the sights and sounds of this wonderful, majestic city.

The New Town and Old Town districts contain much of the beauty and warmth of modern-day Prague. The Old Town Square, as a trading center and marketplace since the 10th century, remains very much active and is, in many ways, the heart and soul of the city. Tourists and locals alike enjoy the 600-year old Astronomical Clock Tower. The clock strikes hourly and includes an astronomical dial and the clockwork Walk of the Apostles and others.

The Old Town Hall overlooks the square, providing an excellent view of Prague from 200 feet. The Church of Our Lady Before Tyn dates from the 14th century, a monumental structure with a Gothic façde and twin spires.

Wenceslas Square in New Town is a broad avenue filled with shops, restaurants,clubs and hotels. The National Museum, founded in 1818, is an enormous Neo-Renaissance structure also located in New Town.

Prague has a long, proud Jewish history. The Gothic-style Old-New Synagogue survived World War II and is the oldest active synagogue in Europe. The Jewish Museum displays a collection of Jewish memorabilia gathered by Jews during World War II. The Pinkas Synagogue contains a moving testament to 80,000 Bohemian Jews—their names are inscribed on the nave walls.

Prague's most prominent landmark is undoubtedly the Charles Bridge. Like much of Prague, the Charles Bridge exists because of the Holy Roman Emperor Charles IV. The bridge was built in the 14th century, and some 30 statues were added 300 years later. These treasures were removed and placed indoors to protect them from pollution; replicas

为战争期间和战后一个颇受欢迎的电影拍摄基地。

光影流金

这座城市据称创建于九世纪,很快它便发展为一个主要的贸易中心,并最终变成波希米亚国王居住的地方。城中大多数恢宏的建筑都建于14世纪,也就是神圣罗马帝国的统治者国王查理四世在位时期,这位国王把布拉格看做是一个新的罗马,1348年,查理还在布拉格创办了第一所大学。

15世纪时,布拉格曾作为胡斯宗教改革的发祥地,并在随后的宗教战争中屡遭破坏。1618年,"三十年战争"由布拉格打响,战争双方为主张新教的波希米亚人和他们所反抗的信奉天主教的哈布斯堡王朝,由于反叛失败,哈布斯堡王朝统治了这座城市以及周边地区,直至第一次世界大战之后。

1918年,布拉格成为新成立的捷克斯洛伐克国家的首都。在第二次世界大战期间,德国军队占领了这座城市,成千上万名捷克斯洛伐克人遭到屠杀,尤其是犹太人。其后,在捷克斯洛伐克共产党的帮助下,前苏联控制了这座城市。

声光景点

布拉格的美,除了其显而易见的艺术和建筑之外,还在于它的布局紧凑合理、易于游玩。布拉格大多数历史古迹都在查理大桥四周,一小时步行的范围之内 —— 而且只需一小时的慢速步行,游客便可以欣赏到这座美妙而庄严的城市内为数众多的景点。

新城和旧城区涵盖了当今布拉格大多数美丽而温馨的景致,自从十世纪起就作为贸易中心的旧城广场,今天依然十分活跃,从很多方面来说,这个广场就是这座城市的心脏和灵魂。无论是游客还是当地人,都同样喜欢那座有600年历史的天文钟楼,那个大钟由一个天文计时指针、名为"使徒的步伐"的机械装置和其他一些部件组成,每过一小时敲响一次。

旧市政厅俯视着广场,从这座200英尺高的大厦向下望去,布拉格的景致尽收眼底。位于泰恩前面的圣母教堂修建于14世纪,这座有纪念性的建筑拥有哥特式的外观和两座尖塔。

位于新城的文西斯劳斯广场是一条宽阔的街道,街道两旁满是商店、餐馆、俱乐部和酒店。创建于1818年的国家博物馆,一座庞大的新文艺复兴时期的建筑就位于新城区内。

布拉格拥有一段漫长的、值得骄傲的犹太人历史,哥特式的新旧犹太教堂在第二次世界大战中得以幸存,成为欧洲依然活跃的最古老的犹太会堂。犹太人博物馆展出了大量在二战期间收集起来的犹太人的纪念品。品卡斯犹太教堂里有一处关于八万波希米亚犹太人的动态展示证明 —— 他们的名字都被刻在教堂的中殿墙上。

布拉格最杰出的地标无疑就属查理大桥,正如布拉格大部分建筑一样,查理大桥的存在是因为神圣罗马帝国的皇帝查理四世。大桥修建于14世纪,在之后的300年间,大桥上先后矗立起了大约30座雕塑,为了防止这些宝贝遭到污染损坏,后来,他们都被移至室内保护起来,如今,取而代之矗立在大桥上的都是他们的复制品。这座大桥为布拉格平添

are in their place now. The bridge offers wondrous views of the city and appears to have different moods throughout the day—from quiet and contemplative early in the morning to festive at night.

Prague Castle reflects the city's historical greatness. The castle is perched on a hilltop where it has stood for more than 1,000 years. The real spirit of the Castle is St. Vitus Cathedral, which was completed over 600 years from 1344 to 1929. The cathedral features a variety of styles from Gothic to Art Nouveau, reflecting the prominent genres of each era. There are 22 chapels in the cathedral, of which the most famous and the most opulent is dedicated to Good King Wenceslas, the patron saint of Prague and Bohemia. Interestingly, Wenceslas was a prince, but never a king.

Two important museums are housed in the castle complex: St.George's Basilica,which contains ancient Czech art; and Sternbeck Palace, known for its fine European art collection. The castle ramparts are particularly favored for their splendid views of Prague.

Beer drinking is a great pastime in Prague. In fact, the Czech Republic is said to have the highest per capita rate of beer consumption in the world. U Fleku, dating back to 1499, is a sprawling beer hall, entertainment venue, and brewery museum. It is said that patrons consume over two million gallons of their dark lager annually.

The Trivia

Fact: Prague is made up of five medieval towns: Prague's Old Town, which dates to the 12th century; Lesser Town, founded in 1257; New Town; the Old Jewish Quarter; and Castle District, established in the 1330s.

Fact: In the late 16th century Prague became a center of the Renaissance. The Emperor Rudolph II selected artists, musicians, philosophers, and others to enrich Prague's cultural landscape. The associated artistic movement became known as European Mannerism.

Why Prague Is a 50 plus one City

A trip to Eastern Europe would be incomplete without seeing the beauty and richness of Prague. The city's rich history, art, and architecture remained largely unscathed during World War II, and so tourists can still appreciate the centuriesold sights and sounds. To visit Prague is to live the good life!

了奇妙的景象，一天之内大桥会呈现出不同的氛围——从清晨的静谧沉思到夜晚的欢快喜庆。

布拉格城堡反映了这座城市历史的伟大，这座城堡栖息在山巅之上长达千年之久，城堡真正的精髓所在是圣维塔斯大教堂，它的建成从1344年~1929年跨越了600年的时空，教堂的建筑也融汇了从早期的哥特式直到近现代艺术等各种风格，对于每个时期的杰出类型都有所反映。大教堂内部包括22个礼拜堂，其中最著名、也是最奢华的是"好国王"文西斯劳斯专用的礼拜堂，有趣的是，这位布拉格以及波希米亚的主保圣人其实只是一位王子，从未真正当过国王。

在这座城堡建筑群内，还有两座重要的博物馆：一座是以古代捷克艺术为主的圣乔治大教堂，另一座是以精美的欧洲艺术品著称的斯顿伯克宫。城堡周围的防御墙也深受游客欢迎，因为，从那里望下去，布拉格的美景一览无余。

在布拉格喝啤酒可谓一大消遣，事实上，据说捷克共和国是世界上人均消耗啤酒最多的国家。可以追溯到1499的尤弗里库是一间延伸开去的啤酒大厅，一个娱乐场所，同时，也是一家啤酒博物馆。据说这里的客人每年要喝掉200多万加仑他们自酿的贮藏啤酒。

奇闻轶事

之一：布拉格由5座中世纪的城镇组成：它们分别是建于12世纪的布拉格旧城，创建于1257年的小镇，新城，古犹太人区，以及14世纪30年代建立的城堡区。

之二：16世纪后期，布拉格成为文艺复兴的中心，当时的皇帝鲁道夫二世挑选了一批艺术家、音乐家、哲学家等来丰富布拉格的文化景观，与此相关的艺术潮流史上称为"欧洲风格主义"。

为什么布拉格入选50 + 1个城市？

假如没有欣赏到布拉格的美丽与丰富，任何东欧之旅都将是有缺憾的。在第二次世界大战期间，这座城市悠久的历史、艺术和建筑几乎毫发无损，因此，游客来到这里仍然能够感受到几个世纪以前的风貌。布拉格之旅，重温美好生活之旅！

Thirty-six

Rio de Janeiro, Brazil

The Basic Facts

Rio de Janeiro, commonly known as Rio, is the second largest city in Brazil and is a major center for trade, economics and tourism. Although the city has problems of class disparity, overcrowding and pollution, it remains a popular South American tourist attraction.

Geography

Rio lies at 22 degrees 50 minutes south latitude and 43 degrees 20 minutes west longitude. The city is roughly 450 square miles in area, and is surrounded by some of the most spectacular scenery in the western hemisphere: green mountains to the north and west and crystal blue waters to the east. The city is famous for its white beaches and Sugar Loaf Mountain, which rises 1,325 feet from the peninsula in the bay.

Climate

Because Rio is located south of the equator, the winter and summer months are opposite from those in the northern hemisphere; winter occurs between June and August and summer occurs between December and February. Annual temperatures do not vary much, and tend to be in the low 70s Fahrenheit. Even so, because the city is at sea level, it is normally humid. Winters can be rainy and are sometimes marked by unusual spikes in temperature; these periods are referred to as veranicos or mini-summers. Spring is considered the most pleasant time of year.

Government

Brazil is divided into 26 states that are further divided into municipos (Rio is one of them). The city is governed by an elected mayor and city council. The state is led by an elected governor and legislature. Each state also elects an 81-member senate and 513-member Chamber of Deputies. The states elect three senators each and a number of deputies based on the state's population.

Demographics

Rio residents are commonly referred to as Cariocas. This moniker may have been created by Portuguese settlers using a Native American expression for white man's house. Unlike all other South American countries, Brazil's official language is Portuguese. Total population is estimated to be more than six million people.

Roman Catholicism is the dominant religion in Rio, but there are groups that practice Macumba, a mixture of Christian and African rites. Like many South American cities, Rio has a large disparity between classes. Impoverished people are segregated into slums, which are plagued with violence and drug problems.

36

巴西里约热内卢

概况

里约热内卢，通常称为里约，是巴西第二大城市以及主要的贸易、经济和旅游中心。尽管这座城市存在着阶级鸿沟、人口过剩和污染等问题，但是，它仍然是南美一处受人欢迎的旅游胜地。

一、地理

里约位于南纬22°50′，西经43°20′，城市面积大约有450平方英里，拥有西半球最为壮观的景致：北面和西面是层峦叠嶂的绿色山峦，东面则是晶莹剔透的蓝色水域。该市著名的景观还包括白色的沙滩，以及矗立在海湾半岛上的海拔1 325英尺的塔糖山。

二、气候

由于里约位于赤道以南，冬夏两季的月份与北半球正好相反，冬季出现在6月~8月，夏季则在12月~2月。年均气温变化不大，一般在华氏71~73度左右。即便如此，由于城市处于海平面，通常来说比较潮湿。冬天雨水较多，有时会出现异常的极端气温。这些时段被称为韦罗尼克或小夏天。春天被认为是一年中最好的季节。

三、政府

巴西全国划分为26个州，每个州再进一步划分为自治县(里约就是其中之一)。这座城市由一位选举产生的市长和一个市政委员会管理，而每个州则由选出的州长及立法机构领导。此外，各州还有自己的参议院，包括81名选举产生的议员，以及一个包括513名议员的下议院。每个州根据本州人数分别推选3名参议员和相应数量的下议院议员。

四、人口

里约市居民通常被称为"卡里奥克人"(里约热内卢人)，这一绰号或许是由葡萄牙殖民者根据印第安人用来指白人住房的词汇创造出来的。与其他南美国家不同的是，巴西的官方语言是葡萄牙语。据估计，全市人口在600万以上。

虽然天主教是里约市的主要宗教，但是，还有一些人遵循的是马库姆巴宗教仪式，这是一种基督教与非洲宗教仪式的混合体。和许多南美城市一样，里约市存在着很深的阶级鸿沟，贫困人口大多远离富人区居住在贫民窟地区，而这些地区一直受到暴力事件和吸毒问题的困扰。

Economy

Tourism is an important part of Rio's economy. The city is also one of Brazil's financial and commercial centers. Rio is responsible for about 10 percent of Brazil's industrial economy, and goods such as processed foods, chemicals, drugs and metals are manufactured here. The shipbuilding industry employs many residents as well. The city is a major transportation center; roads and rail lines link the city with most of the country and other South American cities.

The History

The area that is now Guanabara Bay was occupied by Tupi Indians when Portuguese explorers first arrived in 1502. In fact, present-day Brazil was a Portuguese colony even before the first explorers arrived. Rio de Janeiro was founded in 1565, and 2 years later the French, who had built a small settlement nearby, were expelled from the city. In 1720 gold and diamonds were discovered in nearby Minas Gerais, and Rio's natural harbor made it an ideal port to export riches to Portugal. The city grew rapidly as a result, and became the capital of Brazil in 1763. Brazil declared independence from Portugal in 1822 and Rio remained the capital until 1960, when it was moved to Brasília.

Over the next 100 years, coffee replaced gold as Brazil's top export. In the early 20th century the city was modernized with a redesigned port and an improved infrastructure. The population boomed during this period, with millions of people moving into the city from rural areas. Many of the poorer newcomers found no affordable housing other than Rio's slums, known as Favelas.

The Sights and Sounds

Rio is a city that delights the senses with its exotic mixture of old and new, indigenous and European, wealth and poverty. Where to begin? In the Centro or the city center, of course, the oldest part of Rio.

Think Rome is the only city famous for its aqueduct? Visitors in the know go to the Carioca Aqueduct, built in the middle of the 18th century to carry fresh water into the city. Modern technology has rendered the aqueduct obsolete, however, and today the massive, stone-arched structure carries not water but local trolley cars known as Bondes.

The National Library, completed by 1908, was one of the first institutions of its kind in all of South America. The library's collection dates to the 11th century and includes drawings, prints and manuscripts. The entire collection tops some 13 million books, from rare to contemporary.

While most of Rio's churches date their history and design to colonial times, one stands as an exception to the rule. The Cathedral of St. Sebastian, completed in 1976, is a massive pyramidal concrete structure that can accommodate 20,000 parishioners! Keeping in style with its ultramodern look, the altar is a simple but enormous rock of granite. The leaded windows are said to be some of the best in South America.

Rio has many churches much older than St. Sebastian: the Convent of St. Anthony, completed in 1780; the Church of St. Francis, completed in 1737; and São Bento Monastery, completed in the 1580s. All are stunning in their majesty and each deserves a visit.

Rio's museums offer a tremendous range of exhibits, and in the case of one—the

五、经济

旅游业是里约市经济的一个重要组成部分,此外,这座城市还是巴西金融和商业的一个中心。里约市的工业生产占巴西经济的10%左右,其产品包括加工食品、化学品、药品和金属等。造船工业是当地居民就业的重要渠道。里约市是巴西重要的交通枢纽之一,公路及铁路线将城市与巴西全国以及南美其他大城市连接起来。

光影流金

1502年,当葡萄牙探险者来到现在的关塔那摩湾的时候,这一地区居住的都是图皮印第安人。事实上,在首批探险者抵达之前,今天的巴西所在地区就是葡萄牙的一个殖民地。里约热内卢市创建于1565年,两年以后,那些在附近建立了一个小殖民地的法国人被从这一地区驱逐出去。1720年,人们在附近的米纳斯-杰拉斯地区发现了黄金和钻石,而里约这一天然港口成为这些财富向葡萄牙出口的理想通道。于是,城市迅速发展起来,1763年,里约市成为巴西的首都。1822年,巴西宣布脱离葡萄牙正式独立,里约仍然是巴西的首都,直到1960年,巴西首都才迁至巴西利亚。

在以后的100年间,咖啡取代黄金成为巴西出口量最大的商品。20世纪初,这座城市通过对港口的重新设计以及改善基础设施等,使城市迅速走上现代化。而这一时期,城市人口也迅猛增加,上百万农村人口涌向城市,许多相对贫困的新移民由于买不起住房而只能选择在当地被称为"棚屋"的贫民窟地区居住。

声光景点

来到里约市,你会有一种新奇的感觉,这座城市将古老与崭新、本土与欧洲、富庶与贫困奇妙的融合在一起,从哪里开始呢?当然应该是市中心,从里约最古老的部分开始。

你是否认为只有罗马才以高架渠而著称呢?熟悉里约这座城市的人都会去卡里奥克高架渠,正是这座修建于18世纪中期的沟渠将活水引入了城市。如今,现代科技已经使得这条沟渠变得陈旧过时,然而,今天这座巨大的石拱形建筑仍在发挥着作用,只不过它不再用来运水,而是用来输送被称作"邦德斯"的有轨电车。

建成于1908年的国家图书馆是整个南美洲地区此类建筑的首创,图书馆的馆藏最早可以追溯到十一世纪时的绘画、印刷品和手稿。图书总数共计达1 300万册左右,从珍本到当代图书应有尽有。

尽管大部分里约市的教堂其设计和历史都可以追溯到殖民地时期,但是有一座教堂却是个例外,这就是建成于1976年的圣塞巴斯蒂安大教堂,这座巨大的金字塔形的混凝土建筑足以容纳两万堂区居民!与其超新式的外观风格相匹配的,是一个简洁但宏大的花岗岩制成的圣餐台。那些镶有铅框的窗户据说是南美最好的。

里约市有许多比圣塞巴斯蒂安大教堂更古老的教堂:如建成于1780年的圣安东尼女修院,1737年的圣弗朗西斯教堂,以及完工于16世纪80年代的圣本东隐修院。这几所教堂都拥有雄伟漂亮的外观,每一座都值得一去。

里约市的博物馆馆藏惊人,就以其中的一个——天空小农场博物馆为例——单就这

Museum of the Small Farm of the Sky—a fascinating name. This museum's 20th century European collection is outstanding, with paintings by Degas, Matisse,Picasso, Dalí, and Matisse, among many others. Also here is a collection of historical maps. The National History Museum documents Brazil's lengthy colonial and national history. The museum building itself is historic; its battlements date from 1603. The National Museum of Fine Arts specializes in Brazilian works from the 19th and 20th centuries. The Museum of Modern Art showcases some 1,700 works are displayed in a contemporary building.

The Paço Imperial is the palace built in 1743 for the Portuguese viceroys, the king's colonial administrators. After Brazil declared its independence, the palace became home to the country's first emperors. Today it is a cultural center. The plaza in front of the building was once the site where emperors were crowned and deposed, and also where slavery was abolished.

Visitors flock to two particular sites for marvelous views of the city and surrounding countryside. The first, Pão-de-Açúcar, also known as Sugarloaf Mountain, is a 1,300-foot-tall granite monolith. Glass-paneled cable cars transport visitors to the peak every half hour. Corcovado is another granite mountain,world-famous for the 125-foot-tall statue at its peak named Christ the Redeemer.The statue was dedicated in 1931 and is dramatically illuminated at night. Visitors can reach the summit of Corcovado by train or taxi.

Cafes, restaurants, dance clubs and theatres are active 7 nights a week. Do not forget to visit Rio's wildly popular beaches, however, expect only to sunbathe. Nevertheless, the beach is the place to see and be seen.

The Trivia

Fact: Rio was the only city in the Americas to be an European capital—however briefly. In 1808, Prince John of Portugal fled Lisbon to escape a French invasion and moved the Portuguese capital to Rio. Thousands of wealthy Portuguese followed him and remained in Brazil. Lisbon again became the Portuguese capital when John returned in 1821.

Fact: When the Portuguese explorer Gaspar de Lemos discovered Guanabara Bay in January 1502, he believed it to be the mouth of a major river, which it is not. He called the bay Rio de Janeiro, which is Portuguese for River of January.

Fact: Cariocas crowd the beaches of Rio each New Years' to holding candlelit Macumba ceremonies.

Why Rio Is a 50 plus one City

While Rio is a city of great contrasts, it has a style and appeal all its own. The city blends all of the best of Native American, Portuguese and African cultures into a festive mix of music, art and food.

个名字本身就令人激动。这家博物馆最突出的展品是20世纪欧洲的绘画作品，包括德加、马蒂斯、毕加索、达利等一些画家。此外，这里还收藏了大量历史性的地图。国家历史博物馆着重展出的是巴西漫长的殖民地和国家历史。博物馆建筑本身也颇具纪念意义，那些带枪眼的防御墙最早是1603年修建的。巴西国家美术馆专门用以收藏19~20世纪巴西本国艺术家的作品。现代艺术博物馆是一座当代建筑，里面陈列了大约1 700件艺术作品。

皇宫是1743年为葡萄牙总督，也就是葡萄牙国王的殖民地行政长官而专门修建的宫殿，巴西宣布独立之后，这座宫殿成为早期巴西国王的居住地。今天这里是一个文化中心，宫殿前面的广场过去曾经是国王加冕或被废黜的场所，同时也是奴隶制被废除的地方。

有两个特殊的地方是游客通常用来欣赏城市及其周边郊区风景的绝佳场所，第一个是站在被称为"塔糖山"的高1 300英尺的花岗岩独石柱，另一个是坐在输送游客上山顶的玻璃镶门的缆车内，缆车每隔半小时就发一班。康科瓦多是另外一座花岗岩山，因山顶上一座高125英尺的耶稣基督塑像而举世闻名。这座雕像建成于1931年，夜晚时分，雕像会被灯光照亮，颇为神奇，游客还可以乘坐火车或出租车抵达康科瓦多山巅。

在里约市，那些咖啡馆、餐馆、舞厅夜总会、剧院等每天晚上都会营业，别忘了去参观一下里约市人气最旺的沙滩，不过，最好只是晒晒日光浴。不管怎样，海滩是你欣赏别人以及被别人欣赏的地方。

奇闻轶事

之一：里约是美洲地区唯一一座曾经作为欧洲首都的城市 —— 不过，只是很短的时间。1808年，葡萄牙的约翰王子为了躲避入侵的法国人而从里斯本逃出来，并将葡萄牙的首都迁到了里约市，数千名有钱的葡萄牙贵族也随他来到了这里，并最终留在了巴西。1821年，约翰返回葡萄牙后，里斯本又重新成为葡萄牙的首都。

之二：1502年1月，葡萄牙探险家嘉士伯·德·雷莫斯发现了关塔那摩湾，并且他相信这里一定是某条主要河流的入口，事实并非如此。他将这处海湾命名为里约热内卢湾，在葡萄牙语中就是"元月之河"的意思。

之三：每年的新年，里约热内卢人都会聚集到海滩边，举行烛光照耀下的马库姆巴宗教仪式。

为什么里约市入选50＋1个城市？

虽然，里约市是一座对比鲜明的城市，但是，它仍然拥有自身的风格和魅力，这座城市集南美印第安、葡萄牙以及非洲文化的精华于一身，并将其转化为一道充满喜庆气氛的音乐、艺术和美食的大餐。

Thirty-seven

Rome, Italy

The Basic Facts

Rome is the capital of Italy and one of the most historically significant cities in the world. Following the fall of the Roman Empire, its importance faded, but returned during the Renaissance and then grew rapidly during the late 20th century. Today millions of visitors flock to Rome each year to explore the history and experience the culture of what was once the center of the known world.

Geography

Rome lies at 41 degrees 52 minutes north latitude and 12 degrees 37 minutes east longitude. The ancient city was founded in west-central Italy along the Tiber River, about 10 miles west of the Tyrrhenian Sea. Rome's geography and its distance from the sea made it less conducive to attacks by invaders and pirates. The modern city of Rome covers roughly 500 square miles. Vatican City, a sovereign state just 0.17 square miles in size, lies within the city limits. The Vatican is the administrative and spiritual center of the Roman Catholic Church.

Climate

Rome has a mild Mediterranean climate in.uenced by the colder Alpine climate to the north and the hot and dry climate to the south. Average temperatures are fairly consistent throughout the year; winters average in the mid-50s Fahrenheit and summers average in the mid-80s Fahrenheit.

Government

Rome is governed by a City Council consisting of 80 members, each of whom is elected to a 4-year term. The City Council in turn elects one member from the body to be the city's mayor. The mayor heads the City Executive Committee, which is responsible for administering city services.

Demographics

Rome is homogenous in terms of its language and religion, but diverse in terms of its culture, economics and politics. Most Romans are native Italians; northern African and non-Italian Europeans make up the minority. Rome's population of 2.7 million is large by European standards, and the entire metropolitan area population is more than four million.

Economy

Commerce and government dominate Rome's economic landscape; other important industries are tourism and construction. Rome's few factories produce clothing, textiles, processed foods and other products. Many motion picture studios are located in Rome; this

意大利罗马

概况

罗马是意大利的首都，是世界上最富历史意义
的城市之一。虽然随着罗马帝国的衰落，罗马的重要
性也开始减弱，但是，在文艺复兴时期，它又卷土重
来，并在20世纪得到迅速发展。如今，每年都有数以
百万的游客来到罗马，探寻它的历史，体验这座往昔
世界中心的文化。

一、地理

罗马位于北纬41°52′，东经12°37′，这座古老的
城市地处意大利中西部地区台伯河沿岸，距离第勒尼安海以西大约10英里的地方。罗马
的地理位置及靠海的距离使得它不容易被入侵者或海盗袭击。当今罗马市的面积大约有
500平方英里。梵蒂冈这个面积仅0.17平方英里的主权国家就位于市区范围之内。梵蒂
冈是罗马天主教的管理及精神中心。

二、气候

由于受到北方阿尔卑斯山较冷的气候以及南方干燥炎热气候的共同影响，罗马拥有
温和的地中海气候，平均气温在一年之中变化不大，冬季平均是华氏55度左右，夏季则在
华氏85度上下。

三、政府

罗马市由一个包括80名成员的市政委员会管理，所有成员经选举产生，任期4年。市
政委员会定期从其内部选举一名委员来担任市长一职。市长负责城市行政委员会，该委
员会的职责主要是实施城市的各项服务。

四、人口

虽然在语言和宗教方面，罗马是一座相对单一的城市，但是就文化、经济和政治来
说，罗马却是一座多元化的城市。大多数罗马人为地道的意大利人，来自北非及非意大利
的欧洲移民构成城市的少数民族。罗马的270万人口在欧洲是属于比较多的，整个大市范
围的人口则超过了400万。

五、经济

金融业和政府部门构成罗马经济的主要风景线，其余重要的产业还包括旅游及建筑
业。罗马少数一些工厂主要加工服装、纺织、食品和其他产品。许多电影制片厂都位于罗

beautiful and historic city provides an excellent backdrop for mainstream and independent films.

The History

The first known settlers of Rome, the Latins, established a settlement along the Tiber in the 9th century B.C.. Two hundred years later, the Etruscans gained political control of the region. They held power until Rome became a republic in 509 B.C..

The Roman Republic expanded its sphere of influence throughout the ensuing years; by 275 B.C., Rome controlled most of Italy. The Republic defeated the Carthaginians of North Africa during the Punic Wars in the 3rd century B.C.,thereby assuming power over most of the Mediterranean region. Despite its military successes abroad, internal struggles plagued the city; economic disparity and political skirmishes led to revolt and war among the cities. Eventually, Roman general Lucius Sulla became dictator over the city and restored order.

Rome expanded further overseas under Pompey and Julius Caesar. Caesar returned in triumph to Rome after conquering Gaul, yet the Roman Senate ordered him to relinquish power. His refusal led to a civil war, and when he emerged victorious, he became dictator for life. He was assassinated in 44 B.C. by an angry group of Roman senators, an event which touched off another round of civil wars.Caesar's adopted son and heir, Augustus, became the first Roman Emperor in 27 B.C.. Rome under his reign experienced a notable period of peace and prosperity,which became known as Pax Romana (Roman Peace).

After Augustus's death, a succession of rulers furthered the transfer of power from the Senate to the emperor; over time they achieved virtually absolute power. Over the next 2 centuries the Roman Empire went into decline, so much so that in 293 A.D., the emperor Diocletian divided the Empire into eastern and western regions. The Greek city-state of Byzantium was declared the eastern capital, while Rome remained the capital of the western region. In 410 Rome was sacked by invading Barbarians, which caused the abrupt end of the Western Roman Empire.

Although Rome no longer held political power, its culture and form of government survived and helped shape much of Western civilization. During the middle ages, the Roman Catholic Church became the unifying force of Europe and modeled its administrative structure on the Roman Empire. The history of Rome was more closely examined during the Renaissance and by the 1700s books about ancient Rome began to appear.

The Sights and Sounds

Rome is a city with so many great sights and sounds, not just the Vatican or historic sites such as the Roman Forum. Visitors can wander throughout the city and find exceptional smaller, everyday sights that are as much as 2,500 years old;few cities can make this claim!

The historical center of Rome, containing those buildings that represent ancient Rome, is significant not only to Rome and Italy, but also to the entire western world. The Arch of Constantine is one of the finest examples of 4th century architecture still in existence. The Arch and Christianity go hand in hand, as Constantine first permitted the practice of the new religion.

马,这座风景如画且历史悠久的城市为那些主流和独立制作的影片提供了绝佳的背景。

光影流金

目前已知罗马地区最早的居民是拉丁人,他们于公元前9世纪在台伯河沿岸建立起一个居住地。200年后,伊特鲁里亚人在政治上取得了该地区的控制权,并且将这一权利保持到公元前509年罗马共和国建立之前。

在以后的数年间,罗马共和国不断扩大其势力范围,到了公元前275年,罗马已经控制了意大利的大部分地区。公元前3世纪,罗马共和国在布匿战争中打败了北非的迦太基人,从而重新取得了对地中海大部分地区的控制权。尽管罗马帝国在海外不断取得军事胜利,但是,在罗马城内各派纷争不断,经济上的鸿沟以及政治上的小规模冲突导致了城市之间的叛乱和战争,最终,罗马的统帅卢西乌斯·苏拉恢复了城市的秩序,并成为这座城市的独裁者。

在庞培和尤利乌斯·恺撒统治期间,罗马在海外继续扩张。征服高卢以后,恺撒凯旋返回罗马,然而,罗马的元老院命令他交出权力,他的拒绝导致了内战的爆发,当恺撒最终取得内战胜利之后,他成了终身的独裁者。公元前44年,恺撒被罗马元老院的一群愤怒成员暗杀,这一事件引发了新的一轮内战。公元前27年,恺撒的养子和继承人奥古斯都成为罗马帝国的第一任皇帝。在他统治期间,罗马经历了一段相对和平繁荣的阶段,历史上被称为"派克斯-罗马纳"(即"和平罗马"之意)时期。

奥古斯都死后,他的继任者们不断将元老院的权利转移到自己手中,经过一段时间后,他们几乎取得了绝对的权力。在之后的两个世纪里,罗马帝国开始走向衰落。公元293年,戴克里先皇帝将整个罗马帝国划分为东西两个部分,希腊城邦拜占庭被宣布为东罗马的首都,而罗马则仍为西罗马帝国的都城。410年,罗马遭到了入侵的异族人的劫掠,并最终导致西罗马帝国的突然灭亡。

虽然罗马已经不再是政治权利的中心,但是其文化和政府组织却延续至今,构成西方文明的雏形。中世纪时期,罗马天主教教廷成为欧洲统一的力量,其管理模式也被罗马帝国所效仿。文艺复兴时期,罗马的历史得到深入的挖掘,到了18世纪,大量关于古罗马的书籍开始问世。

声光景点

罗马市内景点众多,不仅仅只有梵蒂冈和诸如罗马论坛之类的历史性遗迹。穿梭于市内,游客可以发现许多特别微小、特别寻常,但却拥有2 500年历史的景观,这样的经历恐怕只有在罗马才能碰到!

拥有大量代表古罗马建筑的罗马历史中心不仅对于意大利人和罗马人来说意义重大,即便对于整个西方世界来说亦是如此。君士坦丁拱门是保存至今的四世纪建筑的完美范例之一,这座拱门与基督教密不可分,因为,正是君士坦丁首先授权人们宣传这一新的宗教。

Considering the massive size of the elaborate Coliseum, it is difficult to believe that it was built in just 8 years, from 72 to 80 A.D.. With seats for 50,000 spectators,this oval–shaped stadium was the principal site for games and spectacles, including gladiatorial combat. The statue of Nero, once adjacent to the Coliseum, is believed to have been the source for its name. The arena was abandoned in 524, after the rise of Christianity sparked outrage that combatants were killed during the games staged there. Over the years, the Coliseum was damaged by several earthquakes and ransacked for its prized travertine stone. Nevertheless, this ancient structure remains one of the world's most magnificent ruins, and today serves as a rallying point for protests against the death penalty.

Nero, the Roman Emperor from 54 to 68 A.D., is famous for his excessively cruel nature; he is believed to have played his violin when Rome burned during the great fire of 64 A.D.. Many historians have concluded that Nero himself ordered the destruction so that he might build the Golden House, his famous palace. More than half of its 300 rooms have been excavated; the massive, opulent building leaves both historians and tourists in awe.

Unfortunately for visitors, the Roman Forum is a shadow of its former self. The ruins of palaces, temples and civic buildings are indeed impressive, yet they provide only a glimpse into its former glory. When in Rome, the Pantheon is another must-see. Built in 27 B.C. as a temple, and later consecrated as a Christian church, this globe-shaped building is a classic example of architectural perfection.

Rome's fountains and squares, known as piazzas, are as famous as any of the city's landmarks. Traditionally, visitors to Rome ensure their return by tossing a coin into the Trevi Fountain, built in the mid-1700s. The Piazza Barberini contains the famous Triton Fountain and the Fountain of the Bees. The Piazzo del Popolo is one of the largest in Rome, famous for its ancient Egyptian obelisk. Piazza di Spagna is home to the young and the chic, who meet at the famous Spanish Steps, a 200-year old staircase named after the nearby 19th century Spanish Embassy.

Sant'Angelo Castle was built as a tomb and memorial to the great Emperor Hadrian; this fortress helped the city to defend itself against Barbarian invasions. The castle was associated with the Vatican, and many popes sought refuge there during troubled times.

Words fail to describe the treasures of the Vatican museums. The entire complex has some five miles of displays; to see everything, visitors must be both patient and dedicated. Periods represented include ancient Egyptian, early Roman and Greek, and the Renaissance masters. The painted ceiling of the Sistine Chapel, Michelangelo's greatest legacy to the world, was commissioned by Pope Julius II in 1508 and took the renowned painter 4 years to complete.

St. Peter's Square was redesigned by Bernini in the 17th century to enable large numbers of devout Catholics to receive papal blessings. St. Peter's Basilica at the square was constructed in the 16th and 17th centuries in tribute to God's greatness. The basilica's famous dome was designed by Michelangelo and is accessible by a spiral staircase. From the top of the dome, visitors can take in a lovely view of the church's intricate interior space.

After a strenuous tour of this magnificent city, tourists need to relax and enjoy life.Like every major European city, Rome has a variety of restaurants, cafes, clubs,bars and entertainment spots to suit every taste. The sights and sounds change frequently, but never fail to delight.

大体育场精美而宏大的气势,让人很难相信它的建设仅仅从公元72年到公元80年,持续了8年的时间,这座能够容纳5万名观众的椭圆形体育场是体育比赛及大型活动的主要举办地,例如,角斗比赛等。人们相信体育场的名字来源于曾经一度与大体育场毗邻的尼禄塑像。524年,由于越来越多的基督徒不满于角斗士们在比赛场上被屠杀,这座大体育场遭到废弃。在以后的岁月里,大体育场经历了数次地震的破坏,那些珍贵的石灰石也遭到洗劫。然而,这座古代建筑至今仍然是世界上最宏伟的遗址之一,如今,它成了那些抗议死刑的人们集会的场所。

公元54~68年在位的罗马皇帝尼禄,因其极度的残酷而出名,人们都相信公元64年,罗马城被大火吞噬的时候,他还在拉他的小提琴。许多历史学家认为正是尼禄本人下令毁掉城市,以便修建他的著名宫殿"黄金屋",这座宫殿包括300间房屋,其中超过一半已经被发掘,无论是史学家还是观光客,无不为这座建筑的宏大和奢华而深感敬畏。

令游客遗憾的是,罗马论坛如今已经所剩无几了,尽管那些宫殿、寺庙和民宅遗址足以令人难以忘怀,但是,那些无疑只是往昔辉煌的惊鸿一瞥。在罗马,万神庙是另一必看的景点,这座建于公元前27年的寺庙后来被改成了基督教堂,球形的建筑堪称建筑史上一项完美的经典之作。

罗马的喷泉和广场被称为"皮亚兹",其名气相当于其他城市的地标建筑。根据传统,来到罗马的游客要通过向特雷维喷泉抛硬币的方式来决定他们的返程安排,特雷维喷泉修建于18世纪中期。巴伯里尼广场内有著名的特莱登喷泉和蜜蜂喷泉。波波罗广场是罗马市内最大的广场,因广场内的古代埃及方尖塔而闻名遐迩,斯巴格那广场是年轻人和时尚者的乐园,这里有著名的拥有200年历史的西班牙台阶,其名称源自于附近的19世纪时的西班牙大使馆。

圣安琪罗城堡是为伟大的哈德良皇帝修建的陵墓和纪念馆,这座城堡在罗马抵御外邦入侵时也发挥了重要作用。这座城堡与梵蒂冈相连,因此,在冲突时期,许多教皇会在这里寻求避难。

梵蒂冈博物馆的宝藏用语言是难以描述的,整座建筑群内的展品绵延5英里左右,要将所有的展品一一看过,你必须非常耐心、非常执著。馆内代表性的展区包括古代埃及、罗马和希腊早期以及文艺复兴时期大师们的作品。作为米开朗琪罗留存于世的最伟大的遗产,西斯廷教堂的天顶画于1508年在罗马教皇尤利乌斯二世授权下创作,花费这位绘画大师四年的时间方才完成。

圣彼得广场是17世纪时由贝尔尼尼重新设计的,目的在于让大批虔诚的天主教徒能够接受教皇的赐福,广场内的圣彼得犹太教堂修建于16世纪和17世纪,以作为向上帝荣耀的贡品。这座犹太教堂著名的穹顶也是由米开朗琪罗设计的,教堂内的旋梯可以直达穹顶。站在穹顶之上,游客可以欣赏到教堂内部复杂精美的布局。

经过城中一天辛苦的旅程,游客需要放松和休息,正如其他欧洲城市一样,罗马城内有各式各样的餐馆、咖啡屋、夜总会、酒吧和娱乐场所,可以满足人们不同的口味。尽管景点在不停地变化,但是不变的是开心的享受。

The Trivia

Fact: Christianity entered Rome in the 2nd century A.D.. The Roman rulers were frightened of this new religious movement and brutally repressed its followers, blaming them in part for Rome's decline. Christianity thrived, however, and in 313 Constantine declared Christianity the official religion of Rome.

Fact: The head of the household in ancient Rome was called the Paterfamilias (father of the family). He had absolute power over the household. A son could not own property as long as his father lived, and so many Roman households included married sons and their families.

Fact: Ancient Romans loved spectacle. The Roman Coliseum was known for its violent games, in which trained gladiators fought wild animals—and sometimes each other—often to the death. Condemned criminals and early Christians were frequently killed for sport. On occasion, the Coliseum was even flooded in order to stage mock naval battles.

Fact: The Circus Maximus hosted chariot races in its large oval arena; today it is a park.

Fact: None of the 300 rooms in Nero's Golden House was a bedroom; the palace was built solely for his entertainment.

Fact: Many historians blame lead poisoning for the eventual decline and fall of the Roman Empire. Most Roman plates and cups were made of lead, and they frequently used lead to sweeten their wine.

Fact: Ancient Romans were proud of their physical fitness and hygiene. Emperors built lavish public baths to encourage the citizens to exercise and bathe. These baths became popular meeting places.

Why Rome Is a 50 plus one City

Throw a coin into the Trevi Fountain and return to experience Rome's beauty all over again. The city's art, architecture and cuisine span the centuries providing visitors one of the world's finest vacation experiences.

奇闻轶事

之一：2世纪时，基督教进入罗马。当时的罗马统治者们对于这一新的宗教运动异常恐惧，对其信仰者严酷镇压，甚至将罗马的衰落也归罪于他们头上。然而，基督教依旧日益发展兴旺，313年，君士坦丁宣布基督教为罗马的官方宗教。

之二：在古代罗马，家庭的领导者被称为"家长"（家里的父亲），在家里他们有绝对的权威。只要父亲还活着，儿子就不能拥有财产，所以，许多罗马家庭里已婚的儿子都和父母住在一起。

之三：古代罗马人非常喜欢看热闹。罗马的大体育场因其疯狂的比赛而著名，那些经过训练的角斗士要么同野兽搏斗 —— 有时角斗士之间进行搏斗 —— 常常到死方休。死刑犯人和早期的基督徒时常成为游戏中被杀的对象。有时，在大体育场上演模拟的海军战役时，甚至会出现人满为患的景象。

之四：在巨大的椭圆形的大竞技场内过去主要举办双轮马车比赛，如今，这里成了一个公园。

之五：在尼禄黄金屋的300间房子里没有一间是卧室，建造这座宫殿仅仅是为了娱乐。

之六：许多历史学家认为铅中毒是最终导致罗马帝国衰落和灭亡的罪魁祸首，大多数罗马人的盘子和茶杯都是铅做的，而且他们还经常用铅来使葡萄酒变得更甜。

之七：古代罗马人以身体的强壮和清洁而自豪，罗马皇帝们修建了大量的公共浴室来鼓励公民锻炼和沐浴，这些浴室也成为受人欢迎的公众集会场所。

为什么罗马入选50 + 1个城市？

将一枚硬币扔进特雷维喷泉，然后返回罗马城去重新体验一遍它的美景吧。这座城市跨越数百年历史的艺术、建筑和美食，足以为游客提供一次世界上最完美的假日体验。

Thirty-eight

San Francisco, United States

The Basic Facts

San Francisco is one of California's largest cities and is a popular tourist destination. Main attractions include Chinatown, the famous cable cars, its steep hills, and its mild climate. It is often known as the City by the Bay.

Geography

San Francisco lies at 37 degrees 45 minutes north latitude and 122 degrees 26 minutes west longitude. The city sits on the northern tip of a peninsula in northern California between San Francisco Bay and the Pacific Ocean. A one-mile-wide strait connects the bay to the ocean and was once named the Golden Gate. San Francisco occupies 121 square miles and is dominated by more than 40 hills; some hills rise as high as 400 feet, and so they have some of the steepest streets in the world. There are several islands in the ocean and bay, including the famous island of Alcatraz. The Port of San Francisco borders the bay and is one of the world's largest natural harbors.

Climate

San Francisco's rapid growth is partly attributed to its climate; annual temperatures range from the mid-50s Fahrenheit in winter to the upper 60s Fahrenheit in the summer. San Francisco experiences significant fogs over the western part of the city, especially at night and in the early morning; warm air flows over the cold ocean waters to form this meteorological phenomenon.

Government

San Francisco has been a consolidated city-county since 1856; the mayor is also the county executive. The city is run both by the mayor and an 11-member city council called the Board of Supervisors. The mayor appoints the heads of city government services and prepares an annual budget. The mayor has veto power over laws and regulations passed by the Board of Supervisors.

Demographics

Caucasians comprise nearly half of the population of San Francisco; significant minority groups include Asians, African-Americans, and Native Americans. San Francisco has the largest Chinese population in the United States, and the city's Chinatown is the largest in the country. Many Chinese immigrated to work in gold mines and on the Central Pacific Railroad. The city's population is estimated at 744,000, but that of the metropolitan area is more than 7.5 million.

Economy

San Francisco is a leading U.S. financial center as well as a commercial and industrial

美国旧金山

概况

　　旧金山是加利福尼亚州最大的城市,也是一座非常热门的旅游城市。旧金山的魅力主要来自于唐人街、著名的缆车、陡峭的山丘以及宜人的气候。旧金山常被人们称为"临湾之城"。

一、地理

　　旧金山位于北纬37°45′,西经122°26′,地处加利福尼亚州北部太平洋与圣弗兰西斯科湾之间的半岛北端。一条宽1英里的海峡将圣弗兰西斯科湾与大海连接起来,该海峡曾被称为"金门"。旧金山面积121平方英里,城内有40多座山丘,因此,一些街道堪称世界上最陡峭的街道。周边海域及海湾地区有几座岛屿,其中最著名的是阿尔特拉兹岛,环绕整个海湾的旧金山港是世界上最大的天然港口。

二、气候

　　旧金山的快速成长,一部分原因是得益于其宜人的气候,年均气温从冬季的华氏55度到夏季的华氏67~69度。城市的西部地区时常大雾弥漫,尤其是在午夜或凌晨时分,温暖的空气与冰冷的海水交汇形成这一气象奇观。

三、政府

　　旧金山是一座于1856年经合并组成的联合市镇,市长同时兼任市镇的行政长官。城市由市长和包括11名成员的被称为"管理会"的市政委员会共同管理。市长任命市政府各服务机构的领导,同时负责准备每年的预算。市长有权否决管理会通过的法律与规章制度。

四、人口

　　白人占了旧金山人口的近一半,此外,主要的少数民族包括亚洲人、非洲裔的美国人和美洲印地安人。旧金山的华人数量是美国最多的,城内的唐人街也是美国最大的。许多华人移民为了在金矿或中央太平洋铁路工作而来到这里。虽然旧金山市区的人口大约只有74.4万,但是大市范围的人口却超过了750万。

五、经济

　　旧金山是美国首屈一指的金融、财政和工业中心,旅游业对于城市的经济至关重要,

center. Tourism is vital to the economy, and many San Franciscans work in the tourist trade. The city is at the heart of California's burgeoning high-tech industry; the area from Palo Alto to San Jose is commonly known as Silicon Valley.

The History

In 1769 Spanish explorer Gaspar de Portolà discovered the area surrounding present-day San Francisco. A few years later, the Spanish built a military fort in the area and established a nearby mission. Mexico declared independence from Spain in 1810 and took control of California for the purpose of cattle ranching. The resulting trade in cattle hides led to the development of a busy port at San Francisco Bay.

In 1847 the United States acquired San Francisco following the Mexican-American War. The port area boomed during the Gold Rush of 1849, and San Francisco was incorporated as a city in 1850. Lawlessness prevailed in the late 1800s, despite the efforts of citizens to curb the trend.

In 1906, the massive San Francisco earthquake killed at least 3,000 people and destroyed nearly the entire city; the resolute citizens quickly rebuilt the area. The expansion of ports in Los Angeles and Oakland lessened the importance of San Francisco's port. The city underwent a major makeover in the 1960s; older dilapidated buildings were replaced by modern row houses. The population became more diverse as the building boom continued through the 1970s.

The Sights and Sounds

The federal penitentiary Alcatraz, known as The Rock in its heyday, was built in 1934 on Alcatraz Island in the middle of San Francisco Bay. Some of the United States' most dangerous criminals were imprisoned there, including the notorious gangster Al Capone. By 1963, however, the prison was closed because it became too expensive to maintain. Today it is a National Historic Landmark, and guided tours are available through the building and around the grounds. The West Coast's oldest lighthouse still in operation is also located on Alcatraz Island.

The collection at the Asian Art Museum spans a period of 6,000 years. Works include art from many Asian countries housed in 30 galleries. Because the space is so large, take the time to look at the special exhibits before you try to browse the whole collection.

The Japanese Trade and Cultural Center, a local area known as Japantown, is organized around the Peace Pagoda. This group of five buildings houses Japanese restaurants, museums, art galleries, bookstores and cultural attractions. Each year, the Kabuki Theatre hosts the Asian American Film Festival.

Golden Gate Park, with its beautiful hills and turquoise waters, is the perfect destination for hikers, bikers and picnickers. The park is a welcome break from the bustle of the city. Noteworthy sites here are the Japanese tea garden, the Victorian-styled Conservatory of Flowers greenhouse, and the Strybing Arboretum and Botanical Gardens.

Built in 1937, the Golden Gate Bridge was once the world's largest suspension bridge. It is the undisputed symbol of San Francisco and a popular tourist attraction. To see the fog rolling in at the bridge is a wonderful treat for tourists.

The collections at the Palace of the Legion of Honor range from ancient artifacts to European paintings and ceramics. The museum is known for its extensive collection of

许多旧金山人都在旅游部门工作,与此同时,旧金山还是加利福尼亚欣欣向荣的高科技产业的核心地区,从帕洛阿图到圣何塞之间的地区通常被称作"硅谷"。

光影流金

1769年,西班牙探险家嘉士帕·波尔塔拉发现了今天的旧金山一带地区,几年之后,西班牙在这一地区修建了一座军事要塞,并在附近地区建立了一个传教机构。1810年,墨西哥宣布脱离西班牙独立,同时他们夺取了对加利福尼亚地区的控制权,以便建立养牛牧场。牛皮贸易的发展使得圣弗朗西斯湾变成了一个繁忙的港口。

1847年,伴随着墨西哥和美国战争的进程,美国人取得了对旧金山的控制权。1849年的淘金热加速了港口地区的迅猛发展,1850年,旧金山市正式建立。19世纪后期,违法行为曾一度在城市蔓延,尽管当时许多市民也力图扼制这一趋势。

1906年,旧金山的大地震夺去了至少3 000人的生命,几乎整座城市都变成了废墟。震后,那些不屈不挠的旧金山人立即开始重建家园。洛杉矶和奥克兰港口的扩大削弱了旧金山港的重要性。20世纪60年代,城市经历了一次大规模的改造,年久失修的破烂建筑被时髦的联排房屋所取代,这种住宅建设的快速发展一直持续到70年代,期间城市人口也变得更加多样化。

声光景点

1934年修建的阿尔卡特拉兹联邦监狱,位于圣弗朗西斯科湾中部的阿尔特拉兹岛上,在其鼎盛时期,人们称之为"罗克"(磐石),美国一些最危险的罪犯都关押在这里,其中包括臭名昭著的匪徒阿尔卡彭。不过,由于监狱的维护费用太高,1963年就被关闭了。今天,这里是一处国家级纪念遗址,有导游专门引导游客参观建筑和周边地区。至今仍在使用的西海岸最古老的灯塔就位于阿尔卡特拉兹岛上。

旧金山的亚洲美术馆,其馆藏跨越了6 000年的历史,来自亚洲许多国家的美术作品分处30个展厅内,由于展厅过于庞大,在你开始浏览所有展品之前,最好先花点时间看一看那些特殊展品。

被称为"日本城"的日本贸易和文化中心是一处颇具地方特色的景点,它位于和平塔周围地区,由五座建筑共同组成,内设日本餐馆、博物馆、美术馆、书店及其他文化特色区。每年,这里的歌舞伎剧场都会举办亚洲美国电影节。

拥有美丽山峦和碧绿水面的金门公园是步行者、自行车爱好者及郊游野餐者的理想天堂,远离城市的喧嚣,这座公园成了游客休憩的绝佳场所,园内值得一去的地方包括日本茶道园、维多利亚风格的鲜花暖房、斯特里兵树木园以及植物园。

修建于1937年的金门大桥,曾经是世界上最大的悬索大桥,它毫无争议地成为旧金山的象征,同时,也是深受游客喜爱的景点。站在大桥上欣赏雾气蒸腾的景象对于游客来说是一种奇妙的体验。

荣誉军团宫内的展品包括从古代的手工艺品到欧洲的绘画和陶瓷,这座博物馆以大

sketches, paintings, and sculptures by Auguste Rodin.

A visit to San Francisco is not complete without a trip to Chinatown; more than 10,000 people live in this neighborhood. Shops cater both to tourists and locals.Take a detour from the main streets and wander the alleys and side streets, and follow your nose to some wonderful Chinese food at reasonable prices.

At Fisherman's Wharf, make sure to visit the sea lions at Pier 39; you will hear them before you see them! Board the ferry to Alcatraz Island here. The San Francisco Maritime National Historic Park is located nearby; explore the maritime museum and tour the turn of the century ships at Hyde Park Pier. This is also a great location for lunch or dinner, with something for everyone; pricy restaurants with bayside views, sidewalk bars, and snack shops. People-watching is a popular activity here as well.

Sonoma Valley, the home of many of California's best vineyards, is a short drive from San Francisco. If you have an extra day, visit the wineries of Sonoma; many offer guided tours and gift shops. The surrounding countryside, with its rolling hills, is a beautiful and relaxing change from the city.

Muir Woods National Park, just 12 miles north of the Golden Gate Bridge, is the home of California's giant redwoods. These towering trees can grow to more than 350 feet and have a life span of well over 600 years.

The Trivia

Fact: Lombard Street in San Francisco is the crookedest street in the world. It is on a hill so steep that the street would be impassible otherwise. There are eight turns, or switchbacks, in one city block.

Fact: San Francisco was closely identified with the counterculture of the 1960s.The Haight-Ashbury area was a major center of the hippie movement. Many well-known musical talents emerged from the scene, including the Grateful Dead and the Jefferson Airplane.

Fact: In October 1989, San Francisco experienced the Loma Prieta earthquake. Although fatalities were few in comparison to the 1906 quake, costs to repair the resulting structural damage were in the billions of dollars. The quake is also known as the World Series quake; it struck before Game 3 of the 1989 Bay Series between the San Francisco Giants and the Oakland Athletics.

Fact: The Spanish army post of the Presidio covers over 1,500 acres in northwestern San Francisco. It was the headquarters of the U.S. 6th Army until 1995, and is now operated by the National Park Service. The Presidio Officers' Club, built in 1776, is the oldest building in the city.

Why San Francisco Is a 50 plus one City

Even the locals leave their hearts in San Francisco. The city is vibrant and metropolitan, with wonderful weather and a great standard of living. The districts within the city invite exploration and discovery, with fine restaurants and ethnic cuisine. The city has a reputation for tolerance, quality employment and unfortunately, exorbitant real estate prices. Once you are there, you cannot afford to leave—for many reasons!

量素描、油画以及奥古斯特·罗丹的雕塑作品而闻名。

来到旧金山如果不去唐人街是很遗憾的,这里居住着1万多人,各类店铺不仅满足了当地居民的需求,而且深受游客的欢迎。在这里的大街小巷多转几圈,你的鼻子会帮你找到一些美味又实惠的中国餐馆。

在渔夫码头,记着一定要到39号桥墩去看一下海狮,你会未见其形,先闻其声!在这儿,你可以乘上开往阿尔卡特拉兹岛的渡轮。旧金山国家海洋纪念公园就位于附近,参观一下海洋博物馆,在海德公园码头登上世纪之交船舶来一次巡游,除此之外,在这里吃一次午餐或晚餐也是不错的选择,因为无论是谁都能找到他想要的东西,在一些价格昂贵的餐馆,可以边就餐,边欣赏海湾风景,街边酒吧、小吃店更是随处可见。许多人来到这里甚至就为了看看过往的行人。

离旧金山不远的索诺玛谷,有许多加利福尼亚州最好的葡萄园,如果你还有时间,不妨参观一下索玛诺的葡萄酒厂,许多酒厂除提供导游服务外,还设有礼品店。周围的乡村地区有连绵的山丘,风景优美,是休闲放松的好去处。

距离金门大桥北面仅12英里的缪尔国家森林公园,是加利福尼亚巨人红杉树的家园,这些高耸的树木能长到350英尺,树龄足以超过600年。

奇闻轶事

之一:旧金山的朗巴德街是世界上最曲折的街道,这条位于一座山丘之上的街道坡度之大,如果不转弯的话,根本无法上去,因此,在一个街区之内就出现了有八处转弯或急转弯的现象。

之二:旧金山与20世纪60年代的反传统文化运动密切相关,海特-阿仕伯里地区曾是嬉皮士运动的主要中心,许多著名的音乐才子从幕后走到了台前,其中包括戈雷特弗·戴德和杰佛森·埃尔珀雷。

之三:1989年10月,旧金山遭到了洛马-珀累塔地震的袭击,尽管与1906年大地震相比死伤人数很少,但是,修复损毁建筑的费用还是达到了数十亿美元。此外,这场地震还被称为"世界职业棒球锦标赛地震",因为它恰好发生在1989年海湾棒球锦标赛旧金山巨人队与奥克兰运动队进行第三场比赛之前。

之四:旧金山西北部的西班牙陆军驻防地占地150英亩,1995年之前,这里一直是美国第六陆军总部,如今,这里属于国家公园服务机构管理。建于1776年的驻防地军官俱乐部是旧金山最古老的建筑。

为什么旧金山入选50 + 1个城市?

旧金山,一个即使是当地人,也会魂牵梦绕的地方,一座充满生机的大都会,一座气候超棒、生活超优的城市,一个拥有出色餐馆和特色美食的地方,期待着你的探寻和发现,不仅如此,这座城市还以宽松的环境和优良的就业渠道而著称,稍感遗憾的是,房价偏高。一旦来到这里,你将不忍离去 —— 原因很多很多!

Thirty-nine

Seattle, United States

The Basic Facts

Seattle is the largest city in the state of Washington and is a manufacturing, trade, and transportation center. The city is a popular tourist destination for shopping, dining, and recreation.

Geography

Seattle lies at 47 degrees 36 minutes north latitude and 122 degrees 20 minutes west longitude. The city is located on the eastern shore of Puget Sound, an arm of the Pacific Ocean. Puget Sound is linked to the Pacific Ocean by the Strait of Juan de Fuca. Seattle covers 84 square miles and its downtown area extends eastward from Elliott Bay, an inlet of Puget Sound. The downtown area is surrounded by so much water, including Lake Washington and Union Bay, that it often seems like an island. The actual metropolitan area of Seattle includes King, Snohomish and Island counties. Seattle is framed by the Cascade Mountains to the east and the Olympic Mountains to the west. Mount Rainier, an active volcano, is part of the Cascades and is clearly visible from the city.

Climate

Seattle is known for its wet weather and temperate climate. Temperatures average in the mid-40s Fahrenheit during the winter and mid-60s Fahrenheit during the summer. Although many believe Seattle is a rainy city, there are cities on the East Coast that have a higher annual average rainfall. Seattle's precipitation tends to be more misty than rainy, and when it is not raining, it is usually overcast.

Government

Seattle's has a mayor-council form of government; the mayor and nine city council members are elected to 4-year terms. All city offices are non-partisan.

Demographics

Almost three-quarters of Seattle's population is Caucasian; most are of German, Irish, English or Scandinavian descent. Asians and African-Americans are the two next largest ethnic groups. The city's population is more than 580,000, while the population of the metropolitan area is roughly 3.8 million.

Economy

Service, manufacturing, and shipping industries are vital to Seattle's economy. Health care, government and the military are the primary employers in the service industry. Manufacturing centers around aircraft, software, and computer supplies. Although the

美国西雅图

概况

西雅图是华盛顿州最大的城市,也是加工、贸易和交通的中心之一。这座城市是深受游客喜爱的购物、餐饮和娱乐的理想场所。

一、地理

西雅图位于北纬47°36′,西经122°20′,地处太平洋狭长的港湾帕格特湾东岸,帕格特湾通过胡安夫卡海峡与太平洋相连。西雅图的面积有84平方英里,市中心地区由帕格特湾的入口之一艾略特湾向东延伸。由于市中心水面众多,例如华盛顿湖和联盟湾,常给人一种身处岛屿的错觉。西雅图大市范围包括金县、斯诺赫米市以及岛屿县。西雅图东面被喀斯喀特山、西面被奥林匹克山环绕。雷尼尔山这座活火山就是喀斯喀特山的一部分,从市区就能够清楚地看见。

二、气候

西雅图的气候潮湿温润,平均气温冬季在华氏45度左右,夏季则在华氏65度上下。虽然许多人人认为西雅图是一座多雨的城市,但是在美国东海岸,有许多城市年均降雨量都超过了西雅图。西雅图的降水多为蒙蒙细雨,不下雨的日子,天空也通常是阴沉的。

三、政府

西雅图市政府的构成属于市长加市政委员会的模式,市长及九名市政委员会成员经选举产生,任期4年。所有的市政官员都属于无党派人士。

四、人口

西雅图几乎3/4的人口都是白人,大多数为德国、爱尔兰、英国或斯堪的纳维亚国家白人的后裔,亚洲人和非洲裔美国人是另两支较大的种族群体。市区人口超过58万,不过,大市范围的人口数则在380万左右。

五、经济

服务行业、加工制造及造船行业是西雅图经济的支柱产业,医疗部门、政府机构和军队是主要的就业渠道。加工制造业以飞机、软件和电脑设备为主。尽管波音公司是该地区

Boeing Company is the region's largest employer, as of 2001 its headquarters are now in Chicago. The software giant Microsoft and the video-game maker Nintendo are headquartered in Seattle.

The History

The area was inhabited by Indian tribes long before it was first settled in 1852 by pioneers from Illinois led by Arthur A. Denny. Their settlement was Alki Point,a beach on Puget Sound. The first sawmill in the area opened the next year, and Seattle became a shipping center for lumber from Washington's forests.

Seattle grew rapidly after rail lines were established in the late 19th century,although in 1889 most of Seattle business districts were destroyed by fire. The city recovered, however, and experienced another growth spurt during the Alaskan and Klondike Gold Rushes soon afterward. The area's economy began to diversify in the early 20th century with the growth of agriculture and the fishing industry.Seattle became important to the war effort during World War Ⅰ, and manufactured ships, aircraft, and related products. The defense industry grew further during World War Ⅱ and the population surged as a result. After a series of ups and downs in the defense industry in the late 20th century, Seattle reinvented itself as a tourist destination.

The Sights and Sounds

Nestled between the Cascade Mountains and Elliott Bay in Puget Sound, Seattle is a metropolitan center with heart. Famous for coffee and grunge rock, this city is known for its laid-back charm and fabulous seafood. The interesting mixture of arts, technology and scenery make Seattle a must-see for outdoor enthusiasts and art lovers.

No visit to Seattle is complete without a trip to the Space Needle, a structure originally built for the 1962 World's Fair. The tower is 605 feet tall, has an observation deck near the top, and a restaurant called Sky City which rotates to give patrons a 360-degree view of the city. The Space Needle is part of the Seattle Center, which includes the Center House, the Pacific Science Center, and two movie theaters.

Pioneer Square is an historic district that is now home to trendy restaurants,antique bookstores and jazz clubs. This location is also rumored to be the hub of Seattle's nightlife. You can wander around, explore the old buildings and peek in at the shops, or visit a trendy restaurant or hot spot.

Pike Place Market is one of the major tourist attractions in Seattle. Built in 1907 and covering an area of nine acres, the market is filled with hundreds of shops,flower markets and restaurants. The original Starbucks store is here, along with dozens of other interesting shops. The open-air setting and the clientele make this a huge people-watching destination. Be sure to take in the flying fish at the Pike Place Fish Market; onlookers delight in watching fishmongers throw fish to one another.

The Experience Music Project is an eclectic museum which was funded by Paul Allen of Microsoft. There are hundreds of interactivie exhibits as well as a gift shop, restaurant and bar. Visitors can play musical instruments and even make their own recordings. The collection also includes rock-and-roll memorabilia from such icons as the Beatles, Jimi Hendrix and Bob Dylan. If visitors need any other enticements, the museum was designed by the avant-garde architect Frank Gehry.

最大的雇主,但是2001年起,其总部已迁到了芝加哥。软件巨头微软公司以及电子游戏制造商任天堂游戏机公司总部都设在西雅图。

光影流金

1852年,由阿瑟·A.丹尼率领的来自伊利诺斯的拓荒者们首先在西雅图地区定居下来,之前,居住在这里的都是印第安部落。阿瑟等人在帕格特湾海滨建立了一个名为阿尔基的要塞。第二年,这一地区的首家锯木厂正式开张,西雅图成为来自华盛顿森林的木材运输航运中心。

19世纪后期,在铁路线建成之后,西雅图得以迅速发展,尽管1889年的一场大火曾经吞噬了西雅图大部分的贸易区,但是,在之后不久阿拉斯加和克朗代克的淘金热期间,这座城市又恢复了生机,并且经历了新的一轮快速成长。20世纪早期,随着农业和渔业的发展,这一地区的经济开始呈现出多元化的趋势。在第一次世界大战期间,西雅图成为重要的战争机器,生产加工了大量的船舶、飞机等战争相关产品。在第二次世界大战期间,随着国防工业进一步发展,城市人口激增。20世纪后期,经过国防工业的一系列兴衰沉浮,西雅图重新确立了其作为旅游中心城市的地位。

声光景点

依偎在喀斯喀特山与帕格特湾内的艾略特湾的怀抱里,西雅图是一座充满灵秀的大都会中心。以咖啡和格郎基摇滚乐而著称的这座城市拥有悠闲迷人的生活方式以及各类海鲜美食,艺术、科技和景观的有趣组合使得西雅图成为户外运动爱好者及美术迷们的必到之处。

来到西雅图不能不去"天线"塔,这是一座最初为1962年世博会而修建的建筑。塔高605英尺,在接近顶端的地方有一处观景台,还有一家名为"天空城"的旋转餐厅,为游客提供360度全方位欣赏整座城市的可能。"天线"塔是西雅图中心的一部分,这个中心包括中央大厦、太平洋科学中心以及两家影剧院。

拓荒者广场是一处具有纪念意义的街区,如今这里有时髦的餐馆、古旧书店和爵士俱乐部。此外,传言都说这里是西雅图夜生活的核心地区,你可以在这里随意地漫步、参观一下那些古老的建筑,也可以瞄一眼店铺里的商品,或者选一家时髦餐厅或热门场所小憩一下。

派克大市场是西雅图主要的旅游景点之一,这个修建于1907年、占地9英亩的市场内有成百上千家商铺、鲜花市场和餐馆。第一家星巴克咖啡店就开在这里,周围还有数十家有趣的商店。广场露天的设计,加之众多的顾客,使之成为观赏各式人等的好去处。一定记着要在派克市场的鱼市上买一条飞鱼回家,许多人都喜欢站在那里看那些鱼贩们把飞鱼抛来抛去。

"体验音乐工程"是一家由微软公司的保罗·艾伦投资兴建的不拘一格的博物馆,这里有数百件互动式的展品,以及礼品店、餐馆、酒吧等。游客不仅可以弹奏乐器,甚至可以自己录制唱片。此外,馆内的展品还包括来自披头士乐队、吉米·亨德里克以及鲍勃·戴兰等偶像人物的摇滚乐纪念品。如果上述一切还不足以诱惑游客的话,那么博物馆本身或许可以,因为它是由先锋派建筑大师弗兰克·盖瑞所设计的。

The Museum of Flight has an extensive collection of aircraft and flight simulators. There are exhibits on famous pilots, what they wore, and what they carried in combat. The flight simulators alone are worth the price of admission.

Most visitors recognize Seattle as the home of Starbucks coffee. The city has a lively coffee culture with many local coffee shops vying for top honors with the big guys. Locals recommend Zeitgeist Coffee for its up-and-coming art, and the excellent java near Pioneer Square. Other hometown heroes include Café Ladro and Vivace. While Starbucks and Seattle's Best on the corner are popular, real java junkies swear by the artistic expression of their local baristas.

Mount Rainier National Park is a few hours southeast of Seattle and is well worth the trip. The views of the coast and the mountains are beautiful, and the hiking trails are first-rate.

The Trivia

Fact: After the disastrous 1889 fire leveled much of Seattle, the city engineers raised the level of the downtown streets several feet above sea level. Doing so left many intact storefronts below street level. The Seattle Underground Tour in Pioneer Square visits this hidden realm.

Fact: The economic boom of World War I led to the rise of powerful labor unions in Seattle. After the war, the unions were afraid they would lose power due to the need for fewer defense workers. In February 1919, 60,000 union workers staged a 5-day strike to voice their concerns. It was the nation's first general strike and was called the Seattle Revolution of 1919.

Fact: Tourism in Seattle was given a major boost when the city hosted the World's Fair in 1962. The fairgrounds are now called the Seattle Center (including the famous Space Needle) and they, and the monorail that was built at the same time, are major tourist attractions.

Fact: The Nisqually Earthquake struck Seattle in 2001, causing injuries and significant property damage but no fatalities.

Fact: Seattle has been on the forefront of several cultural movements. The most famous (and most contrasting) is the birth of the Northwest School of Painters in the 1930s and 1940s and the creation of grunge rock in the 1990s.

Fact: Seattle is home to 25 theatre companies. The only U.S. cities with more theatres are New York City and Chicago.

Why Seattle Is a 50 plus one City

Seattle is environmentally beautiful, virtually surrounded by water and mountains; few can resist its magnificent setting. In addition, the city is clean, safe, culturally alive, and simply an inviting and invigorating place to live and visit.

飞行博物馆收藏了大量飞机和飞行模拟装置，这里还展出了一些著名飞行员的物品，例如他们穿的制服、在战斗中携带的物品等。仅那些飞行模拟装置就会让你觉得门票花得值。

许多游客都把西雅图当成是星巴克咖啡的发祥地，这座城市拥有一种鲜活的咖啡文化。市内许多当地的咖啡店利用那些成功人士为自己宣传，以期在竞争中获得最高的荣誉。当地居民会向你推荐"时代精神咖啡"，因为它代表了一种积极进取的艺术，以及拓荒者广场附近的"完美爪哇"。颇受推崇的其他一些咖啡品牌还包括兰瓦咖啡屋以及"维瓦奇"。虽然星巴克和拐角处的西雅图"最佳"都很受欢迎，但在真正喝爪哇咖啡上瘾的人眼里，拥有艺术气质的当地咖啡才是最值得信赖的。

雷尼尔山国家公园距离西雅图东南只有数小时的车程，一个值得一去的地方。那里不仅有秀丽的海滨及群山景致，而且对于徒步旅行者来说，那里的林间小径绝对一流。

奇闻轶事

之一：1889年，西雅图灾难性的大火将城市的大部分化为灰烬，之后，城市的工程设计师们将整个中心城区的街道水平地向上提升了数英尺，结果造成许多保存完好的店面沉入街面以下。位于拓荒者广场的西雅图地下之旅，目的就是安排游客参观这些被掩藏起来的地方。

之二：第一次世界大战期间的经济增长使得西雅图的工会组织日益强大，战后，由于工人们维权意识的降低，工会组织担心自身的力量会被削弱，于是1919年2月，6万名工会工人组织了持续五天的罢工来呼吁工人们的维权意识，并表达他们的担心，这次罢工是美国历史上第一次大规模的罢工，被称作1919年西雅图革命。

之三：西雅图主办了1962年的世界博览会，这期间西雅图的旅游业得以快速发展。博览会的会址如今成了西雅图中心（其中就有著名的"天线"），这一地区连同当时修建的单轨火车，都成了今天西雅图重要的旅游景点。

之四：2001年，一场大地震袭击了西雅图，造成了许多人受伤以及大量的财产损失，但是，没有人在这次地震中死亡。

之五：西雅图是几次文化运动的排头兵，最著名的（也是对比最鲜明的）包括20世纪三四十年代的西北派画家运动以及20世纪90年代的"颓废"摇滚乐创作。

之六：西雅图设有25家戏剧公司，其数量之多在美国所有城市中仅次于纽约市和芝加哥。

为什么西雅图入选50 + 1个城市？

西雅图市环境优美，四周青山绿水环绕，几乎没有哪座城市其自然风光能与之匹敌。此外，这座城市整洁、安全、文化氛围浓郁，生机盎然、魅力无限，的确是一个旅游兼生活的好地方。

Shanghai, China

The Basics

Shanghai is the largest city in China, the country's largest port, and a world center of finance, trade and industry. Shanghai experienced a building boom in the late 20th century, as thousands of new buildings and a new subway system were added. The new development included the Pudong Area, on the east side of the Huangpu River, as an international financial center.

Geography

Shanghai lies at 31 degrees 14 minutes north latitude and 121 degrees 29 minutes east longitude. The city is located on the Huangpu River in the eastern part of China. The Huangpu and Yangtze Rivers meet and empty into the South China Sea only 14 miles north of Shanghai. This location helped establish Shanghai as China's leading port.

The city of Shanghai actually lies within the Shanghai Municipality, which is divided into three areas: the old foreign section in the north, the original Chinese settlement in the south and the suburban areas that surround both sections. Some rural counties and offshore islands are also included in the municipality.

Climate

Shanghai has a moderate climate in the winter with temperatures averaging in the 40s Fahrenheit. Summers can be warm and humid with temperatures averaging in the high 80s and low 90s Fahrenheit. Rainfall is prevalent, especially in the spring. Winters can be gray and dreary with some snow. Shanghai is also affected by periodic typhoons, which are the Pacific Ocean's equivalent of hurricanes.

Government

The Shanghai Municipality is divided in 18 districts and one county. The municipality is ruled directly by the national government.

Demographics

Few Shanghai residents are descended from the original inhabitants of the old walled city. Nearly all registered residents of Shanghai are descended from 19th and 20th century immigrants from the adjacent provinces of Jiangsu and Zhejiang. This sense of local identity has been diluted in recent years as people from other Chinese regions have moved here. The population of greater Shanghai is estimated at a staggering 17 million.

Economy

Shanghai is China's leading port and one of its most important industrial areas. Major manufacturing industries include machinery, ships, cement, electrical equipment, textiles, and furniture. Shanghai also has a strong agricultural base; suburban farmers raise cereal

中国上海

概况

上海是中国最大的城市,最大的港口以及世界金融、贸易和工业的中心之一。20世纪后期,上海经历了一次大规模的住宅建设高峰期,上千座新建筑拔地而起。与此同时,新的地铁线路建成通车,新开发的地区包括浦东新区,即黄浦江东岸地区,目前这里已经成为一个国际金融中心。

一、地理

上海位于北纬31°14′,东经121°29′,地处中国东部的黄浦江沿岸。黄浦江与长江在此汇合,并流入上海以北仅14英里的中国南海。这一地理位置促使上海成为中国首要的港口城市。

事实上,上海市属于上海直辖市的一部分,而上海直辖市共分为三个地区:北面的旧上海外国领事区、南面的老上海居住区以及环绕这两个地区的城郊地区。一些农村县镇和近海岛屿也包括在大市范围内。

二、气候

上海冬季气候温和,平均气温在华氏40度上下。夏季炎热潮湿,平均气温在华氏87~93度。降水比较多,特别是在春季,冬天下雪的日子会比较阴霾烦心。此外,上海还会定期遭受台风的影响,台风就类似于太平洋上的飓风。

三、政府

上海直辖市划分为18个区和1个县,整个直辖市由中央政府直接管理。

四、人口

上海市的居民几乎都不是本地土生土长的后代,几乎所有的居民都是19~20世纪期间从周边的江苏或浙江省迁移过来的。近些年来,随着来自中国其他地区人口的涌入,上海当地居民的身份进一步被弱化。据估计,上海大市范围的人口有大约1 700万。

五、经济

上海是中国最主要的港口和最重要的工业中心之一,主要的加工制造业包括机械、船舶、水泥、电动设备、纺织和家具。此外,上海还拥有很强的农业基础,郊区的农民种植

grains, vegetables, pigs and fish. In recent years, the communications industry has gained in economic importance.

The History

The city of Shanghai began in 1553, which is rather late in comparison to other major Chinese cities. However, there is evidence that it was a trading center as early as 960. Because the city was not considered a major center until the 19th century, there are few ancient artifacts or historical buildings.

The city was a small trading center before 1842, when the British opened the area to international trade at the end of the Opium War. Other Western nations quickly followed Britain into Shanghai, yet foreign infiuence came under fire in the early 20th century by Shanghai citizens.

The Japanese captured Shanghai in 1937 and occupied the area until the end of World War II. The Chinese communist government enlarged Shanghai and expanded its industrial base.

The Sights and Sounds

Shanghai is a cosmopolitan city with two sides. The old foreign city, (called Pu Xi or West City) includes colonial buildings, while the Chinese City across the river (called Pu Dong or East City) includes modern skyscrapers. Both the old and new Shanghai are visible in almost every block. At night, the city seems to glow from the lights atop the newer buildings.

The Bund (Zhongshan Road) is in the old foreign side of the city; colonial buildings in every architectural style cover the main thoroughfare. At night, visitors can see the lights on the skyscrapers across the river in the Chinese City. A boat cruise down the river at night includes beautiful sights and scenery on both sides.

An old racecourse, the People's Square is now an open-air park in the middle of the city. Surrounded on all sides by buildings, the park is a wonderful green space in the middle of a busy metropolis. Trees, gardens and benches make this a good place to take a much-needed break from the action.

The Shanghai Museum is near to the People's Square. Reputed to be the best museum in all of China, this structure is four stories tall with thousands of artifacts in its collection. Each gallery is huge and full of explanatory placards in both Chinese and English. The museum is so large and the collection so extensive that visitors can spend several days trying to see everything.

Jade Buddha Temple is one of the most important Buddhist temples in China. The temple's exterior is not architecturally significant, but the large statue of the sitting Buddha inside the temple is well worth a visit. This statue is made of white jade and weighs more than a ton.

Nanjing Lu Street is Shanghai in a microcosm. Visitors can walk from the People's Square down this street to the Bund. All along the way, tourists and locals mingle in a mélange of shops, restaurants, snack bars and businesses. At night, the gleam of neon makes this street the Chinese version of Times Square.

The soaring Pearl Tower is a symbol of the new Shanghai to locals. The tower is a huge tourist attraction with a restaurant and museum. There can be long lines on the

稻谷、蔬菜、养猪、养鱼。近年来,上海在通讯领域也占据了重要的经济地位。

光影流金
上海市的发展开始于1553年,同其他中国城市相比,是属于起步比较晚的。然而,有证据表明早在960年时,上海就已经是一个贸易中心了。因为在19世纪之前,没有人把这座城市当成是发展中心,所以市内几乎没什么古代的手工艺品或历史建筑。

1842年之前,这座城市一直是一个小的贸易中心,鸦片战争末期,英国人迫使开放了这一地区进行国际贸易,于是,其他西方国家迅速跟随英国进驻上海,然而,外国势力的影响在20世纪早期遭到一些上海市民的猛烈抨击。

1937年,日本人攻克了上海,并且长期占领了这一地区,直到第二次世界大战结束。1949年后,中国共产党政府扩大了上海市的面积和工业基础。

声光景点
上海是一座国际化的大都会,城市由两部分组成,老的外国租界区(称为"浦西"或西城)有一些殖民地时期的建筑,而河对岸的中国城(称为"浦东"或东城)主要为现代化的摩天大楼。无论在哪一个街区,新旧上海都清晰地展现在你的面前。夜晚降临之后,一些较新的建筑上灯光闪烁,似乎整座城市都被点亮。

沿江街道"外滩"(中山路)位于上海古老的外国租界区,街道两旁殖民地时期的建筑以各种不同的风格矗立在那里。晚上,游客在此可以欣赏到对岸中国城摩天大楼上璀璨的灯光。浦江夜游可以带你领略两岸美丽的灯光景致。

一处古老的赛马场现在叫人民广场,是市中心一处露天公园,广场四周都是高楼大厦,在这座繁忙的大都市里,这里可谓一个不错的绿色空间,由绿树、花园、长椅组成的这一广场,为那些走累的人们提供了一个必需的休憩场所。

上海博物馆就位于人民广场附近,这座号称全中国最棒的博物馆有四层楼高,收藏了成千上万件手工艺品,里面的每个展馆都很大,并且配有丰富的中英文的解说牌。这座博物馆如此之大,馆藏如此之丰,游客要想把所有的展品都看一遍,可能需要几天的时间。

玉佛寺是中国最重要的佛教寺庙之一,虽然这座寺庙的外观并不起眼,但是庙内的巨大的坐姿佛像却值得一看,这座佛像由白玉雕刻,重达一吨多。

上海的南京路是一处繁华的小天地,游客可以沿着这条街步行从人民广场一直走到外滩,一路上在那些各式各样的商店、餐馆、小吃店和商务大楼里,可以看到本地人和外地客混杂在一起。夜幕降临之后,街道两旁的闪烁的霓虹灯将南京路变成了中国版的"时代广场"。

高耸入云的东方明珠塔,对于当地人来说,就是新上海的象征,这座塔上设有餐厅和博物馆,因而成为一处重要的旅游景点。周末时,会出现排队的长龙,所以建议你最好早

weekends, so go early. The views of the city are marvelous and especially beautiful at sunset and as the lights go on at night.

The Trivia

Fact: During the pre-World War II years, Shanghai became synonymous with exploitation and vice. The city featured opium dens, gambling halls and brothels. These areas were actually guarded by the Western nationals who occupied the city.

Fact: After the British opened the city to international trade, the city created special areas, or concessions, in order to segregate foreign nationals from the rest of the population.

Fact: China's Communist Party was founded in Shanghai in 1921.

Why Shanghai Is a 50 plus one City

The explosive growth and dynamism of this city attracts people from throughout China and the world. While very young compared to many Chinese cities, Shanghai has attracted world attention for its bustling streets and its modern ways—mixed, of course, with the old.

些出发。站在塔上欣赏整座城市,令人心旷神怡,尤其是在傍晚,夕阳西下,华灯初上之时。

奇闻轶事

之一:在第二次世界大战之前的一段时间,上海曾经是剥削和邪恶的代名词,城中众多的鸦片馆、赌博厅和妓院成为特殊的一景,而事实上,这些地方当时都受到那些占据上海的西方国家的保护。

之二:英国将这一地区变为国际贸易开放地后,上海开辟了特殊的区域或称租界区,以便将那些外国人与其他人群区分开来。

之三:1921年,中国共产党在上海成立。

为什么上海入选50 + 1个城市?

这座城市爆炸性的增长以及勃勃生机吸引着来自中国乃至世界各地的人群,尽管和中国其他城市相比,上海还很年轻,但是上海以其繁华的街道和现代的生活方式吸引了全球的目光 —— 当然,也不乏古老韵味的混合。

Forty-one

Singapore

The Basic Facts

Singapore is an independent city-state, a bustling center of finance, trade and manufacturing. During the late 20th century, Singapore grew into one of the most stable and populous nations in Asia.

Geography

Singapore lies at 1 degree 18 minutes north latitude and 103 degrees 52 minutes east longitude. It is located at the southernmost tip of the Malay Peninsula where the South China Sea and Indian Sea converge. Singapore consists of one large island, covering 221 square miles, and over 50 smaller islands covering another 18 square miles. The large island, also called Singapore, contains the capital and houses most residents.

Singapore is built around the harbor with warehouses and docks lining the port. The city is roughly divided between the commercial section and the Jurong area, an industrial park west of the city.

Climate

Singapore's temperature is consistent throughout the year with highs averaging about 80 degrees Fahrenheit. Thanks to cool sea breezes, the temperature rarely rises above 95 degrees Fahrenheit. The climate, however, is rainy; Singapore annually receives about 95 inches of rain. The rainiest months are during the monsoon season, from November to March. June to October is the driest period of the year.

Government

The city-state of Singapore is ruled by a democratic government. Members of the Unicameral Parliament are elected to 5-year terms. The prime minister and cabinet administer government functions.

Demographics

Singapore is one of the world's most densely populated areas. Chinese constitute three-quarters of the population, Malays constitute 15 percent and Indians make up the remainder. Singapore has no official religion. Various ethnic groups practice Buddhism, Islam, Christianity, Taoism and Hinduism, among others.

Economy

Prior to the 1960s, Singapore's economy was based on trade. Its economy has become more varied of late and now includes the financial and transportation industries. Singapore's annual per-capita income is one of the highest in Asia, and it has a low rate of unemployment. Singapore is a major manufacturing center, producing chemicals, electrical and electronic equipment, machinery, rubber, plastics, and other goods. Tourism is an

新加坡

概况

新加坡是一个独立的城市国家,也是一个繁忙的金融、贸易和生产中心。20世纪后期,新加坡发展成为亚洲最稳定、人口密度最大的国家之一。

一、地理

新加坡位于北纬1°18′,东经103°52′,地处南中国海与印度洋交汇处的马来半岛最南端。新加坡由一个221平方英里的大岛,以及另外50多个面积共计18平方英里的小岛组成。大岛,又称新加坡岛,是新加坡的首都,也是新加坡大多数人居住的地方。

新加坡沿港口修建了很多仓库和码头,城市被粗略地划分为商业区和裕廊区,即城西的工业园。

二、气候

新加坡的气温一年四季变化不大,平均气温始终徘徊在华氏80度左右,得益于凉爽的海风,气温很少高于华氏90度。然而,气候的另一特点是多雨,新加坡年均降水在95英尺左右,雨水最多的月份在11月~3月间的季风季节,6月~10月则属于全年最干燥的时期。

三、政府

新加坡这座城市国家由一个民主政府管理,一院制的议会成员经选举产生,任期5年,总理和内阁负责行使政府的行政功能。

四、人口

新加坡是世界上人口密度最大的地区之一,华人占总人口的三分之一,马来人占15%,其余为印度人。新加坡没有官方的宗教,各种民族团体信仰的有佛教、伊斯兰教、基督教、道教和印度教等。

五、经济

20世纪60年代之前,新加坡的经济以贸易为基础,之后,经济呈现出多元化,如今,还涵盖了金融业和交通业。新加坡人均年收入属于亚洲最高的之一,失业率较低。新加坡还是主要的加工制造中心,生产的产品包括化学品、电器及电子设备、机械产品、橡胶、塑料和其他产品等。旅游业是新加坡经济一个重要的组成部分,每年大约要接待800万

important part of Singapore's economy; some eight million tourists visit every year.

Cars overcrowd the city, so much so that drivers have to pay a fee to enter during peak traffic periods. Singapore's mass-transit system has helped alleviate some of the traffic congestion. Singapore is linked to nearby Malaysia via a bridge and causeway, but most visitors arrive through Changi International Airport, located on the eastern end of the large island.

The History

It is believed the Singapore islands were a small trading center when the Chinese arrived in the area in the 1300s. In 1390, a Sumatran prince named Parameswara took over the area. Ten years later the city became known as Shingapura and later Singapore.

The Portuguese occupied the city in 1511 and eventually destroyed most of it in 1613. Trade emerged in the early 1800s when Sir Thomas Stamford Raffles of the British East India Company arrived and established a trading colony to offset the Dutch influence in the region. The new port was a huge success, and shipping facilities were enlarged in the 1850s.

The opening of the Suez Canal in 1869 was a boon for Singapore, which exported Malaysian tin and rubber. Mass immigration led to lawlessness, however, until the early 20th century. During the Great Depression in the 1930s, Singapore deported many immigrants to their home countries.

Although Singapore was heavily forti.ed by the British, the Japanese invaded and conquered the area in World War II. After the war, the British regained control of Singapore for a short time before an independence movement emerged in the city. Singapore declared independence from Britain in 1963 and the government allied itself with nearby Malaysia. The relationship between the two countries was tenuous.

The Sights and Sounds

The north bank of the Singapore River was originally the seat of colonial government for the island. This area is now known as the Historical District, where the British and others built most of the government buildings. The Asian Civilizations Museum, located in the Empress Place Building, is said to be one of the best museums in Singapore. First opened in 2003, the museum houses an excellent collection of art, artifacts, jewelry and relics from the various cultures represented in Singapore. The Empress Place Building was originally constructed by the British to run the colonial government.

The Padang in downtown Singapore is a large open field where the British and other Europeans participated in sports and outdoor ceremonies. During World War II the Japanese used the field as a holding pen for British and other non-Asian residents. The area is surrounded with the symbols of colonialism and government, including City Hall, Parliament House, and the Cricket Club.

The Raffles Hotel, named after Sir Stamford Raffles, was built in 1887 to accommodate the upper classes that were making their fortunes in Singapore. The Raffles Hotel symbolizes Singapore's boom-and-bust history. In the 1920s it was the place to be; its famous dining room and ballroom were all the rage. But the Great Depression, World War II, and stiff competition from newer hotels nearly bankrupted the grand dame. In the 1980s the hotel was restored to its original beauty and gained prominence again in the city.

游客。

新加坡市内车满为患，以至于交通高峰期开车的司机必须缴费才行。新加坡的公共交通系统一定程度上缓解了交通拥堵现象。虽然新加坡与邻国马来西亚有一座大桥和公路相连接，但是大多数游客还是经由位于新加坡岛东端的樟宜国际机场抵达这里。

光影流金

人们相信，在14世纪华人来到该地区之前，新加坡岛只是一个小的贸易中心。1390年，一位名为拜里米苏拉的苏门答腊的王子取得了对该地区的控制权，十年之后，这座城市众所周知地成为"新加普拉"，再后来就变成了新加坡。

1511年，葡萄牙人占领了这座城市，并于1613年最终破坏了新加坡城的大部分地区。19世纪早期，英国东印度公司的托马斯·史丹福·莱佛士爵士抵达这里，并建立了一个贸易领地以削弱荷兰人在该地区的影响，贸易的出现使得这一新兴港口获得了巨大的成功。19世纪50年代造船设施进一步扩大。

1869年，苏伊士运河的开通使新加坡受益无穷，因为他们可以将马来西亚的锡和橡胶向外出口。然而，由于大批移民的涌入，违法活动一度变得猖獗，并且这一现象一直持续到20世纪早期。在20世纪30年代的大萧条时期，新加坡将许多移民驱逐出境，迫使他们重新回到自己的国家。

第二次世界大战期间，虽然新加坡得到英国的重重设防，但是日本军队还是入侵并占领了这一地区。战争结束之后，英国重新取得了对新加坡的控制权，然而好景不长，很快一场独立运动席卷全城。1963年，新加坡宣布脱离英国独立，此后，新加坡政府与邻近的马来西亚结成联盟。不过，两国之间的关系始终若即若离。

声光景点

新加坡的北岸最早是殖民地政府所在地，由于英国和其他外国人都将政府大厦建在这一地区，因此，如今这里被称为历史街区。据说位于皇后坊内的亚洲文明博物馆，是全新加坡最好的博物馆之一。这家博物馆于2003年开馆，里面收藏了大量精美的代表新加坡各种文化的美术品、手工艺品、珠宝、古董等。皇后坊最初是英国殖民者为了方便殖民政府的管理而建造的。

位于新加坡市中心的巴东是一大型露天场所，从前英国人及其他欧洲人会在这里参加体育活动或室外庆典仪式。第二次世界大战期间，日本人曾将这里作为英国人和其他非亚洲居民的临时隐蔽所。环绕这一地区的建筑大都是殖民主义和政府的象征，例如，市政厅、议会大厦和板球俱乐部。

以史丹福·莱佛士爵士的名字命名的莱佛士酒店建于1887年，专门为那些在新加坡发财致富的上流社会人士提供服务。莱佛士酒店印证了新加坡大繁荣紧接着是大萧条的历史。20世纪20年代是其大繁荣的阶段，酒店内著名的餐厅和舞厅曾风靡一时。然而，大萧条、二战以及来自新建酒店激烈的竞争，一度将这座辉煌宫殿挤入破产的边缘。20世纪80年代，酒店恢复了最初的美丽，并再次确立了其在城市中显赫的位置。酒店内的长酒吧

Its Long Bar is still the place for the movers and shakers of Singapore society.

The Chinatown Heritage Centre keeps alive the history of the ethnic Chinese in Singapore. Three shops in this enclave have been restored to give visitors a glimpse into life in old Chinatown. The displays include antiques from the time of immigration and re-creations of shops, houses and public buildings.

The religious traditions of Singapore are a fascinating mix of East and West. The Armenian Church dates back to 1836 and services are still held there—but not by its own members. St. Andrews Cathedral, rebuilt in the 1850s, is the oldest Anglican church in Singapore, although its old English Gothic style may look somewhat out of place in this Asian setting. Other notable religious structures include Nagore Durgha Shrine, dedicated to a Muslim holy man who visited Singapore spreading the message of Islam; Sri Mariamman Hindu Temple, the oldest Hindu temple in Singapore; Thian Hock Keng Temple (the temple of heavenly bliss), the city's oldest Chinese temple; Wak Hai Cheng Bio Temple, also Chinese; and Sri Veerama Kaliamman Temple, a Hindu temple dedicated to the goddess Kali.

Singapore has delightful parks and reserves, among them Tiger Balm Gardens, Jurong Bird Park (with a collection of some 8,000 birds) and the Singapore Botanic Gardens. Most visitors take a trip to Sentosa Island either by monorail or by ferry from the World Trade Center on the main island. Sentosa is an oft-visited island resort with lovely beaches and luxury hotels. Its attractions include the 360-foot-tall Carlsberg Sky Tower, Underwater World, the Musical Fountain, and Fort Siloso.

Night life in Singapore centers on two areas called Boat Quay, which once was a notorious opium den, and Clarke Quay, which was a former industrial site. Both have the nightlife, cafes, restaurants, bars and clubs that visitors enjoy late into the night.

The Trivia

Fact: The original name of Shingapura is a puzzle. The name means lion city, but lions are not native to Singapore. The actual name might have been Singapura which is connected to Buddhism (Buddha was often symbolized by a lion in ancient Indian art).

Fact: As part of his plan for modern Singapore, Sir Thomas Raffles divided the city into distinct enclaves known as kampongs; immigrants were segregated according to their ethnic groups. In many respects, these divisions exist to this day.

Fact: In the early 19th century Singapore was plagued by pirates who plundered exports from departing ships. This problem continued into the 1850s and beyond, despite the efforts of local merchants and British colonialists to stem the raids.

Fact: Between 1825 and 1873, India used Singapore as a penal colony. Many of the Indians who later settled in the area were convicts sent to Singapore to work as laborers.

Fact: Many locals speak Singlish, a hodge-podge regional dialect with English, Chinese, and Malay roots.

Why Singapore Is a 50 plus one City

Visitors to this remarkable city will understand its signi.cance in the pantheon of the world's greatest cities. Modern, prosperous and multicultural, Singapore stands among the economic giants of Asia. The city is safe and clean, and visitors are invited to explore and enjoy the sights and sounds without any concern.

至今仍是新加坡社会有权势的人聚会之所。

　　牛车水原貌馆将新加坡华人生活的历史活生生地展现出来，馆内的3家商店是在原有基础上的复原，为的是向游客提供早期华人生活的一瞥。展品包括移民时期的古董以及店铺、房屋、公共建筑的再现。

　　新加坡的宗教传统是东西方神奇的混合，可以追溯到1836年的亚美尼亚人的教堂至今仍在使用 —— 当然参加的人已经不一样了。圣安德鲁大教堂是19世纪80年代重建的，也是新加坡最古老的英国圣公会教堂，不过，其古老的英国哥特式风格与所处的亚洲背景多少显得有些不协调。其他著名的宗教建筑还包括为纪念来新加坡传播伊斯兰教福音的一位穆斯林圣人而修建的纳宫清真寺，新加坡最古老的印度教寺庙马里安曼兴都庙，新加坡最古老的华人寺庙圣后宫庙(天福寺)，同样为华人寺庙的粤海清庙，以及为印度教卡莉女神而修建的维拉玛卡里雅曼兴都庙。

　　新加坡拥有令人开心的公园和自然保护区，其中包括虎豹别墅、裕廊飞禽公园(有大约8 000只鸟类)以及新加坡植物园。大多数游客会从位于主岛的世界贸易中心乘坐渡轮或单轨列车到圣陶沙岛游玩。圣陶沙是一个游人众多的度假小岛，拥有迷人的海滩以及豪华的酒店，岛上的景点包括360英尺高的皇帽摩天塔、海底世界、音乐喷泉和西乐索炮台。

　　新加坡的夜生活以两个地区为中心：驳船码头过去曾是一家臭名昭著的鸦片馆，克拉码头是原来一处工业遗址。两个地方都有咖啡馆、餐馆、酒吧、俱乐部等夜生活场所，游客可以尽情享受到深夜时分。

奇闻轶事

　　之一：新加坡最初的名字"新加普拉"至今都是个谜，虽然这个名字的意思是"狮城"，但是狮子并不是新加坡的特产，事实上这个名称或许是与佛教有关的"辛加普拉"(在古代印度艺术当中，佛教常用狮子作为象征)。

　　之二：作为发展现代新加坡计划的一部分，托马斯·莱佛士爵士将城市划分为明显的区域，称为"卡彭"(小村庄)，移民们根据其所属的民族被区分开来，在很多方面，这些区分至今依然存在。

　　之三：19世纪初，新加坡曾遭到海盗的劫掠，他们主要从离港船只上抢劫出口商品，尽管当地商人和英国殖民者花了很大力气来阻止海盗的袭击，但是这一问题还是持续到19世纪50年代之后

　　之四：1825年~1873年，印度曾将新加坡作为罪犯流放地，许多后来在新加坡定居下来的印度人，都是被送到新加坡接受劳动改造的囚犯。

　　之五：许多当地人讲新加坡英语，这是一种混合了英语、汉语和马来语词根的当地方言。

为什么新加坡入选50 + 1个城市？

　　来到新加坡，游客就会明白为什么这座杰出的城市能够跻身世界最伟大的城市之列，现代、繁荣、多元文化、亚洲经济巨人，这就是新加坡，这座安全、干净的城市，让所有的游客可以毫无顾虑地探寻和欣赏它的风光景致。

Forty-two

St. Petersburg, Russia

The Basic Facts

St. Petersburg is the second largest city in Russia. It is a major port and the former capital of the country. The city is one of the largest industrial and cultural centers in the world. The city takes its name from the Russian czar Peter the Great who founded the city in 1703.

Geography

St. Petersburg lies at 59 degrees 57 minutes north latitude and 30 degrees 20 minutes east longitude. The city is located in northwestern Russia at the eastern end of the Gulf of Finland (an arm of the Baltic Sea). Peter the Great wanted to create the city in the style of Western European cities, and so its design mimics that of cities such as London, Paris and Vienna.

St. Petersburg lies on a marshy lowland where the Neva River flows into the Gulf of Finland. The city center is located on the southern bank of the Neva.

Climate

St. Petersburg's climate is generally damp and rainy, thanks to its location near the Baltic Sea. Winters are cold with temperatures averaging in the 20s Fahrenheit. Summers are cool with average temperatures in the upper 60s Fahrenheit. In winter daylight is minimal, because the city is so far north of the equator. Conversely, during the summer months twilight lasts all night, giving rise to the white nights for which the city is famous.

Government

St. Petersburg is divided into 18 city districts; the city itself is the capital of a provincial area known as the Leningrad Oblast. The governor controls city government, territorial and industrial branches, and administrative boards.

Demographics

City residents are primarily of Russian heritage, from a variety of ethnic groups. In an attempt to curb the recent rapid population increase, the government has instituted a strict policy: potential residents must either have a job and residence or marry an existing resident. Despite this restriction, a large number of undocumented residents have contributed to the city's congestion. The population is estimated to be 4.5 million.

Economy

Shipbuilding has been an important industry since the city was founded. During the Industrial Revolution the city emerged as an important manufacturer of machine tools; this manufacturing segment comprises nearly 40 percent of the city's industry. Other industries

俄罗斯圣彼得堡

概况

圣彼得堡是俄罗斯第二大城市,是一个主要的港口和俄罗斯原来的首都。同时也是世界上最大的工业和文化中心之一。这座城市的名字是由俄罗斯沙皇彼得大帝所取,正是他于1703年建立了这座城市。

一、地理

圣彼得堡位于北纬59°57′,东经30°20′,地处芬兰湾(波罗的海的一个海湾)东端俄罗斯西北部地区,彼得大帝想要根据西欧城市的风格创建这座城市,因此,在设计上效仿了伦敦、巴黎和维也纳之类的城市。

二、气候

由于受到附近波罗的海的影响,圣彼得堡的气候通常潮湿而多雨。冬季寒冷,气温平均在华氏20度左右,夏季凉爽,平均气温在华氏67~69度。因为城市距离赤道以北很远的地方,因此冬季的日照强度最低,反之,夏季月份里曙暮光会持续整个晚上,形成圣彼得堡著名的白夜现象。

三、政府

圣彼得堡市被划分为18个区,同时城市本身还是列宁格勒州的首府。州长负责市政府、地方和工业部门以及行政工会等。

四、人口

圣彼得堡的居民主要为俄罗斯血统,但分属不同的民族。作为遏制近年来人口快速增长的一种措施,政府实行了一项严格的政策:那些想成为正式居民的人必须拥有一份工作和住房,或者与现有城市居民结婚才行。尽管有这样的限制,但是,大量非在册的居民仍然造成了城市交通拥堵现象。据估计,圣彼得堡的人口有450万左右。

五、经济

自从圣彼得堡建立以来,造船业一直是这座城市重要的工业之一。在工业革命期间,该市成为机械工具的重要加工制造点,此类加工部门在城市工业中占了近40%。其他工业还包括化学品、电动设备、纺织、核设施和木材等。圣彼得堡拥有一个优良的港口、完善

include chemicals, electrical equipment, textiles, nuclear equipment and timber. St. Petersburg has an excellent port and railroad network, and so is a major national trade and distribution center.

The History

Peter the Great intended to make St. Petersburg the first Western city in Russia, and he hired Western architects to design its layout. The city soon became the intellectual and social center of Russia, and it grew rapidly during the 18th century. In the late 19th and early 20th centuries, several popular movements against czarist rule were centered here.

The Russian Revolution toppled the czarist government of Nicholas II and enabled the Bolsheviks to seize power; their leader V.I. Lenin became head of their new government. The capital was moved back to Moscow in 1918 as Lenin fled from potential foreign invasion. Lenin died in 1924, and St. Petersburg—which had been known as Petrograd since 1914—was renamed Leningrad in his honor.

Leningrad was the site of one of the most famous battles of World War II, when the German army laid siege to the city for almost 3 years. Even though more than a million Soviets perished—mostly from starvation—the city did not fall to the Germans. After World War II, many of the city's historic structures were rebuilt, and the government began a massive campaign to build new housing. The city's official name reverted to the original St. Petersburg in 1991.

Many of St. Petersburg's classic buildings fell into disrepair through neglect. Restoration is now underway, due largely to the fact that Russia's leader, Vladimir Putin, was born and raised in the city. In 2003, St. Petersburg celebrated its 300th anniversary.

The Sights and Sounds

Palace Square and the adjoining Winter Palace certainly are St. Petersburg's most famous landmarks of the city. The Italian architect Bartolomeo Rastrelli designed the sprawling structure—all 1,057 rooms—as well as many of the adjoining buildings. The palace is now part of the State Hermitage Museum, with a collection so vast that visitors are often overwhelmed by the sheer number of exhibits. Of particular import are the Egyptian collection and the works of the Italianate masters and the Impressionists. The 155-foot-tall Alexander Column, built as a tribute to Emperor Alexander I, features prominently in the center of Palace Square.

The Peter and Paul Fortress, located on an island in the Neva River, was the original military stronghold of the city. Until 1917, its prison housed political prisoners including Dostoyevsky, Trotsky, and Peter the Great's own son, Alexei. Peter and Paul Cathedral, with its needle-thin spire and rich baroque style, dominates the center of the fortress. The church is the burial site of nearly all Russia's former emperors and empresses.

In the center of St. Isaac's Square is its namesake, the magnificent St. Isaac's Cathedral. This church, built in the 19th century, is in the Neoclassical style and has a striking golden dome. Its ornate interior includes granite and marble fixtures, paintings, and mosaics. Until 1917 this was the main cathedral of the Russian Orthodox Church. The monument to Nicholas I on the square is unique among equestrian statutes, in that it has only two support points: the legs of his horse.

Decembrists Square is named for the revolutionaries of 1825 who rebelled against

的铁路网,因而成为俄罗斯主要的贸易和流通的中心之一。

光影流金

　　彼得大帝试图把圣彼得堡建成俄罗斯第一座西方城市,因此,他聘请了西方建筑师进行城市的整体设计,很快,这座城市就成了俄罗斯社会和知识分子的中心。18世纪时,城市发展尤为迅速。19世纪后期和20世纪初,数次反对沙皇统治的民众运动就以这座城市为中心。

　　俄罗斯革命推翻了沙皇尼古拉斯二世的统治,布尔什维克党取得了政权,该党领袖列宁成为新政府的领导。1918年,为躲避可能的外国入侵,列宁将首都迁回莫斯科。1924年列宁去世,为了纪念他,圣彼得堡——从1924年起它被称为彼得格勒——被重新命名为列宁格勒。

　　第二次世界大战期间,列宁格勒曾作为几次最著名战役的战场,当时德国军队围攻这座城市长达3年,即便如此,有超过100万苏联士兵失去了生命 —— 大多数是死于饥饿 —— 但是这座城市始终没有落入德国人之手。二战之后,城市里的许多历史性建筑被重新翻修,政府也开始了大规模兴建新型住宅的运动。1991年,这座城市也恢复了其最初的官方名称圣彼得堡。

　　圣彼得堡许多经典建筑由于无人维护而日益破败,如今,重建工作正在进行,这在很大程度上归功于俄罗斯领袖弗拉吉米尔·普京,因为这里是生他养他的地方。2003年,圣彼得堡举行了建市300周年的庆典活动。

声光景点

　　冬宫广场和毗邻的冬宫无疑是圣彼得堡最著名的地标,意大利建筑师巴托洛梅奥·拉斯特雷利设计了这座蔓生的建筑 —— 总共有1057间房子 —— 还有许多毗邻的建筑。现在这座宫殿是国家爱尔米塔什博物馆的一部分,该博物馆馆藏之丰富,仅其展品数量就足以令游客叹为观止,其中来自国外的特殊展品有埃及、意大利艺术大师以及印象派画家的作品。高155英尺的亚历山大柱矗立在冬宫广场中心的显著位置,它是作为献给亚历山大大帝的礼物而建造的。

　　位于涅瓦河一个小岛上的彼得和保罗要塞最初是圣彼得堡的一个军事要塞,1917年之前,这里的监狱曾关押过的政治犯包括陀思妥耶夫斯基、托洛茨基和彼得大帝的亲儿子阿列克谢。以尖塔和巴洛克风格著称的彼得和保罗大教堂位于要塞中心的显著位置,这座教堂是俄罗斯以前几乎所有的皇帝和皇后埋葬的地方。

　　在圣伊萨克广场中央是与之同名的圣伊萨克大教堂,这座修建于19世纪的教堂属于新古典主义风格,拥有一个引人注目的金色穹顶,教堂内部华丽的装饰包括花岗岩和大理石的固定装置、绘画及马赛克等。直到1917年以前,这座教堂一直是俄罗斯东正教主要的大教堂,广场上的尼古拉一世纪念碑在众多骑士塑像中显得非常独特,因为整座塑像只有两个支撑点:马的两条腿。

　　十二月党人广场,是以1825年那些反对俄罗斯独裁政府的革命党人命名的广场,广

Russia's autocratic government, The Bronze Horseman, an imposing monument to Peter the Great, is a short distance away and faces the Neva River; its pedestal resembles a wave and reflects Russia's then merging sea power.

Arts Square is named for the series of museums and concert halls in the area, including: the Russian Museum, the world's largest museum of Russian art, with over 400,000 works; the Ethnography Museum, which represents all the ethnic cultures of the former Soviet Union; the St. Petersburg Philharmonic; and the Maly Theatre for opera and ballet. A statue of the Russian poet Pushkin stands in the middle of Arts Square.

The Church of Our Savior on the Spilled Blood is built on the site at which Czar Alexander II was mortally wounded by a dissenter—this in spite of his openness to Russian reform. The church was intentionally modeled after St. Basil's Cathedral in Moscow's Red Square.

The palace and park of Petergof (Peter's Court) is a jewel of St. Petersburg. It is nicknamed the Russian Versailles for its series of parks, palaces, and fountains. The palace, which originally served as an exquisite summer residence for the Russian czars, is now a museum surrounded by masterful landscaping.

The Trivia

Fact: This beautiful and grand city was built on a mosquito-ridden swamp using thousands of Swedish prisoners of war as slave labor.

Fact: St. Petersburg was designed in the 19th century by a commission including the noted Italian architect Carlo Rossi. Empress Elizabeth carefully reviewed and refined the commission's plans, and Catherine the Great extended the designs into the Neoclassical genre.

Fact: St. Petersburg has played a pivotal role in Russian literature and is the setting for works by Alexander Pushkin, Fyodor Dostoyevsky and Andre Bely.

Fact: St Petersburg's nearly 500 bridges gives the city's its nickname, the Venice of the North.

Fact: The entire city of St. Petersburg has 140 museums that display more than three million art objects.

Why St. Petersburg Is a 50 plus one City

Imagine the sheer tenacity to build a beautiful city in a swamp and build it with the finest minds in art and architecture of the day—and have it survive for 300 years through every sort of political and social upheaval. Not even wars and massive destruction could destroy St. Petersburg. Not only does the city survive, but it thrives, with it culture and art being restored after years of neglect. Visitors are awed by the city, its museums and its culture.

场不远处的铜制骑士是一座气势不凡的彼得大帝的纪念塑像,塑像面朝涅瓦河,基座形似波浪,反映了当时俄罗斯正在逐步联合的海上力量。

艺术广场因其众多的系列博物馆和音乐厅而得名,其中包括世界上最大的关于俄罗斯艺术的俄罗斯博物馆,内有超过40万件艺术品,代表前苏联所有民族文化的人种博物馆,圣彼得堡爱乐乐团,专门上演歌剧和芭蕾舞的魅力剧院,俄罗斯诗人普希金的一座塑像矗立于艺术广场中央。

我们流血的救世主教堂,建在沙皇亚历山大二世被一名持不同政见者致命袭击的地方 —— 尽管他对俄罗斯改革保持着开放的态度。这座教堂刻意地模仿了莫斯科红场上的圣巴西勒大教堂。

彼得高夫(彼得宫)的宫殿和花园是圣彼得堡的珍宝,宫内一系列的花园、宫殿和喷泉为它赢得了俄罗斯的凡尔赛宫的美称。这座当初被俄罗斯的沙皇们当做夏季住所的宫殿,如今是一座风景秀丽的博物馆。

奇闻轶事

之一:圣彼得堡这座美丽而宏伟的城市是建在一个曾经蚊虫肆虐的沼泽之上的,并且动用了成千上万的瑞典战犯来做苦役。

之二:圣彼得堡市的设计,是19世纪由一个包括著名意大利建筑师卡洛·罗西在内的委员会共同完成的,女皇伊丽莎白仔细审核并完善了该委员会的方案,皇后叶卡捷琳娜进一步将设计风格确定为新古典主义。

之三:圣彼得堡在俄罗斯文学领域占据着轴心的位置,亚历山大·普希金,费尔多·陀思妥耶夫斯基和安德·贝利等人的创作都是以这里为背景的。

之四:圣彼得堡有近500座大小桥梁,因此有"北方威尼斯"之称。

之五:圣彼得堡全城有140家博物馆,展出的艺术品多达300万件。

为什么圣彼得堡入选50 + 1个城市?

设想一下,在一处沼泽之上建立起一座美丽的城市,并且以当时最完美的艺术和建筑思维来建造它 —— 此外,历经300年的岁月沧桑和社会政治动荡,甚至战争的炮火和大规模的破坏依然无法摧毁这座城市,这就是圣彼得堡,仅这些就足以令人惊叹了。如今,圣彼得堡不仅魅力不减,而且随着那些以往被遗忘的文化及艺术作品的修复,这座城市愈加兴旺繁荣,游客惊叹的目光不仅因为城市本身,还因为它的博物馆、它的文化。

Stockholm, Sweden

The Basic Facts

Stockholm is the capital of Sweden and is the country's largest city. Gentrification efforts in the 20th century replaced entire sections of the city with modern architecture; Stockholm continues to renew itself today.

Geography

Stockholm lies at 59 degrees 23 minutes north latitude and 18 degrees east longitude. Stockholm is located on the east coast of Sweden, between Lake Mälaren and the Baltic Sea, on the mainland and 14 islands. The city is connected by 53 bridges. Thousands of other islands are located near Stockholm and are a recreational haven for city residents.

Climate

Stockholm's weather is normally cool and temperate, and precipitation is moderate throughout the year. The summers are mild and usually sunny, with average temperatures in the upper 60s and lower 70s Fahrenheit. Winters are dark, cold and snowy, with average temperatures in the lower 30s Fahrenheit.

Government

The city and its environs comprise the Stockholm Municipality, an administrative region that is further subdivided into 18 district councils or boroughs. Each borough is responsible for its own elementary education, social services, and leisure and cultural services. Stockholm County's responsibilities include healthcare, public transportation, and various cultural institutions.

Demographics

Stockholm's population, like most of Sweden, consists mainly of Scandinavians of Germanic descent. In recent decades immigration has led to a sharp rise in the city's population and ethnic diversity. Many immigrants, most of whom are from the neighboring countries of Finland, Norway, and Denmark, come to the city as guest workers. Some recent immigrants have fled the conflicts in the former Yugoslavia. The population of the city itself is roughly 1.2 million.

Economy

Stockholm is the center of Sweden's economy and government. Most city residents are employed in the service industry and more than 30 percent are employed in local or national government. Insurance, commerce and banking are important to the city's economy, as is manufacturing, which includes publishing, chemicals, machinery, and metal products.

瑞典斯德哥尔摩

概况

斯德哥尔摩是瑞典的首都和最大的城市。20世纪的拆移改造将城市所有地区都变成了现代化的高楼大厦,如今,这种更新依旧进行着。

一、地理

斯德哥尔摩位于北纬59°23′,东经18°,地处瑞典东部海岸,梅拉伦湖和波罗的海之间。市内有53座大小桥梁,斯德哥尔摩附近还有数千座大小岛屿,对于城市居民来说,这些地方无疑是休闲娱乐的好去处。

二、气候

斯德哥尔摩的天气凉爽宜人,全年降水比较平均。夏季温和,通常阳光明媚,平均气温在华氏67~73度,冬季天气阴沉、寒冷、多雪,平均气温在华氏31~33度。

三、政府

斯德哥尔摩市和附近郊区构成斯德哥尔摩行政区,该行政区进一步划分为18个地区或区,各区负责自己的基础教育、社会服务以及休闲、文化服务等。斯德哥尔摩行政区的职责在于医疗、公共交通以及各类文化机构。

四、人口

和大多数瑞典城市一样,斯德哥尔摩的人口主要为日耳曼后裔中的斯堪的纳维亚族人,最近数十年间,由于移民的大量涌入,城市人口急剧增长,民族多样化的趋势也开始呈现。许多移民,尤其是那些来自邻国芬兰、挪威和丹麦的人,都是作为临时工人来到这座城市的,近些年,还有一些移民是为了躲避前南斯拉夫的政治冲突而来到这里的。斯德哥尔摩的城市人口大约有120万。

五、经济

斯德哥尔摩是瑞典经济和政府的中心,大多数城市居民从事服务行业,还有超过30%的人在国家或地方政府部门就职。保险业、商业和银行业在城市经济中占着非常重要的地位,加工制造业的主要产品有出版物、化学品、机械和金属制品。

The History

The name Stockholm first appears in the Chronicle of Eric, thought to be written between 1322 and 1332. According to the chronicle, the city was founded by Birger Jarl, who built a castle in the area now known as Gamla stan. Stockholm became a major trading center because goods being transported between the lake and the sea had to be transported by land through the city. The iron trade was particularly important to the city of Stockholm and the surrounding area. During Stockholm's early years, the city was vastly overcrowded and suffered from frequent destructive fires.

In 1523, Gustav Vasa became the first king of Sweden, and led a rebellion against Denmark, which at the time controlled most of the country. Sweden's independence had a major impact on Stockholm, and the city moved further toward economic and political importance.

Stockholm became the capital of the Swedish empire in 1634. Trading regulations gave the city a monopoly on trade with foreign merchants. Also during this period, prosperous city residents built palaces and large castles, and immigration to the city increased dramatically.

By the beginning of the 18th century, Sweden's and Stockholm's influence had begun to wane. The Black Death struck the city in 1713, and several areas of the city were destroyed in 1721. Stockholm revived, however, and in the 19th century acquired a reputation as a European cultural center—a reputation that continues to this day. New hospitals, post offices, and transportation systems helped to modernize the city, and its economy thrived due to increased trade and commerce.

The Sights and Sounds

Stockholm's great sights are located in a relatively compact area, mainly in Gamla stan. This is the old city, also known as the town between the bridges. This part of the city is on an island south of the city center and is known for its streets and squares that date to medieval times. The earliest inhabitants of this area were German, and the house designs and architecture reflect their cultural influences. The large square in the middle of the district, known as Stortorget, was the site of the Stockholm Massacre in 1520, when the Swedish nobles and clergy were slaughtered by Danish forces under King Christian II. This event prompted Sweden's move toward eventual independence.

The Royal Palace is the official residence of the Swedish monarchy, although the royal family resides at Drottningholm Palace outside Stockholm. In the 13th century Birger Jarl built a fortress on this site to defend against foreign naval invasion. The fort was converted to a palace in the late 16th century, and rebuilt a century later in the Baroque style. Tourists and locals enjoy the ceremonial changing of the guard outside the palace, which takes place each day at noon.

The Stockholm City Hall, completed in 1923, is an unusual and imposing building. The famous Blue Hall (which is not blue at all) is the site of the annual Nobel Prize banquet. The building's 348-foot tower dominates the area.

Stockholm has many world-class museums. The Museum of Modern Art, which opened in 1998, features some of the finest works of both regional and international artists. The National Museum's collection focuses on the Old Masters, while the exhibits at the Nordic Museum display folk art, costumes, and artifacts from Sweden's 500-year

光影流金

斯德哥尔摩的名字最早出现在埃里克编年史中，这部编年史据说完成于1322年~1332年。根据这部编年史中的记载，这座城市是由比耶·亚尔建立的，是他在现今被称为盖姆拉斯坦(老城)的地方修建了一座城堡。因为那时来往于梅拉伦湖和波罗的海之间的商品，都必须经过该地区进行路上交通，所以，斯德哥尔摩成为一个主要的贸易中心，对于斯德哥尔摩市和周边地区来说，铁制品的交易尤其重要，在斯德哥尔摩发展的早期阶段，由于人口过于拥挤，城市时常发生严重的火灾。

1523年，古斯塔夫·瓦萨成为瑞典首位国王，他率领军队反抗丹麦统治，夺取了全国大部分地区的控制权。瑞典的独立对于斯德哥尔摩市产生了深刻的影响，城市的政治和经济地位被进一步提升。

1634年，斯德哥尔摩成为瑞典王国的首都，贸易法规使得这座城市在与外国商人进行贸易时处于垄断地位。此外，在这一时期，富裕的城市居民开始修建宫殿和大型城堡，移民人数急剧增长。

到了18世纪初，瑞典以及斯德哥尔摩的影响开始减退。1713年，黑死病袭击了全城，1721年，城市的数个区域遭到破坏，然而，斯德哥尔摩并没有消失，它重新站立了起来，到了19世纪，该市进一步确立了其作为欧洲文化中心之一的地位——这一地位延续至今。新建的医院、邮局和交通系统使得城市更加现代化，随着贸易和商业的增长，城市经济日益繁荣。

声光景点

斯德哥尔摩最著名的景点位于相对集中的区域，主要就在盖姆拉斯坦。这里是老城区，也被称为桥梁之间的市镇。该地区位于市中心以南的一座岛上，以中世纪时期的街道和广场而著称。这一区域最早的居民是德国人，因此，房屋的式样和建筑反映出德国文化的影响。位于这一地区中心的大广场被称为斯托托盖特，是1520年斯德哥尔摩大屠杀的旧址，当年，许多瑞典贵族和牧师遭到丹麦国王克里斯蒂安二世军队的屠杀，这一事件也推动了瑞典最终的独立运动。

皇宫是瑞典王室的官方住址，尽管王室成员住在斯德哥尔摩城外的德洛特宁哥尔姆宫。13世纪时，比耶·亚尔在这个地方修建了一个要塞以抵御外国海军的入侵，16世纪后期这座要塞被改造成宫殿，一个世纪之后又以巴洛克风格重建。无论是游客还是当地人都喜欢在每天正午时分，观看王宫外警卫正式的换岗仪式。

斯德哥尔摩市政厅建成于1923年，这是一座奇特而宏伟的建筑，著名的蓝厅(其实根本不是蓝色)是每年诺贝尔颁奖典礼的举办地，这座建筑高达348英尺的塔楼在整个区域非常显眼。

斯德哥尔摩有许多世界级的博物馆，现代艺术博物馆1998年开馆，里面有一些本地和全球艺术家最精美的作品。国家博物馆的藏品以传统大师的作品为主，而斯堪的纳维亚博物馆展出的是瑞典500年历史中积累下来的民间工艺品、服饰和手工艺品等。斯堪森是一处露天博物馆，其中包括重建的传统建筑、一个动物园、一家水族馆以及一个游乐

history. The Skansen is an open-air museum that includes traditional buildings that have been rebuilt, as well as a zoo, an aquarium, and an amusement park. The Vasa Museum displays the only surviving 17th century ship, the Vasa; this is the most popular and most-visited museum in all of Scandinavia. The collection of 19th century carriages at the Royal Stables in Stockholm is the finest collection in the world; among the most famous is the Seven-Glass Coach. Visitors must take guided tours to see the museum's treasures.

For the best view of Stockholm, visitors flock to the Kaknastornet, a television tower owned by the National Swedish Broadcasting Company, Teracom. The 508-foot-tall tower has both indoor and outdoor observation decks that allow for impressive views of the city.

The Trivia

*Fact:*The fires that plagued Stockholm during the 14th century were a benefit to the city. Newer, safer buildings retained the medieval charm of the old structures.

*Fact:*Stockholm features nearly 70 performing arts venues, 60 museums, and various art galleries. It is the home of Sweden's Royal Ballet and Stockholm University.

*Fact:*Residential suburbs were built in the 1950s and 1960s on land that was purchased in the early 20th century for future redevelopment; this is but one example of Stockholm's reputation for far-sighted city planning.

*Fact:*There are more restaurants per person in Stockholm than in any other European capital. The traditional lunch buffet is the big meal of the day and is an enjoyable occasion.

Why Stockholm Is a 50 plus one City

Stockholm is one of the cultural capitals of Europe, as well as an important trade and commercial center. The city's blend of culture, architecture, natural beauty, and charm makes it a popular destination for international tourists. If nothing else, visitors enjoy the city based on its sheer physical beauty, its cleanliness, and its sense of order.

场。瓦萨博物馆内有一艘17世纪唯一保存下来的名为"瓦萨"的船只,在所有斯堪的纳维亚国家中,这家博物馆是最受游客欢迎、参观人数最多的博物馆。斯德哥尔摩的皇家赛马训练场收藏的19世纪的马车在世界上首屈一指,其中最著名的是七层玻璃大马车,要欣赏馆内的宝贝,游客必须有专门的导游介绍才行。

为了从最佳角度欣赏斯德哥尔摩全景,成群的游客会聚集到电视塔上,这是属于瑞典国家广播公司和网络运营商Teracom所有的电视塔,这座高508英尺的电视塔既有室内也有室外的观景台,可供游客一览城市美景。

奇闻轶事
之一:14世纪时肆虐于斯德哥尔摩的火灾对于这座城市来说也有好处,因为那些更新、更安全的建筑延续了中世纪古老建筑的风韵。

之二:斯德哥尔摩有近70座艺术表演会场、60座博物馆和各种各样的美术馆。瑞典皇家芭蕾舞团和斯德哥尔摩大学都位于这里。

之三:斯德哥尔摩以城市发展的远瞻性而著称。20世纪早期,市政府购买了一些土地用于未来的再发展,20世纪50~60年代,那些郊区住宅就是在这些土地上建造的,而这仅仅是其中的一个例子。

之四:在欧洲所有的首府城市当中,斯德哥尔摩是人均餐馆最多的城市,传统的自助午餐是一天中的大餐,也是一次愉快的聚会。

为什么斯德哥尔摩入选50 + 1个城市?
斯德哥尔摩是欧洲文化首府之一,同时也是贸易和商业的中心。城市中文化、建筑、自然美景以及魅力的融合使得它成为深受国际游客欢迎的目的地。如果不为别的,仅仅这座城市的自然景观、洁净程度以及有条不紊就足以令人感到无比的享受了。

Forty-four

Sydney, Australia

The Basic Facts

Sydney is the oldest and largest city in Australia and is also the capital of New South Wales. It is an important industrial city and has a major international port.

Geography

Sydney lies at 33 degrees 55 minutes south latitude and 151 degrees 17 minutes east longitude. Sydney lies on a large natural harbor known as Port Jackson, which is commonly called Sydney Harbour. Sydney and its suburbs cover nearly 500 square miles in southeast Australia. Downtown Sydney occupies the south side of Sydney Harbour and the oldest section of the city lies near the waterfront. Sydney has suburbs to the north and south. Ku-Ring-Gal Chase National Park is north of the city and is famous for its Aboriginal rock paintings and carvings.

Climate

Sydney's climate is consistently mild throughout the year, with moderate precipitation. Winter temperatures average in the mid-60s Fahrenheit, and summer temperatures average in the upper 70s Fahrenheit. Because Sydney is located south of the equator, the winter and summer months are opposite from those in the northern hemisphere; winter occurs between June and August and summer occurs between December and February.

Government

The metropolitan area of Sydney lacks an overall governing body, but is managed by local government areas; the state government of New South Wales designates duties to these areas. The city itself is run by an elected Lord Mayor of Sydney and a council.

Demographics

Most Sydney residents, known colloquially as Sydneysiders, are Australian-born of British descent. Many of their ancestors came to Australia either as settlers or as convicts (New South Wales was originally a British penal colony). Sydney's population includes Italian, Greek, and Asian immigrants, and a small number of Aborigines, those native to Australia. The population of Sydney's metropolitan area is more than 4.2 million.

Economy

Sydney is a major manufacturing center for Australia; its industries produce machinery, chemicals, paper goods, and food products. The city is also a major international livestock and wool market, thanks to the expansive cattle and sheep ranches in the outback. Sydney is also Australia's business and financial hub.

澳大利亚悉尼

概况

悉尼是澳大利亚最大也是最古老的城市,同时,还是新南威尔士州的州府。此外,它是一座重要的工业城市和主要的国际港口。

一、地理

悉尼位于南纬33°55′,东经151°17′,地处一个巨大的被称为杰克森港的天然港口,通常人们称这个港口为悉尼港。悉尼在澳大利亚东南部,城市和郊区面积近500平方英里。悉尼市中心位于悉尼港的南部,而城市最古老的部分则在靠近码头的地区。悉尼的郊区在城市的南北两面。库灵盖国家公园位于城市北面,那里以土著居民的岩画和雕刻而闻名于世。

二、气候

悉尼一年四季气候温和宜人,降水平均,冬季平均气温在华氏65度左右,夏季平均气温在华氏77~79度。因为悉尼位于赤道以南,冬夏两季的月份与北半球正好相反。冬季出现在6月~8月,夏季则为12月~2月。

三、政府

悉尼大市范围缺乏一个统一的政府管理机构,因此,城市由各地方辖区政府负责管理。新南威尔士州政府为这些地区指定相应的职责,城市本身由一位选举产生的悉尼市长大人以及一个市政委员会负责管理。

四、人口

俗称为"悉尼人"的大多数悉尼居民都是在澳大利亚出生的英国后裔,他们中许多人的祖先要么是来到澳洲的殖民者,要么是囚犯(新南威尔士最初是英国的一个流放地)。悉尼的人口包括意大利人、希腊人以及亚洲移民,此外还有一小部分土著居民,就是那些土生土长的澳大利亚人。悉尼大市范围的人口超过了420万。

五、经济

悉尼是澳大利亚的一个主要的加工制造中心,主要生产机械、化学品、纸制品以及食品类产品。这座城市还是主要的国际家畜及羊毛市场之一,这些无疑得益于其广阔的位于内陆地区的牛羊牧场。此外,悉尼也是澳大利亚商业和金融业的核心地区。

The History

Aborigines are believed to have inhabited the area for perhaps 40,000 years. Captain James Cook of Britain first visited the Sydney region in 1770, and by 1788 the British had established a penal colony there. A smallpox epidemic swept through the native population in 1789; by 1820 only a few hundred Aborigines remained in the area.

The area became troubled by conflict, not only with Aboriginal tribes, but also between landowners and freed convicts. Sydney was incorporated in 1842, and in 1850 the British penal colonies were closed.

The city boomed during the late 1850s, thanks in part to the discovery of gold in the nearby town of Bathurst. The city population grew rapidly during the 20th century, especially after World War II, and Sydney became a sprawling urban center with the usual problems that plague fast-growing cities: overcrowding, pollution, and traffic congestion.

Many historic buildings were demolished in the mid-20th century to make way for modern skyscrapers. Various districts sprung up to reflect the city's many ethnic groups. Sydney hosted the 2000 Summer Olympics.

The Sights and Sounds

This is a hip and happening city. Sydney has something for everyone: white-sand beaches, warm ocean waters, beautiful mountains, and a captivating cityscape. Whatever you like to do on vacation, you can find it in Sydney.

Critics and locals despised the Sydney Opera House when it opened in 1973, but today this striking building is the city's most-recognized landmark. For a small fee, visitors can tour the interior, but those short on cash can enjoy the fabulous view of Sydney Harbor from the Opera House.

The Royal Botanic Garden, near the Opera House, is home to over 7,500 species of plants. The location is a restful spot for people-watching or for a picnic lunch under the shade trees. A train shuttles patrons around the facility.

The Rocks is the oldest conclave in Sydney, with fine restaurants and trendy local art galleries. Although the area has been recently renovated, its old-world charm remains in the buildings and streets. The Rocks' tourist center offers both guided and self-guided walking tours at reasonable rates.

Darling Harbor offers further people-watching opportunities. This popular tourist attraction includes a maritime museum, aquarium, the Chinese garden, and an IMAX theater. Major shopping attractions are also here, of course, as well as a variety of family-friendly restaurants.

The Queen Victoria Building is a shopper's dream. This center, known as the QVB, is an indoor mall containing dozens of shops and restaurants in a Byzantine architectural setting.

Fox Studios is a family-friendly location that includes theaters, an ice rink, and an operating movie studio (the recent motion picture *Moulin Rouge* was filmed here). Visitors can tour the movie-making factory and enjoy interesting interactive exhibits on makeup and cartooning.

Hyde Park is an expansive outdoor park with many statues and memorials. Two notable memorials are the Anzac War Memorial honoring Australia's dead in WWI, and Lady Macquaire's Chair, a memorial to the wife of Governor Lachlan Macquaire, the park's

光影流金

人们相信,土著居民在这一地区居住的历史或许已经有四万年了。1770年,英国的詹姆士·库克船长第一次到达悉尼地区,到了1788年,英国已经在这一地区建立了一个流放地。1789年,流行病天花在土著人群中传播,到了1820年,生活在这一地区的土著居民只剩下了区区数百人。

该地区长期冲突不断,不仅土著部落之间存在着冲突,而且土地所有者与那些获得自由的囚犯之间也有冲突。1842年,悉尼合并为一座城市,1850年,英国的流放地被关闭。

19世纪50年代后期,城市发展迅猛,其中部分原因是在附近的巴瑟斯特镇发现了黄金。20世纪时,该市人口快速增长,尤其是在第二次世界大战之后,悉尼成为无计划扩展的城市中心,一些快速发展城市常见的问题随之产生:例如,过度拥挤、污染以及交通拥堵。

20世纪中期,许多有纪念意义的建筑都被拆除,以便为那些摩天大楼腾出空间。市内各种各样反映民族特色的街区如雨后春笋般出现。悉尼主办了2000年夏季奥运会。

声光景点

悉尼是一座时尚而又鲜活的城市,在这里,人人都可以找到他想要的东西:白沙的海滩、温暖的海水、美丽的群山以及迷人的市景。无论你对自己的假期有何种设想,悉尼都可以满足你的需求。

1973年,当悉尼歌剧院开张之时,评论家和当地人都对这座建筑嗤之以鼻,然而,时至今日,这座引人注目的建筑已经成为悉尼最著名的地标。只需一点点费用,游客就可以进入歌剧院内部参观,但是,如果你觉得钞票有限的话,从歌剧院欣赏一下悉尼港的美景也是一个不错的选择。

位于悉尼歌剧院附近的皇家植物园拥有超过7 500种植物品种。作为一处绝佳的休憩场所,你可以坐在园内的树荫下来一次野餐或者欣赏一下往来的人群。园内的火车往来穿梭,将游客送到各个景点。

岩石区是悉尼市最古老的集会场所,有很棒的餐馆和时髦的地区美术馆。虽然,近些年这一地区已整修一新,但是,原有建筑和街道的迷人风貌依然保留着。岩石区的旅游中心可以提供导游或自助游服务,且收费合理。

达令港是又一处欣赏各色人等的地方,这个游人众多的景点由一座海洋博物馆、水族馆、中国园林和一家巨幕影院组成,一些大型的购物商场也位于这一地区,当然,还有适合家庭聚会的各类餐馆。

维多利亚女王大厦是购物者的天堂,这家通常被称为QVB的购物中心是一座室内的商业步行街,在拜占庭风格的建筑背景衬托下,琳琅满目的商店和诱人的餐馆遍布其中。

福克斯电影公司是一个适合家庭游玩的地方,这里有剧院、溜冰场,还有至今仍在运作的电影制片厂(最近的电影《红磨坊》就是在这里拍摄的)。游客可以参观电影制作工厂,欣赏有趣的化妆及动画制作方面的互动展品。

海德公园是一处大型的户外公园,内有大量的雕塑和纪念物,其中最值得关注的两处纪念物,一是为纪念二战中阵亡的澳大利亚士兵而修建的澳新战争纪念馆,另一个是麦格里夫人的椅子,而麦格里夫人正是海德公园的设计者拉赫兰·麦格里总督的妻子。海

designer. This vantage point provides an excellent view of Sydney Harbour.

Sydney boasts a number of white-sand beaches beside beautiful turquoise waters. Two of the best known are Bondi and Manly Beaches; everyone from families with children to serious surfers and beach bunnies come to soak up the sun. Visitors who choose not to sunbathe may stroll the two-mile Beach Walk from Coogee Beach to Bondi Beach; the views from the Walk are beautiful, and there are plenty of places to rest as well at nearby shops and restaurants.

Cricket and rugby are popular Australian sports, but the Aussies are mad for footy. This unique brand of football is played on an oval field that may be as much as 200 yards long, and the players' uniforms resemble those worn in rugby (i.e., without any padding). Take in a game if you have time.

The Trivia

Fact: During the early part of World War II , four Japanese midget submarines were discovered in Sydney Harbour and were sunk. Shortly thereafter, the Japanese mother submarine shelled the waterfront suburbs of Bondi and Rose Bay; many panicked residents left the city for the nearby Blue Mountains.

Fact: The city was named by the first governor, Arthur Phillip, in honor of British nobleman Thomas Townshend, the Viscount Sydney.

Fact: The government, troubled by the loss of many historic buildings during the boom of the 20th century, restored many historic buildings in the oldest section of the city, known as the Rocks. The area is now a major tourist center.

Fact: Sydney is sometimes referred to as the gateway to Australia, because most international tourists enter the country through Sydney's Kingsford Smith International Airport.

Why Sydney Is a 50 plus one City

Sydney is a friendly, vibrant city that invites visitors to enjoy its hospitality and warmth. A visit to the Sydney Opera House makes the trip to the city worthwhile in its own right— whether you are an opera buff or not.

德公园优越的地理位置为欣赏悉尼港提供了绝佳角度。

让悉尼引以为傲的不仅有美丽碧蓝的海水，还有众多的白沙海滩，其中最著名的要数邦迪海滩和曼丽海滩，海滩上有专门带孩子来玩的家长，有专门来冲浪的勇士，还有专门来晒日光浴的漂亮女士。那些不想晒日光浴的游客不妨沿两英里长的海滨大道漫步，你可以从古基海滩一直走到邦迪海滩。大道两侧风景秀丽，附近还有大量商店和餐馆，你可以随时停下来休息一下。

虽然板球和英式橄榄球在澳大利亚都是颇受欢迎的体育项目，但是令澳大利亚人为之疯狂的却是澳式足球，这种独特的足球运动是在一个椭圆形的足有两百码长的球场上进行的，球员的运动服看上去和英式橄榄球的服装差不多（就是没有填塞物的那种）。假如有时间，建议你看一场比赛。

奇闻轶事

之一：第二次世界大战初期，四艘小型的日本潜水艇在悉尼港被人们发现已经沉没，之后不久，日本的母舰潜水艇对邦迪和玫瑰湾附近的码头地区进行了炮轰，许多惊慌失措的居民离开城市逃到了附近的蓝山地区。

之二：悉尼市名是第一任总督亚瑟·菲利普所赐，为的是纪念英国贵族托马斯·汤森，又称悉尼子爵。

之三：由于在20世纪的快速发展时期，大批的古建筑被拆除，令悉尼政府苦恼不已，因此，他们在城市最古老的区域重修了许多建筑，这一地区被称为岩石区，如今是主要的旅游中心之一。

之四：悉尼有时被称为通往澳大利亚的门户，因为大多数国际游客都是通过悉尼的金斯福—史密斯国际机场进入这个国家的。

为什么悉尼入选50+1个城市？

悉尼是一座友好而充满生机的城市，它以自己的好客和温暖向八方来客敞开双臂，仅悉尼歌剧院一地游就足以令你不虚此行 —— 不管你是不是歌剧爱好者。

Forty-five

Tokyo, Japan

The Basic Facts

Tokyo is the capital of Japan and one of the world's largest and most modern cities. It is the seat of Japan's government and is a center of business, culture and education. Tokyo was largely destroyed by bombing in World War II ; after the war, Tokyo was rebuilt and the economy and the population boomed.

Geography

Tokyo lies at 35 degrees 42 minutes north latitude and 139 degrees 46 minutes east longitude. The Tokyo urban area includes the manufacturing cities of Chiba and Kawasaki. The city is on the southeastern coast of Honshu, the largest island in Japan, and is located in the southern part of the Kanto Plain. It is bordered by the Edo River to the northeast, Tokyo Bay to the east, and the Tama River to the south. The Sumida River flows through the eastern part of the city and empties into Tokyo Bay. Mount Fuji, Japan's highest and most famous mountain, is about 60 miles southwest of Tokyo.

Tokyo is divided into 23 wards. The land on the city's far eastern side was reclaimed from Tokyo Bay, and thus is prone to seasonal flooding.

Climate

The climate in Tokyo, and all Japan for that matter, varies widely due to its location in the Pacific Ocean. Summers are generally hot and humid and winters are typically dry. Average temperatures range from the upper 40s Fahrenheit in the winter to the upper 80s Fahrenheit in summer. On clear days, Mount Fuji is clearly visible and often appears to float in the clouds.

Government

Tokyo's official name is Tokyo Prefecture. This area consists of the city, or ward area; 25 suburban areas west of the ward area; several towns in a mountainous western area; and the Izu and Bonin Islands. The governor heads the Tokyo Metropolitan Prefecture and is publicly elected to a 4-year term. The legislative body is the 127-member Metropolitan Assembly, all of whom are elected to 4-year terms. In addition to the central government, each ward, suburb, town, or village in the Prefecture has a form of local government with an elected council, mayor, or other administrator. Their power is limited by the prefecture.

Demographics

Tokyo's population density is among the highest in the world at 33,000 people per square mile. More than 12.5 million people live in the city itself, while more than 36.5 million live in the Greater Tokyo Area. Tokyo's population is overwhelmingly Japanese, with small concentrations of Chinese, Koreans, Filipinos, Americans, and Britons.

日本东京

概况

东京是日本的首都,是世界上最大、也是最现代化的城市之一。它是日本政府所在地,还是商业、文化和教育中心之一。第二次世界大战中,东京大部分地区遭到炮火毁坏,战争结束之后,城市得以重建,其经济和人口也迅速增长。

一、地理

东京位于北纬35°42′,东经139°46′。东京城市区域包括加工城市千叶和川崎。东京地处日本最大的岛屿本州岛的东南岸和关东平原的南部。城市周边河流环绕,东北面是江户河、东面是东京湾、南面是多摩川,隔田川从城市东部穿城而过流入东京湾。日本最高、最著名的山脉富士山距离东京西北大约60英里。

东京被划分为23个区,城市最东端的土地是经东京湾填海造地而成的,因此,常会爆发季节性洪水。

二、气候

由于地处太平洋中,东京乃至整个日本的气候变化巨大,夏季通常炎热潮湿,冬季则非常干燥。平均气温在冬季的华氏47~49度到夏季的华氏87~89度。在晴朗的日子里,远处的富士山清晰可见,并且时常在云雾中若隐若现。

三、政府

东京的官方名称是东京地方行政区,该地区包括东京市或行政区地区、行政区以西的25个郊区地区、西部山区地区的几个町(镇)以及伊豆诸岛和小笠原群岛。东京大市行政区由行政长官主管,行政长官经公众选举产生,任期4年。立法机构是包括127名成员的城市议会,议会成员同样经选举产生。除中央政府之外,行政区内的各市区、城郊、城镇或乡村也有自己的政府体系:一个选举产生的市政委员会、市长或其他行政官员。他们的行政权限范围由地方行政区来规定。

四、人口

东京的人口密度排在世界城市前列,每平方英里的人口数达到了3.3万人。市区本身的人口数就超过了1 250万,而在大东京范围内则居住着3 650万人。东京人口中日本人占了压倒多数,其他主要为中国人、朝鲜人、菲律宾人、美国人和英国人。

Economy

Tokyo is a world center of economic activity and traditionally was the heart of the Japanese manufacturing industry. Goods manufactured in Tokyo include chemicals, food, electronics, furniture and paper. In the late 20th century, service industries such as communication, finance and trade supplanted manufacturing as the most important part of Tokyo's economy. Many of the world's largest electronic firms, such as Hitachi, Toshiba, Sony and NEC are headquartered in Tokyo.

Tokyo Bay is rather shallow for a successful port, so most imports and exports pass through nearby Yokohama. Tokyo has an extensive public transportation system of rail lines and buses, yet an increasing number of residents drive cars and cause significant traffic congestion. High-speed shinkansen, or bullet trains, link Tokyo to Osaka and other Japanese cities. The city's two major airports are Tokyo International, or Haneda, and Narita International.

The History

In 1457 a warrior named Ota Dokan built a castle there to take advantage of the site's strategic military location; the town of Edo formed around the castle. In 1590, a warrior named Tokugawa Ieyasu made Edo his headquarters when he became shogun, the military ruler of Japan. Edo became the nation's political center, but Kyoto remained the official capital of Japan because it was there that the emperor resided.

Tokyo and Japan voluntarily isolated themselves from the Western world in the early 17th century. In 1853 the United States naval officer Commodore Matthew C. Perry sailed into Tokyo Harbor to negotiated trade agreements with the Japanese rulers.

Emperor Meiji (also known as Mutsuhito) seized control of Japan in 1867, moved the capital to Edo, and renamed it Tokyo. A powerful earthquake destroyed much of the city in 1923; the subsequent reconstruction increased the westernization of the city that had begun in the 19th century. Tokyo was devastated by the United States during World War II bombing raids, and many buildings were destroyed. After the war, skyscrapers and other modern buildings were constructed in the city, and strict building codes were implemented to prevent future earthquakerelated damage. Tokyo's population tripled between 1945 and 1960; this rapid growth, combined with insufficient city planning, led to housing shortages and traffic congestion. Tokyo improved its air and water quality in the 1990s, but overcrowding and skyrocketing property values continue to be a problem.

The Sights and Sounds

Tokyo is a crowded, bustling city, but its crime rate is low, enabling visitors to feel safe even in the wee hours of the morning. Many sights and sounds are familiar to Westerners, but still more are traditionally Japanese. Many people take time from work to admire the cherry blossoms in April.

The Tokyo National Museum, housed in eight buildings, exhibits an unmatched collection of Asian antiquities including paintings, sculpture, archaeology, calligraphy and decorative arts. The National Museum of Modern Art showcases the works of modern Japanese artists in three buildings: the Art Museum, the Crafts Gallery, and the National Film Center. Visitors may need a whole day to explore just one of these buildings.

The Kabuki-za Theater, located in the Ginza, was built especially for Kabuki performances, which include traditional Japanese music, dance and theater. Most Kabuki

五、经济

东京是世界经济活动的中心,也是传统的日本加工工业中心,东京生产的产品包括化学品、食品、电子产品、家具和纸张。20世纪晚期,诸如通讯等服务行业、金融和贸易行业取代加工制造业成为东京经济最主要的组成部分。许多世界上最大的电子公司,例如日立、东芝、索尼和NEC等公司都把总部设在了东京。

对于一个成功的港口来说,东京湾的吞吐量相当有限,因此,大多数进出口货物都经由附近的横滨港进出。虽然东京拥有一个由轨道交通和公交汽车构成的全面的公共交通系统,但是,由于有越来越多的城市居民驾驶私家车上路,交通拥堵时常发生。高速的新干线列车,或称子弹头列车,将东京和大阪以及其他日本城市连接起来。东京的两个主要机场是东京国际机场,又称羽田机场,以及成田国际机场。

光影流金

1457年,一个名为太田道灌的武士在现今东京所处地区修建了一座城堡,以便充分利用该地区有利的军事战略位置,江户镇就是围绕这座城堡建立起来的。1590年,一个名为德川家康的武士在成为幕府将军,也就是日本的军事领袖以后,把江户变成了他的大本营。虽然江户成了日本的政治中心,但是京都却一直是日本的官方首府,因为日本天皇就住在那里。

17世纪早期,日本和东京主动断绝了与西方世界的来往,1853年,美国海军军官马修·C.佩里准将航行来到东京湾,与当时的日本统治者进行了贸易谈判。

1867年,明治天皇(又称睦仁天皇)取得政权,他将都城迁到了江户,并将江户更名为东京。1923年,一场强烈的地震摧毁了城市的大部分地区,接下来的重建过程加速了城市的西方化,而这种西化倾向自19世纪起就已经开始了。第二次世界大战期间,东京遭到了美国飞机的狂轰滥炸,许多建筑被夷为平地。战后,摩天大楼和其他现代建筑在城市中拔地而起,而日本执行的严格建筑规范确保了这些建筑在以后的地震中能安然无恙。1945至1960年间,东京人口增加了两倍,这种快速的增长,加之城市规划的不完善导致了住房短缺和交通堵塞等问题。20世纪90年代,东京市政府采取措施改善了城市的空气和饮水质量,然而,人口的过度拥挤以及猛涨的房地产价格仍是困扰他们的大问题。

声光景点

虽说东京是一座拥挤而喧嚣的城市,但是犯罪率却很低,因此,即使是凌晨一二点钟,游客也可放心游玩。许多景点是西方游客非常熟悉的,不过,更多的景区则具有传统的日本特色。三月里,很多人会忙里偷闲去欣赏樱花盛开的美景。

由8幢建筑组合而成的东京国家博物馆展品数量无与伦比,其中出自亚洲地区的古董包括绘画、雕塑、考古、书法和装饰艺术品等。国家现代艺术馆展出的是日本现代艺术家的作品,博物馆由3幢建筑构成,分别是美术馆、工艺美术馆和国家电影中心。这3幢大厦中的任何一个都够你参观一天的。

位于银座的歌舞伎剧院是专为歌舞伎表演而修建的,歌舞伎表演展示的是日本传统的音乐、舞蹈和舞台。虽然大多数歌舞伎表演长达数小时,但是早晨剧院会提供较短的演

performances are several hours long, but the theater offers a shorter performance in the morning. Visitors may also watch from the fourth floor and leave when they wish without disturbing other theatergoers.

Ginza is the high-end shopping district in the city with many department stores, boutiques, designer outlets and trendy restaurants. This district never seems to sleep; the sidewalks are crowded both day and night. The neon signs in the Ginza District rival Times Square in their brightness and variety. If you are looking for electronics, Akihabara is the place to go. The latest techno-gadgets are on display in hundreds of shops that specialize in all types of electronic devices.

The Ryogoku Kokugikan is the heart of sumo wrestling in Tokyo; three annual tournaments are held here. The attached Sumo Museum displays woodblock prints, ceremonial garb, and other historical items related to this popular sport. Local restaurants offer a hotpot dish called chanko-nabe, the staple diet of sumo wrestlers. Training facilities, called stables, are located near the stadium, and some stables allow visitors to watch practice sessions.

The Meiji Shrine is a Shinto temple dedicated to Emperor Meiji and his wife Empress Shoken. Located amidst beautiful tree-lined grounds, this shrine is a good place to rest and relax without battling the crowds. Tours of the buildings are available. The Zojo-ji Temple is a Buddhist temple located in Shiba and is surrounded by a public park. The Sangedatsu Gate at the entrance to the temple was the only structure on the site that survived World War II. Six members of the Tokugawa shogunate are buried here.

Two of the finest Japanese gardens in Tokyo are Koishikawa Korakuen and Rikugien. Koshikawa Korakuen was built during the time of the Tokugawa shogunate and displays landscapes of China and Japan in miniature. Rikugien (or six poems garden) recreates scenes from 88 famous Japanese poems in a network of pools, islands, and teahouses. Both gardens charge a nominal entrance fee.

The Trivia

Fact: Tokyo means eastern capital in Japanese.

Fact: Tokyo was spared by the atomic bombs that the United States dropped on Japan in 1945; bombing raids earlier that year had already destroyed at least onethird of the city and killed hundreds of thousands of residents.

Fact: The Imperial Palace in Tokyo is the home of the Japanese emperor. It consists of several buildings connected by beautiful landscaped grounds. The palace buildings and inner grounds are only open to the public on January 2nd and the emperor's birthday, December 23rd.

Fact: Shinto and Buddhism are the major religions of Tokyo, and many shrines and temples are available for worshippers and visitors.

Fact: Tokyo's subways and commuter trains are so crowded during rush hours that oshiya (literally pushers) are employed to shove commuters into the packed trains.

Why Tokyo Is a 50 plus one City

Tokyo's traditions and its prominence in the global economy make it a great city. The sheer beauty of Mount Fuji, ever-present against the cityscape, awes visitors from around the world. Visitors and locals alike cherish the city for its excitement, history and power. Tokyo is a modern metropolis, crowded and clamorous, yet also artistic and culturally aware.

出。游客还可以选择从四楼观看表演,这样就可以在不影响其他观众的前提下随时离开剧院。

银座是东京购物的终极地区,这里有大量的百货商店、时装店、专卖店和时髦的餐馆。这一地区似乎永远不会休息,无论白天黑夜,人行道上总是熙来攘往。银座区的霓虹灯箱其明亮程度、花样之多堪比美国的时代广场。假如你想寻找电子产品,秋叶原就是你该去的地方。这里有数百家专门出售各类电子设备的电器商店,柜台里展出的是最新的小巧精致的数码产品。

两国国技馆是东京相扑运动的中心,每年三次的锦标赛都在这里举行。与此相连的相扑博物馆展出的是与这项在日本广受欢迎的体育运动相关的版画印刷品、正式比赛的服装以及其他纪念品。当地的餐馆提供一种名为"力士火锅"的炖锅食品,是相扑手们的主食。被称为"马房"的训练设施位于体育馆附近,有些"马房"允许游客一旁观看选手训练。

明治神宫是献给明治天皇和他的妻子昭宪皇后的神道寺庙,位于绿茵环绕的墓地之中,这座神庙是远离尘嚣的人们休憩和放松的好地方。神庙提供导游服务。增上寺是位于此地的佛教寺院,寺院周边就是一个公园,入口处通往寺院的"三解脱门"是二战中唯一幸存下来的建筑。有六位德川幕府时代的将军就葬在这里。

在东京有两座最完美的日式庭园,分别是小石川后乐园和六义园。修建于德川幕府时代的小石川后乐园,是中国和日本山水的微缩展示。六义园(或称"六首诗花园"),通过一个以池塘、岛屿和茶室构成的网络,再现了88首日本著名诗歌中的景象。两座花园都只是象征性地收一张门票钱。

奇闻轶事
之一:东京的意思就是日本东部的首府。

之二:1945年,东京躲过了美国人在日本投下的原子弹,因为在那之前,飞机轰炸已经将东京至少1/3的地区完全破坏,成百上千的居民在轰炸中丧生。

之三:位于东京的日本皇宫是日本天皇居住的地方,它由建在美丽景观基础之上的数座建筑构成,宫殿建筑和其内部区域只有每年的1月2日以及12月23日天皇生日之时才向公众开放。

之四:神道和佛教是东京的主要宗教,许多神庙和寺院都向信徒和游人开放。

之五:东京的地铁和通勤列车在高峰期都异常拥挤,因此,"奥仕轧"(字面意思就是"推手")应运而生,这些人受雇把那些上下班的人推进拥挤的车厢。

为什么东京入选50 + 1个城市?
东京的传统和它在全球经济中的杰出地位使之成为一座伟大的城市,富士山以其纯粹之美,成为城市风景永久的背景,吸引着来自全球惊艳的目光。无论外来的访客,还是当地的居民都同样难忘这座城市带给他们的激动、历史和力量。东京是一座现代化的大都会,在其拥挤而喧闹的外表之下,还隐藏着艺术和文化的觉醒。

Toronto, Canada

The Basic Facts

Toronto is the largest city in Canada and the capital of the province of Ontario. It is a principal center for the nation's manufacturing, financial, and communications industries.

Geography

Toronto lies at 43 degrees 40 minutes north latitude and 79 degrees 23 minutes west longitude. The city occupies 243 square miles on the northwest shore of Lake Ontario, and the metropolitan area of Greater Toronto covers more than 2,700 square miles. Three rivers travel south through the city and empty into Lake Ontario: the Humber, the Don, and the Rouge.

Climate

Toronto has a fairly mild climate relative to the rest of Canada, thanks to Lake Ontario's moderating effect. Temperatures range from the 30s Fahrenheit in winter to the 70s Fahrenheit in summer. Autumn and spring days can be spectacular with clear and cool weather. Winter temperatures occasionally drop below freezing, and the area typically has one or two major snowstorms every winter.

Government

Toronto was once composed of six locally-controlled metropolitan areas. In 1997, however, the Ontario Provincial Legislature merged these six entities to create the city of Toronto. This unified city is run by a single government and is directed by the Toronto City Council. The council, which consists of a mayor and 44 council members, is responsible for nearly all city services and operates a variety of municipal agencies, boards, and commissions.

Demographics

Toronto's population is among the world's most ethnically diverse; more than 100 languages are spoken by some 150 ethnic groups. Toronto experienced significant population growth during the mid-20th century with an influx of European immigrants, primarily from Italy and Portugal. The city's population is roughly 2.5 million and the Greater Toronto Area has more than five million residents.

Economy

Toronto is the major industrial center for the nation. Chief industries include food processing, printing and publishing, and paper, rubber and wood manufacturing. Toronto is also the country's banking and financial center, and is the home of the Toronto Stock Exchange.

The History

The area's first inhabitants were Algonquin and Iroquois Indians, who portaged across

加拿大多伦多

概况

多伦多是加拿大最大的城市，也是安大略省的省会，是加拿大加工业、金融业和通讯工业的一个重要中心。

一、地理

多伦多位于北纬43°40′，西经79°23′，地处安大略湖西北岸，占地面积243平方英里。大多伦多都市范围的面积则在2 700平方英里以上。有3条河流向南穿过城市，汇入安大略湖：坎伯河、顿河和红河。

二、气候

相对于加拿大其他地区来说，多伦多的气候相当温和，这多亏了安大略湖的调节作用。气温在冬季的华氏30度至夏季的华氏70度。春秋季节，天空晴朗，气候凉爽，令人心旷神怡。冬季气温偶尔会降到零度以下，一般每年冬天，这一地区都会经历一两次暴风雪。

三、政府

过去多伦多曾经分为6个自治的行政地区，然而，1997年，安大略省立法机构将这6个实体进行合并，组成了多伦多市。如今，这一联合城市由一个单一政府管理，并受多伦多市政委员会领导。市政委员会由一位市长和44位市政委员组成，他们负责管理几乎所有的市政服务，并保证各类政府部门、理事会和委员会等的运作。

四、人口

多伦多的人口构成使之处于世界上民族最为多样化的城市行列，共有大约150个民族的人讲着100多种语言。20世纪中期，随着欧洲移民潮的涌入，多伦多的人口经历了一次显著增长，这些欧洲移民主要为意大利人和葡萄牙人。如今，该市人口大约为250万，而大市范围的人口则超过了500万。

五、经济

多伦多是加拿大主要的工业中心，其工业集中在食品加工、印刷和出版、纸张、橡胶以及木材加工等。此外，多伦多还是加拿大银行和金融业的中心，多伦多证券交易所就位于多伦多。

光影流金

这一地区最早的原住民是阿耳冈昆和易洛魁印第安人，因为这一地区是他们在休伦

the site between Lake Huron and Lake Ontario. In the mid-18th century, French explorers built a trading post and began to colonize the area. During the French and Indian War, the French burned Fort Rouillé (later Fort Toronto) to prevent it from falling to the British. Britain won the war, and in 1763 the French ceded most of their Canadian territory in the Treaty of Paris.

John Graves Simcoe established a permanent settlement on the site in 1793 and replaced Newark as the capital of Upper Canada. He named the settlement Fort York in honor of the Duke of York. York was later renamed Toronto and received its city charter in 1834. The rise of transportation and the manufacturing industry caused the city to grow rapidly in the late 1800s. Toronto became a major market for grain and livestock once the Canadian government opened new areas in the west.

Toronto's industrial economy expanded during both World Wars due to the demand for war materials; European immigration rose as a result. To help the area meet the demands for these new immigrants, the Ontario legislature in 1954 created the Municipality of Metropolitan Toronto, a federation of Toronto and 12 of its suburbs. In 1967, the legislature merged the 13 units into six. Toronto underwent significant urban renewal in the late 1960s with the creation of improved transportation systems, housing and shopping areas. To avoid duplication of services, the Ontario legislature merged the six municipalities into the unified city of Toronto in 1997.

The Sights and Sounds

Toronto is a metropolitan center with a comfortable small town feel. While it offers everything a visitor could want in a city center such as art, theater, museums, fine dining and the like, it also offers quirky attractions such as the Bata Shoe Museum and bohemian areas like the old Distillery District. With its low crime rate, Toronto may well be the safest big city in North America.

The shopping mecca of Eaton Centre is one of Toronto's main tourist attractions. The mall contains more than 500 shops and restaurants, as well as a movie theater and a police station. Eaton Centre is the model of a successful indoor mall; visitors can find nearly everything they wish to buy. This is a fine place to wander out of the elements in winter when bitter winds blow.

Hockey is to Canadians as baseball is to Americans: it is the national pastime, and fans are loyal to their favorite teams. The Hockey Hall of Fame is located in downtown Toronto and is a must-see for fans of this fast-paced sport. Attractions include the historical hockey jerseys, plaques dedicated to former players and broadcasters, interactive exhibits popular with children, and a gift shop. The showcase of the museum is a vault—literally a former bank vault—within which the Stanley Cup and other National Hockey League trophies are displayed.

Bata Shoe Museum, located near the University of Toronto, is a museum that presents the history of footwear. Among the collection's 10,000 pairs of shoes are those of Elton John, Madonna, Michael Jordan, Picasso, and even a sock worn by Napoleon. Three of the 50 tallest buildings in the world are located in Toronto: First Canadian Place (72 stories); Scotia Plaza (68 stories); and TD Canada Trust Tower (53 stories). All three offer good views of the city and many camera-worthy angles.

Harbourfront Centre has interesting shops and restaurants, and offers plenty of people-watching opportunities. Local artists and artisans practice their crafts here, including

湖和安大略湖之间进行运输的陆上必经之地。18世纪中期,法国探险家在这一地区修建了一个贸易驿站,并且开始了殖民统治。在法国人与印第安人进行战争期间,法国人将这座要塞(即后来的多伦多要塞)付之一炬,以防其落入英国人手中。最终,英国人赢得了战争胜利,1763年,在《巴黎条约》中,法国将其位于加拿大的大部分领土割让给了英国。

1793年,约翰·格雷夫斯·西姆克在这个地区建立了一个永久性的殖民地,并使之取代巴瑞克而成为上加拿大的首府。他将这一殖民地取名为约克城堡,以表示对约克公爵的敬意。约克后来被重新命名为多伦多,并于1834年,达成城市宪章。19世纪后期,交通的增长以及加工制造业的兴起推动城市迅速发展,一旦加拿大政府开放了西部的新兴地区,多伦多便一跃成为一个谷物和牲畜的主要市场。

在两次世界大战期间,由于对战争物资的需求,多伦多的工业经济进一步扩展,其结果是欧洲移民人数的上升。为了满足该地区这些新移民的需求,1954年,安大略立法机构创建了多伦多自治城市,包括一个多伦多联邦政府以及12个郊属县。1967年,立法机构又将这13个行政单位合并为6个。20世纪60年代后期,多伦多市改善了城市交通系统,兴建了住宅和购物中心,城市面貌焕然一新。为了避免市政服务方面的重复劳动,安大略省立法部门于1997年将六个行政区合并成了统一的多伦多市。

声光景点

多伦多虽是大都会的中心,却有着小城市舒适的感觉。它既为游客提供了大城市所必需的诸如美术、剧院、博物馆、美食店之类的场所,同时又有一些与众不同的景点,例如贝塔鞋类博物馆以及像老酿酒厂区这样的波希米亚地区。由于犯罪率很低,多伦多或许是北美地区最安全的大城市。

购物天堂伊顿中心是多伦多最主要的旅游景点之一,这条步行街上有超过500家商店和餐馆,还有一家影剧院和一个警察局。伊顿中心可谓成功的大型室内购物区的典范。在这里,游客几乎能够找到他们想要的任何东西。在冬季室外寒风凛冽的日子里,这里无疑也是令人徘徊留恋的美妙场所。

冰球对于加拿大人来说,就如同棒球对美国人一样的重要:它是全民族的体育项目,那些球迷对于自己喜爱的球队忠心耿耿。冰球名人堂位于多伦多市中心,是所有爱好这项快速运动的球迷们必到之处。馆内收藏了历史上冰球运动的球衣以及奖给过去一些运动员和播音员的勋章等,那些互动式展品非常受孩子们的喜爱,此外,这里还有一家礼品店。博物馆的陈列柜是一个保险库 —— 表面意思就是原来银行的一个金库 —— 里面陈列的有史丹利杯和其他国家冰球联合会的奖杯。

坐落于多伦多大学附近的贝塔鞋类博物馆是一家以展示鞋类历史为主的博物馆,馆内收藏的一万双鞋子里包括埃尔顿·约翰、麦当娜、迈克尔·乔丹、毕加索等名人穿过的,甚至还有一只拿破仑穿过的袜子。世界上50座最高的建筑中有三座位于多伦多:第一加拿大广场(72层);斯科亚广场(68层);加拿大信托银行大厦(53层),这三座建筑都是俯瞰全市,抑或摄影取景的好去处。

湖畔中心广场除了有许多特色商店和餐馆之外,还为欣赏各色人等提供了很多机会。当地的艺术家及工匠都以这里为展示才华的地方,例如,吹玻璃和首饰制作等。在这座地处市中心以南水岸边的建筑群内,还有许多小型美术馆、咖啡屋,以及一家巨幕影

glass blowing and jewelry making. Many small art galleries and cafes are also within this complex, which is on the waterfront south of the city center. Other attractions include an IMAX theater, musicals, and dance productions.

Toronto Island Park is divided into three sections: Centre Island, Ward's Island and Hanlon's Point. Centre Island includes a children's playground called Centreville with rides appropriate for little people. This section also includes a hedge maze, lots of green space, and plenty of room for children to explore. Both Ward's Island and Hanlon's Point are quieter spaces with more green space and no rides. Families can bike, rollerblade, walk or picnic in all three sections, and the local ferry stops at each.

Old Fort York was destroyed during the War of 1812—by Canadians, who ignited the city's gunpowder supply and blew up the fort. The structure was later rebuilt, and today it houses the world's finest collection of buildings from that area as well as exhibits on the war's history.

Tourists flock to Casa Loma, a majestic 98-room castle north of the city. This structure, built for the financier Sir Henry Pellatt, has secret passageways, hidden doors and beautiful period decorations. The five-acre gardens are also welldesigned and lovely almost any time of the year.

The Royal Ontario Museum—also known as the ROM—houses a collection of over five million pieces. Its most interesting exhibit is the display of Chinese art and artifacts. The facility is currently undergoing renovation, which will create a dramatic new entranceway and new gallery spaces.

Niagara Falls is 2 hours away by car, and this is a great side trip if you have time. There are observation areas on both the U.S. and Canadian sides, but the latter has a better view of the famous Horseshoe Falls. Among the most popular attractions here is the Maid of the Mist boat ride, which takes tourists almost to the very base of the falls; the rushing water creates a deafening roar.

The Trivia

Fact: The CN Tower, at 1815 feet tall, is the world's tallest free-standing tower. Television and radio transmissions, including those of the Canadian Broadcasting Corporation (CBC), emanate from the tower.

Fact: U.S. troops captured Toronto during the War of 1812 and burned parts of the town including the fort. The troops looted the town and took the Mace, the ceremonial staff used by the legislature. President Franklin D. Roosevelt ordered the Mace returned in 1934.

Fact: Many Canadians were unhappy with British rule during the 19th century. In 1837, William Lyon Mackenzie led a revolt in the Toronto area, but the protest was quickly crushed by British troops. Mackenzie later became the first mayor of Toronto.

Fact: Toronto's film industry has experienced a tremendous boom, as its labor costs are much lower than those of United States studios. The city frequently doubles for cities such as New York and Chicago. Casa Loma appears prominently in the first X-Men film as the School for Gifted Mutants.

Why Toronto Is a 50 plus one City

Toronto is beautiful, sophisticated, and one of the safest cities in the world. This global city prides itself on its cosmopolitan atmosphere and sophisticated urban environment, a view that is not lost on the countless tourists who visit each year.

院、音乐剧以及舞蹈制作产业等。

多伦多海岛公园分为三个部分：中央岛、沃德岛和汉兰角。中央岛包括一个名为森特维尔的儿童游乐场，内设专为小朋友设计的游乐设施，此外，这里还有一个树篱迷宫、大片的绿色空地以及足够孩子们探寻的空间。沃德岛和汉兰角都是相对安静的地方，绿色更多，没有游乐设施。家庭可以选择在这三个区域内骑自行者车、玩滑板、散步或野餐。当地的渡轮在这三个地方都有停靠。

约克旧城堡在1812年战争中被加拿大人自己摧毁 —— 他们点燃了城中的弹药库炸掉了要塞。后来，这座城堡又被重建，如今，城堡内收藏了大量关于战争历史的纪念品，以及来自那一地区的世界上最完美的建筑。

卡萨罗马是位于城市北部的一座拥有98间房屋的宏伟城堡，时常游客如织。这座专为金融家亨利·佩拉提爵士而修建的建筑内设秘密通道、暗门以及那一时代漂亮的装饰物。城堡四周方圆5英亩的花园设计精美，一年四季景致不断。
皇家安大略博物馆 —— 又称为ROM —— 收藏了500多万件艺术品，其中最有趣的要数来自中国的美术和手工艺品。最近，博物馆的设施正在进行改造，一个新的入口以及新的美术馆空间将为游客带来惊喜。

尼亚加拉瀑布距城市大约两小时的车程，假如时间充足的话，这无疑会是一次很棒的附带行程。瀑布在美国和加拿大境内都有观赏点，但是，后者更适合欣赏著名的马蹄瀑布景观。这里最受游客欢迎的景点有乘坐"雾中少女号"游船，它可以把游客到几乎是瀑布的最底部。在那里你可以听到飞泻的水花发出的震耳欲聋的声音。

奇闻轶事
之一：高1815英尺的加拿大国家电视塔是世界上最高的无其他支撑的电视塔，广播和电视节目的播出，包括加拿大广播公司(CBC)的节目都是从这座塔上发射出去的。

之二：1812年战争期间，美国军队曾经一度占领了多伦多，并且焚烧了要塞在内的大部分地区。美国兵在城内大肆掠夺，抢走了立法会所使用的权杖"美思"。1934年，在弗兰克林·罗斯福总统的命令下，这根权杖才重新回到多伦多的怀抱。

之三：19世纪时，许多加拿大人不满英国的统治，1837年，威廉·里昂·麦肯齐在多伦多地区领导了一支叛军，然而，他们的抗议很快便被英国军队镇压下去，后来，麦肯齐成了多伦多的首任市长。
之四：由于劳动力开支较之美国电影公司要低很多，多伦多的电影业经历了一个迅猛发展的阶段，其电影产品的数量时常是纽约和芝加哥等大城市的两倍。卡萨罗马作为培养异种战士的学校出现在首部《X战警》影片当中，引起全球的关注。

为什么多伦多入选50 + 1个城市？
多伦多是世界上一座美丽、成熟而又异常安全的城市，它以大都会的氛围及其发达的城市环境而傲立于全球大都会之林，尽管每年有数不清的游客来到这里，依然无法改变它原有的美丽风貌。

Forty-seven

Vancouver, Canada

The Basic Facts

Vancouver is the largest city in British Columbia and the busiest port in Canada. The growth of trade between Canada and Japan in the late 20th century made Vancouver's seaport even more important. The city became a modern metropolis as a construction boom continued into the 1990s. Vancouver will host the Winter Olympics in 2010.

Geography

Vancouver lies at 49 degrees 16 minutes north latitude and 123 degrees 6 minutes west longitude. The city is located in southwestern British Columbia, approximately 25 miles north of the U.S.-Canadian border. The port is in the natural harbor of Burrard Inlet; the Strait of Juan de Fuca to the south is the main water route to the Pacific Ocean.

Climate

The protection of the Coast Mountains, combined with warm winds from the Pacific Ocean, gives Vancouver a mild climate for its latitude. Average temperatures range from mid-30s Fahrenheit in winter to the mid-60s Fahrenheit in summer. Snow is common in the nearby mountains, but rare at sea level. Because Vancouver is so far north, there are less than 8 hours of darkness around the summer solstice. Although Vancouver is popularly believed to be a rainy city, measurable rainfall averages only 166 days out of the year.

Government

Vancouver has a mayor-city council form of government. The mayor and 10-members city council are elected to 2-year terms. Property taxes fund most city services, but the federal and provincial governments contribute funds toward improvements to the city's infrastructure.

Demographics

Roughly half of Vancouver's population is native-born, most of whom are descended from the British. Asian and western European immigrants are among the city's largest ethnic groups. The city's population is estimated at 545,000, and that of the entire metropolitan area is estimated at 2.2 million.

Economy

Vancouver's port drives most of Vancouver's economy. International freight shipping accounts for 75 million short tons annually. Vancouver is also a major port-of-call for cruise ships. Other industries include wholesale and retail trades, food processing, and lumber, and wood products. Vancouver is the largest financial center in western Canada, and nearly every large business in the province is headquartered here. Tourism is a rapidly growing industry, and the film and television industry is on the rise due to lower production costs in the country.

The History

The Vancouver area was inhabited by Salish Indians more than 2,000 years ago. The first European to visit the area was Spanish explorer Don Jose Marie Narvaez, in 1791. One year later, Captain George Vancouver of Britain sailed into what eventually became

加拿大温哥华

概况

温哥华是加拿大不列颠哥伦比亚省最大的城市,是加拿大最繁忙的港口。20世纪后期,加拿大与日本之间的贸易发展使得温哥华海港变得尤为重要。伴随着一轮持续到20世纪90年代的大规模建设热潮,这座城市已经变成了一座现代化的大都市。2010年,温哥华将要主办冬季奥林匹克运动会。

一、地理

温哥华位于北纬49°16′,西经123°6′,地处不列颠哥伦比亚省西南地区,距离美国与加拿大边界以北近25英里。温哥华的港口位于布立德内湾的天然良港内,南部的胡安−德−富卡海峡是通往太平洋的主要水路。

二、气候

海岸山脉的保护,加之来自于太平洋温暖的海风,赋予了温哥华同一海拔地区得天独厚的宜人气候。平均气温在冬季的华氏35度至夏季的华氏65度。虽然,在附近的山区时常下雪,但是平地地区却降雪极少。由于温哥华位于赤道以北很远的地方,夏至前后,黑夜只有不到8个小时。尽管人们都认为温哥华是一座多雨的城市,但是,据测量,实际上全年平均降水只有166天左右。

三、政府

温哥华市政府的构成属于市长加市政委员会形式,市长和总共包括10名成员的市政委员会都是选举产生,任期两年。大部分市政服务开支来自于征收的财产税,但是,基础设施的改善则主要靠联邦和省政府提供资金。

四、人口

温哥华约一半的人口都是在当地出生的,其中大部分为英国人的后裔。亚洲及欧洲移民是城市中最大的少数民族。据估计,温哥华的人口有54.5万,整个大市范围则有大约220万人。

五、经济

温哥华的港口是城市经济的主要推动力,每年国际海上货运量达7 500万吨。此外,温哥华也是游轮的主要停靠港,其他产业还包括批发和零售业、食品加工、木材和木制品等。温哥华是加拿大西部最大的金融中心。省内几乎所有的大公司都把总部设在这里。旅游业发展迅速,电影及电视产业由于成本较低也正成为这个国家的新兴产业。

光影流金

2000多年前在温哥华地区居住的是萨利希印第安人,首批造访这里的欧洲人是于1791年到来的西班牙探险家唐·荷赛·马利·拿瓦耶兹。一年后,英国的乔治·温哥华船长

Burrard Inlet. The actual settlement was founded in 1865, when the Hastings Mill sawmill was built on the site. In 1884, the Canadian Pacific Railway chose the area for its western terminal. The city was incorporated in 1886. A major fire that same year destroyed much of the city, but reconstruction was swift.

Vancouver became the fastest-growing Canadian city between 1900 and 1910; the population swelled with immigrants from around the world, most of whom arrived to work in the fish- and wood-processing industries. The city grew further still during the Great Depression of the 1930s, as many unemployed Canadians tried (unsuccessfully) to find work. Vancouver began to prosper again during World War II, when it was the headquarters for the Canadian Army's coastal defense staff. Many skyscrapers and high-rise residential buildings were built following the war, forever changing the city's landscape.

The Sights and Sounds

Vancouver has a variety of museums and attractions to suit every taste. For art lovers, there is the Vancouver Museum, which frequently stages exhibitions from Canada and around the world. Its permanent collection provides a glimpse into the city's rich cultural heritage. The Vancouver Art Gallery is downtown and displays international art and artifacts both ancient and modern. The Vancouver Maritime Museum in Heritage Harbour displays many historic seagoing vessels including the schooner St. Roch.

Scientific history is well represented in Vancouver's many science museums. Science World of British Columbia enables visitors to enjoy interactive exhibits while they learn about fascinating scientific discoveries of the past. At the H.R. MacMillan Space Centre, patrons can take part in a space-travel simulator and view multimedia shows and demonstrations at the museum's planetarium. The Vancouver Aquarium's extensive animal collection includes beluga whales, sea lions, dolphins, seals, and fascinating tropical fish. Special presentations include the popular shark dives and dolphin shows. To get a dramatic 360-degree view of the city and surrounding Coast Mountains, visit the Vancouver Lookout at Harbour Centre.

Vancouver also has beautiful and captivating outdoor treasures for nature lovers. The VanDusen Botanical Garden displays live plant collections, including species such as cherry trees, water lilies, and perennials. Leaf-peepers must visit in fall, when the trees display their full palette of colors. The Classical Chinese Garden is in the downtown area, and is named for Dr. Sun Yat Sen, the Father of Modern China. This authentic Chinese garden is an urban oasis of peace and tranquility. Guided tours are available, and a stop at the garden gift shop is a pleasant way to end your visit.

The Trivia

Fact: Vancouver's harbor is open all year because the harbor's water never freezes.

Fact: Vancouver's Chinatown is one the largest Chinese communities in North America. More than 17,000 people of Chinese descent live in the area, which is filled with restaurants, gift shops and nightclubs.

Why Vancouver Is a 50 plus one City

Vancouver is a great city in the making. Like many locations in North America, it has a relatively short history and its potential lies in its future. The city dominates the Pacific coast of Canada, in the midst of natural beauty and a temperate climate. Vancouver is a fine place to visit any time of year.

航行来到了最终成为布立德内湾的地方。事实上,这里的殖民地是于1865年才建立起来的,当时,在这一地区修建了黑斯廷斯–穆勒锯木厂,1884年,加拿大太平洋铁路选择这一地区作为其西部的终点站。1886年,这座城市进行了合并,同年,一场大火将城市的大片地区化为灰烬,然而,重建工作异常迅速高效。

1900至1910年间,温哥华成为加拿大发展最快的城市,人口数量快速膨胀,世界各地的移民大量涌入,其中大部分都是到当地鱼类及木材加工企业工作的。20世纪30年代的经济大萧条时期,这座城市依然在发展,因为许多失业的加拿大人仍在试图(徒劳地)寻找工作。第二次世界大战之后,温哥华开始再次繁荣起来,当时,这里是加拿大陆军海岸防御指挥部总部。战后,众多的摩天大楼以及高层住宅拔地而起,不断改变着这座城市的风景线。

声光景点

温哥华有着各种各样的博物馆和旅游景点,能够满足各种不同的口味。对于美术爱好者来说,这里有温哥华博物馆,时常展出来自加拿大本国以及世界各地的艺术品,其中的永久性收藏为人们提供了了解这座城市丰富文化遗产的机会。温哥华美术馆位于市中心,展出的是从古代直到今天世界各地的美术及手工艺品。位于遗产港的温哥华海洋博物馆展出了许多具有纪念意义的航海船只,其中就有著名的"圣劳殊号"皇家骑警帆船。

科学的历史在温哥华众多的科学博物馆中得到了很好的反映。不列颠哥伦比亚科学世界在为游客提供了解过去神奇的科学发现的同时,还使他们能够在互动式的展品中获得享受。在麦克米伦太空中心,游客除了可以坐进宇宙飞船模拟器以外,还可以在馆内的太空馆观看多媒体表演和展示。在温哥华水族馆所展出的大量动物中,游客能够欣赏到白鲸、海狮、海豚、海豹以及各种神奇的热带鱼。其中富有特色的表演还有鲨鱼潜水和海豚表演。如果想要360度全方位地欣赏这座城市及其周边海岸山脉动人的景致,就去海港中心的温哥华瞭望台看一看吧。

此外,对于那些热爱大自然的人们来说,温哥华也拥有美丽而迷人的户外风景。范杜森植物园所展出的植物包括樱桃树、睡莲和多年生植物等鲜活的品种。钟爱绿叶的人们最好选择秋天光临此地,因为到了那时,五颜六色的树木将会组成一幅浓郁的画卷展现在你的面前。位于市中心的中国古典园林,是以现代中国之父孙逸仙的名字命名的。这座地道的中国园林是城市中一处和平而安宁的绿洲,这里有导游为游客提供讲解,到园林内的礼品店逗留一下,将会为你的旅程画上一个圆满的句号。

奇闻轶事

之一:由于温哥华港口的水域从不结冰,因此这里一年四季开放通航。

之二:温哥华的唐人街是北美地区最大的华人社区之一,有超过1.7万名华人后裔居住在这里,因此,该地区拥有众多的餐馆、礼品店和夜总会。

为什么温哥华入选50＋1个城市?

温哥华是一座成长中的伟大城市,如同北美其他地区一样,这里的历史相对较短,但未来的潜力却很巨大。这座城市在加拿大太平洋沿岸占据着显著位置,天然美景,再加上宜人的气候,温哥华是一个你一年四季随时可以游览的好地方。

Forty-eight

Venice, Italy

The Basic Facts

Venice is one of the world's most famous and unusual cities. Venice developed as an independent city-state ruled by nobles and was briefiy a colonial power in the 15th century.

Geography

Venice lies at 45 degrees 25 minutes north latitude and 12 degrees 18 minutes east longitude. The city's geography is unique among world cities; it is located on several islands in the Adriatic Sea northeast of Italy. The islands make up the historic center of Venice, but the mainland communities of Marghera and Mestre are also part of the city. The waterway that separates Venice from the mainland is the Venetian Lagoon, and a roadway connects the islands to the mainland. Venice is divided into six zones: San Marco, San Polo, Cannaregio, Dorsoduro, Castello and Santa Croce.

Climate

The weather in Venice can change drastically through the seasons; this is due in large part to the in.uence of Alpine and North African winds that blow across the area. Average temperatures range from the 80s Fahrenheit in summer—often spiking into the high 90s— and the lower 40s Fahrenheit in winter. Venice has high humidity regardless of the season.

Government

Venice is the center of an Italian government unit known as a comune. The chief executive of the comune is the mayor, who may delegate functions to subordinate councilors. Most officials are democratically elected.

Demographics

The population of the city of Venice is approximately 270,000 and the metropolitan area, which includes the city of Padua has a population of 1.6 million. More than 95 percent of the population is Italian; the remainder includes immigrants from Turkey, Ukraine, Tunisia and the Balkans

Since 1950 residents have moved from the islands to the Marghera and Mestre to escape Venice's annual floods. These areas also have better employment opportunities, a lower cost of living, and better housing than the city itself. New housing construction is essentially nonexistent on the islands of Venice because of geographic restrictions.

Economy

Tourism is the prime mover of Venice's economy since there are no manufacturing industries on the islands. Marghera and Mestre are the comune's industrial centers.

意大利威尼斯

概况

威尼斯是世界上最著名、也是最独特的城市之一,15世纪时,威尼斯发展成为一个独立的由贵族统治的城邦,并一度成为权利巨大的殖民地。

一、地理

威尼斯位于北纬45°25′,东经12°18′,在世界所有城市当中,这座城市的地理可谓独一无二。它建在意大利东北亚得里亚海中的数个小岛之上。尽管这些岛屿构成了威尼斯的历史中心,但是,位于大陆的玛格哈和梅斯特社区也属于城市的一部分。将威尼斯与大陆分隔开来的水路是威尼斯泻湖,此外,还有一条陆路连接这些岛屿与大陆。威尼斯分为六个区:圣马克区、圣波罗区、坎纳雷乔区、道索杜罗区、卡斯特罗区和圣十字区。

二、气候

随着季节的变换,威尼斯的天气波动剧烈。其原因主要是受到阿尔卑斯山的影响,加之来自北非的风从这里吹过。平均气温在夏季的华氏80度 —— 经常可能飙升至华氏97~99度 —— 到冬季的华氏41~43度。一年四季,威尼斯的湿度都很大。

三、政府

威尼斯是一个被称为"社区"的意大利行政单位的中心。社区的主要行政官员是市长,他代表下属的政务委员会行使职权,大多数官员都通过选举产生。

四、人口

威尼斯城市人口有近27万,包括帕多瓦市的大市范围拥有人口160万。95%以上的人口是意大利人,剩下的是来自土耳其、乌克兰、突尼斯和巴尔干的移民。

自1950年起,许多居民从岛上搬迁至玛格哈和梅斯特以躲避威尼斯每年发生的洪水。此外,这些陆上区域较之老城本身,就业机会也更多,生活开支相对较低,住房条件相对较好。由于受到地理条件的制约,在威尼斯的岛屿地区,新的住宅建设基本上是不存在的。

五、经济

由于在岛上不存在基础设施工业,因此,旅游业就成了威尼斯经济的主要动力。玛格哈和梅斯特是社区工业的中心。

The History

In the 5th century Italians fled from invading Barbarians and poured into Venice. The early Venetian economy was based on fishing and trading, and by the 9th century was a major trading partner with the Italian mainland, Constantinople, and Africa. Venice was ruled by nobles and was a virtual city-state during this period of growth. Venice rivaled Genoa for trading privileges and the two regions battled in the 14th century; Venice eventually prevailed in 1380. The city's wealth and naval power helped to control the expansion of Islam into southern Europe.

In the 15th century Venice began to colonize the Mediterranean, and added Crete, Cyprus and Dalmatian (now part of Croatia) to its burgeoning empire. Venice also became a major trading center between Asia and the rest of Europe during this era. Trade declined in Venice after the discovery of America, as European trade shifted to the Atlantic coast. The Venetian empire was split between France and Austria when Napoleon occupied the city in the late 18th century.

Venice became part of the independent kingdom of Italy in 1866, and Marghera and Mestre began to industrialize in the early 20th century. After the Nazis seized Venice during World War II, the Allies bombed the mainland communities but spared the islands. Venice was devastated by a flood in 1966, during which many of the city's famous artworks were destroyed. The international community helped to restore the priceless artwork, and in the wake of the flood the city government instituted flood control measures to circumvent future disasters.

The Sights and Sounds

Unfortunately, years of environmental degradation and neglect have eroded much of Venice's storied history. Still, its romance and charm continue to attract tourists from around the world.

St. Mark's Basilica and the Plaza of St. Mark are perhaps the most famous of Venice's historical treasures. The Basilica was built to house the remains of St. Mark, who is the patron saint of Venice. This church is actually the third built on the site; the first was built in the 9th century. The Basilica's exterior is a fine example of Byzantine architecture, and its interior combines both Byzantine and Gothic elements. It is a grand and ornate Catholic church, and one of the world's great tourist attractions. Venice appropriated much of the church's art, mosaics and other riches from other areas of the Mediterranean; the renowned Triumphal Quadriga, a grouping of four bronze horses, were taken from Constantinople when that city was sacked during the Fourth Crusade.

Many consider St. Mark's Square to be loveliest in the world. On a typical day, visitors crowd the square to enjoy its elegant shops and cafes. The square is recognized worldwide for its ever-present flocks of pigeons. Napoleon is said to have remarked that the square is the finest drawing room in Europe.

The Campanile di San Marco, a 325-foot-tall bell tower, stood majestically in St. Mark's Square for 1,000 years—until it collapsed in 1902 for no apparent reason. It was rebuilt soon afterward in its original 16th century style. The view from the top of the tower is said to be the best in all of Venice.

The Doge's Palace, constructed of marble and limestone and finished in 1424, was the residence of the Doge (Duke), the seat of government, and the hall of justice. The

光影流金

五世纪时,意大利人为逃避入侵的野蛮人而大批涌入威尼斯,早期威尼斯的经济是建立在渔业和贸易的基础之上的。到了19世纪,威尼斯成为意大利本土、君士坦丁堡以及非洲的一个主要贸易伙伴,在这一发展阶段,威尼斯由贵族统治,事实上是一个城邦国家。14世纪,为了争夺贸易特权,威尼斯和热那亚两个地区进行了战争,最终,威尼斯于1380年取得胜利,城市的财富及其海军势力使其控制了从伊斯兰教国家直到欧洲南部的辽阔地区。

15世纪,威尼斯开始了对地中海地区的殖民统治,将克里特岛、塞浦路斯岛和达尔马提亚(即现今克罗地亚的部分地区)并入了当时正迅速发展的帝国疆土,此外,在这一时期,威尼斯也成了连接亚洲与欧洲其他地区的主要贸易中心。美洲大陆被发现之后,由于欧洲贸易的重心开始向大西洋沿岸转移,威尼斯的贸易日渐衰落。18世纪后期,拿破仑占领这座城市的时候,威尼斯帝国分裂为法国与奥地利两部分。

1866年,威尼斯成为独立的意大利王国的一部分。20世纪初期,玛格哈和梅斯特开始了工业化的进程。第二次世界大战期间,纳粹夺取了威尼斯,盟军部队对威尼斯的陆上地区进行了轰炸,但是岛屿地区幸免于难。1966年,威尼斯被一场洪水所淹没,当时城中许多著名的艺术品遭到破坏。在国际社会的帮助之下,这些无价之宝得以修复。受到洪水的警示,威尼斯政府采取了滞洪措施,以防止未来类似灾难的发生。

声光景点

不幸的是,常年的环境退化和疏于保护,使得威尼斯累积起来的历史日益被吞噬,即便如此,这座城市的浪漫和魅力依然吸引着来自世界各地的游客。

圣马可大教堂和圣马可广场或许是威尼斯历史宝库中最为著名的地方了,教堂是为存放威尼斯神圣保护者圣马可的遗骸而修建的。事实上,现在的教堂已经是在此修建的第三座教堂了,第一座教堂修建于九世纪,教堂的外部是拜占庭建筑风格的完美表现,内部则吸收了拜占庭及哥特式建筑风格的双重元素。这是一座宏伟而华丽的天主教堂,世界上最伟大的景点之一。威尼斯政府拨出专款为教堂购买了大部分的艺术品、马赛克和来自地中海其他地区的财富。其中著名的"胜利四驹",由四匹青铜马组成,来自君士坦丁堡,是第四次十字军东征时期由那座城市掳掠而来的。

许多人都把圣马可广场当成世界上最可爱的地方,每天,人们聚集到广场上,留恋于各类典雅的店铺和咖啡馆,广场上那些似乎从未离去的成群的鸽子成为其广为熟知的典型象征,据说,拿破仑曾经说过:圣马可广场是欧洲最完美的绘画室。

圣马克钟楼是一座高325英尺的钟楼,它以雄伟的姿态矗立于圣马可广场上已经有1 000年了 —— 直到1902年不知何故而倒塌。之后,人们很快按照最初16世纪的风格重新修建了这座钟楼,据说,钟楼顶上是俯瞰威尼斯全城的最佳位置。

总督府是一座大理石和石灰岩建筑,完成于1424年,它既是总督(公爵)的官邸,政府所在地,又是司法厅。罪犯裁决地是与此相连的一座建筑,而将两者连接起来的就是著

prisoner's holding area is attached to the building by the famous Bridge of Sighs.

The Grand Canal is a two-mile main route through town. During the short voyage, sightseers pass some 200 Gothic and Renaissance palaces and grand estates that represent 1,000 years of history and culture. Locals suggest that visitors take a trip on the water bus once during the day and then again at night. Along the way are such sights as Ca' d'Oro (Golden House), which was built in the 15th century, its marble façade once enhanced with real gold; Ca' Rezzonico, a sumptuous palace built in the 1660s; and the Rialto Bridge, which dates from 1591 as the first stone bridge across the canal.

The Church of Saints John and Paul, second only to St. Mark's in size and opulence, was the traditional site where Doges were crowned. It was built in the 13th and 14th centuries and is the resting place of some 25 Doges.

The Trivia

Fact: After Venice defeated Genoa in 1380, the city celebrated the victory with a symbolic marriage ceremony, in which the Doges were wed with the Adriatic Sea. The ceremony was celebrated with great pomp on a huge gilded gondola called the Bucentaur.

Fact: Venice was essential to the Fourth Crusade which lasted from 1201 to 1204. Venice provided the transportation necessary for the crusaders and joined them in battle against the Byzantine Empire. The 4th Crusade ended with the invasion and defeat of Constantinople.

Fact: Venice's 150 canals take the place of streets. Boats rather than cars are the city's primary means of transportation. The famous flat-bottomed gondolas were employed for centuries but have been replaced by motorboats and waterbuses. More than 400 bridges traverse the canals, and narrow alleys called calli run between the buildings and the islands.

Fact: Until the mid-1970's, Venice sank at a rate of about one-fifth an inch per year. Experts believed that well drilling was largely responsible for this phenomenon. Although the Italian government later restricted the drilling process, many believe that the city is still sinking today.

Why Venice Is a 50 plus one City

Venice is a romantic, artistic, historically significant, and unique city. Tourists often outnumber residents in this city that has attracted sightseers for hundreds of years.

名的"叹息桥"。

　　大运河是从城中穿过的一条长两英里的主要航线,尽管航程很短,但是观光客能够经过大约200处哥特式及文艺复兴时期的宫殿和宏大庄园,他们代表了1 000年的历史和文化。当地人会建议游客在白天坐一次水上巴士,然后再在晚上坐一次,河道两旁可以看到诸如修建于15世纪的"卡多洛"(黄金屋),其大理石的外表曾经一度被真正的黄金所覆盖,雷佐尼可宫是一座修建于17世纪60年代的豪华宫殿,横跨运河之上的第一座石桥里阿尔托桥,其历史可以追溯到1591年。

　　圣约翰和圣保罗教堂在规模和富裕程度上仅次于圣马可大教堂,这里是历史上总督加冕的地方,教堂修建于13世纪和14世纪,大约有25位总督死后葬在这里。

奇闻轶事

　　之一:1380年,威尼斯打败热那亚之后,为了庆祝胜利,在城中举行了一场象征性的婚礼仪式,总督和亚得里亚海结婚,仪式在一艘巨大的名为"布森托"的镀金凤尾船上隆重举行,盛况空前。

　　之二:威尼斯在1201年~1204年的第四次十字军东征中至关重要,一方面,威尼斯为十字军战士提供了必要的交通通道,另一方面,他们还与十字军一道参与了反抗拜占庭帝国的战役。第四次十字军东征以君士坦丁堡的入侵和失败而告终。

　　之三:威尼斯大大小小150条运河取代了城市的街道,船只取代汽车成为城市主要的交通工具,著名的平底船"贡多拉"在被使用了几个世纪之后,如今已经被摩托艇和水上巴士所取代。运河上有400多座大小桥梁,在建筑物与岛屿之间能够看到一些被称为"卡里"的狭窄街巷。

　　之四:20世纪70年代之前,威尼斯一直在以每年大约1/5英尺的速度下沉,专家们认为,造成这种现象的原因主要在于过度钻探,虽然后来意大利政府限制了这种钻探作业,但是,许多人认为这座城市至今仍在继续下沉。

为什么威尼斯入选50 + 1个城市?

　　威尼斯是一座温馨浪漫、精致典雅、历史悠久、独一无二的城市,在这座城市里,游客常常多于当地居民,在数百年间,它的魅力始终如一。

Forty-nine

Vienna, Austria

The Basic Facts

Vienna is the capital of Austria and the country's largest city. It is a leading cultural, political and economic center, and one of Europe's most beautiful and culturally rich cities.

Geography

Vienna lies at 48 degrees 13 minutes north latitude and 16 degrees 22 minutes east longitude. The city is located in northeastern Austria on the south bank of the Danube River, in a narrow plain between the Carpathian Mountains and the Alps. Just east of Vienna is a mountain gap through the Carpathians that helped the city become a major trading center.

Climate

Vienna has a climate that is typically dry and largely influenced by the rest of continental Europe. Frigid winds from Eastern Europe and Russia can bring cold winters. Average temperatures range from the 30s Fahrenheit in winter to the upper 70s Fahrenheit in summer.

Government

Vienna is the capital of the Republic of Austria and is both a city and a federal province. The city's mayor is also the governor of the province, and the city council also acts as the provincial government. Both the mayor and city council are democratically elected.

Demographics

Austrians constitute the majority of Vienna residents; the city also has a large number of Czechs and Hungarians. German is the primary language of Vienna. The city's population is 1.6 million and the metropolitan area's population is roughly 2.2 million.

Economy

Vienna is the center of the nation's industrial economy. Manufacturing industries include chemicals, clothing, leather goods and medicine. Tourism and government services are also important to the local economy.

The History

The area of present-day Vienna was originally a Celtic settlement founded around 500 B.C.. In the 1st century A.D. the Roman Empire used Vindobona (the empire's name for Vienna) as a base to guard against invading Germanic forces. The Emperor Marcus Aurelius lived there until his death in 180. The Goths sacked Vindobona in the 4th century and

奥地利维也纳

概况

　　维也纳是奥地利的首都和最大的城市,同时,也是文化、政治和经济中心,是欧洲最美丽、文化最为丰富的城市之一。

一、地理

　　维也纳位于北纬48°13′,东经16°22′,地处奥地利东北部,多瑙河南岸,喀尔巴阡山与阿尔卑斯山之间的一个狭窄平原之上。就在维也纳的东部,是通往喀尔巴阡山的一处峡谷地带,它使得维也纳成为一个主要的贸易中心。

二、气候

　　主要由于受到欧洲大陆其他地区的影响,维也纳气候的典型表现是干燥,来自东欧和俄罗斯凛冽的寒风使得冬季异常寒冷,年均气温在冬季的华氏30度左右至夏季的华氏77~79度。

三、政府

　　维也纳是奥地利共和国的首都,它既是一座城市,同时也是一个联邦省,城市的市长同时兼任联邦省的省长,市政委员会同时也发挥着省政府的作用。市长和市政委员会通过民主选举产生。

四、人口

　　奥地利人占维也纳居民的大部分,此外,城市里还有很大数量的捷克人和匈牙利人,德语是维也纳的主要语言。维也纳的人口有160万,大市范围的人口大约是220万。

五、经济

　　维也纳是奥地利工业经济的中心,加工行业包括化学品、服装、皮革产品和药品等。此外,旅游业和行政服务对于当地经济也非常重要。

光影流金

　　如今的维也纳地区最早是公元前500年左右,凯尔特人建立起的一个殖民地。公元1世纪,罗马帝国利用"温多波纳"(维也纳的帝国名称)作为防御入侵的日耳曼军队的一个基地,皇帝马可·奥勒利乌斯就住在这里,直至公元180年去世为止。4世纪时,哥特族人洗劫了"温多波纳",并且将罗马人驱逐出去,之后,该地区经历了一系列的入侵者,直到

ousted the Romans. A series of invaders occupied the area until the 12th century, when Leopold I of Austria assumed control.

In the 13th century Henry II of Austria moved the capital to Vienna, and in 1281 the city became the official residence of the House of Habsburg. In 1857 the walls of the original city were razed to permit expansion; the walls' original location became the tree-lined boulevard known as the Ring. The city survived sieges by the Turks and their Hungarian allies over the next several centuries, and by the 18th century began a new set of fortifications. The city also began to erect some magnificent buildings during this period.

In the late 19th and early 20th centuries, Vienna flourished as a center of the arts and sciences, and in 1918 became the capital of the First Austrian Republic. During this period, Vienna improved its urban infrastructure and built new housing for the city's poor.

Austria was annexed to Germany in the Anschluss of 1938, and in March of that year Hitler's troops entered Vienna and were greeted warmly by crowds. Allied bombing during World War II heavily damaged Vienna, and the Nazi extermination of Austrian Jews decimated the city's population. At the Potsdam Conference in 1945, Austria and Vienna were each divided into four occupation zones. Austria was reunited as a neutral state in 1955 and Vienna again became the nation's capital.

The Sights and Sounds

The old-world culture, art and architecture of Vienna make it a comfortable and charming city. It is also an accessible city; most of the major sights are in the oldest section of the city within the Ring.

Vienna is well regarded for its museums, which are some of the finest in Europe. The Albertina is popular for its collection of drawings, sketches, engravings, and etchings by the Old Masters. Efforts have been made in recent years to restore the Albertina and to enhance the quality of its exhibits. Classical music fans will enjoy the Mozart Memorial Rooms, a small museum in a house near St. Stephen's Cathedral. Mozart lived here for about 4 years, and today a full array of Mozart memorabilia is on display. From this intimate apartment, progress to the House of Music devoted to the classical greats, including Haydn, Strauss, Beethoven and Mahler. Individual rooms are dedicated to each composer and many display the artists' original scores.

Conflict, war, and ethnic chaos occurred throughout Austria's history and the history of its predecessor, the Austro-Hungarian Empire. The Museum of Military History displays the full range of arms and armaments implemented in the region's major conflicts. A notable exhibit contains the car in which Archduke Franz Ferdinand was assassinated; his death led to the start of World War I.

In 2001 the Imperial Court Stables became the Museum Quarter, a vast cultural center that includes four museums, a concert hall, theatres, dance facilities, exhibition halls, and even a children's museum. The museum is conveniently located near the Hofburg Imperial Palace.

Much of the Hofburg dates to the 13th century. This glamorous, formal complex of buildings and courtyards currently serves as the residence of the Austrian president.

On Sundays and religious holidays, the world-famous Vienna Boys Choir performs at the court chapel in the Hofburg. Their High Mass performances are so popular that tickets are expensive and in short supply. The court chapel is a small venue, but lucky ticket

12世纪,奥地利的利奥波德一世重新取得政权。

13世纪,奥地利国王亨利二世将都城搬迁到维也纳。1281年,这座城市成为哈布斯堡王朝的官邸。1857年,为了扩建城市,原有的城墙被拆除,取而代之的是被称为"环线"的3条林荫大道。在接下来的几个世纪里,这座城市曾遭到土耳其人及其盟友匈牙利人的围攻,到了18世纪,城市开始修建一套新的防御体系,在这一时期,一些宏伟建筑也拔地而起。

19世纪后期到20世纪初,维也纳作为艺术和科学中心日益繁荣,1918年,这座城市成为首个奥地利共和国的首都,与此同时,维也纳的城市基础设施得到改善,为城市的贫困人口修建了新的住宅。

1938年,在所谓的"联合"名义下,奥地利被纳粹德国并吞,同年3月,希特勒的军队进驻维也纳,并受到人群的热烈欢迎。第二次世界大战期间,盟军的炸弹使维也纳城市遭到严重破坏,纳粹对奥地利犹太人进行的种族灭绝行动屠杀了大部分城市人口。1945年的波茨坦会议上,奥地利和维也纳分别被划分为4个就业区域。1955年,奥地利作为一个中立国家重新统一,维也纳也再次成为奥地利的首都。

声光景点

维也纳古老的文化、艺术和建筑使它成为一座舒适而迷人的城市,此外,它也是一座易于游览的城市,大多数主要的景点都位于环线内城市最古老的区域。

维也纳的博物馆享有很高的声誉,其中有不少被公认为是欧洲最完美的博物馆。阿尔贝蒂纳博物馆以收藏传统大师们的素描、速写、雕刻及蚀刻作品而著称,近些年来,博物馆下大力气对一些原有作品进行修复,以期加强展品的质量。古典音乐迷们一定会喜欢莫扎特纪念馆,这是靠近圣史蒂芬大教堂的一座小型博物馆,莫扎特在这里生活了大约4年,如今,这里展出有一系列关于莫扎特的纪念品。从这套私人公寓向前就可以进入到音乐大厦,这是专为那些古典音乐大师,如海顿、施特劳斯、贝多芬和马勒等修建的博物馆,每一位作曲家都有一间个人展厅进行专门介绍,其中许多展厅还包括作曲家创作的曲谱原稿。

冲突、战争及民族纷争贯穿了奥地利的历史以及这个国家的前身——奥匈帝国。军事历史博物馆展出的是在该地区所发生的主要冲突中,人们使用过的全套武器及军事装备。一件值得关注的展品是弗朗茨·斐迪南大公被暗杀时所乘坐的轿车,正是他的死直接导致了第一次世界大战的爆发。

2001年,皇家御用赛马场成为博物馆区,这是一个由4座博物馆、一家音乐厅、数个剧院、舞蹈设施、展览大厅、甚至还有一个儿童博物馆所共同组成的规模巨大的文化中心,博物馆位于霍夫堡皇宫附近,游览起来非常方便。

霍夫堡皇宫的大部分修建于13世纪,这座富丽堂皇而又风格严谨的建筑群及其庭院目前是奥地利总统的官邸。

在周日和宗教节日里,世界著名的维也纳少年合唱团都会在霍夫堡内的宫廷小教堂进行表演,他们的大弥撒表演人气之高,常常一票难求,或者票价昂贵。虽然宫廷小教堂

holders will cherish the experience.

The revered Vienna Philharmonic Orchestra performs in the fabulous Musikverein, a beautiful concert hall where the orchestra performs its annual New Year's Concert. The Staatsoper is the home of the popular Vienna State Opera. Much of the original structure was destroyed during World War II, but in 1955 the restored building opened to great acclaim.

Near the Hofburg is another must-see: the Spanish Riding School, the training grounds of the renowned Lipizzan horses. Formal shows take place on Saturday and Sunday in the indoor Winter Riding School, where the beauty and grace of these majestic creatures are enhanced by the hall's pure white walls and crystal chandeliers. If weekend shows sell out— which they often do—tickets to morning practice sessions during the week are also available.

The cathedral known as Stephansdom is an architectural masterpiece, its Gothic spires reaching heavenward to dominate the city's landscape. The church is a literal maze of tombs, altars, and sculptures. Also heavily damaged during World War II, the church has not lost its medieval mystery and fascination. Many Habsburg royals are entombed in the underground crypt. Those visitors able to manage the 343 steps up the south tower will be rewarded with a delightful view of Vienna.

Outside of the inner zone, the Schönbrunn Palace is popularly known as the Versailles of Vienna, which exemplifies Baroque art and architecture at its best. The palace and formal gardens were built by the Habsburgs between 1696 and 1713. Guided tours are available, although only a fraction of this sprawling complex is open to the public. State dinners and other formal events are held here.

Vienna is known for its numerous restaurants, cafes and coffee houses, and especially its famous torts and pastries. Evening in Vienna offers a wealth of opportunities as well, from theatres and concerts to nightclubs and wine taverns. There truly is something for everyone in this world-famous city.

The Trivia

Fact: Vienna attracted noteworthy composers such as Brahms, Mahler, Strauss and Schoenberg during its golden age of the late 19th and early 20th centuries. Also at this time, the important Austrian neurologist Sigmund Freud developed his theories and techniques in psychoanalysis.

Fact: Vienna is the home of international organizations such as the International Atomic Energy Agency and the Organization of Petroleum Exporting Countries (OPEC).

Fact: In 1961 the city hosted the historic Vienna Summit, at which U.S. President John F. Kennedy and Soviet Premier Nikita Khrushchev attempted to resolve a variety of diplomatic concerns. The conference ultimately proved to be a failure, however, as the Cuban Missile Crisis of 1962 plunged the world further into the lengthy Cold War.

Why Vienna Is a 50 plus one City

Vienna has constantly survived wars and other conflicts to retain its greatness, sophistication, and old-world culture. The entire city is a treasure to be seen and cherished.

面积很小,但是那些有幸买到票的人们都非常珍惜这样难得的经历。

广受尊崇的维也纳爱乐交响乐团在神奇的金色大厅表演,每年,交响乐团表演的新年音乐会也是在这座美丽的音乐大厅内进行的。斯塔特索泊是维也纳国家歌剧院所在地,第二次世界大战期间,原有建筑的大部分遭到破坏,但是,1955年,修复后的大厦对外开放,并受到广泛赞誉。

在霍夫堡附近还有另外一处不可错过的地方:西班牙骑术学校,这是著名的利皮扎马的训练基地,每当周六和周日的时候,在冬季骑术学校的室内都有正式的马术表演,这些尊贵的动物们在大厅纯白色的墙壁和水晶枝形吊灯的映衬下,显得愈发美丽而优雅。假如周末表演的门票已经售罄——这种事经常发生——你还可以购买周内马匹晨练的观摩票。

被称为"史蒂芬斯顿"的大教堂是一个建筑奇迹,它哥特式的尖顶耸入云霄,成为维也纳一处亮丽的风景,这座教堂是一座不折不扣的由墓地、圣坛和雕塑所构成的迷宫。二战期间,这座教堂也遭到了严重破坏,然而,教堂原有的中世纪的神秘和动人风格并未消失。许多哈布斯堡王室成员,死后都埋葬在教堂的地下室内。那些有勇气征服343级台阶登临教堂南塔的游客,将有幸欣赏到维也纳的空中美景。

在内环区的外围,最著名的要数香布伦皇宫,人们通常称之为维也纳的凡尔赛宫,这座宫殿堪称巴洛克艺术和建筑的最佳范例。宫殿及其周边的花园修建于1696~1713年,是哈布斯堡王室的杰作。这里有导游服务,不过,这座庞大的建筑群只有一小部分对公众开放。国宴及其他一些官方事务都在这里举行。

维也纳之所以出名,还因为这里有不计其数的餐馆、咖啡屋、咖啡馆,尤其是著名的果子奶大蛋糕以及肉馅饼。维也纳的夜晚同样有着丰富的内容,从影剧院、音乐厅到夜总会和小酒店,这座世界著名的城市真可谓应有尽有。

奇闻轶事

之一:在19世纪后期到20世纪初,维也纳发展的黄金时期,这座城市吸引了众多著名的作曲家来到这里,例如,勃拉姆斯、马勒、施特劳斯和勋伯格等。此外,在同一时期,一位重要的奥地利神经病学家西蒙·弗洛伊德在精神分析领域发展了他的理论和技术。

之二:维也纳是一些重要的国际组织的所在地,例如,国际原子能机构和石油输出国组织。

之三:1961年,维也纳主办了具有历史意义的维也纳峰会,在这次会议上,美国总统约翰·肯尼迪与前苏联总理尼基塔·赫鲁晓夫试图就彼此关心的外交事务寻求解决办法,然而,会议最终以失败告终,1962年,古巴的导弹危机使全世界进一步陷入长期的冷战之中。

为什么维也纳入选50 + 1个城市?

历经战争和民族冲突的洗礼,维也纳依然保持着它的伟大、成熟和古老的文化。这座城市就是一座值得观赏和珍惜的宝库。

Washington, D.C., United States

The Basic Facts

Washington, D.C. (also known as Washington or D.C.), is the capital of the United States and is one of the nation's most beautiful and historic cities. Apart from its status as the seat of the federal government, it has a wealth of historical monuments and museums.

Geography

Washington lies at 38 degrees 50 minutes north latitude and 77 degrees west longitude. It is located along the Potomac River and is bordered by Maryland and Virginia. The city itself is composed of four quadrants arranged in grids, and its metropolitan area consists of the District of Columbia and 26 counties in West Virginia, Virginia and Maryland.

Climate

Washington's weather varies significantly throughout the year. Summers are usually hot and humid, especially in the city center. Winters are often cold and snowy, and heavy snowfalls are common. Annual temperatures vary widely, from the mid-20s Fahrenheit in winter to the low 90s Fahrenheit in summer.

Government

Washington's local government is unique among U.S. cities. Although the city's mayor and council are democratically elected, the federal government has power to veto any legislation passed by the council. In the 1870s, Congress took over government rule of Washington after it found that the city's governor mismanaged funds. Because the city is a government entity and not a state, it has no representation in the U.S. Congress—a fact that has led to much consternation among Washingtonians, who believe that they deserve equal status in the federal government.

Demographics

Washington's population of 550,000 is small in comparison to most major world cities, but the metropolitan area's population is currently 4.8 million and ever on the increase.

Economy

Washington's economy is dominated by the federal government and nongovernmental organizations including think tanks and lobbyists. The service industry is accordingly large to accommodate this significant workforce. Tourism is vital to the economy as well; millions arrive every year to visit the city's many historical sites. Trade and industry are virtually nonexistent.

美国华盛顿

概况

华盛顿市(又被称为华盛顿或D.C.)是美国的首都,也是这个国家最美丽、最具有历史意义的城市之一。除了作为联邦政府所在地的特殊地位外,这座城市还拥有宝贵的历史纪念地和众多的博物馆。

一、地理

华盛顿市位于北纬38°50′,西经77°,地处由马里兰州和弗吉尼亚州环抱的波托马克河沿岸地区,城市本身由四个扇形区域组合成一个网状地区,其大市范围包括哥伦比亚特区和位于西弗吉尼亚、弗吉尼亚和马里兰州内的26个县。

二、气候

华盛顿的天气四季分明,夏季通常炎热而潮湿,尤其是市中心地区,冬季时常寒冷多雪,下大雪的日子并不少见。年均气温变化幅度很大,冬季在华氏25度左右,夏季则可达华氏91~93度。

三、政府

在美国所有的城市当中,华盛顿市地方政府可谓独树一帜,尽管市长和市政委员会都是民主选举产生,但是联邦政府有权否决市政委员会通过的任何立法。19世纪70年代,国会在发现城市主管对资金管理不善之后,接管了华盛顿市政府的管理工作。由于这座城市就是政府的一个实体,而非一个独立的州,因此,在美国国会中不占有席位——这一事实令华盛顿市民异常震惊,因为他们认为自己在联邦政府中理应享有平等的权利。

四、人口

相比世界上大多数城市来说,华盛顿55万的人口只是个小数目,然而,目前华盛顿大市范围的人口已经达到480万,并且仍在继续增加。

五、经济

华盛顿市的经济主要由联邦政府及包括智囊团和说客在内的非政府组织所支配,为了给这些不可忽视的劳动力提供方便,城市的服务行业相应变得庞大,同样,旅游业对于经济也至关重要,每年有数百万的游客光临这座城市众多的历史景点。而贸易和工业在这座城市基本不存在。

The History

The French-born architect Charles L'Enfant designed the street plan for the city, and chose the Capitol Building as its focal point. The U.S. Congress held its first session at the Capitol in 1800.

British soldiers invaded Washington in 1814 during the War of 1812 and most public buildings were destroyed by fire but by 1819 the buildings were restored. A territorial government was established in Washington after the Civil War, and the city began to improve its infrastructure. After World War II, Washington's population declined in the 1950s as many residents moved to the expanding suburbs in the metropolitan area.

Washingtonians began demanding more control over their government, and in 1967 President Lyndon Johnson reorganized the city government to include a mayor and city council.

The Sights and Sounds

Tourists flock to Washington because there is so much to see and do in a relatively small area. The city has a useful public transportation system, and many of the city's districts are easily accessible on foot.

The National Mall is the heart and soul of Washington. Locals and visitors alike fill the place each day to enjoy life, view the sights, and gather for recreation or political purposes. It is a vast open space roughly two miles long, bounded by the U.S. Capitol and the Lincoln Memorial at either end and the Washington Monument at its center. The Mall's hundreds of cherry trees—a gift from Japan in 1912—are abloom each spring.

Washington D.C. is well known for its memorials to past presidents. The Washington Monument, completed in 1884, is a marble, granite, and sandstone obelisk that rises 555 feet over the National Mall. This monument, named for the country's first president, is beautifully mirrored in the adjacent Reflecting Pool. The Lincoln Memorial is a masterpiece of U.S. architecture, and undoubtedly the single most evocative structure in the nation. Built as a tribute to the nation's 16th president, Abraham Lincoln, its marble-and-limestone architecture recalls the Doric temples of Greece. Within its large open-air interior, a 19-foot-tall of the seated president gazes somberly out onto the Mall. The Jefferson Memorial is visible from the Mall, located in West Potomac Park on the Tidal Basin. The city's beloved cherry trees grow and bloom here. A 19-foot-tall bronze statue of Thomas Jefferson, the architect of the Declaration of Independence, stands majestically under the memorial's rotunda. The Franklin Delano Roosevelt Memorial, completed in 1997, is a new arrival on the Mall. Four outdoor galleries—one for each term of Roosevelt's presidency—are enhanced by a series of waterfalls and pools.

Among the many memorials to fallen war heroes on the National Mall, three cannot be overlooked. The National World War II Memorial is a more elaborate display, with 56 pillars surrounding a central plaza. The Korean War Veterans Memorial, dedicated in 1995, is a triangular arrangement with life-sized statues of soldiers on patrol. Its design provokes contemplation of the horrors of war and the terrible hardships that the soldiers endured. The Vietnam Veterans Memorial Wall, an expansive yet unobtrusive monument of black granite, is inscribed with the names of the more than 58,000 dead or missing who served in the Vietnam War. Families, friends, and others are drawn to the memorial to pay their respects to the men and women who gave their lives for their country. Reverent visitors fall

光影流金

法国籍的建筑大师查尔斯·朗方设计了这座城市的街道蓝图,并选择国会大厦作为其设计的焦点。1800年,美国国会在国会大厦举行了第一次会议。

1812年战争期间,英国士兵于1814年入侵华盛顿市,大多数公共建筑被大火烧毁,然而,到了1819年,这些建筑得以重新修复。美国内战之后,在华盛顿建立了一个准州政府,并且开始改善城市的基础设施。第二次世界大战之后的20世纪50年代,随着大都会地区向周边扩张,许多居民搬离市中心,华盛顿人口一度减少。

华盛顿市市民开始为自己争取更多的政府管理权利,1967年,林登·约翰逊总统对市政府进行重新组阁,建立了包括一位市长和一个市政委员会的组织机构。

声光景点

在这个相对较小的城市,你却能够看到如此众多的东西,这就是华盛顿吸引游客纷至沓来的原因。这座城市拥有便利的公共交通体系,城市的许多区域步行便很容易到达。

国家广场步行街是华盛顿市的心脏和灵魂,每天,当地居民和外来游客充斥这一地区,享受生活、观光赏景,为了娱乐抑或政治目的聚集到这里,这片宽敞的露天区域绵延大约两英里,其中心区域是华盛顿纪念碑,两端则是美国国会大厦和林肯纪念馆。街道两旁数百株樱花树 —— 这些都是1912年来自日本的礼物 —— 每年春季都会盛开。

华盛顿市以众多美国前总统的纪念物而著名,建成于1884年的华盛顿纪念碑是位于国家广场步行街上的一座高555英尺的由大理石、石灰岩和砂岩制成的方尖碑,这座以美国第一任总统的名字命名的纪念碑在毗邻的反射池中可以看到其优美的倒影。林肯纪念碑是美国建筑的杰作,毫无疑问,它也是最能令人遐思的建筑,作为献给这个国家第16任总统、亚伯拉罕·林肯的纪念碑,这座大理石和花岗岩构成的建筑令人想起希腊的多利斯神庙。在其巨大的敞开的内部空间里,一尊19英尺高的总统坐姿塑像似乎正严肃地凝望着外面的步行街。从步行街望过去,能够看见不远处的杰弗逊纪念碑,它位于通潮闸坝上的西波托马克公园内。华盛顿市最受人喜爱的樱花树就生长和开放在那里。一座高19英尺的美国《独立宣言》的设计师托马斯·杰弗逊的青铜雕像就威严地矗立在那里,在雕像的顶端是圆形的纪念大厅。富兰克林·德拉诺·罗斯福纪念碑建成于1997年,是广场步行街上的新成员。四座户外美术馆 —— 每一个代表了罗斯福总统的一届任期 —— 在系列喷泉和水池中分外醒目。

在国家广场步行街上,还有许多阵亡战争英雄纪念碑,其中有三个不应忽视,美国二战纪念碑是一个由56根纪念柱围成的中心广场,复杂而又匠心独运。朝鲜战争老兵纪念碑建于1995年,由真人大小的正在巡逻的士兵塑像组合而成,雕塑呈三角形分布。整个设计唤起人们对于战争的恐怖以及那些士兵所经历的艰难困苦的思考。越战老兵纪念墙是一堵面积很大但并不引人注目的黑色花岗岩纪念碑,上面铭刻着超过5.8万名在越南战争中阵亡或失踪的士兵的名字。他们的家人、朋友和那些素不相识的人都被吸引到这里,以缅怀那些为了这个国家而献出生命的男男女女。当目睹那些人用手抚摸他们所认

silent to witness loved ones touching the names of those they knew.

A grassy ellipse connects the National Mall to the White House, surely one of the most frequently photographed and recognized residences of the world. Recently-enhanced security has unfortunately limited tours of the building's interior, but its exterior is breathtaking in its design. Among its 132 rooms are the Oval Office, Lincoln's bedroom, and the Blue Room, where heads of state are traditional received.

The Smithsonian Institution is a complex of 19 museums, each dedicated to a distinct period of art or science history. Of note are the National Air and Space Museum, with the world's largest collection of aircraft and spacecraft, the National Museum of American History, the National Museum of Natural History, and the Freer Gallery of Art.

The Capitol Hill area is a must for first-time visitors. The U.S. Capitol building, the Supreme Court Building, and the Library of Congress are all located within a short distance of one another, yet security restrictions periodically restrict access to these areas.

The Georgetown neighborhood of Washington is an enclave for the rich and the powerful. Charming old homes, cafes, restaurants and bars line its streets. Georgetown University, the oldest Jesuit university in the United States, is located here.

The Trivia

Fact: On September 11, 2001, terrorists hijacked a commercial airliner and crashed it into the Pentagon, the headquarters of the U.S. Department of Defense. Although all passengers and crew perished in the crash, there were few fatalities on the ground because that area of the building was unoccupied due to construction.

Fact: In 1862, slavery was abolished in Washington D.C. before President Lincoln signed the Emancipation Proclamation, which would abolish the practice nationwide. Slave owners who swore an oath of loyalty to the United States exchanged their slaves for an average of $300 each.

Fact: The steps of the Lincoln Memorial have served as a fitting backdrop to many speeches, including the famous I Have a Dream speech delivered by Martin Luther King, Jr. in 1963. The footage of the speech figures prominently in documentaries of the city's history.

Fact: Ford's Theatre, where Abraham Lincoln was assassinated in 1865, is both a museum containing Lincoln memorabilia and a venue for live performances.

Fact: All 50 U.S. states are represented in the names of the city's diagonal roads.

Why Washington, D.C. Is a 50 plus one City

As the center of United States government, as a planned city with world-famous monuments, as the repository of the nation's treasures, and as a city famous for its restaurants, people and power brokers, it is fabulous!

识或深爱的人的名字时,游客们都保持沉默,以示恭敬和哀悼。

连接国家广场步行街和白宫的椭圆形草坪肯定是世界上曝光率最高、最为人们熟知的一个地方。最近,出于安全考虑,白宫内部限制游客进入,这一点颇为令人遗憾,然而,白宫的外围设计依然令人心旷神怡。在132间房子中,有总统的椭圆形办公室,林肯的卧室以及蓝厅,那里通常是接见国家首脑的地方。

史密森尼学会是一个由19座博物馆组成的建筑群,每间博物馆专门反映艺术或科学历史的一个显著阶段,值得关注的有国家航空航天博物馆——这里有世界上规模最大的飞行器和航天器展品,美国国家历史博物馆、国家自然历史博物馆以及自由美术馆。

对于初次到访的游客来说,国会山应是必游之地。美国国会大厦、联邦最高法院以及国会图书馆都在咫尺之内,遥相呼应。不过,定期的安全限制常使游客无法进入这些区域。

华盛顿市的乔治敦区是有钱有势的人聚居地区,街道两旁,有迷人的老式住宅、咖啡馆、餐馆、酒吧等。美国最古老的耶稣会会士大学乔治敦大学就坐落于这里。

奇闻轶事

之一:2001年9月11日,恐怖分子劫持了一架商用飞机撞进美国国防部总部所在的五角大楼,虽然,在这次空难中机上所有的乘客和机组成员都不幸遇难,但是,在地面却几乎未造成任何伤亡,因为,当时由于建筑施工,大厦的这一地区恰巧无人。

之二:1862年,华盛顿市废除了奴隶制,之后,林肯总统签署《解放宣言》,旨在于全美范围内废除奴隶制,那些宣誓忠于美利坚的奴隶主们用他们的奴隶换回了人均300美元的补偿。

之三:林肯纪念碑的台阶曾经作为许多人演讲的恰当背景,其中就包括马丁·路德·金于1963年发表的《我有一个梦》的著名演讲。在这座城市的历史文献中,此次演讲的连续镜头成为杰出的代表。

之四:福特剧院是1865年亚伯拉罕·林肯遇刺的地方,如今,这里既是一家收藏了林肯纪念物的博物馆,又是一家现场表演场所。

之五:美国的50个州在这座城市的对角线道路名称中都可以找得到。

为什么华盛顿市入选50 + 1个城市?

作为美国政府的中心,作为一座拥有著名纪念碑的有计划的城市,作为美国的财富宝库,作为一座餐馆林立、人物众多、权力经纪人聚集的城市,华盛顿是一个传奇!